The Transformational Helping Professional

A New Vision

Yvonne Gold
*Bellflower and Downey Beginning Teacher
Support and Assessment (BTSA) Program*

Robert A. Roth (Deceased)

Allyn and Bacon
Boston • London • Toronto • Sydney • Tokyo • Singapore

Series Editorial Assistant: Karin Huang
Marketing Manager: Susan E. Brown

Copyright © 1999 by Allyn & Bacon
A Viacom Company
Needham Heights, MA 02494

Internet: www.abacon.com

All rights reserved. No part of the material protected by this copyright notice may be reproduced or utilized in any form or by any means, electronic or mechanical, including photocopying, recording, or by any information storage and retrieval system, without written permission from the copyright owner.

Library of Congress Cataloging-in-Publication Data

Gold, Yvonne.
  The transformational helping professional : a new vision / Yvonne Gold, Robert A. Roth.
    p.   cm.
  Includes bibliographical references and index.
  ISBN 0-205-19559-8
  1. Mentoring in business.   2. Supervisors.   I. Roth, Robert A.
II. Title.
HF5385.G65   1998
658.3' 124—dc21

98-8738
CIP

Printed in the United States of America
10 9 8 7 6 5 4 3 2 1   02 01 00 99 98

The Transformational Helping Professional model is dedicated to all of the mentors, supervising teachers, and helpers who give of themselves so freely to enhance the lives of others and is dedicated to all those who have touched our lives. May God bless each one and guide them all through the transformations in their own lives.

Prologue

During the writing of this book, Dr. Roth was diagnosed with skin cancer. His dedication to the profession and his desire to continue his work helped him fight a long and courageous battle. In February 1997, the battle ended. However, his ideas live on through his writing. I believe Dr. Roth would be pleased with the completion of *The Transformational Helping Professional: A New Vision*.

May you, the reader, continue the vision and touch the future.

Yvonne Gold

About the Authors

Yvonne Gold is a psychotherapist in private practice in Los Alamitos, California, and director of the Beginning Teacher Support and Assessment (BTSA) Program in Bellflower and Downey, California. For over fifteen years she has conducted extensive research on teacher stress and burnout, as well as the use of psychological support with teachers and mentors. Dr. Gold is a former professor from California State University, Long Beach (CSULB), where she was the Director of the Curriculum and Instruction Master's Program for ten years. She was awarded the three prestigious faculty awards at CSULB, which has a faculty of about 2,000. Dr. Gold was awarded University Distinguished Faculty Scholar in 1991, the University Outstanding Professor in 1992, and honored with the Outstanding Teaching Award in 1993. Recently, the National Advisory Board on Recruiting New Teachers invited Dr. Gold to join a "distinguished list of educators and policy analysts" on the Advisory Board to contribute her empirical perspective and professional experience. Other contributions to professional organizations include invited membership into the National Induction Task Force for the Association of Teacher Educators and the Commission on the Role and Preparation of Mentors. Her research and psychological support programs have been incorporated into teacher preparation programs and professional development programs nationwide. In addition, professors from Great Britain and Africa have conferred with her regarding her research, books, numerous publications and utilization of her professional health programs with teachers, mentors, and administrators in their schools.

Robert A. Roth had a distinguished career until his long and courageous battle with cancer ended on February 23, 1997. He had over 150 publications, including books, chapters, monographs, and articles. His topics cover program evaluation and teacher development. Recognition of Dr. Roth's work has come from a variety of sources and in a number of forms. He was past national president of three professional organizations: the National Association of Teacher Educators (ATE), the National Association of State Directors of Teacher Education and Certification (NASDTEC), and the Interstate Certification Compact (ICC). He had been president of numerous state and regional units, including chapters of Phi Delta Kappa and the American Society of Training and Development. A number of honors had been awarded to Dr. Roth in acknowledgment of his contributions to the profession. He was named by the national ATE as one of the seventy Distinguished Leaders in Teacher Education, awarded the University Distinguished Faculty Scholar at California State University, Long Beach, named Distinguished Teacher Educator by the California ATE, and selected as a Distinguished Member of the Association of Teacher Educators. Dr. Roth had been a classroom teacher, program administrator, State Director of Teacher Education and Certification, university professor, and university administrator as Chair of the Department of Teacher Education.

Contents

Preface   xiii

PART I   A New Vision

1   Context of the New Vision   1
Changing Perspectives   2
Juxtaposition of Roles   3
The Literature of Supervision   4
The Literature of Mentoring   6
Definitions of Supervision and Mentoring   9
Helping and Evaluating   10
A New Vision—New Dimensions   11
Summary   12
Issues and Questions for Review and Reflection   13
References   13
Related Readings   17

2   A New Vision of the Helper: The Helping Professional   18
Contemporary Fundamental Elements   18
Pervasiveness of Philosophy   21
The Transformational Helping Professional: Philosophy and Theory   22
Characteristics of the Transformational Helping Professional   34
Comparison of Philosophies   38
Definition of the Transformational Helping Professional   40
Issues and Questions for Review and Reflection   40
References   40
Related Readings   42

3 Beyond Change: A Process of Transformations 43
Process Theories and Models of Change 44
Helping Professionals Assisting Teachers through Change 50
Educational Change Models 51
Implications of the Educational Change Literature for Helping Professionals 55
A Transformational Model: Beyond Change 55
The Role of the Helping Professional in the Transformational Model 63
Exercises That Help in Understanding the Transformational Process 66
Closing Remarks 67
References 67

PART II Domains of Needs: Dimensions of Helping

4 Personal and Psychological Needs: Domain One 69
Personal and Psychological Needs of Teachers 71
Physical Needs 73
Emotional Needs 75
Social Needs 83
Spiritual Needs 88
Meeting Personal and Professional Needs: A Life Process 90
References 90

5 Instructional and Professional Needs: Domain Two 93
Teachers' Instructional and Professional Development 94
The Relationship between Teacher Thought and Action and the Role of the Helping Professional 99
A Constructivist View 102
Teachers' Instructional Needs: Learning to Teach 104
Meeting Teachers' Professional Needs 107
Meeting Teachers' Needs 115
References 116

6 The Five Dimensions of Helping 120
Self-Enhancement for Helping Professionals: Dimension One 121
Interpersonal Effectiveness—Communication and Helping Strategies: Dimension Two 122
Assessing and Diagnosing: Dimension Three 123
Guidance and Support: Dimension Four 125
Revitalizing the Helping Professional: Dimension Five 127
Summary 128
References 128
Related Readings 129

PART III Dimension One: Self-Enhancement for the Helping Professional

7 Self-Enhancement for Helping Professionals (Dimension One)   **130**
Self-Enhancement: An Essential Aspect to Growth   *131*
Healthy Self-Valuing: The Fundamental Purpose of Helping   *132*
Promoting Self-Esteem in Self and Others   *134*
Developing Empathy: A Feeling of Oneness   *138*
Meeting Personal and Psychological Needs: The Foundations for Helping   *140*
Adding to Our Life Plan: Self-Enhancement   *146*
Summary   *147*
References   *147*

PART IV Dimension Two: Interpersonal Effectiveness

8 Interpersonal Effectiveness—Helping Strategies (Dimension Two)   **149**
Interpersonal Support   *150*
Developing and Maintaining Positive Relationships   *151*
Helping Strategies: Essential Tools for Groups   *155*
The Helping Professional: Personal Qualities   *162*
Summary   *163*
References   *164*
Related Readings   *164*

9 Interpersonal Skills and Communication   **165**
Application and Scope   *165*
Approaches and Strategies   *166*
Acquiring the Strategies   *168*
Specific Communication Skills   *169*
Summary   *179*
Issues and Questions for Review and Reflection   *180*
References   *180*
Related Readings   *181*

PART V Structure and Content

10 Models for Assessing, Diagnosing, Guiding, and Supporting   **183**
The Nature of Models   *183*
Operational Elements of Clinical Models   *185*
The Role of Observation and Assistance   *187*
The Transformational Helping Professional Model   *190*
A Template for Review of Models   *192*
Closing Thoughts   *194*
Issues and Questions for Review and Reflection   *194*
References   *194*
Related Readings   *195*

11 A Focus on Content   196
Setting the Stage   196
Content As Meaning   197
Cognitive Complexity   198
Curriculum and Planning   200
Standards for Teachers   203
Closing Remarks   207
References   207

PART VI   Dimension Three: The Assessing and Diagnosing Process

12 Assessing and Diagnosing (Dimension Three)   209
Purpose of Assessing and Diagnosing   209
The Focus of Assessing and Diagnosing   210
The Process of Assessing and Diagnosing   210
Personal-Psychological Needs   211
Instructional-Professional Needs   217
Assessment and Diagnosis in the Instructional-Professional Domain   220
Assessment Approaches Matrix   228
Assessing Teachers' Professional Needs   229
Issues and Questions for Review and Reflection   230
References   231
Related Readings   231

PART VII   Dimension Four: The Guidance and Support Process

13 The Process of Guidance and Support (Dimension Four)   233
Guidance and Support within the Personal-Psychological Domain   234
Instructional-Professional Needs   239
Conferencing with Teachers   241
The Progress of Observation   242
Closing Remarks   250
Issues and Questions for Review and Reflection   251
References   251
Related Readings   252

PART VIII   Dimension Five: Revitalizing

14 Managing Stress and Preventing Burnout: Keeping the Flame Burning Brightly   253
A Conceptualization of Teacher Stress   254
The Evolving Definition of Stress   254
Sources of Teacher Stress   256
Guidelines for Stress Management and Lifestyle Changes   260

The Deleterious Consequences of Burnout   265
Effective Coping Strategies to Prevent Burnout   272
Concluding Remarks   275
References   276

15 Revitalizing the Helping Professional (Dimension Five)   280
Recognizing the Risks of Helping   281
Personal Fulfillment   283
How Can I Revitalize Myself?   290
The Rewards of Revitalizing Yourself   292
Concluding Thoughts   293
Activities for Revitalizing   294
References   294
Related Readings   295

PART IX Creating the Future

16 Now the Vision Shall Be Real   296
Reference   298

Index   299

Preface

This book and the model it describes are intended for use by individuals in a wide range of roles. These include mentor teachers who provide leadership and work with the full spectrum of teacher experience, school supervisors and administrators, university student teacher supervisors, master teachers in the schools who work with student teachers, new teacher induction personnel, professional development leaders and staff, and school-based teacher educators providing initial teacher preparation or new teacher support. The thread that unifies these roles is the function of serving as a Helping Professional. The focus of this book is thus on the nature of the helping process and the Helping Professional, and how to function at maximum levels of effectiveness as a mentor or supervisor.

Over the years we have worked closely with large numbers of mentor teachers, school supervisors, university student teacher supervisors, master teachers, and classroom teachers. We have learned a great deal from these exemplary practitioners and are grateful for the knowledge and insights acquired through these affiliations.

We also have been serious students of the theory and practice of mentoring, supervising, and helping. We have closely reviewed and analyzed the literature, noting the historical and current theoretical perspectives and the recent findings of research as they emerged. We also have engaged in our own research on several aspects of these roles and functions. As a result, we have developed great respect for the earlier generations of scholars, researchers, and outstanding practitioners who have contributed to creating the current state of the art.

From all of these experiences and inquiry, over time we formulated perspectives on the varied aspects of the mentoring and supervision functions and recognized the fundamental theme of helping as being central to these roles. We have continually engaged in better articulating the theoretical framework or belief system on which our practice is founded. We have tested, refined, and modified the practical applications, learning from real situations and from those we have worked with using the new approach.

The results derived from working with the model have been extremely gratifying for us, both personally and professionally. The feedback we have received from teachers, mentors, and supervisors tells us of the great strides they have made in their instructional-professional levels of competence and effectiveness and the meaningful transformations they have experienced in changing their professional as well as personal lives. These outcomes are not only most meaningful to us; they are the essence of our new model.

The development of the Transformational Helping Professional model is a culmination of years of inquiry and analysis. It is a vision of helpers, the helping process, and the nature of schools. We have been urged by many with whom we have helped to share this vision and its processes with a wider audience so that others may enter the realm of and experiment with the transformational principles and practices.

Our purpose in this text is to create reality from the vision. We believe a vision must be translated into concrete terms, yet not be set in stone. This means that in order for the vision to be operationalized, it is necessary to clearly and specifically address the means by which the concepts of the vision are transformed into reality in actual practice. On the other hand, the strategies and techniques may be refined or adapted and new ones developed as the model is put into practice. The model is thus a fluid system within the theoretical framework of beliefs, values, and premises.

Sections of the Book

The first section of the book, Part I, provides an overview of The New Vision. It begins with a brief historical treatment of mentoring and supervision, highlighting the major philosophical eras and key dimensions of these roles. The second chapter presents the essence of the Transformational Helping Professional model through a description of the philosophy of the model and characteristics of the Helping Professional. The third chapter addresses a major component of the model, the process of transformations, moving beyond change to significant alterations and growth.

Part II consists of the Domains of Needs and Dimensions of Helping. Chapters 4 and 5 clarify the two broad domains of need, personal-psychological and instructional-professional. These form the basis of assessment, guidance, and support that constitute the professional development plan. Chapter 6 introduces the Five Dimensions of Helping. These serve as the focus of much of the remainder of the book.

Part III includes Chapter 7, Self-Enhancement of the Helping Professional, which focuses on professional and personal development of the Helping Professional. Part IV addresses Dimension Two: Interpersonal Effectiveness. This consists of two groups of strategies and skills, helping strategies (Chapter 8), and interpersonal skills and communication (Chapter 9). Collectively these provide a powerful set of resources for effective functioning in the role of mentor or supervisor.

Part V relates to the structure of clinical observation and assisting and the content or focus of observations in instructional settings. Chapter 10 deals with models for clinical assistance, such as the structure or steps involved in the process.

Chapter 11 offers a wide array of competencies to be observed and assessed as found in several sets of new national standards for teachers.

Part VI relates to Dimension Three: The Assessing and Diagnosing Process. Chapter 12 is a detailed treatment of the assessing and diagnosing process, as it pertains to both the instructional-professional and personal-psychological domains.

Part VII follows the assessment section with an extensive analysis of the Guidance and Support Process. This is contained in Chapter 13, which provides strategies and skills for guiding and supporting in both domains.

Part VIII: The Fifth Dimension of Helping describes alternative styles for helping based on research and analysis of best practice. Assisting educators with the most serious threats to professional practice—stress and burnout—is the substance of Chapter 14. The purpose here is to alert educators to the destructive effects of stress and burnout and assist them in learning how to function at peak levels of personal and professional performance. Chapter 15, Revitalizing the Helping Professional, is of particular importance in that it provides guidance for helping professionals in sustaining their vitality and finding personal fulfillment in their role and responsibilities.

Finally, Part IX delves into the future. Chapter 16, Now the Vision Shall Be Real, suggests that helpers must transform the philosophy into future practice. It challenges the reader to assimilate the transformational philosophy and operationalize it so it becomes real.

Acknowledgments

Our appreciation goes to the following reviewers for their comments on the manuscript: Wendy Doty, Downey Unified School District; Jennifer L. Shepard, Ontario-Montclair School District; and Sally J. Zepeda, University of Oklahoma.

The Transformational Philosophy

The Transformational Helping Professional model has evolved as a result of a deep commitment to enhancing people's lives, to improving instructional practice and learning experiences in the schools, and to enhancing the profession. We envision the Transformational model as a means of developing Helping Professionals for creating schools of the future characterized by a culture of significance, where individual worth, achievement of one's potential, and personal fulfillment are highly valued.

We hope the reader will not only engage in the activities and substance of the text, but also become fully immersed in the philosophy expressed in the values, beliefs, and dispositions of the Transformational model. We ask that you perceive this as an intellectual and personal journey to be experienced, rather than only a text to be studied. We truly hope that by the end of the journey you will have experienced meaningful personal and professional transformations.

An Invitation

We would very much like to hear from readers regarding their experiences in using the model in their particular professional roles. We would appreciate learning of personal insights or transformations of the Helping Professionals themselves, as well as those they assist. All names used in examples given throughout the book have been changed to protect the privacy of teachers and mentors. Situations and examples used are authentic. We wish you Godspeed on your journey.

Chapter 1

Context of the New Vision

> *I don't know what your destiny will be,
> but one thing I know; the only ones among
> you who will be truly happy are those who
> will have sought and found how to serve.*
> —ALBERT SCHWEITZER

The theory and practice of assisting, supervising, and mentoring teachers is at a threshold in its evolution. A new vision is emerging based on an analytical view of the essential elements of the processes, an integration of various theoretical perspectives, and the introduction of new concepts. The focus of this book is to describe the underlying tenets of the new vision, clarify its philosophical basis, and operationally define it to illustrate the ways and means of putting the vision into practice.

The interest in providing assistance to teachers takes many forms and has experienced a variety of changes through several phases over the decades. Each of the phases has added to the knowledge base. The focus, procedures, and guiding premises have been recast over time in accordance with prevailing attitudes and themes. Supervision and mentoring tend to be a reflection of the intellectual beliefs and social attitudes of the times. The prevailing philosophy of the culture, organizations, and the profession sets the direction for supervision and mentoring, creating a shadow history.

Currently there are quite divergent philosophies and models in use, and their historical roots cast light on their present form and function (for an analysis, see Tracy, 1995). A review of the changing perspectives of supervision and mentoring over time reveals the foundation of current practice and the evolving nature of the process.

Changing Perspectives

The field of supervision has a long history and a distinct position in the educational system. Original treatments of supervision date as far back as 1875 in William Payne's *Chapters on School Supervision*. Most of the early texts focused on supervision as an inspection function to improve efficiency, including teacher performance and student achievement.

It was in the early 1900s that supervision began to develop on its own, separate from administration. In the 1930s the field of supervision more clearly separated itself from administration and aligned with the process of curriculum development and the newly organized Association for Supervision and Curriculum Development (Callahan & Button, 1964).

Tracing this historical path is significant for understanding the position occupied by supervision in schooling today and its influence on mentoring. Its niche is defined by the function of supervision that is distinct from, although often within the purview of, the role of school administration. Historical perspective explains the source of most writing and model development in the field of supervision. Of particular importance is the influence of this history on the direction and focus of supervision.

A related function of supervision is conducted by university student teacher supervisors and cooperating teachers. Their role is to provide guidance and support to the student, just as the school supervisor assists teachers in improving practice. Although these are seemingly the same responsibilities, they have not been studied in the same ways or viewed as the same process. This is due primarily to the fact that the student teaching setting is not the same context and involves different role relationships and different people. The student teacher is still perceived as a learner, not yet a beginning professional. The university supervisor's role is that of the expert, as is the role of the cooperating teacher.

Because teacher preparation has been a function of the university, student teacher supervision has its own history. The general literature on supervision, however, often addresses and is used by both school supervisors and student teaching supervisors. Analyzing the competencies needed for the supervision function thus benefits both school and university personnel.

A more recent phenomenon is the emergence of the role of mentor. This role is variously referred to as support provider, professional helper, coach, peer, teacher, buddy, professional associate, and, more commonly, mentor. Its origins provide insight into the niche it occupies within the profession.

In the 1970s there was a heightened awareness of the needs of beginning teachers and the high dropout rate among those new to the profession. One of the initial treatments was prepared by Kevin Ryan in *Don't Smile until Christmas: Accounts of the First Year of Teaching* (1970). This anecdotal discourse provided insights into what would become a major area of study. The First Year Teacher Study conducted by Ryan and others in 1977 and other publications (Howey & Bents, 1979; Veenman, 1984) provided a picture of the first-year experience as perceived by beginning teachers.

These concerns with beginning teacher needs led to the study and design of practices for the induction of teachers into the profession. A comprehensive review of induction programs reported that, "prior to 1980, only a few isolated induction programs, most of which were initiated by local districts or individual schools, were in operation in the United States... the movement toward induction programs grew dramatically in the 1980s" (Huling-Austin, 1990, p. 536). By the late 1980s, about thirty-one states, plus the District of Columbia, had implemented or were planning to implement induction programs (Hawk & Robards, 1987). In the early 1980s, other studies of induction were conducted as the movement grew, including McDonald (1980); Grant and Zeichner (1981); Marshall (1983); and a host of others that followed. A study by Sclan and Darling-Hammond in 1992 found that forty-five states and the District of Columbia had initiated systematic programs to evaluate beginning teachers.

A major component of induction programs that was quickly realized is that of the support provider or mentor. "Probably the most consistent finding across studies is the importance of the support teacher" (Huling-Austin, 1990, p. 542). Thus, a new role for assisting teachers emerged, although mentor teachers had already been developed for teacher assistance at all levels in some states, such as California. Mentors, or professional helpers, deal with the teacher's professional growth, curriculum, and other related issues. Their role in the schools is unique, as is that of supervisors, as described previously.

Juxtaposition of Roles

What has evolved are two different roles, supervisor and mentor, that perform essentially the same functions, the only difference being that supervisors ultimately may have to make evaluation decisions. Since the 1980s, however, perspectives of instructional supervision have separated supervision from the evaluative function of administration, as noted by Glatthorn (1984). The two positions continue to grow closer in the nature of their work, their purposes, techniques, and intended outcomes. Their historical precedents account for their different positions in the workplace.

What has been discovered is that these two fields or roles are essentially the same in function and require the same skills and competencies. This is particularly true of clinical supervision, which primarily focuses on teacher performance. This similarity of function translates to a common body of knowledge, drawn from the research and practices of each and enriching the efficacy of both. This synergistic relationship is an underlying theme of this book, providing the impetus to serve the different professionals who require this knowledge and competence. These professionals include administrators, supervisors, mentors, student teacher supervisors, and any other personnel who function as professional helpers in schools.

Despite the similarity in function, an apparent dichotomy between supervision and mentoring evidences itself in several ways. These various professionals belong to different professional associations and interact in separate circles of colleagues. The professional literature of each is also quite distinct, as shown in the following pages.

The Literature of Supervision

The objective here is to summarize some essential perspectives, models, and purposes of school supervision. It is not intended to be a comprehensive review, due to both space limitations and the purpose of analysis in relation to the theme of this book. For a comprehensive and in-depth treatment of supervision, we refer the reader to "Histories, Antecedents, and Legacies: Constructing a History of School Supervision" by Jeffrey Glanz, in the *Handbook of Research on School Supervision* (1998) published by the Association for Supervision and Curriculum Development (ASCD) and Macmillan Publishers.

Perspectives of Supervision

The practice of supervision has been viewed from several different theoretical perspectives. General supervision has been based on either one or a combination of at least three different schools of thought. These include classic scientific management, human relations, and human resources or revisionist theories. Some would include a new scientific approach that is an adaptation of the scientific management theory.

In the early 1920s, school populations grew and schools became more bureaucratic. This called for more specialized roles for administrators such as superintendents, leading to a more distinct role of school supervisor. By 1929, supervision had advanced far enough to establish a separate department in the National Education Association (Karier, 1982). The emerging emphasis of philosophy and practice after about 1920 was democratic supervision.

In the late 1930s and 1940s, the impact of the depression and war had extended the human relations discussion to the notion of a democratic society and school systems, emphasizing the inherent democratic values of shared decision making. "By the 1940s, it was widely recognized that curriculum programs would be stronger if teachers were involved in their development. [In the 1940s, 1950s, and early 1960s,] many who were interested in the democratic, cooperative group process became taken with new theories related to group dynamics and human relations" (Bolin & Panaritis, 1992, pp. 38, 40). According to Kimball Wiles, a human relations supervision advocate, the supervisor's role was becoming one of *supporting, assisting,* and *sharing* rather than directing (Wiles, 1967). The form of supervision that emerged in the 1960s to accommodate this shift was clinical supervision.

The human resources approach has its origins in the work of such proponents as Douglas McGregor (1960), Warren Bennis (1961), Chris Argyris (1957), and Rensis Likert (1961). The focus is on "individual competence, commitment, self-responsibility, fully functioning individuals, and active, viable, vital organizations..." (Argyris, 1964, p. 4). It is contrasted with human relations in that human relations is limited by its failure to provide maximum opportunity for growth: Achievement, challenge, and responsibility are not attended to sufficiently. The human resources approach seeks to integrate the accomplishment needs of individuals with the purposes and goals of the school (Sergiovanni, 1982). Whereas the human relations approach uses teacher satisfaction to achieve individual and school effectiveness, the human resources model employs individual achievement and school effectiveness to achieve teacher satisfaction (Sergiovanni & Starratt, 1988).

Major contemporary proponents of the human resources supervision theory are Sergiovanni and Starratt (1993). Other approaches popular in the mid-1990s relate to influencing and enhancing the teacher's cognitive processes. These include the work of Schön (1983, 1987) and Costa and Garmston (1994).

Clinical Supervision

The varied theories of general supervision are reflected, to some extent, in the approaches to clinical supervision. It emerged during the 1960s and significantly redefined the process of supervision.

Pajak (1993) organized approaches to clinical supervision into four categories: original clinical, humanistic/artistic, technical/didactic, and developmental/reflective. Original clinical models emerged in the 1960s to early 1970s, humanistic/artistic models in the mid-1970s to early 1980s, technical/didactic models in early to mid-1980s; and developmental/reflective in mid-1980s to early 1990s.

Clinical supervision as a process also has experienced change in its emphasis and orientation during the decades from the 1970s to 1990s. Goldhammer, Anderson, and Krajewski (1993) described this progression in accordance with six aspects of clinical supervision: emphasis, use in schools, supervisor role, rapport and mutual trust, literature emphasis, and observation methodology. The emphasis has changed from method to synthesis of method and concept through facilitating conditions; supervisory role from traditional to collegial; and observation methodology from authoritarian to objective analysis system. The role of rapport and mutual trust has moved from cursory in the 1970s to crucial in the 1990s.

Student Teacher Supervision

Studies of the supervisory function in student teaching for the most part have related to the role of the individuals in the triad (university supervisor, cooperating teacher, student teacher), the relationships among these individuals, and the interpersonal component of the process. Most of the interest has been in the interpersonal nature, as this is consistently recognized as a critical component of the process.

A review of the early history of student teaching may be found in Hughes (1982).

The Literature of Mentoring

It is difficult to pinpoint the emergence of the formal mentor role, as it was practiced in a variety of forms prior to the development of induction programs. Informal approaches to teacher assistance included strategies such as peer clinical observation described by Withall and Wood (1979), Freeman, Palmer, and Ferren (1980), and McFaul (1983); peer observation by Glatthorn (1984) and Sparks (1986); and peer coaching by Strother (1989), Chase and Wolfe (1989), and Raney and Robbins (1989). These are forms of peer support derived from the principle of encouraging collegiality and support.

The term "mentor" had its origins in Homer's *Odyssey*. Mentoring as such had an early foothold in business (Clawson, 1980), and higher education (Schmidt & Wolf, 1980). A substantial body of literature exists related to mentoring in business. Some of the early reviews of business mentoring include Shapiro, Haseltine, and Rowe (1978), "Moving Up: Role Models, Mentors, and the Patron System"; Klauss (1979), "Formalized Mentor Relationships for Management and Development Programs in the Federal Government"; Woodlands Group (1980), "Management Development Roles: Coach, Sponsor and Mentor"; Philips-Jones (1982), *Mentors and Protégés*; Hunt and Michael (1983), "Mentorship: A Career Training and Development Tool"; and Merriam (1983), "Mentors and Protégés: A Critical Review of the Literature." As noted by Clawson (1980), the importance of having someone to counsel and guide another in a career has been the topic of much research and deliberation since the mid-1970s.

The impetus of induction programs for beginning teachers and the experience of mentoring in business and related fields initiated the development of more formal mentor programs in education. It was in the early 1980s that mentoring in education received greater visibility and implementation, primarily through beginning teacher assistance programs. Studies of this function began to appear shortly after (Butler, 1987; Huling-Austin & Murphy, 1987). Several projects and programs were designed to assist in the preparation of educators for the role of mentor. These included the Teacher Advisor Project in California (Little, Galagaran, & O'Neal, 1984). In this program, teachers were on special assignment, released from the classroom full-time and paid according to the established teachers' pay scale. This clearly was a formal role for mentors that extended the earlier peer advisor informal relationships.

The California Mentor Teacher Program, which has been in effect since January 1, 1984, was developed to capitalize on this type of relationship and benefits of the program. A 1985 evaluation of the first year of this program revealed the early developmental nature of the mentor role in education, referring to the "mentors' dilemma" (Byrd, 1986).

Another project was the Leadership Resource book for the State of Ohio, which was developed to assist the beginning teacher (Gordon, 1990). It includes a number of topics for mentor training. North Carolina also developed an extensive preparation program for mentors and produced the North Carolina Trainer's Manual for the Mentor/Support Team Training Program (North Carolina Department of Public Instruction, 1986). The California Beginning Teacher Support and Assessment Program (BTSA) also has developed an extensive program for the preparation of support providers who are assigned to beginning teachers. A comprehensive manual is used in a two-day preparation program.

Preparation of Mentors

As the process of assisting teachers moved from informal peer relationships to more formal roles, interest turned to defining the knowledge and skills needed. It was evident that just being an excellent teacher in the classroom was not sufficient. Other specialized skills, particularly working well with other adults, were necessary. The State of Ohio Leadership Resource book (Gordon, 1990), the North Carolina Mentor/Support Team Training Program (1986), and the California BTSA include topics such as helping relationships, diagnostician, the adult learner, resource broker, and conferencing (California Commission of Teacher Credentialing and California Department of Education, 1994b). The findings about important skills have implications for several aspects of teacher support, including structure of these programs, attention to individual needs, and special training for mentors. The need for special training is of particular importance in providing effective support.

In an analysis of mentor preparation, Wolfe (1992) cited the following components: adult development, interpersonal skills, coaching and modeling, nonevaluative styles of supervision, needs of beginning teachers, and the mentoring process. She concluded that mentors "should be prepared for their complex roles and functions of mentoring through a well-designed, multi-faceted, and ongoing training program" (p. 108). She also emphasized the importance of training programs that allow mentors to direct their own learning to fulfill the need for autonomy. This is an essential yet often overlooked domain.

Related to the need for autonomy is another domain of training that none of the other programs has identified: a psychological support preparation component, which provides insights on psychological needs, stress, and burnout. It enables support providers to deal with their needs in these areas and it prepares them to assist other teachers with these issues (Gold & Roth, 1993).

It is evident from the efforts of these programs that specialized preparation for the role of mentor is necessary to enhance the effectiveness of those who serve in this capacity. The approaches to this preparation are quite varied. Many different topics are addressed, and there seems to be a lack of a conceptual framework or philosophical basis for the design and development of mentor preparation programs.

Critics of mentor preparation programs express concerns about their prescriptiveness. One review indicated that training favors procedural knowledge derived from research and minimizes the members' own experiences, wisdom, and expertise acquired in their career (Feiman-Nemser, 1992).

The training programs as they exist are very useful, however, particularly because of the significant need they address. To advance this role to new levels, a new type of program needs to be designed. It must be a cohesive program grounded in adult learning principles and research on mentoring, one that recognizes teaching as an intellectual and personal experience and accounts for the mentor's need to exercise professional judgment. This is one objective of the model presented in this book.

Roles and Responsibilities

A study of 150 mentor–beginning teacher dyads during the 1989–90 academic year was conducted by Wildman and others (1992). Their analysis revealed eight ways of providing assistance to beginning teachers that are divided into three broad categories: direct professional assistance, direct personal/professional assistance, and indirect personal/professional assistance (Wildman et al., 1992).

In order to explore the nature of these mentor activities, in an earlier analysis, Wildman and others (1988) provided specific examples reported by 150 mentors surveyed in their study. These were traced across five categories of beginning teacher concerns: getting students to cooperate, instruction, administrative tasks, parents, and school/working environment. In order to encourage beginning teachers to reflect on their teaching, mentors talked about individual children, showed different grading systems, discussed procedures, modeled a parent conference, and discussed unwritten school policies. This is somewhat different from other approaches to promoting reflection found in Schön (1983, 1987) and Costa and Garmston (1994).

In a review of literature by Gold (1996), several criteria for selection were identified that relate to the role of mentors. These include mentor teachers viewed as experts by their peers (Byrd, 1986; Galvez-Hjornevik, 1986; Ward, 1987), the demonstrated ability of the mentor teacher to be reflective and analytical about teaching (Borko, 1986), a keen desire to be a mentor and to work with a new teacher (Varah, Theune, & Parker, 1986), and an uncommon commitment to their role of leadership (Howey & Zimpher, 1986).

Much of what has been described thus far regarding the role of mentor or support provider appears to emanate from observation and reports from practitioners. A cohesive framework or philosophical context is not provided to any meaningful extent. This often leads mentors to make inferences or assumptions about their responsibilities. As noted by Gold (1996): "Perceptions of the role and the functions of support providers are too often ambiguous. The literature has documented uncertainties of mentors, teachers, and administrators regarding the central purpose of mentoring, specific behaviors that mentors might engage in, and assessment procedure they should or could use" (p. 577).

Similarly, confusion develops when teachers as mentors are left to "invent their roles as they went along" (Hart, 1990, p. 26). Smylie and Denny (1990) found that teacher leaders "were much less certain about whether their fellow teachers understood their leadership roles and what those teachers and their principals expected of them in those roles" (p. 246). Ganser's (1993) study of twenty-four mentor teachers found they emphasized the curriculum and instructional needs of beginning teachers while "their focus on these topics was largely to the exclusion of other broader topics, both personal and professional" (p. 8). This is a very significant finding that will be revisited later in this chapter and throughout the book. It again reflects the early developmental status of peer support and mentoring.

Gold (1996) summarized that "It is easily seen that ambiguity and conflict accompany role definition and have an effect upon teachers' perceptions of mentoring. This is especially true throughout the case literature where support providers are so fearful of collegial criticism that they often are too humble in regard to their own expertise" (p. 578).

The literature on mentoring and the role of support provider or helper reflects the embryonic stage of this activity as a designated role. There is need for a conceptual frame to provide direction to move this area to a new phase of development. One intent of this book is to contribute to that development.

Definitions of Supervision and Mentoring

There are a number of varied perspectives of the supervision and mentoring roles and functions. Some of these are as follows:

- "A comprehensive effort directed toward helping . . . develop the attitudes and behaviors (skills) of self-reliance and accountability within a defined environment" (Kay, 1990, pp. 26–27)
- "A vehicle for developing professionally responsible teachers who were capable of analyzing their own performance, who were open to change and assistance from others, and who were, above all, self-directing" (Pajak, 1993, p. 6)
- "Direct psychological and technical support, service and help to teachers" (Sturges, Krajewski, Lovell, McNeill & Ness, 1978, p. 45)
- "Seek improved methods of teaching and learning; . . . create a physical, social, and psychological climate or environment favorable to learning . . ." (Sergiovanni & Starratt, 1988, p. 31)

Which of the preceding are definitions of mentoring and which are definitions of supervision? The definition by Kay is of mentoring, while all the remaining definitions and statements apply to supervision. It is difficult to differentiate among these statements. In each instance the terms *mentor* and *supervisor* can be used interchangeably. The point being made is to illustrate again the similarities in the two roles, and that most of the research, theory, and literature can be used to inform both roles. How this expansive knowledge base is used in the development of the new vision will be described.

A common thread that runs through the concepts of supervision and mentoring is that of process. Viewing the commonality of process may be much more informative than analyzing roles and functions. Process is perhaps best viewed as the means of making function operational. It is these processes that will be given particular attention here, illustrating how they are embedded in or woven into the fabric of the various roles.

Helping and Evaluating

It has been suggested that the concepts and skills presented in this book are applicable to a variety of roles, such as school supervisor (assistant superintendent for instruction, principal, department head, etc.), student teacher supervisor, mentor teacher, and school-based teacher educator. All of these perform helping roles.

Supervisors also have a responsibility for evaluation of personnel. This function is considered to be incongruent with the function of helping, particularly when the evaluation is for purposes of job retention, tenure, or passing student teaching. The evaluation function interferes with the process of helping, which requires trust and an absence of threat.

In analyzing the mentor's role, several writers have emphatically stated that one who serves in the role of mentor should not be an evaluator as well: "... [There are] inherent differences between providing unconditional support and measuring acceptable performance; ... the activities of mentoring and evaluating teacher performance are on opposite ends of a continuum; ... the disparate purposes of mentoring and evaluating as functions of school personnel are incompatible activities" (Neal, 1992, pp. 35–36). Gold (1996) noted that evaluation hinders the development of trust and teachers may refrain from confiding in support persons.

When conducting observation-assessment activities, the relationship between the helper and teacher is not likely to be contaminated, particularly if trust and rapport have been established. This may be facilitated by attending to several factors identified by Gold (1996). The first of these is making clear the purpose of the observation or assessment. Is it to provide information to share with the teacher to gain insights on his or her practice? Is it intended to serve as a baseline for designing professional development? Is it to enable mutual analysis of strengths and weakness to promote growth? Is it a formative assessment to identify areas needing further development to address in preparation for a future summative evaluation? Is it to serve as the basis for making decisions about retention or passing? Knowing how the information will be used obviously contributes greatly to setting the tone of the interaction.

Clarification of assessment versus evaluation is not only informative, but it also provides guidance and contributes to establishing a supportive environment. Nevertheless, those who supervise student teachers and interns and those who have the responsibility of making judgments about retaining teachers are called upon to perform an evaluation function. This is a necessary component of quality assurance and fulfills a responsibility to the school and its students.

It would be naive to assume that evaluation has no effect on the relationship with the teacher. This does not mean, however, that the supervisor is unable to have an effective helping relationship. Sergiovanni and Starratt (1993) suggest that as supervisors provide support to help teachers grow and commit to teaching, the need for quality control becomes less important. Goldhammer, Anderson, and Krajewski (1993) refer to *supportive supervision* that is directed toward both organizational and individual goals, thus employing both evaluating and facilitating growth. Acheson and Gall (1992) propose that, in some respects, evaluation and helping are compatible as they both lead to growth.

Hunter and Russell (1990) suggest that formative followed by summative evaluation must be a sequential process, not simultaneous or discrete. Glickman, Gordon, and Ross-Gordon (1995) believe that one person can have both responsibilities of direct assistance and formal evaluation and do both well. However, this is achieved with difficulty, and only by a person who can maintain trust and credibility with teachers.

The way the evaluation is conducted can temper the impact of this activity. Also, if a context is established in which evaluation is viewed as a necessary part of feedback and growth, the process will have a less deleterious effect on the helping relationship. Evaluation does not diminish the use of helping skills. Indeed, these skills are needed even more so. The relationship between evaluation and helping within the role of supervision may best be viewed in terms of the purpose of supervision.

In a conceptual framework for effective supervision, Anderson (1982) characterizes the supervisor as mentor and collaborator. "The supervisor is portrayed not only as one who participates in the supervisory process (collaborator), but also as one who provides guidance and instruction (mentor and trainer) . . ." (p. 188). Collectively, such perspectives clearly lead to the conclusion that the supervisory role is one of professional helping. Even the evaluation function may be perceived as helping in that it provides constructive feedback.

The purpose of the preceding discussion is to support the concept that supervision is appropriately characterized as a helping, supportive function. In view of this, the preparation of supervisors should be focused on developing helping skills. This is the theme of this book and the basis for the new vision.

A New Vision—New Dimensions

Helping others grow in their profession is a significant endeavor. It also is very complex. Taking an in-depth look at professional roles that are dedicated to this purpose is informative. By analyzing these functions from different viewpoints, greater insights may be derived and integrated into the design of a new theory of professional support that focuses on helping teachers bring about changes that will transform their lives. This theory emphasizes a diagnostic-prescriptive model to meet individuals' needs for the purpose of enhancing their lives which will in turn affect the psychological well-being of the organization.

In addition to the analysis of existing functions, looking at unique perspectives of the nature of helping contributes significantly to understanding the helping process. These perspectives emanate from several fields of study including supervision, psychotherapy, motivation theory, communications, relationship theory, change processes, and professional development.

The relevant concepts, strategies, and skills from these domains, as well as specific analyses of current roles and functions, are analyzed and selected aspects are integrated into a new configuration. A new framework based on understanding and developing the professional and psychological needs of individuals is presented. This collective set of understandings and perspectives is formulated into a new vision of supervision and mentoring that creates the role of a professional helper. The focus of the model is on supporting teachers as they make necessary personal and professional transformations in their lives that in turn impact the very essence of the organization. In the next chapter the philosophy and operational elements of the new vision will be explained.

Summary

This introductory chapter began by noting the existence of different domains of knowledge and practice related to the process of helping educators with professional development. Each has its own history, emanates from different sources, and addresses different clientele, but all are strikingly similar in process and purpose.

The history of general supervision was briefly traced, noting the varied philosophies and theories that govern its practice. There is no one prevailing model or set of principles guiding school supervision today. Scientific, human relations, and human resource management ideologies all have some degree of influence. A primary focus is on clinical supervision of various sorts. In general, the evolution of supervision has moved from a regulatory role to one that is more needs-sensitive and people-centered.

More recently, mentoring has emerged mostly as a response to the need to assist beginning teachers. It derives from the need to provide support for new teachers as they make the transition to independent teacher in their own classrooms. Mentoring is conceived of as being a helping function because its purpose is to address the needs of beginning teachers. Mentoring is in its early stages of development in professional education. Paradoxically, "the practice of mentoring is on the increase, . . . [yet] the concept remains relatively underdeveloped in practice" (Peper, 1994, pp. 6–8). An analysis of the functions of mentors, as reported in the literature, reveals these functions are virtually indistinguishable from those of supervisor. Definitions of each of these are such that the terms *supervision* or *student teacher supervision* and *mentoring* are essentially interchangeable.

The student teaching literature also clearly indicates how this field fits neatly into the realm of general supervision and of mentoring. The background of student teaching supervision is very congruent with general supervision and particularly consistent with clinical supervision.

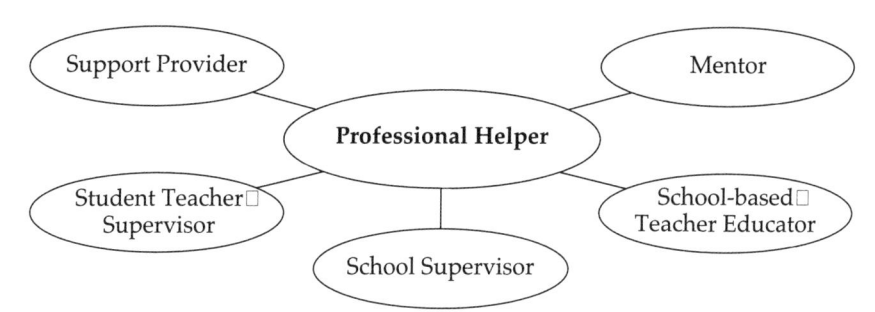

FIGURE 1-1 The Roles of the Professional Helper

```
   Support Provider                              Mentor
                     Professional Helper
   Student Teacher                         School-based
     Supervisor                           Teacher Educator
                     School Supervisor
```

There also is an apparent contradiction between helping and evaluating. The function and influence of evaluation was duly noted, but not emphasized. Assessment was defined in such a way as to clarify its compatibility with helping and supporting. Further, the evaluation function need not interfere with the process of assisting, and the helping function is the essence of the various roles.

A fundamental conclusion is that semantically, philosophically, and operationally the various roles referred to are essentially the same in that the dominant and common thread through all of these is the role of helping. This is depicted in Figure 1-1.

Issues and Questions for Review and Reflection

1. Historically there have been a variety of philosophies that direct the nature of supervision, mentoring, and helping. Identify the key elements of some of these approaches.
2. Describe how a supervisor would function using a particular philosophy.
3. Role play a particular approach, demonstrating the sense of the underlying philosophy.
4. List pros and cons of the various philosophies, and compare them.
5. What are the similarities and differences between the role and functions of the supervisor and mentor?
6. Supervision and mentoring each have their own research and literature base. Given the similarities of these roles, what are the implications for using the literature of both for each role? What are the implications for the knowledge and skills required of each?

References

Acheson, K. A., & Gall, M. D. (1992). *Techniques in the clinical supervision of teachers: Preservice and inservice applications* (3d ed.). New York: Longman.

Anderson, R. H. (1982). Creating a future for supervision. In T. J. Sergiovanni (Ed.), *Supervision of teaching*. Alexandria, VA: Association for Supervision and Curriculum Development.

Argyris, C. (1957). *Personality and organization.* New York: Harper & Row.

Argyris, C. (1964). *Integrating the individual and the organization.* New York: Wiley & Sons, Inc.

Bennis, W. (1961). Revisionist theory of leadership. *Harvard Business Review, 39*(1), 26–38.

Bolin, F. S., & Panaritis, P. (1992). Searching for a common purpose: A perspective on the history of supervision. In C. Glickman (Ed.), *Supervision in transition: 1992 yearbook.* Alexandria, VA: Association for Supervision and Curriculum Development.

Borko, H. (1986). Clinical teacher education: The induction years. In J. Hoffman & S. Edwards (Eds.), *Reality and reform in clinical teacher education* (pp. 45–63). New York: Random House.

Butler, E. D. (1987). Lessons learned about mentoring in two fifth year teacher preparation-induction programs. Paper presented at the annual meeting of the Association of Teacher Educators, Houston, TX.

Byrd, T. (1986). *The mentors' dilemma.* San Francisco: Far West Laboratory for Educational Research and Development.

California Commission of Teacher Credentialing and California Department of Education. (1994b). *A guide to prepare support providers for work with beginning teachers: Training module.* Sacramento: CA: Author.

California Commission of Teacher Credentialing and California Department of Education. (1994b). *Report on implementation of the Beginning Teacher Support and Assessment Program.* Sacramento: CA: Author.

Callahan, R. E., & Button, H. W. (1964). Historical change of the role of the man in the organization: 1865–1950. In D. E. Griffiths (Ed.), *Behavioral science and educational administration.* (The sixty-third yearbook of the National Society for the Study of Education, Part II). Chicago: University of Chicago Press.

Chase, A., & Wolfe, P. (1989). Off to a good start in peer coaching. *Educational Leadership, 46*(8), 37.

Clawson, J. (1980). Mentoring and managerial careers. In C. B. Derr (Ed.), *Work, family, and the career* (pp. 144–165). New York: Praeger.

Costa, A. L., & Garmston, R. J. (1994). *Cognitive coaching: A foundation for renaissance schools.* Norwood, MA: Christopher-Gordon.

Feiman-Nemser, S. (1992). *Helping novices learn to teach: Lessons from an experienced support teacher* (Report No. 91-6). East Lansing: Michigan State University, National Center for Research on Teacher Learning.

Freeman, G., Palmer, R. C., & Ferren, A. S. (1980). Team building for supervisory support. *Educational Leadership, 37*(4), 356–358.

Galvez-Hjornevik, C. (1986). Mentoring among teachers: A review of literature. *Journal of Teacher Education, 37*(1), 6–11.

Ganser, T. (1993). How mentors describe and categorized their ideas about mentoring roles, benefits of mentoring, and obstacles of mentoring. Paper presented at the annual meeting of the Association of Teacher Educators, Los Angeles.

Glatthorn, A. A. (1984). *Differentiated supervision.* Alexandria, VA: Association for Supervision and Curriculum Development.

Glickman, C. D., Gordon, S. P., & Ross-Gordon, J. M. (1995). *Supervision of instruction: A developmental approach* (3d ed.). Boston: Allyn and Bacon.

Gold, Y. (1996). Beginning teacher support: Attrition, mentoring, and induction. In J. Sikula (Ed.), *Handbook of research on teacher education* (pp. 548–594). New York: Macmillan.

Gold, Y., & Roth, R. A. (1993). *Teachers managing stress and preventing burnout: The professional health (PH) solution.* London: Falmer Press.

Goldhammer, R., Anderson, R. H., & Krajewski, R. J. (1993). *Clinical supervision: Special methods for the supervision of teachers* (3d ed.). New York: Harcourt-Brace.

Gordon, S. P. (1990). *Assisting the entry-year teacher: A leadership resource.* Columbus: Ohio Department of Education, Inservice Education.

Grant, C., & Zeichner, K. (1981). Inservice support for first-year teachers: The state of the scene. *Journal of Research and Development in Education, 14*(2), 99–111.

Hart, A. W. (1990). Impacts of the school social unit on teacher authority during work redesign. *American Educational Research Journal, 27*(3), 503–532.

Hawk, P., & Robards, S. (1987). Statewide teacher induction programs. In D. Brooks (Ed.), *Teacher induction: A new beginning* (pp. 33–44). Reston, VA: Association of Teacher Educators.

Howey, K. R., & Bents, R. H. (1979). *Toward meeting the needs of the beginning teacher.* Minneapolis, MN: Midwest Teacher Corps Network.

Howey, K. R., & Zimpher, N. L. (1986). *Requisites for the teacher-mentor: Uncommon commitment and commonplace knowledge.* Unpublished manuscript. Columbus: Ohio State University.

Hughes, R., Jr. (1982). Student teaching: The past as a window to the future. In G. A. Griffin & S. Edwards (Eds.), *Student teaching: Problems and promising practices.* Austin: University of Texas at Austin, Research and Development Center for Teacher Education.

Huling-Austin, L. (1990). Teacher induction programs and internships. In W. R. Houston (Ed.), *Handbook of research on teacher education: A project of the Association of Teacher Educators* (pp. 535–548). New York: Macmillan.

Huling-Austin, L., & Murphy, S. C. (1987). Assessing the impact of teacher induction programs: Implications for program development. Paper presented at the annual meeting of the American Educational Research Association, Washington, DC (ERIC Document Reproduction Service No. ED 283 779).

Hunt, D. M., & Michael, C. (1983). Mentorship: A career training and development tool. *Academy of Management Review, 8*(3), 475–485.

Hunter, M., & Russell, D. (1990). *Mastering coaching and supervision* (Principles of Learning series). Thousand Oaks, CA: Corwin Press.

Karier, C. (1982). Supervision in historic perspective. In T. J. Sergiovanni (Ed.), *Supervision of teaching* (pp. 2–15). Washington, DC: Association for Supervision and Curriculum Development.

Kay, R. S. (1990). A definition for developing self reliance. In T. M. Bey & C. T. Holmes (Eds.), *Mentoring: Developing successful new teachers* (pp. 25–38). Reston, VA: Association of Teacher Educators.

Klauss, R. (1979). Formalized mentor relationships for management and development programs in the federal government. *Public Administration Review,* 489–496.

Likert, R. (1961). *New patterns of management.* New York: McGraw-Hill.

Little, J. W., Galagaran, P., & O'Neal, R. (1984). *Professional development roles and relationships: Principles and skills of "advising."* San Francisco: Far West Laboratory for Educational Research and Development.

Marshall, F. G. (1983). Perceived effectiveness of induction practices by beginning teachers in public school districts in the greater Houston area. (Doctoral dissertation, University of Houston). *Dissertation Abstracts International, 43,* 7.

McDonald, F. (1980). *The problems of beginning teachers: A crisis in training: Vol. 1. Study of induction programs for beginning teachers.* Princeton, NJ: Educational Testing Service.

McFaul, S.A. (1983). A case study of the implementation of peer clinical supervision in an urban elementary school. *Dissertation Abstracts International, 43,* 3527A.

McGregor, D. (1960). *The human side of enterprise.* New York: McGraw-Hill.

Merriam, S. (1983). Mentors and protégés. A critical review of the literature. *Adult Education Quarterly, 33*(3), 161–173.

Neal, J. C. (1992). Mentoring: A teacher development activity that avoids formal evaluation of the protégé. In T. M. Bey & C. T. Holmes (Eds.), *Mentoring: Contemporary principles and issues.* Reston, VA: Association of Teacher Educators.

North Carolina Department of Public Instruction (1986). *North Carolina Mentor/Support Team Training Program: Trainers manual.* Raleigh, NC: Division of Program Approval, Personnel Services Area.

Pajak, E. (1993). *Approaches to clinical supervision: Alternatives for improving instruction.* Norwood, MA: Christopher-Gordon.

Payne, W. H. (1875). *Chapters on school supervision.* New York: Wilson, Hinkle.

Peper, John B. (1994). "Mentoring, Mentors and Protégés." Paper presented at the annual meeting of the American Educational Research Association, New Orleans, LA, April 4–10, 1994.

Philips-Jones, L. (1982). *Mentors and protégés.* New York: Arbor House.

Raney, P., & Robbins, P. (1989). Professional growth and support through peer coaching. *Educational Leadership, 46*(8), 35–38.

Ryan, K. (1970). *Don't smile until Christmas:*

Accounts of the first year of teaching. Chicago: University of Chicago Press.

Schmidt, J. A., & Wolf, J. S. (1980). The mentor partnership: Discovery of professionalism. *National Association of Student Personnel Administration Journal, 17*, 45–51.

Schön, D. A. (1983). *The reflective practitioner: How professionals think in action.* New York: Basic Books.

Schön, D. A. (1987). *Educating the reflective practitioners.* San Francisco: Jossey-Bass.

Sclan, E., & Darling-Hammond, L. (1992). *Beginning teacher performance evaluation: An overview of state policies. Trends and issues paper No. 7.* Washington, DC: ERIC Clearinghouse on Teacher Education.

Sergiovanni, T. J. (1982). The context for supervision. In T. J. Sergiovanni (Ed.), *Supervision of teaching.* Alexandria, VA: Association for Supervision and Curriculum Development.

Sergiovanni, T. J., & Starratt, R. J. (1988). *Supervision: Human perspectives* (4th ed.). New York: McGraw-Hill.

Sergiovanni, T. J., & Starratt, R. J. (1993). *Supervision: A redefinition* (5th ed.). New York: McGraw-Hill.

Shapiro, E. C., Haseltine, F. P., & Rowe, M. P. (1978). Moving up: Role models, mentors, and the patron system. *Sloan Management Review, 19*(3), 51–58.

Smylie, M. A., & Denny, J. W. (1990). Teacher leadership: Tensions and ambiguities in organizational perspective. *Educational Administration Quarterly, 26*(3), 235–259.

Sparks, G. M. (1986). The effectiveness of alternative training activities in changing teaching practices. *American Educational Research Journal, 23*(2), 217–225.

Strother, D. B. (1989). Peer coaching for teachers: Opening classroom doors. *Phi Delta Kappan, 70*, 824-827.

Sturges, A. W., Krajewski, R. J., Lovell, J. T., McNeill, E., & Ness, M. G. (1978). The roles and responsibilities of instructional supervisors. *Report of the ASCD Working Group on the roles and responsibilities of supervisors.* Alexandria, VA: Association for Supervision and Curriculum Development.

Tracy, S. J. (1995). How historical concepts of supervision relate to supervisory practices today. *The Clearing House, 68,* 320–325.

Varah, L. J., Theune, W. S., & Parker, L. (1986). Beginning teachers: Sink or swim? *Journal of Teacher Education, 37*(1), 30–34.

Veenman, S. (1984). Perceived problems of beginning teachers. *Review of Educational Research 54*(2), 143-178.

Ward, B. A. (1987). State and district structures to support initial year of teaching programs. In G. A. Griffin & S. Millies (Eds.), *The first years of teaching: Background papers and a proposal* (pp. 35–64). Chicago: University of Illinois State Board of Education.

Wildman, T. M., Magliaro, S. G., Niles, J. A., McLaughlin, R. A., & Drill, L. (1988). Sources of teaching problems and the ways beginners solve them: An analysis for the first two years. Paper presented at the meeting of the American Educational Research Association, New Orleans, LA.

Wildman, T. M., Magliaro, S. G., Niles, R. A., & Niles, J. A. (1992). Teacher mentoring: An analysis of roles, activities, and conditions. *Journal of Teacher Education, 43*(3), 205–213.

Wiles, K. (1967). *Supervision for better schools* (3d ed.). Englewood Cliffs, NJ: Prentice-Hall.

Withall, J., & Wood, F. H. (1979). Taking the threat out of classroom observation and feedback. *Journal of Teacher Education, 30*(1), 55–58.

Wolfe, D. M. (1992). Designing, training, and selecting incentives for mentor programs. In T. M. Bey & C. T. Holmes (Eds.), *Mentoring: Contemporary principles and issues* (pp. 103–110). Reston, VA: Association of Teacher Educators.

Woodlands Group.(1980). Management development roles: Coach, sponsor, and mentor. *Personnel Journal, 59*(11), 918–921.

Zahorik, J. A. (1988). The observing-conferencing role of university supervisors. *Journal of Teacher Education, 39*(2), 9–16.

Zeichner, K. M., & Liston, D. P. (1985). Theory and practice in the evolution of an inquiry-oriented student teaching program. Paper presented at the meeting of the American Educational Research Association, Chicago.

Zeichner, K. M., & Tabachnick, R. (1982). The belief systems of university supervisors in an elementary student teaching program. *Journal of Education for Teaching, 8*(1), 34–35.

Related Readings

Darling-Hammond, L., Wise, A., & Pease, S. (1986). Teacher evaluation in the organizational context: A review of the literature. *Review of Educational Research, 53*(3), 285–328.

Duke, D. L., & Stiggins, R. J. (1986). *Teacher evaluation: Five keys to growth.* Washington, DC: (joint publication) AASA, NAESP, NASSP, NEA.

Educational Leadership. (1987c). Theme issue: Progress in evaluating teaching, *44*(7).

Glickman, C. D., & Pajak, E. (1986). The supervisor as evaluator or helper: Research on a controversial issue. *Canadian School Executive, 6*(3), 3–5.

Hunter, M. (1988). Effective reconciliation between supervision and evaluation. A reply to Popham. *Journal of Personnel Evaluation in Education, 1,* 275–279.

Jones, K., & Sherman, A. (1980). Two approaches to evaluation. *Educational Leadership, 37,* 553–557.

Krechevsky, M. (1991). Project spectrum: An innovative assessment alternative. *Educational Leadership, 48*(5), 43–48.

McCarthy, D. J., Kaufman, J. W., & Stafford, J. C. (1986, April). Supervision and evaluation: Two irreconcilable processes. *Clearing House, 59,* 351–353.

McIntyre, D. J., & Byrd, D. M. (Eds.) (1996). Preparing tomorrow's teachers: The field experience. Teacher education yearbook IV. Thousand Oaks, CA: Corwin Press.

McLaughlin, M. W., & Pfeifer, R. S. (1988). *Teacher evaluation: Improvement, accountability, and effective learning.* New York: Teachers College Press.

Stanley, S. J., & Popham, W. S. (Eds.). (1988). *Teacher evaluation: Six prescriptions for success.* Alexandria, VA: Association for Supervision and Curriculum Development.

Chapter 2

A New Vision of the Helper: The Helping Professional

The search for a significant theory and more effective practice of the professional helping role has taken many paths, with each contributing to the knowledge base and processes of mentoring and supervising. Insights from these efforts led to identification of several essential elements of the helping process theory. These basic elements include the following: (1) the role of the mentor/supervisor as support provider, (2) the function of interpersonal relationships and helping, (3) motivation for growth and helping, (4) the mentor/supervisor as role model and leader, (5) a focus on the individual, (6) communication skills, (7) self-responsibility, (8) a concern for the vitality of the organization through integration of organizational and individual goals, (9) personal growth, and (10) an emphasis on cognitive processes. These issues are embedded in the classical and contemporary theories of supervision and the models of mentoring that are now in use. These are factors that have survived through time and are of sufficient importance to be integrated with new perspectives and elements into a new vision of the professional serving in a helping capacity. A brief summary of these is of value in providing a basis for the elaboration of the overall philosophy of a new model of the helping professional.

Contemporary Fundamental Elements

The ten fundamental elements just cited will be reviewed as basic components of a model for helping. These elements define some of the categories of information that need to be included in a new philosophy. The elements may be identified with similar headings in the new vision or may be infused throughout the set of additional principles described in the philosophy of the helping model. Although conceptualized, translated, or operationalized in unique ways in the new vision, these elements as described here provide context and an understanding of the legacy of the existing models of supervision and mentoring. In the context of the new vision, these elements may be viewed from different perspectives, operationalized in significantly different ways, or integrated with new components to form unique configurations that provide more significant meanings.

Support Provider/Helper

A number of existing programs and models have incorporated the concept of support provider or helper. The North Carolina Mentor/Support Team Training Program addresses the area of helping relationships. It includes the roles of supporter/helper, facilitator, and similar functions. The program identifies factors in a helping relationship such as trust, empathy, acceptance, caring, individuation, and communication (NC Dept. of Public Instruction, 1986).

An analysis of several studies of student teaching by Glickman (1990) concluded that there is a strong need for establishing a helping relationship between the supervisor and student teacher. A study by Koehler (1984) concluded that university supervisors believe their primary responsibility centers on support to student teachers while facilitating growth. Among the roles identified by Koehler is giving support for student teachers in both personal and professional areas. The study of mentors by Wildman and colleagues (1992) revealed eight ways of providing assistance. One of these is direct personal/professional assistance that includes encouraging and supporting.

In each of these studies these roles consistently are characterized as having an embedded responsibility for helping and supporting. The function of support provider or helper thus is fundamental to the role of supervisor or mentor.

Interpersonal Relationships

The necessity for interpersonal relationship skills has been identified by several studies and authors. Goldhammer, Anderson, and Krajewski (1993) note that the element of rapport and mutual trust has moved from a cursory treatment in clinical supervision in the 1970s to a crucial place in the process in the 1990s. Kimball Wiles (1967) notes that in the human relations supervisory approach the role becomes one of supporting, assisting and sharing rather than directing. Sergiovanni and Starratt (1988) emphasize the importance of relationships and that supervision is defined as "creating a physical, social, and psychological climate or environment favorable to learning . . ." (p. 31). Gold and Roth (1993) describe the essential nature of interpersonal relationships in meeting teachers' needs for professional health. Interpersonal relationships thus pervade every approach to training for mentors, supervisors, or other support providers.

Motivation and Growth

The emphasis on motivation and growth is manifest in several different ways in the literature. Cuff (1978) found that increasing motivation and stimulating growth are goals of cooperating teachers. Herzberg (1966) cites the need for psychological stimulation by which the individual is activated toward self-realization needs. Koehler (1984) also emphasizes the need for motivation and growth as part of the function of university supervisors. Sergiovanni (1982) identifies accomplishment needs as a means of providing a challenge and motivation. Identifying an orientation to motivation as a growth stimulus is an important element of a model for supervision, mentoring, or helping.

Role Model/Leader

The North Carolina mentor training program (NC Dept. of Public Instruction, 1986) identifies several roles of the support provider, one of which is that of teacher/model. Anderson (1982) characterized the supervisor as a mentor and collaborator who provides guidance and instruction. In her analysis of mentor preparation, Wolfe (1992) cited coaching and modeling as important components of such a training program.

Individual Competence/Technical Proficiency

One of the strands of emphasis in most of the models is a focus on the individual and the individual's competence. Developing technical proficiency is an objective of all the mentoring programs.

Communication Skills

Communication skills have been identified in all of the approaches to preparation and are embedded in other categories such as the support provider/helper and interpersonal relationships. It is a topic in the preparation programs for Ohio, North Carolina, and California.

Self-Responsibility

Taking responsibility for one's self as a teacher and professional and making a commitment to personal growth and the growth of the organization also are given high priority. The human resources model places more emphasis on commitment to the organization than other models; however, their focus is on self-responsibility (Argyris, 1964). This is a fundamental principle of adult learning theory. As noted by Malcolm Knowles (1978), "Adults have a deep need to be self directing" (p. 31).

The Ohio Department of Education Training Program and the North Carolina program also emphasize adult learning principles that focus on teacher self-responsibility as an adult learner.

The Organization and the Individual

Goldhammer, Anderson, and Krajewski (1993) refer to "supportive supervision." This type of supervision is directed toward both organizational and individual goals. The human resources approach to supervision seeks to integrate the accomplishment needs of individuals with the purposes and goals of the school (Sergiovanni, 1982).

Personal Growth

As noted in Chapter 1, the emphasis in supervision is moving more toward that of the individual rather than focusing solely on the needs of the organization. This is an essential change because teachers need assistance in their individual growth if they are going to be effective.

Cognitive Development

In recent years a great deal of emphasis is placed on the cognitive development of the teacher including reflection on his or her own thinking (metacognition). This is a fundamental basis of the approaches by Schön (1983, 1987) and Costa and Garmston (1994). Ziechner and Tabachnick (1982) state that one of the goals of student teacher supervision is to help student teachers become more reflective and analytical about their teaching.

Summary of Elements

The preceding ten elements provide an important historical framework for the creation of a new vision. These elements continue to be of importance and form part of the foundation of the vision of effective helping. Combined with a sound philosophical perspective and associated elements, collectively these create the role we refer to as the *Helping Professional*. The Helping Professional engages in a process of self-transformation to higher levels of personal and professional competence and assists teachers in their self-transformation as well. We thus refer to the overall approach as the *Transformational Helping Professional model*.

Pervasiveness of Philosophy

Most practitioners do not ordinarily engage in dialogue about their particular philosophy or the basic philosophical premises that undergird and guide their practice. Philosophy is viewed as abstract, obtuse, and unrelated to the real world of daily decision making. Paradoxically, virtually all of our professional practice is driven by a tacit philosophical orientation. The mentor, supervisor, and teacher are influenced by their visions of teaching, learning, and assisting other professionals.

Given the pervasive influence of one's philosophy on practice (e.g. teaching, mentoring, helping), it is of paramount importance for educators to understand their own philosophy. This means to reveal or discover it for themselves. Further, and of greater importance, it is essential that professionals examine, analyze, test, and reconsider the nature and substance of their basic professional philosophy.

As a beginning, we might inquire what we mean by professional philosophy. What is philosophy, and how is it characterized? In essence, philosophy is a set of values and beliefs. The role of philosophy is to guide understanding through identification of patterns and by creating organization or structure. Thus, philosophy is an organizational framework that enables one to conceptualize the whole.

Philosophy also guides one's judgment about the value or worth of events, issues, or entities. Congruency with the premises of the philosophy predisposes one's perspective and judgment of situations or ideas. Philosophy enables one to analyze or critique and to determine meaning in different contexts.

A professional philosophy relates to elements of particular relevance to that profession. In education, and specifically in professional helping, these include elements such as the nature of knowledge (epistemology), motivation, personal development, and the nature of helping. Four fields had a major influence on theories of supervision: leadership theory, communication theory, organization theory, and change theory (Alfonso, Firth, & Neville, 1981). Other fields having an impact include sociology and anthropology (Bowers & Flinders, 1991), psychology and educational psychology (Hunter & Russell, 1990), counseling theory (Costa & Garmston, 1994), and communications and linguistics (R. J. Roberts, 1992; G. B. Roberts, 1992; Waite, 1993). From these philosophical perspectives we can develop a theory or model of how the helping process works, thus putting the philosophy into operational terms.

The Transformational Helping Professional: Philosophy and Theory

Given the importance of clearly identifying a philosophy, at this point we turn to describing the values, beliefs, and related components that make up the Transformational Helping Professional philosophy.

We will present here the basic tenets of the Transformational model in accordance with the following framework: (1) identification of beliefs, (2) description of the related theoretical understandings and hypotheses, (3) specification of goals and intended outcomes, (4) analysis of necessary content, (5) clarification of roles and responsibilities, and (6) delineation of processes.

Values and Beliefs of the Transformational Helping Model

Eight fundamental values and beliefs of the Transformational Helping Model can be identified:

1. Clearly conceptualized and well-thought-out values and beliefs must underlie professional practice.
2. The worth of the individual is a fundamental value.
3. Meeting healthy personal and psychological needs is the foundation of personal fulfillment and growth.
4. Meeting individual professional needs is the foundation of effective professional practice.
5. Learning is a personal experience and best achieved when meaningful to the individual.
6. Professional helping is a process of support and guidance for enhancing personal fulfillment and realization of potential.
7. Change is endemic to the process of helping and growth.
8. The well-being of the organization and achievement of the common good depend, in large measure, upon the psychological health and professional competence of the individuals within it.

In this section each of the beliefs/values will be expanded upon in terms of the framework we described, such as the related theoretical understandings.

Belief/value 1: Clearly conceptualized and well-thought-out values and beliefs must underlie professional practice. From this it follows that the Helping Professional clearly understands, articulates, and adheres to a set of values and beliefs. The goal of this component of the model is to have Helping Professionals who use the beliefs and values of the Transformational model in their responsibilities to assist teachers and themselves in professional growth.

The related content of the model consists of the values and beliefs of the Transformational Helping Professional model, as well as the associated knowledge, skills, and dispositions. The role of the Helping Professional is to act consistently with these beliefs and values in performing the responsibilities of helping. The belief system of the Helping Professional guides practice and is periodically revised for relevance. The processes of the model emanate from and are consistent with the stated values and beliefs.

Belief/value 2: The worth of the individual is a fundamental value. Each person has worth that must be recognized, validated, and appreciated. The goal then is to provide and demonstrate acceptance of and respect for the individual. The desired outcome is that individuals feel accepted and respected in connection with the helping process. This includes students, teachers, administrators, and Helping Professionals. The content of the model here consists of interpersonal and related skills to create the possibility for each individual to feel worthwhile. The responsibility of the Helping Professional is to serve as a role model in this regard. The process requires interacting in ways and creating conditions in which an individual feels accepted, of worth, and free to develop.

A principle based on this belief is that the organization and its processes, such as helping, must be conducted in such a way that they provide acceptance of and respect for the individual. A corollary is that individuals want to feel that they have worth and thus seek respect from others. This clearly suggests that the helping process should be conducted in an environment of respect, and the Helping Professional needs to be an individual who accepts others for their worth and value and encourages and guides their growth and development. Interpersonal skills are necessary in order to develop optimum conditions. It is the accepting and encouraging aspects of the Helping Professional that create the environment for growth.

Belief/value 3: Meeting healthy personal and psychological needs is the foundation of personal fulfillment and growth. The Helping Professional philosophy holds firmly to the belief that individual personal and psychological needs are the foundation of the helping process. The helping theory thus provides that these needs must be identified and addressed. The content consists of the range of personal and psychological needs. The Helping Professional's role is one of guide, facilitating the teacher's identification of needs and means of addressing them through a relationship of trust. The processes required are those of assessing, diagnosing, guiding, and supporting.

Motivation to achieve or change is driven primarily by unmet personal and psychological needs and a desire to meet them. Thus, if the Helping Professional can assist the teacher in clarifying unmet needs and in discovering meaningful ways of fulfilling them, the teacher's motivation for personal and professional growth will be increased. The personal and psychological framework is defined to cover a broad range of needs, such as social needs, intellectual needs, and emotional needs.

Belief/value 4: Meeting individual professional needs is the foundation of effective professional practice. Instructional and professional needs are those that must be met in order to perform one's professional role. These needs also must be identified and addressed, and motivation is partly driven by a desire to meet these needs. Professional needs include the knowledge, skills, and dispositions of the practitioner. Of particular importance is an emphasis on cognitive processes—what teachers think about while planning, making decisions during instruction, and subsequent to teaching. The content also includes reflection on their own thinking processes, or metacognition.

The role of the Helping Professional is to provide for meaningful assessment and self-analysis of the teacher's instructional needs, as a foundation for planning professional growth. The Helping Professional also has a responsibility to be a guide and supporter of the teacher's professional growth process. In order to fulfill this role and responsibility, the Helping Professional establishes a relationship of trust and openness so that the teacher freely engages in a mutual exploration and assessment of instructional and professional needs. Furthermore, the Helping Professional collaborates and consults with the teacher in the design of professional growth activities to respond to the needs identified in the assessments. These processes require a significant knowledge base in instructional practice, technical skills of teaching, and strong interpersonal skills in order to establish the productive relationship.

Belief/value 5: Learning is a personal experience and best achieved when meaningful to the individual. Meaning is derived from one's personal perspective. The resultant principle of the theory is that learning best occurs when personal meaning is associated with the process and content. Furthermore, the breadth and depth of what is learned and remembered are affected by a variety of factors such as affect, emotion, personal growth, personal expectations of success, and general states of mind. Learning is facilitated by social interactions in communication; self-esteem facilitates learning and is heightened when individuals are in a respectful and caring relationship with others who see their potential. Learning is also influenced by beliefs and thoughts resulting from prior learning and based on unique interpretations (American Psychological Association, 1991).

The goal then is to establish a conducive environment and conditions for learning so that the teacher being helped may derive meaning and achieve the maximum level of professional growth. The content of the model relates to all the various factors and conditions that promote the learning principles previously described.

The responsibility of the Helping Professional is to create the conditions in which the individual perceives meaning and will be able to achieve maximum growth. In order to meet this responsibility, the Helping Professional engages in processes that utilize the knowledge, skills, and dispositions that support the learning principles. The processes include the creation of meaningful experiences, development of trust, and establishment of positive working relationships with which the teacher feels comfortable. All of this suggests that the Helping Professional has a keen understanding of the teachers being helped by becoming aware of their values, beliefs, and interests and by determining how learning experiences can be designed to guide and encourage them to formulate their own meaning out of their experiences.

Belief/value 6: Professional helping is a process of support and guidance for enhancing personal fulfillment and realization of potential. Professional helping is conducted in such a way as to provide for support and guidance that leads to the personal fulfillment of teachers and guides them toward the realization of their full potential. The goal is that teachers will achieve a sense of fulfillment and function at their maximum potential as a result of the helping process. The content consists of the full range of professional helping skills derived from a professional knowledge base.

The process of helping in its most significant form is both a personal and interpersonal experience. Helping is reinforced by relationships that are formed through healthy interactions. Deeper levels of helping are achieved when there is mutual growth. The helper also continually seeks to learn and grow in both personal and professional domains.

Helping in its true form is not derived from an authority base or a power base. Rather, it is a function that is influence-based. This influence may be out of respect for another's expertise as in the classic mentor-protégé relationship. The influence also may be derived from the interpersonal skills of the helper. A third possibility is that the influence is some combination of expertise and relationship skills.

Influence due to interpersonal skills does not imply a lack of content. It is a vehicle for developing a relationship that provides conditions conducive to growth. It is not a process of playing to the needs of the teacher as a ploy or manipulation, but it is an honest and open bonding that opens the mind to insights and substantive issues.

Helping is not viewed as a control mechanism, but as a means of freeing the teacher to explore and obtain new levels of personal competence, effectiveness, and satisfaction. It does not create a dependency on the helper, but rather collegiality and healthy interdependence (Glickman, 1990). It is a process to assist teachers to derive more meaning in who they are as persons, as well as what they do professionally. The goal is to achieve more meaning in life and in the profession. Helping enhances the teacher's feelings of worthwhileness and competence and the feeling that what he or she does can have a powerful and positive effect (efficacy). In its most productive form, helping not only assists the other person to grow, but it also contributes to building the other person's capacity for personal and professional growth.

Belief/value 7: Change is endemic to the process of helping and growth. Change must be recognized as an integral part of the helping process. Change is inevitable, and making it rewarding and productive is a primary goal. An important element of the helping theory is that managing change must be an essential component of the helping strategy, and that failure to assist teachers with strategies to bring about personal-professional change is failure to function effectively as a Helping Professional. A goal is to use change productively to promote the growth of each teacher, each Helping Professional, and the organization itself. The Transformational Helping Professional model includes a considerable body of knowledge related to the nature and process of change. The model for change and the related processes that emanate from the Transformational philosophy constitute the content of change in the model. The role of the Helping Professional is to provide for an acceptance of change so that it is viewed and effectively used for positive growth. The Helping Professional engages in processes that provide for the identification and acceptance of change, the management of change, and the utilization of change for meeting individual personal goals as well as the goals of the organization. The Helping Professional thus is highly skilled in using the process of change as a tool for development. In its most effective form, participants and the organization move through change to significant transformations.

Belief/value 8: The well-being of the organization and achievement of the common good depend, in large measure, upon the psychological health and professional competence of the individuals within it. In order for the organization to thrive, each person must be psychologically healthy and possess the necessary professional competence to perform the assigned roles and responsibilities. Thus, the Transformational model provides for a stable professional staff that is characterized by technical proficiency, professional efficacy, and psychological maturity. An essential belief is that the psychological state is a critical factor in human capability. This relates to capability in learning, teaching, and helping. The theoretical counterpart of this belief provides that the more one's personal and psychological needs are met, the more capable one will be at the assigned task, be it learning, teaching, or helping. This is not meant to imply, however, that a healthy psychological state is the only necessary factor. Human capacity is a composite of proficiency and psychological state. One without the other is not sufficient. Technical skills of the profession must be at a sufficient level, and psychological factors must be satisfactory. Psychological maturity cannot compensate for underdeveloped skills, and even high levels of skill can be masked by unmet or dysfunctional psychological factors.

The content of the model addresses the personal-psychological and instructional-professional needs as delineated in the instruments used to assess these. The nature of the culture of a significant organization is part of the knowledge base of the model as well. Included also is the understanding of how the needs of individuals relate to the common good.

The role of the Helping Professional is to provide for conditions that nurture psychological health and professional competence, as well as the integration of personal goals and the common good. The processes engaged in by the Helping Professional relate to culture building, assisting individuals in striving for both psychological and professional levels of maturity, and directing energies toward achievement of the organization's goals toward the good of the community.

Elements of the Transformational Helping Professional Model

The eight basic beliefs and values just detailed form the philosophy of the Transformational Helping Professional model. They lead us to specification of additional components of the new model, which are described here.

The Transformational Helping Professional model has several major components that distinguish it from other models. It incorporates the basic ten elements described at the beginning of this chapter, and in addition it builds upon, expands, and reconfigures these into new perspectives. It also provides for several other important dimensions. Taken collectively, these construct the new vision. Added to the ten contemporary fundamental elements are the following eleven:

1. A personal-psychological foundation
2. Motivation theory underlying the Transformational Helping Professional model
3. The change factor
4. Building capacity
5. An individualized/personalized approach
6. Personal and professional competence
7. Personal and professional efficacy
8. Creating conducive conditions
9. Self-enhancement of the Helping Professional
10. Viable dispositions
11. Revitalizing the Helping Professional

All of these apparently random threads are woven together to form the fabric of the Transformational Helping Professional model.

As we noted, an integral part of the role of mentor or supervisor is that of providing support and being a helper. This is a fundamental element carried forth through history and one that has evolved as a central focus. The dominant function of individuals who operate in these professional roles is that of *helper*. This is an all-inclusive term that encompasses a wide variety of needed skills, competencies, and strategies. The ten fundamental elements and the eleven components of the helping philosophy reflect a capacity that is highly professional, rather than casual or simply well intentioned but not well informed. The integration of this rationale, fundamental elements, and a professional philosophy creates a new vision and the role of the Transformational Helping Professional.

In general, the Transformational Helping Professional is a leadership role. It intends to maximize the teacher's intellectual, personal, and psychological skills. A goal of the Transformational Helping Professional model is to create and sustain growth, dispositions, and functional attributes so that the teacher is personally productive and contributes to the goals of the school.

At this point we turn our attention to the specifics and dynamics of the new vision. Essential to building the new model is constructing meaningful foundations of the helping process. We thus will describe each of the additional eleven components of the Transformational Helping Model and how they contribute to creating the new vision.

A Personal-Psychological Foundation

Some of the approaches to supervision in the past have recognized the need to deal with psychological issues. The term *psychological* has been used very broadly and differentially in the literature. The human relations advocates, for example, identify teachers' social needs and comfortable relationships as important factors in the model. Although these are related to deeper psychological needs, the approach is to work more with the social interaction than with the psychological needs of the individual. Blumberg's (1980) humanistic clinical supervision model addresses psychological barriers between teachers and supervisors. Its emphasis is on the establishment of trust and positive working relationships. It focuses on emotional and relational rather than on deeper psychological concerns. This is evident in the way the model is operationalized.

In the Transformational Helping Professional philosophy the personal factors of importance are derived from specifically identifiable psychological needs. The philosophy asserts that these needs affect both the personal and professional performance of the individual teacher. Collectively, these constitute professional health (Gold & Roth, 1993). The Transformational Helping Professional Model requires addressing two major domains: the instructional-professional as well as the personal-psychological. The Helping Professional strives to enhance the intellectual skills and psychological growth of teachers and their ability to apply these skills.

The psychological foundation of the Transformational Helping Professional model relates to the needs of the Helping Professional, the teacher, and their relationship. It maintains that a healthy concept of self is important to both the Helping Professional and the teacher. The Helping Professional is committed to establishing a healthy psychological environment that provides an appropriate context for nurturing, growth, and maximum professional performance.

One factor that contributes to the development of positive psychological health is a strong set of beliefs and values. It is held that both the organization and individuals must have a clearly defined set of beliefs and values, and that they function comfortably within the framework of these values and beliefs. This contributes to the condition of having a healthy concept of self and knowing what one stands for. Having pride in one's values and living these values are important components in establishing a productive helping relationship.

The Transformational Helping Professional model is a therapeutic approach that rests on the assumption that a psychologically healthy individual who has the appropriate knowledge, skills, and intellectual capacity for adapting to changing conditions is a person who is most likely to perform effectively. It is important to note that these factors are applicable to teachers, supervisors, mentors, and other helpers. Each must be psychologically healthy, have appropriate skills and strategies, and have the ability to work with individuals in an analytical mode on a person-to-person basis.

Perspectives of Motivation

The Transformational Helping Professional model views basic psychological and personal needs of the individual as motivating factors. When related to organizational needs, these produce a productive dynamic. Issues such as emotional needs, personal satisfaction, and achievement needs identified in other models are compatible and acceptable perspectives. The missing piece is that in the Transformational Helping Professional model, these are identified as emanating from more fundamental personal and psychological needs. These needs also include the emotional needs as well as a broader spectrum of social, intellectual, physical, and spiritual needs as they contribute to psychological growth. This combination of needs makes up the personal and psychological needs of the model that work in harmony to create a healthy individual.

It also should be noted that not all individuals have the same degree of motivation based on achievement or personal needs. Achievement may be highly motivating for some individuals, but not so important for others. Some educators may have a strong desire for their personal needs to be met in order to be fully productive, whereas for others they may not be as critical. Personal needs or achievement needs may not even be enough. The central issue is that these are individualized. The motivation component of the Transformational Helping Professional model must account for the fact that various needs have different effects and are experienced to different degrees depending upon the individual.

It is thus necessary to determine the individual's needs, how these relate to his or her motivation, and how to address these for both personal satisfaction and the good of the organization. The personal and achievement needs, for example, are tied to a more fundamental underlying set of premises that suggest that when psychological needs are met, one is in a much better position to be productive or meet the personal needs emanating from these. The individual also has a greater capacity for growth, will have greater motivation, and will be more self-enhanced. This, in turn, will lead to greater effectiveness in the classroom and in the professional role.

How does meeting one's psychological needs relate to achievement? Achievement could be an essential part of psychological needs, as achievement may relate to the individual's need for recognition. In this instance it is a cyclical relationship. The more one achieves, the more the underlying need is met. The more the need is met, the greater the motivation to achieve.

An important consideration is to discover what one's needs are and relate them back to the goals of the organization. It is not the achievement itself as the factor causing the motivation, but the underlying need that is met.

The role of the Helping Professional, therefore, is to support and assist the teacher in: (1) identifying his or her needs, (2) assessing the extent to which these needs are met, and (3) relating achievement of these needs to measures of effective performance in terms of both personal and organizational goals.

If an individual's performance is not satisfactory, or if there is an interest in increasing effectiveness, it is of value to investigate whether the current performance level is related to a need for improvement of instructional skills, working conditions, unmet psychological needs, or some combination of these. Productive or effective performance is not just related to feeling comfortable and happy in the workplace. This may lead to complacency, as was noted in the analysis of the human relations theory. It also does not provide for adequate feedback on performance that is diagnostic and specific.

Motivation is a complex set of factors, but these factors ultimately lead back to the individual's needs. In some instances these are very fundamental, such as survival. In other cases they are basic, such as affiliation and related social needs. They also can be of a higher order, such as enhancing the well-being of others (e.g., students, the community). Abraham Maslow (1954) proposed five categories of human need: physiological, safety, belonging and love, esteem, and self-actualization. Porter (1963) substituted autonomy for physiological, suggesting that physical needs are not realistic motivating factors in work settings. In our work with teachers, however, we have found that the physiological needs are indeed relevant to work motivation (e.g., safety and health). Maslow believed that need gratification is the most important single principle underlying all human development and motivation. In the Transformational model we will look at a broad array of needs and in more specific terms.

In the Transformational model we suggest that the more intrinsically motivated the individual, the more he or she will achieve. For example, if the individual has a feeling of commitment and belonging to the school and students, several types of significant needs may be met. These may include many of the social and emotional needs such as collegiality, belonging, relationships, and a sense of worth. Also, if individuals feel significant, and what they do is perceived to be of significance in some way, they will have more sense of affiliation with their work and be motivated to commit themselves to it. Wlodkowski (1986) bases his approach to motivation and teaching on the needs gratification principle.

We support the premise of *intrinsic motivation* as being more powerful and long lasting. The Transformational Helping Professional model asserts in subsuming personal needs for the moral good, one is responding to a higher-order need that derives from a fundamental value system. Meeting needs is not necessarily a self-centered motivation. For example, if one is compelled to respond to moral imperatives, needs such as feeling worthwhile and engaging in matters of significance can help to develop a healthy self-esteem.

Motivation is an individual-specific characteristic. The Transformational Helper assists teachers in identifying their values, the needs base for their motivation, and thus the manner in which they are motivated. The skills related to this process are incorporated in assessing and diagnosing the needs of the individual, as well as the subsequent processes of guidance and support.

The Element of Change

Productive change is embedded in the Transformational Helping model. The philosophical framework indicates change is pervasive, and thus the question is not whether one should consider change, but rather how it can be channeled and leveraged for effective growth. Understanding the theories of change, change models, the process of change, the phases of change that an individual must experience, the need for resistance to change, and how to facilitate change are threads that must be woven throughout the theory and practice. Change is integral to transformation; in fact, it is an essential part of life, and we thus devote an entire chapter (Chapter 3) to the nature and practice of change. Change is considered in relation to self-enhancement of the Transformational Helper as well as the teacher.

Capacity for Growth

Transformation does not occur through externally imposed directives. It is primarily internally driven. Allowing growth to occur requires capacity to do so. Capacity is the companion to motivation. The role of the Transformational Helper is to assist in increasing this capacity for growth.

Building personal capacity involves empowering the teacher to direct his or her self-growth, increase self-understanding, enhance motivation and ability to engage in meaningful lifelong learning, bring about necessary changes, improve and enlarge the repertoire of skills, receive constructive feedback, and continually acquire new modes of perceiving and understanding. The guidance and support of the Helping Professional are essential in building capacity. The entire dimension of self-enhancement of the Helping Professional also is concerned with building personal capacity for growth.

Individualized/Personalized Focus

An integrating theme throughout the model is individualizing the process of helping. We have described motivation as an individual-specific characteristic and noted the basis of the Transformational philosophy as being centered on individual personal and professional needs.

The helping process needs to be constructed as a personalized approach. The Helping Professional must assess and diagnose the status of the individual's personal and professional skills in order to be of assistance. The plan for personal and professional development and the associated guidance and support takes into account the unique personal and professional needs of the teacher and the teacher's personal style for learning. The helping relationship is most effective when it is an interpersonal one.

Competence

An obvious goal of supervision, mentoring, and helping is to increase personal and professional competence and engender an attitude of striving toward the highest levels of quality in one's own performance and that of one's students. In the Transformational model the vision of competence extends beyond technical proficiency. The intent is to maximize intellectual and psychological skills and the decision-making capacity to apply these skills and techniques appropriately to the needs of the students, the context, the nature and level of content, etcetera. It is the artistry of teaching and helping that transforms technical skills into effective, context-appropriate strategies. This transformation is developed through a unique set of complementary strategies, such as reflection, metacognition, and acquiring personal insight. The Helping Professional orchestrates this quest for competence through a variety of guidance and support modes.

Sense of Efficacy

Inspiring a sense of efficacy involves guiding teachers in believing in their personal-professional resources to effect significant growth in other individuals and productive change in organizations. It involves building an environment that validates teachers' capacities to make a difference and create meaningful results that have powerful influences on the lives of learners and cultures of organizations. Efficacy has been related to several positive student outcomes and professional effectiveness (Ashton & Webb, 1986). Personal- and professional efficacy is integral to the foundation of the Transformational Helping model.

Creating Conducive Conditions

A premise of particular importance to the Transformational model is nurturing the individual's growth. This is created through the efforts of the Helping Professional and the nature of the environment that is established. Of the issues identified through decades of practice and research in supervision, a salient component emerging as a critical factor is nurturing the individual. Contemporary conditions in schools clearly indicate a need to encourage and stimulate teachers and provide conducive conditions for change, growth, and ultimately transformation.

Helping is a process that when legitimately conducted requires developing trust and rapport with and commitment to others. Part of that commitment is to build a supportive environment, including understanding, a positive tone, freedom to risk, and access to assistance when needed. The helping dimension of guidance and support specifically is concerned with this element, as is the helping dimension of interpersonal relationships. The conducive conditions relate to physical, intellectual, and psychological characteristics.

Self-Enhancement of the Helping Professional

The Helping Professional faces a number of serious challenges in the pursuit of change and in helping others change. One of the more essential elements of the challenge is the Helper's own personal and professional growth. The Transformational model recognizes the concomitant growth of the helper and helpee, in what is referred to as a *growth dynamic*. The dynamic is the interchange that occurs in the process.

Viable Dispositions

There are a number of dispositions or attitudes that are of value in the Transformational model both on the part of the Helping Professional and the teacher. Each must enter the relationship with a commitment to productivity and quality. If this commitment is not strongly present, the Helping Professional seeks to engender it.

The concept of mutual engagement in seeking common goals and achieving both individual and organizational objectives is part of the disposition profile. Other factors relate to developing a sense of belonging among all participants and a feeling of open communication that is honest and constructive.

A disposition that underlies the entire process is that of integrity. This provides for the building of trust and rapport cited as a building block of the model. Compromised integrity will seriously deteriorate the process and the relationship.

Revitalizing the Helping Professional

An essential dimension of the life of a Helping Professional is to revitalize at appropriate times and in ways that are personalized. Understanding the factors that interfere with the Helper's skills and competencies also is of value. Although one may have effective helping strategies, often they cannot fully be utilized because of interference factors, such as stress and burnout, that provide static in an otherwise smoothly operating process.

It also is critical to understand the toll that helping takes on Helping Professionals in the transformational process. They are giving support and guidance much of the time, and they often acquire a sense of responsibility for those with whom they work. These pressures begin to wear over time and are classic conditions for burnout in the helping profession. The needs of the support provider for his or her own growth must be identified and met to prevent burnout.

Characteristics of the Transformational Helping Professional

The foundation of a Transformational Helping Professional is the concept of self. In order to help others, Helping Professionals must be secure in a clear conception of who they are. A positive self-image is integral to their psychological make-up. They accept that helpers do not have to be perfect. What is essential is an accurate, realistic view of themselves, their assets, and their limitations. They have a high degree of self-worth and experience deep feelings of identification with others. They are readily approachable by those they can help, and they have a strong desire and commitment to helping others.

Mature Helping Professionals demonstrate a clear understanding of their beliefs and values and live consistently with them. They continually evaluate their own beliefs, which provides for introspection and enhances practice. Of importance to helping individuals, as professionals, is that they have a high degree of integrity and do not violate the process for self gain or for any other reasons. They maintain an internal set of principles to which they adhere as individuals and as Helping Professionals.

Helping Professionals are constantly growing, seeking new skills and insights about themselves and the process of helping. They are committed to the process of growth in both their personal and professional lives. Helping Professionals recognize their own immediate and long-term needs and develop specific strategies to meet them.

In order to be effective in their role, Helping Professionals have a variety and range of skills and strategies. They have a strong knowledge base about effective practices, including classroom instruction; interpersonal relations; and working with parents, students, and co-workers in their teaching role. They also maintain active participation in professional associations in order to remain current and to continually enlarge their knowledge base.

Helping Professionals are expert observers of classrooms, events, and other individuals in the educational environment. They use the information gained from observation ethically to enhance the transformational helping relationship. In addition, they are flexible and adaptable to changing conditions, situations, and contexts. Of critical importance is that they have strong interpersonal relationship skills and use these effectively in performing the functions of the role of Helping Professional. The helping process involves establishing rapport and building trust, for which interpersonal skills are essential.

The essence of being a Helping Professional is a deep and sincere commitment to enhancement of others and their growth. The prime focus of helping is on the individual and his or her personal and professional development. It involves assisting others in becoming increasingly self-sufficient, reflective, and personally and professionally competent. Enhancement of individuals both personally and professionally is the essential component of the helping process. It involves understanding the nature of the helping process, having insights into the persons being helped, and recognizing the dynamics of the supportive relationship. It is acknowledged that adult learning principles serve as a guide in the helping process, and this is integral in understanding the nature of the persons being assisted.

The process of helping is based on the principle that learning often is a social activity deeply affected by feelings of belonging. The primary purpose of assisting others is to help them in their search for personal and professional fulfillment and to enhance their ability to provide benefit to the clients they serve. Teachers derive satisfaction from challenging work related to the goals of the organization and the needs of students (Sergiovanni & Starratt, 1993).

Part of the purpose of the helping relationship is to assist others in attaining technical proficiency. The Helping Professional identifies and provides access to resources that are available for those purposes. One of the critical components of assistance to others is not only enabling them to acquire skills, but increasing capacity for growth as well.

The entire helping process is centered around a personal and psychological basis relating to individual psychological needs and the means of satisfying these in order to enhance the achievement of personal and organizational goals. These needs relate to the physical, emotional, intellectual, social, and spiritual domains. It is the composite of these needs that drives motivation. Individual and personal needs thus provide insights into strategies the Helping Professional might use that are unique to the individual. Of course, certain needs are more critical to some individuals than to others, and it is not assumed that certain factors motivate all individuals equally.

The nature of the relationship between the Helping Professional and the teacher is of critical importance to the Helping Professional. The Transformational Helping Professional Philosophy reflects a helper–teacher relationship that is one of collaborative inquiry, in which collegiality builds a shared vision that translates into common goals. Concomitant growth of the Helping Professional and the person being assisted is both valued and practiced. This is approached and accomplished in meaningful ways, utilizing both introspection and interpersonal feedback as vehicles. The relationship is built on rapport, trust, respect, confidentiality, and a sincere concern for the interests, growth, and achievements of each other.

The nature of the helping process is one of encouraging, assisting, guiding, collaborating, and achieving. It is held that the professional role defines the responsibilities and appropriate ways of behaving toward others. Further, personal meaning is best acquired and internalized through situations that can be identified with and then accepted as being meaningful for the individual. The process may be one of seeking meaningful resolutions, questions, and events, and when necessary through confronting dilemmas.

Perspectives on the nature of the teacher are fundamental in defining the philosophy of the helping process. The Helping Professional's viewpoint is that of the whole person, one who becomes self-directed in both his or her personal and professional life. Satisfaction in the workplace is achieved through meeting personal needs and experiencing satisfying results. Teaching is viewed as a search for meaning.

The focus of the Helping Professional's philosophy can be characterized as person-centered, needs-based, and achievement-focused. It is directed at satisfaction through meeting personal needs and through the achievement of common goals.

TABLE 2-1 The Transformational Helping Professional Model

Beliefs/Values	Theory and Understandings	Goals
Clearly conceptualized and well-thought-out values and beliefs must underlie professional practice	H.P.s understand, articulate, and adhere to a set of values and beliefs.	H.P.s use the beliefs and values of the T. H. P. M. to assist individuals' growth.
The worth of the individual is a fundamental value.	Each person's worth must be recognized, validated, and appreciated.	Provide and demonstrate acceptance of and respect for the individual.
Meeting personal and psychological needs is the foundation of personal fulfillment and growth.	Personal and psychological needs are the foundation of the helping process.	Personal and psychological needs are identified and met.
Meeting individual professional needs is the foundation of effective professional practice.	Instructional and professional needs are essential to the professional role.	Instructional and professional needs are identified and met.
Learning is a personal experience and best achieved when meaningful to the individual.	Learning best occurs when personal meaning is associated with the process and content.	Conducive environments for meaningful experiences and professional growth.
Professional helping is a process of support and guidance for enhancing personal fulfillment and realization of potential.	Helping provides support for personal fulfillment and full potential.	Each teacher achieves a sense of fulfillment and functions at maximum potential.
Change is endemic to the process of helping and growth.	Change must be supported and managed to meet organizational and individual goals.	Use change productively for participants and organization.
The well-being of the organization and achievement of common good is dependent upon the psychological health and professional competence of the individuals within it.	Each individual's psychological health and professional competence determines organizational health.	Each person functions at peak psychological and professional levels.

H.P. = Helping Professional. T. H. P. M. = Transformational Helping Professional Model.

It is concerned with helping one another find significance and satisfaction in both personal and professional endeavors. Specifically within the school context, the ultimate objective is to enhance student learning and growth for the maintenance and further development of a democratic society. It is intended to assist all of those in the learning community to find meaning in and through the experience. This includes students in the classroom, teachers, and other personnel. The Helping Professional provides leadership in creating a culture conducive to growth and development for all participants. These are the fundamental premises of the Transformational Helping Professional philosophy.

Content	Roles and Responsibilities	Process
Values, beliefs of T. H. P. M. and associated knowledge, skills, and dispositions.	H.P.s act consistently with beliefs and values.	The processes emanate from and are consistent with values and beliefs.
Interpersonal and related skills create conditions for individuals to feel worthwhile.	H.P. as role model.	Interact in ways to create conditions of acceptance and worth.
Personal and psychological needs: social, physical, spiritual, emotional, intellectual.	Guide, facilitator, establish trust, develop rapport, use of empathy.	Assessing, diagnosing, guiding, supporting.
Knowledge, skills, dispositions, cognitive and metacognitive processes.	Guide, support, and provide for meaningful assessment, self-analysis through trust and openness.	Require a significant knowledge base, technical and interpersonal skills.
Factors and conditions related to beliefs of the T. H. P. M. and helping relationships.	Create conditions for meaning in learning for teachers.	Understanding of teacher, positive relationships, meaningful experiences.
Entire set of H.P.s knowledge base and skills.	Support and guidance, collegiality, and personal growth.	Mutual growth, freeing, capacity builders, personal enhancement strategies.
Change model, knowledge base on change, processes of change.	Provide acceptance of change and productive use of the phases of change.	Identification and acceptance of change, use as tool for development.
Personal, psychological, instructional and professional needs; knowledge and process of helping; and nature of the culture.	Provide conditions that nurture psychological health and professional competence and common good.	Culture building, guiding and supporting, integrating individual and organizational goals.

A discussion of the philosophy of helping would not be complete without addressing the issue of effective implementation of change. Change is a fundamental requirement for growth. Essential to the helping process are understanding the nature of change, forces creating and contributing to change, dynamics related to resistance to change, factors providing conducive conditions for change, essential strategies to promote change, and the processes and procedures that bring about successful change.

We have described the basic elements and characteristics of the Transformational Helping Professional model throughout this chapter. Table 2-1 provides a summary of the model in terms of the six categories.

Comparison of Philosophies

Philosophies of mentoring, supervising, and helping can be analyzed in a variety of ways. One of these is to identify certain essential components that help define and characterize each of the models and allow for a comparison across these variables with relative ease. These components include the following:

1. Supervisory/helping style (e.g., autocratic, collaborative)
2. The view of the nature of the worker/teacher (e.g., tool of the organization, self-directed)
3. The supervisor/helper–teacher relationship (e.g., prescriptive, participative)
4. The nature of supervision/helping (e.g., inspection, nurturing)
5. The view of the nature of teaching (e.g., prescriptive, search for meaning)
6. The primary focus of the philosophy (e.g., directing, guarding)
7. Essential characteristics (e.g., accountability, insights)

The comparative philosophies reviewed include the scientific model, the human relations model, the neo-scientific approach, the human resources management philosophy, and the Transformational Helping Professional model. Table 2-2 summarizes the similarities and differences of the philosophies in terms of the seven components.

The scientific model can be characterized by the terms *control, accountability,* and *efficiency*. This is clearly a direct approach in which achievement is the driving force. The human relations philosophy can be identified with the areas of social needs, relationships, and harmony. These are the key elements; once these are achieved, other elements will follow. The neo-scientific approach again can be seen in terms of control and accountability through externally imposed standards. Human resources supervision is task-motivated. It maintains that growth requires task achievement. It is concerned with a viable organization and successful work. As noted by one of the early proponents of human resources supervision, Argyris (1964), "We're interested in developing neither an overpowering manipulative organization nor organizations that will 'keep people happy.' Happiness, morale, and satisfaction are not going to be highly relevant guides. . . . [I]ndividual competence, commitment, self-responsibility [and] active viable organizations will be the kinds of criteria that we will keep foremost" (p. 4).

The Transformational Helping Professional model emphasizes insight, meeting psychological needs, and mutual respect and growth. It is concerned with developing psychologically healthy individuals who find significance in who they are and what they can contribute to others. It is intended to provide insights, dispositions, and processes to transform the mentor or supervisor into a true Helping Professional and to guide the transformation of the teacher and school toward a psychologically healthy and productive culture of significance.

TABLE 2-2 Supervision and Helping Philosophies Comparison

	Scientific (early 1900s)	Human Relations (1930s–1950s)	Neo-scientific (1980s–1990s)	Human Resources (1960s–1990s)	Helping Professional (mid-1990s)
Supervisory Style	Autocratic	Democratic	Autocratic with external authority	Commitment to organization; accountable	Satisfaction through personal needs and results; psychologically healthy; technical proficiency; growth-oriented
View of Teacher	Compliant tool	Whole person with needs	Compliant	Self-directed	Person of value and worth; self-directed; personal and professional; integrated personality; seeking fulfillment for self and others
Supervisor–Teacher Relationship	Follow management directives; prescriptive curriculum; management–subordinate relation	Participation; shared decision making	Prescriptive; impose standards	Participate in decision making with responsibility and accountability; Self-responsible; shared decision making for results	Respect; collaborative inquiry; trust; genuineness; openness
Nature of Supervision	Inspection; closely monitor	Comfortable relationship; permissive	Monitor with external standards	Motivate for common goals; commitment	Helping; guiding; collaborating; facilitating; enhancing
Focus of the Philosophy	Product	Satisfaction through relationships; social needs to achieve results	Results through external standards	Competence; results to achieve satisfaction	Significance; personal and professional growth, psychological growth of the individual; enhancing the organization
View of Teaching	Follow prescribed methods	Open; flexible	Adhere to performance objectives	Objective-focused	Search for meaning; discovery; inquiry; reflection
Characteristics	Control; accountability; efficiency	Social needs; relationships; harmony	Control; accountable	Task-motivated; growth requires task achievement; viable organization; successful work	Insight; personal and psychological needs; helping; contributing; transforming

Definition of the Transformational Helping Professional

The Transformational Helping Professional is one who believes and acts consistently with the premises of the Transformational Helping Professional Model; has specialized expertise to engage effectively in creating a professionally meaningful relationship by establishing rapport, providing support, and developing collegiality and collaboration; assists others in gaining insights and increasing capacity for personal and professional growth by addressing personal and professional needs; identifies resources for development; enhances his or her own and other's effectiveness in their professional role; serves as a change agent; encourages and works toward developing a psychologically healthy culture; maintains ethical standards; and continually seeks to enhance his or her own personal and professional development.

Issues and Questions for Review and Reflection

1. The focus of the Helping Professional philosophy is characterized as person-centered, needs-based, and achievement-focused. Discuss what this means in terms of how to work with teachers.

2. The matrix identifies seven categories for describing and characterizing philosophical approaches. Compare and contrast these approaches in relationship to the categories.

3. A fundamental premise of the Helping Professional model is building capacity for growth. Discuss the ways this can be accomplished. What is the role of the Helping Professional and the organization in helping educators achieve this?

4. What do teacher's psychological needs have to do with improving instruction in the classroom? What do they have to do with improving the school environment?

5. Discuss the role of teacher self-esteem in building professional competencies.

References

Alfonso, R. J., Firth, G. R., & Neville, R. F. (1981). *Instructional supervision: A behavior system.* Boston: Allyn and Bacon.

American Psychological Association. (1991, June). *Learner-centered psychological principles: Guidelines for school redesign and reform.* Washington, DC: American Psychological Association.

Anderson, R. H. (1982). Creating a future for supervision. In T. J. Sergiovanni (Ed.), *Supervision of teaching* (pp. 180–190). Alexandria, VA: Association for Supervision and Curriculum Development.

Argyris, C. (1964). *Integrating the individual and the organization.* New York: Wiley.

Ashton, P. T., & Webb, R. B. (1986). *Making a difference: Teachers' sense of efficacy and student achievement.* New York: Longman.

Blumberg, A. (1980). *Supervisors and teachers: A private cold war* (2d ed.). Berkeley, CA: McCutchan.

Bowers, C. A., & Flinders, D. J. (1991). *Culturally responsive teaching and supervision.* New York: Teachers College Press.

Costa, A. L., & Garmston, R. J. (1994). *Cognitive coaching: A foundation for renaissance schools.* Norwood, MA: Christopher-Gordon.

Cuff, W. A. (1978). Indirect versus direct influence in supervisory conferences and student teacher's levels of needs. (Doctoral dissertation, New York University). *Dissertation Abstracts International, 39,* 4877A.

Glickman, C. D. (1990, Fall). Right question, wrong extrapolation: A response to Duffy's "supervising for results." *Journal of Curriculum and Supervision, 6*(1), 39–40.

Gold, Y., & Roth, R. A. (1993). *Teachers managing stress and preventing burnout: The professional health (PH) solution.* London: Falmer Press.

Goldhammer, R., Anderson, R. H., & Krajewski, R. J. (1993). *Clinical supervision: Special methods for the supervision of teachers* (3d ed.). New York: Harcourt Brace.

Herzberg, F. (1966). *Work and the nature of man.* New York: World.

Hunter, M., & Russell, D. (1990). *Mastering coaching and supervision* (Principles of Learning series). Thousand Oaks, CA: Corwin Press.

Knowles, M. S. (1978). *The adult learner: A neglected species.* Houston, TX: Gulf.

Koehler, V. (1984). University supervision of student teaching. Paper presented at the annual meeting of the American Educational Research Association, New Orleans, LA.

Maslow, A. (1954). *Motivation and personality.* New York: Harper & Row.

North Carolina Department of Public Instruction (1986). *North Carolina Mentor/Support Team Training Program: Trainers manual.* Raleigh, NC: Division of Program Approval, Personnel Services Area.

Porter, L. (1963). Job attitudes in management I: Perceived deficiencies and need fulfillment as a function of job level. *Journal of Applied Psychology, 46*(6), 386–397.

Roberts, G. B. (1992). The relationship of power and involvement to experience in supervisory conferences: Discourse analysis of supervisor style. Paper presented at the annual meeting of the American Educational Research Association, San Francisco.

Roberts, R. J. (1992). Face threatening acts and politeness theory: Contrasting speeches from supervisory conferences. *Journal of Curriculum and Supervision, 7*(3), 287–301.

Schön, D. A. (1983). *The reflective practitioner: How professionals think in action.* New York: Basic Books.

Schön, D. A. (1987). *Educating the reflective practitioner.* San Francisco: Jossey Bass.

Sergiovanni, T. J. (1982). The context for supervision. In T. J. Sergiovanni (Ed.), *Supervision of teaching* (pp. 108–130). Alexandria, VA: Association for Supervision and Curriculum Development.

Sergiovanni, T. J., & Starratt, R. J. (1988). *Supervision: Human perspectives* (4th ed.). New York: McGraw-Hill.

Sergiovanni, T. J., & Starratt, R. J. (1993). *Supervision: A redefinition.* New York: McGraw-Hill.

Waite, D. (1993). Teachers in conference: A qualitative study of teacher–supervisor face-to-face interactions. *American Educational Research Journal, 30*(4), 675–702.

Wildman, T. M., Magliaro, S. G., Niles, R. A., & Niles, J. A. (1992). Teacher mentoring: An analysis of roles, activities, and conditions. *Journal of Teacher Education, 43*(3), 205–213.

Wiles, K. (1967). *Supervision for better schools* (3d ed.). Englewood Cliffs, NJ: Prentice-Hall.

Wlodkowski, R. J. (1986). *Motivation and teaching: A practical guide.* Washington, DC: National Education Association.

Wolfe, D. M. (1992). Designing, training, and selecting incentives for mentor programs. In T. M. Bey & C. T. Holmes (Eds.), *Mentoring: Contemporary principles and issues* (pp. 103–110). Reston, VA: Association of Teacher Educators.

Zeichner, K. M., & Tabachnick, R. (1982). The belief systems of university supervisors in an elementary student teaching program. *Journal of Education for Teaching, 8*(1), 34–35.

Related Readings

Argyris, C., & Schön, D. A. (1974). *Theory in practice: Increasing professional effectiveness.* San Francisco: Jossey-Bass.

Bourdieu, P. (1977). *Outline of a theory of practice* (R. Nice, Trans.). Cambridge, England: Cambridge University Press.

Bruner, J. S. (1966). *Toward a theory of instruction.* New York: Norton.

Glickman, C. D., & Bey, T. M. (1990). Supervision. In W. R. Houston (Ed.), *Handbook of research on teacher education: A project of the Association of Teacher Educators* (pp. 549–566). New York: Macmillan.

Hersey, P., & Blanchard, K. H. (1982). *Management of organizational behavior: Utilizing human resources* (4th ed.). Englewood Cliffs, NJ: Prentice-Hall.

Hunt, D. E. (1987). *Beginning with ourselves.* Cambridge, MA: Brookline Books.

Pratte, R. (1971). *Contemporary theories of education.* Scranton, PA: Crowel.

Chapter 3

Beyond Change: A Process of Transformations

Life is change, rhythm and development. To live is to adapt. Each new situation demands a giving beyond ourselves and our habits, which is far from easy. —F. HARRY DANIEL (LETTING GO)

Over the past 10 years much has been written about the need for change in education—a call for educational renewal. The focus has been on how schools can change and improve. One of the outcomes of the renewal movement has been the realization that changing schools involves a difficult and complex process. Another realization has been that it is essential for teachers to be included in this process if change is to take place at all. The call for empowering teachers was heard and was echoed by teachers becoming more involved in decision making and in school management. Teachers had to feel valued and be given opportunities to be active in successful change. Inservice programs were initiated to prepare teacher leaders who would initiate changes in the culture of the organization; provide programs to involve parents; develop excellence in teaching; increase student motivation; and create dynamic, future-oriented curriculum that responded to multicultural diversity.

A variety of models of change were developed by a number of people to assist individuals and organizations with the overwhelming task of bringing about effective change. Because change is a complex process and involves both individuals and organizations, change theories for each will be reviewed. A new model of change will be presented that includes the necessity of bringing about personal change before initiating organizational change. An overview of the Helping Professional as an agent of change for individual and organizational growth will be provided.

Process Theories and Models of Change

Theories and models related to individual and organizational change will be examined beginning with a focus on individual change.

Theories of Individual Change

One of the most familiar models of individual change in the health field is that of Bandura's social learning approach (Bandura, 1969; Elder et al., 1986). In this approach the individual is viewed as a self-determined organism who acts on and reacts to environmental stimuli, which then aids the individual in acquiring new ideas and behaviors through modeling the ideas and behaviors learned from selected others. Therefore, this type of change is promoted by exposure to special role models. For this to be accomplished, mass media need to be employed to increase visibility of the ideas and behaviors that are to be learned. Prominent people need to be included as change initiators, and existing social networks that will maximize interpersonal contact should be used (Bandura, 1969; Lasater et al., 1984). To improve the likelihood that a target individual will learn and adopt a new behavior by observing those around her or him, creation of social networks or "networking" among people is encouraged.

Bandura's (1969) social learning approach proposes that simple cognitive acquaintance with new material is not sufficient to motivate individual change. The social norms and values of an individual set limits on what will be considered and how easily it will be accepted. Therefore, a change in norms, however accomplished, will contribute to a change in people's learning and in their eventual behaviors. Replacing norms that contribute to high-risk behavior or maladaptive behavior with norms that support healthier lifestyles is essential when working with individuals. These types of changes in thinking and in behavior will bring about eventual changes in an individual's life.

Bandura's theory holds strong implications for Helping Professionals who model personal characteristics and teaching skills appropriate for other teachers. Positive changes will occur when teachers: (1) acquire new ideas and behaviors that they have observed from Helping Professionals, (2) apply the new ideas and strategies they have seen modeled by Helping Professionals, and (3) share the new ideas with other teachers in support groups that encourage growth and healthier lifestyles.

Another theory of change was developed by Lewin (1947), who reconceptualized the social change process. Prior to Lewin's theory, two major theories existed (Hawkinshire & Liggett, 1990). The first one, *the organismic or evolutionary position* derived from Comte's (1852/1875) theory, stated that change is naturally smooth and relatively continuous. Any disruption during the process is taken as a sign that the goals and the implementation are inappropriate or faulty. A second theory, *the conflict or revolutionary position*, was held by theorists such as Marx and Engels (1988). Their position stated that change is inherently discontinuous and primarily disruptive. This view considers fundamental change to be characterized by disruption of the existing social system.

Lewin's (1947) model combined aspects of both theories into what has been described as a *holistic model of planned change*. His model focuses on genotypic (latent) change processes that apply equally well to individuals, groups, or whole societies. Lewin believed that change is a multiphased and continuous process. He proposed that some of the phases of change, "moving" and "freezing," are smooth and individuals demonstrate few disruptive symptoms as they progress through them. However, one phase, "unfreezing," was described as discontinuous and disruptive. This phase paralleled the conflict view of change in which individuals demonstrated many actions similar to those that conflict theorists described. This phase is filled with stress and strain that must take place if the individual is to change old patterns and learn new ones.

Lewin attempted to identify in his social change model the latent processes common to all types of change. These latent concepts are summarized here in the form of seven propositions and may be beneficial for Helping Professionals in their own lives and when giving assistance to others:

1. A conflict exists between opposing forces of change, and resistance occurs among individuals.
2. Conflicting forces exist in all structures such as within individuals, between individuals, or between groups of individuals.
3. Whenever there is movement within the equilibrium of a structure, social change will occur; the movement results from impinging change forces becoming stronger than the resistant forces.
4. Maintenance of existing structures is affected by the resistant forces within the system.
5. For change to take place, existing habits must be released within the social system. This is referred to as unfreezing or making structural changes.
6. Whenever there is a letting go of existing social habits through the change process, there always will be emotional reactions and some type of catharsis.
7. Whenever there is a changing of social structures, there will be several phases associated with the changes. The two transition phases, called *unfreezing* and *moving*, take place between the time when the original point of equilibrium is departed from and the time when the new equilibrium is established, known as freezing.

To test whether the seven concepts of Lewin's holistic model were contained within the theories put forth by other investigators, Hawkinshire and Liggett (1990) reviewed the writings of twenty-nine classical and contemporary authors. These investigators reported that there did "not appear to be a real difference between the two theoretical positions" (p. 320). The authors also reported that disruption is a natural part of the change process, regardless of the rate of change. Thus, Lewin's (1947) model was found to be the paradigm of planned change, and he was deemed the father of modern change theory.

Helping Professionals who use Hawkinshire and Liggett's (1990) research on Lewin's model of change may apply the following concepts when helping teachers and organizations during times of change:

1. The first attempts at change are likely to be the period of most intense turmoil. This phase was labeled unfreezing by Lewin (1947).
2. The termination, or final phase, is also a time of intense turmoil.
3. Strong reactions during these two phases are brought about by a number of factors as individuals attempt to act in new ways and are usually not prepared for the difficulties of changing.
4. The turmoil experienced during the termination phase is a result of anticipating the loss of support that individuals felt had helped them through the change.
5. Fortunately, these two phases of unfreezing and termination are temporary periods of disruption.
6. Offering support to people during these two difficult phases of the change process; helping individuals identify their feelings of fear, pain, loss, and insecurity; and helping them identify their need for support will allow change to progress and individuals to feel less threatened.
7. Educating individuals about the phases of change and what takes place during the phases will help to prepare them for the unknown and allow the process to continue.

In summarizing Lewin's change model, his three phases of change (unfreezing, moving, and freezing) include two transition phases (unfreezing and moving) that exist between the time when the old point of quasi-stationary equilibrium is left and the time when the new equilibrium is established (freezing). Helping Professionals will find it worthwhile to become acquainted with Lewin's phases of change and then to observe the dynamics in their own lives as they go through each of the phases when they experience change. Becoming familiar with the phases and gaining awareness of what they themselves are experiencing will be of tremendous assistance to Helping Professionals when they are working with others. As helpers encourage teachers to identify their feelings, and especially their resistances, the process of change will be facilitated.

In summary, there are a number of theories that subscribe to the belief that individuals can be changed by exposure to special role models (Kelly, 1979; Kelly, Snowden, & Munoz, 1977). This philosophical position was presented in Bandura's (1969) social learning model, in which the individual is viewed as a self-determined organism who acts on and reacts to environmental stimuli. The important role of an influential model is introduced so that an individual will choose to adopt new behaviors and learn new ideas through the modeling process. Thus, change is brought about through the modeling principle.

Being aware of types of reactions to change will assist the Helping Professional when working with teachers at all levels of experience. The awareness is of utmost importance in working with restructuring schools, new curricula, and professional development schools. Whenever teachers are placed in new environments, or new situations are created, they are faced with the challenges of change. Beginning teachers, student teachers, teachers who move to another school, and teachers finding themselves in changing school environments experience the change phenomenon.

Beginning teachers in particular are involved in the change process as they attempt to adjust to new teaching situations that in most instances are very different from their student teaching experiences. Guiding them through the phases of change, helping them to identify their feelings and resistances, acquainting them with new coping strategies, and developing support groups to encourage and affirm them will assist these teachers in managing the challenges confronting them during their first years of teaching.

We have focused on two major theories of individual-level change, looked at the importance of assisting individuals as they manage the difficulties involved in the change process, and discussed the essential role of Helping Professionals who assist teachers during times of change. Because the individual cannot be the only source of change within the system, it is necessary to also review significant aspects of educational change.

Educational Change: Truth or Fiction

Teachers and educators who work with elementary and secondary school students are constantly involved in small- and large-scale change. Thus, it is essential to understand educational change and forces that influence it.

Reform, Renewal, and Reality

The wave of educational reform began in 1983 when *A Nation at Risk* was published by the National Commission on Excellence in Education. The sharp criticism of the condition of public education, along with rhetoric regarding the threat to the nation's economic future, gained the attention of the nation. High schools became a main target of criticism, as critics stated that they must change if the economic and political future of the United States was to be ensured. Response to these criticisms was rapid, and related political activity affected the nation's schools. In looking at the results, we find that since 1983, states have generated more educational rules and regulations than they had enacted in the previous 20 years. Between 1984 and 1986, states passed more than 700 statutes that affected directly or indirectly some aspect of public schooling (Timar & Kirp, 1989). The majority of the statutes could be placed in four categories: higher academic standards for students, recognition of the importance of the role of the teacher, ways to reward teachers for superior work, and higher standards to enter the profession (Passow, 1989). These reforms fit Cuban's (1988) category of "first-order" changes that improve the effectiveness of what schools do at the present time. They do not aim for "second-order" reform that would bring new goals or even alter the fundamental goals of education, which would change the ways that traditional roles are performed within the organization. Renewing schools at all levels in the 1990s is mainly an effort to bring about second-order change.

A major difficulty today in bringing about change is the lack of finances in most states. Massive deficits in at least thirty states blocked attempts at school reform (Tye, 1990). In fact, governors and legislators reported that the prospects for new educational reform initiatives, or any increased aid to schools, "are dim or nonexistent" (Harp, 1991, p. 22). Some even had doubts that basic aid programs could be maintained.

One of the major problems that schools must face, according to Kirst, is "how to improve schools without spending more money" (1982, pp. 6–8). He sees a return to the emphasis on "alterable variables" such as curriculum content, time, instructional methods and materials, and teacher quality as the focus for improvement. Bloom (1980) would put the focus on similar variables and emphasize those that are more closely related to learners and learning. He maintains that we can have a great impact on the quality of education if we will focus more of our efforts on using what we know from research about these variables. Most changes in schools take place slowly, and, as Elmore and McLaughlin (1988) suggested, "school systems respond to external pressure for change, not by highly visible, well-specified, sequential actions, but by subtle shifts over time" (p. 7).

As with most perspectives, there are elements of significance in both of Cuban's categories of change. Improving the effectiveness of what schools are now doing in curriculum development, instructional methods and materials, and teacher quality and rewards would greatly benefit teachers and students now and in the future (first-order changes). Developing new goals and altering the ways in which traditional roles are performed within the schools could help to change the ways that schools are now organized (second-order changes). These types of changes may bring about new organizational structures that are greatly improved over those being used at the present time. Unfortunately, bureaucratic needs and political survival become the focal points within the organization and in many cases drain the life from effective and lasting educational change efforts.

The central issues here are that change is inevitable and that every organization changes; solutions of today will be obsolete tomorrow. Rapid changes in technology and society itself demand that schools change. Whether changes are voluntary or mandated, changes will take place within programs, departments, and individuals.

Restructuring

In the 1990s, the battle cry for "reform" and "renewal" has been replaced with the call for restructuring. The well-known educational historian David Tyack stated that "as U.S. education enters the 1990s, restructuring has become a magic incantation" (1990, p. 170).

Even though there is much written about restructuring, and even more discussed about it, Timar argues that there is little agreement on what restructuring means, what it looks like in practice, and how it should be implemented. Timar believes it to be a reform strategy (1989).

In attempting to define the term, one finds that it is nearly impossible to trace its exact origin. However, restructuring is found to be associated with crises and with questions concerning survival of the organization. Specific themes such as examining our basic beliefs about teaching, learning, the nature of human beings, and the kinds of environments that maximize growth for teachers and students; changing the nature of schools from the interior; creating new relationships for children and teachers; and opening up the process of learning and teaching, of human interaction and decision making are major concerns (Lewis, 1989).

Because restructuring has been defined differently by educators, politicians, and others, many complications exist. Educators have a responsibility to understand the definitional differences, to work toward agreement at the local level, and to educate all of these groups involved about the meaning of restructuring. If educators fail to accomplish these tasks, the real issues involved will become lost and possible solutions will not become a reality.

Restructuring is an admirable goal with considerable potential to bring about change and to improve schools in essential ways. The focus must not be lost. As Fullan argues, "We are still at the early stages of restructuring experiments, which should serve to help clarify the concept and debug how it might best be implemented" (1991, p. 88).

Educational Change: Its Meaning

If change is to be accomplished in education, models for change must involve the school district, the school, and the teacher. In order to accomplish educational change, beliefs must be examined; curriculum and curriculum materials must be evaluated, revised, and in some instances replaced with new curriculum materials; and new teaching strategies must be developed.

In most instances, changes take place in schools without teachers being actively involved in developing the underlying purposes and beliefs regarding change. Teachers often are required to make changes without understanding the principles and rationale involved. Bussis, Chittenden, and Amarel (1976) have stated that ". . . action based on valuing and faith is not very likely to lead to an enlargement or strengthening of the teacher's own understanding. The potential informational support available in feedback to the teacher is not received because it is not recognized" (p. 74).

For change to have meaning and for it to be successful, teachers and other individuals within a school must cooperate and work together to clarify any new practices they plan on implementing. They must first have clearly defined their beliefs and goals. Questions regarding specific educational practices to be used must be addressed, and teachers need to be actively involved in discussing how these new practices will be used—that is, what changes do they plan on implementing, how will they implement them, and how are these two aspects of change interrelated.

To help clarify educational change, Fullan (1991) brought together the ideas of researchers (Berman & McLaughlin, 1978; Huberman & Miles, 1984) and described three broad phases of the change process: Phase I, initiation, mobilization, or adoption; Phase II, implementation or initial use; and Phase III, continuation, incorporation, routinization, or institutionalization.

The initiation phase involves the process that leads up to and includes a decision to adopt or to proceed with a change. The implementation phase addresses the first experiences of attempting to put an idea into practice. The continuation phase includes whether the change is built as an ongoing part of the system or whether it disappears by way of a decision to discard, or possibly through attrition. Fullan (1991) added a fourth phase to the original phases and called it "outcome," which was to provide a more complete overview of the change process.

One of the important concepts of this model is that change is a process, not an event (Fullan & Park, 1981). The initiation phase may take years. Implementation for most changes takes 2 or more years, and continuation takes place over an indefinite time period. Fullan stated that implementation is the "means to achieving certain outcomes" (1991, p. 49). He also reported that each stage of the process strongly affects subsequent stages, and he identified the main factors and their influences at each stage.

Helping Professionals Assisting Teachers through Change

Teachers need to be able to interact with other teachers to share ideas, clarify concepts, and gain support in carrying out their ideas. Little's (1982) extensive research of work conditions in six schools over a 1-year period resulted in a report that school improvement occurred when:

> *1) teachers engaged in frequent, continuous, and increasingly concrete and precise talk about teaching practice; 2) teachers are frequently observed and provided with useful critiques of their teaching; 3) teachers plan, design, research, evaluate, and prepare teaching materials together ... confirm their emerging understanding of their approach; and 4) teachers teach each other the practice of teaching. (p. 331)*

What this information demonstrates is the fact that teachers are, in most instances, eager and willing to adopt changes in their classrooms, and they do so when encouraged and validated for their efforts.

Helping Professionals can be key agents of change when: (1) they offer teachers information about new programs and practices, (2) they provide support groups so teachers can discuss their frustrations and concerns in an atmosphere that is free from criticism, and (3) teachers can problem solve and work through their concerns.

In too many instances, teachers are not given adequate information about the changes that need to take place in their schools. They do not have enough time or energy to bring about the innovations they would like, and they do not receive the support necessary to work through the stages in the change process.

Helping Professionals can stimulate change, especially during the initiation phase when decisions are being made as to whether or not new practices should be adopted. They also can help teachers choose among a range of new practices, develop plans for implementation, arrange any training that is needed, and offer emotional support throughout. Subsequent chapters in this book will discuss ways to meet teachers' personal-psychological needs and instructional-professional needs. These chapters will be especially beneficial as teachers meet the challenges brought about by change.

All change involves loss, anxiety, and struggle (Marris, 1975). The Helping Professional can be a key person in informing teachers about the essential aspects of the change process and in helping them identify their own fears and anxieties. The needs inventories described in Chapter 4 will be especially useful in assisting teachers to identify their emotional needs and to plan specific ways to meet them during the insecure phases of change. Marris stated that, "Once the anxieties of loss were understood, both the tenacity of conservatism and the ambivalence of transitional institutions became clearer" (1975, p. 2).

Teachers need to discuss their concerns, to learn that they are not alone in their feelings, and to acknowledge that people experience anxiety when they move from the familiar to the unknown. They must be encouraged to share their feelings and receive support during difficult periods of adjustment. They need to know that change brings with it anxiety and insecurity, and that what they are experiencing is a natural part of the change process. Meaning must be shared for it to be assimilated and accepted.

Helping Professionals are in a position to encourage teachers as they work through changes. They can help them with their personal and psychological needs as they make necessary adjustments during times of change. Too often teachers are only offered assistance with instructional needs and the personal-psychological needs are neglected.

Successful change, then, requires that both personal and professional growth are attended to. The outcome will be a sense of accomplishment and appreciation on the part of all who are involved in the change process.

Educational Change Models

The educational change literature provides a number of models of change. A selected number of these models will be reviewed. Three of these models were articulated by Havelock (1971, 1973a) and were selected for review due to his extensive record of research and his change model development. They are the Social Interaction model; the Research, Development, and Diffusion model; and the Problem Solving model. The Organizational Development model, the Rand Change Agent Study, and the Concerns-Based Adoption model will also be described.

The Social Interaction Model

Within the Social Interaction model the assumption is made that the change to be accomplished and the innovations to be adopted are already fully developed and ready for dissemination. There are five phases that typically characterize the innovation adoption process. Phase one, or the initial phase, includes developing an awareness of the innovation. Phase two is characterized by an increased interest in and a search for more information about the innovation. Next, the evaluation phase is when a decision is made to adopt the innovation, and the final phases are called trial and adoption.

The major emphasis of this model is on understanding the change process, which is accomplished through a series of decision phases. The individual adopter progresses through these phases in relation to how an innovation is diffused throughout a social system.

Information flow and media sources are important in this model. Individuals who belong to a specific network tend to rely on each other rather than on outsiders who may be less credible for their information about innovations. Principals and other individuals in the role of change agent will not have as much influence in the natural process of this model in bringing about change.

The Research, Development, and Diffusion (RD&D) Model

The RD&D model presents change as an orderly and planned sequence. It begins with the identification of the problem or problems, finds or produces a solution, and finally diffuses the solution. Researchers are mainly the ones who produce the knowledge, while systematic development and dissemination follow. The receivers or adopters are perceived of as passive consumers (Guba & Clark, 1976).

The RD&D model describes the national curriculum development projects of the 1960s. The results of the research on this model were used in the comprehensive development projects that resulted in modern materials and processes that were later used in the classroom. Unfortunately, most of the programs were never widely used, which may well be related to the fact that they were not well received by educators.

The Problem Solving Model

The Problem Solving model involves the adopter, who throughout the process is collaboratively solving problems. It also includes consultants working as resource guides along with the receivers. Havelock (1971) discussed five positions proposed by the problem solving perspective: (1) Consideration of user need is the most important position and of primary concern to the change agent, (2) diagnosing need is an integral part of the change process, (3) the change agent is nondirective with users, (4) the internal resources should be fully realized, and (5) self-initiated and self-applied innovations are the strongest commitments from users.

The emphasis of this model is on the receivers and their interactive and collaborative problem-solving activities. However, it is essential for the consultant to play a significant role in training, supporting, and assisting the client system to develop problem-solving skills. Havelock believed that "the concept and role of the change agent are central to the formulation and implementation of [this] strategy" (1973b, p. 239).

The Organizational Development (OD) Model

The OD model had its beginning in business settings and aims to help people in organizations learn to solve their own problems more effectively (Sashkin & Egermeier, 1992). In the late 1960s, the model was adopted for use in schools. It is one of the best-known strategies for change, and it uses a problem solving approach. The focus of OD is on organizational problems rather than on problems that deal with just a part of the organization or with certain technical skills of organization members. It is based on a set of assumptions about change, is made up of distinct components or dimensions, and has definite implications for how change should be accomplished. These characteristics are similar to those of many of the other models. Schmuck et al. (1977) applied the OD model in school settings and reported, "It is the dynamics of the group, not the skill of individual members, that is both the major source of problems and the primary determiner of the quality of solutions" (p. 3).

The ultimate goal of this model is to improve subsystem effectiveness and interpersonal skills, which are believed to be the core strategies for the development of organizational adaptability. The skills have been described as: (1) clarifying communication, (2) establishing goals, (3) uncovering and working with conflict, (4) improving group procedures in meetings, (5) solving problems, (6) making decisions, and (7) assessing change (Schmuck et al., 1977).

The OD model has been implemented and sustained and carefully documented by Fullan, Miles, and Taylor (1981). However, Hall and Hord (1987) believe "its ultimate goal is all too infrequently attained" (p. 36).

The Rand Change Agent Study

The Rand Change Agent Study took place between 1973 and 1978 under the sponsorship of the U.S. Office of Education and has been extensively cited due to the implications this research has had for change in educational settings. Four federal "change agent programs" were identified for study: (1) Title III of the 1965 Elementary and Secondary Education Act, (2) Title VII of ESEA-supported district bilingual education efforts, (3) programs financed by the 1968 Vocational Educational Act that encouraged practitioners to develop new approaches to career education, and (4) the Right-to-Read program that funded local efforts to eliminate illiteracy (McLaughlin, 1989). These programs had a common purpose, which was the stimulation and spread of educational innovations. Temporary funds or seed money to support the new practices was also provided. Two major phases in the study were reported: Phase one concentrated on initiation and implementation of the projects, and phase two focused on incorporation and continuation of the project activity. There were 293 individual projects from eighteen states that were funded by the four federal programs, and brief reports were published each year that contributed to the widespread awareness.

At this time there were those, like Fullan and Pomfret (1977), who were beginning to investigate the implementation phase of the change process. This brought more attention to the Rand study because it included an investigation of the implementation and institutionalization phases.

The findings of the change agent study marked an important shift in the ways practitioners, researchers, and policymakers thought about effecting and understanding planned change in education. The results of the Rand Change Agent Study reported that schools change as new practices gain support, as they are adapted to the local situation, and when they become integrated into the regular operation of the school. Three stages in the change process were emphasized: (1) initiation (securing support), (2) implementation (based on change in the innovation and the school through a process of mutual adapting), and (3) incorporation or institutionalization (when changes become a permanent part of the system). However, according to Sashkin and Egermeier (1992), the findings were disappointing. They reported that "the amount of money and effort invested in the project made little difference" (p. 4).

In the 1980s, the emphasis shifted more to district and statewide decision making in all aspects of schooling. However, there are important implications for Helping Professionals. These include: (1) the Rand study's message of the importance of being supportive; (2) giving moral support to the staff; (3) developing local, interinnovator support systems; (4) supporting local users in adapting change to their particular setting and in adapting materials to match local needs; (5) giving support to new practices; and (6) supporting the principal so that he or she can offer more active support to the project.

The Concerns-Based Adoption Model (CBA)

The CBA approach was begun in the early 1970s by Hall and Hord and their colleagues. Several assumptions underlie the model: (1) It is critical to understand the point of view of the participants in the change process; (2) change is a process, not an event; (3) it is possible to anticipate much that will occur during a change process; (4) innovations come in all sizes and shapes; (5) innovation and implementation are two sides of the change process coin; (6) to change something, someone has to change first; and (7) everyone can be a change facilitator (Hall & Hord, 1987).

The model places a high priority on the change facilitator. The facilitator can be a principal or a staff member. The facilitator must make the decisions about which resources to use, when to use them, and how to use them. Change facilitators in this model are continually probing to assess teachers in each of the three dimensions of resource use. Diagnosis is ongoing, and conferences range from systematic questionnaires to less-structured meetings. Change facilitators continually make interventions, seldom miss opportunities to do something, and watch for opportunities to take action to assist teachers in gaining mastery of new programs and procedures.

It is believed that CBA empowers individuals to make changes, supports their rational assessment of needs and means, and brings them together so they can deal with change as an organized group (Sashkin & Egermeier, 1992).

In reviewing the change models, it is evident that change is more than just planning and developing new and improved practices. Rather, change is an ongoing, fluid process with numerous, unexpected, and hidden conditions that challenge educators today.

Implications of the Educational Change Literature for Helping Professionals

Bringing about educational change involves a number of essential issues. These include: (1) clearly defining beliefs and goals, (2) understanding the process of change and how to assist individuals and organizations successfully through the process, (3) involving teachers in frequent and continuous planning, (4) assisting teachers and administrators in working together, (5) selecting a model of change that will meet the needs of specific schools and individuals, (6) training Helping Professionals to become successful agents of change, and (7) meeting both the personal and the professional needs of those who are involved in the process of change.

Because conflict exists in every type of change, regardless of the degree of differences experienced, it is essential that individuals who are involved in the process of change find ways of working together at a new level of solving and resolving conflict. Conflict results mainly as an outcome of fear of the unknown. Every person feels fear and uncertainty with change. The differences among people exist in the ways they handle their fear. Along with feelings of fear are feelings of loss that must be recognized and dealt with. The Helping Professional is a key person to assist people in recognizing their feelings and in learning coping strategies to help them handle the pressures of change.

In the next section we introduce a new model of change. We have found it to be successful in our work with Helping Professionals, individual teachers, administrators, schools, and organizations involved in the process of change.

A Transformational Model: Beyond Change

Because progress will not be possible without some type of change taking place, it is essential that all change agents be aware of the process that individuals and organizations must experience if change is to be successful. Michael Fullan, after a number of years of research and study on change in schools, stated that there will be "a certain amount of ambiguity, ambivalence and uncertainty for the individual about the meaning of change" (1991, p. 106). He also argued "that conflict and disagreement are not only inevitable but fundamental to successful change" (p. 106). Thus, dissonance is an integral part of the change process and ought to be accepted and worked with.

Understanding why most individuals have some difficulty with change and knowing how people move through the phases of change will assist Helping Professionals in guiding people through the most difficult phases of the change process. In order for this process to be successful, it is essential that a self-transformational model for change be adopted. The model must identify the phases and clarify what will take place within an individual in each of the transformational phases of change. Also, the model will need to include coping strategies for dealing with the stressors and problems individuals will encounter. In

FIGURE 3-1 A Transformational Model: Beyond Change

Readiness ↔ Awareness ↔	New Insights ↔	Resistance to Change ↔	Adjustment ↔	New Commitment ↔	Continuation
Feelings of self-doubt	Anger, grief despair, fear	Cautious	Longer periods of exploration	Developing sense of belonging	Loss of previous support systems
Intellectually grasps the need for change	Threatened	Awkward	Begins to let go of past attitudes and behaviors	More creative	Feelings of loss
Intellectualizes need for change	Withdrawn, lonely, isolated	Many attempts to change ideas and behaviors	Gaining personal rewards	Increased confidence	New personal identity
Apprehensive	Denies reality	Apprehensive	Gaining in confidence	More open to ideas	Higher levels of creativity
Emotionally threatened	Resists new ideas	Begins to look at alternatives	Anxious	Personal rewards	Strong commitment to new programs
Feels emptiness and aloneness	Sense of loss	Denies feelings		Learning new skills	Gaining confidence in new skills
Anxious	Defensiveness	Anxious		Redefined roles and responsibilities	New energies
Anxious and frustrated	Regression			Low anxiety	Periods of anxiety
Fearful	High anxiety				
Highly resistant					
Resistant					
New insights are accepted					

Transitions

fact, Fullan, argued that "... problem-coping models based on knowledge of the change process are essential" (1991, p. 107).

A number of researchers of the change process identify three broad phases: Phase I, initiation, mobilization, or adoption; Phase II, initial use or implementation; and Phase III, incorporation, continuation, routinization, or institutionalization.

Models based on these three phases have been helpful in that they assist people in understanding the three major areas of change. However, when people are involved in trying to make essential changes and they are attempting to cope with the many adjustments that are necessary, what is essential is a model that includes the multiple phases of change that people are experiencing. A model of this type is more practical in bringing about self-transformation.

If the use of a model for change is to be successful, one of the outcomes must be to produce individuals and organizations that are healthy and productive. To accomplish this, individuals must first be guided through the transformational process. For example, when we work with families in counseling, we focus on the family system and each person within the family. Whenever one member is physically ill or demonstrates maladaptive coping strategies, the entire family is affected. However, when each person is given healthy coping strategies to change maladaptive behaviors and make positive changes, the entire family system is improved. Therefore, in organizations it is essential to first focus on the growth of the individual and then on the organization, which in turn will bring about healthier and more productive change for both the individuals and the organization.

The model for change presented in the next section focuses on the transforming of individuals and then of the organization. The transformation of the individual is the central theme of the model: A Transformational Model: Beyond Change (Figure 3-1).

The model is a comprehensive and detailed model for transforming the lives of people. As stated previously, we have found it essential to first understand the dynamics of an individual if change is to be meaningful and lasting. We view the process of change as being fluid, as people move back and forth through the phases, because change is not a linear process. When individuals are involved in any one of the phases, they can move back to a previous phase as they work through their own growth process. Fullan (1993) supports this concept when he describes "change as a journey, not a blueprint" (p. 24). When people gain insights about themselves as well as the project they are involved in, decisions can be made and altered at any one of the previously experienced phases. An example of this is when individuals make a decision to look for new alternatives in their lives, they are demonstrating the "Readiness for Change" phase of the model. New information gained at one phase of the model may lead individuals to explore decisions they made during previous phases. Also, gaining information about the first two phases of the model may help individuals clarify why they initially felt so threatened and why they resisted any of the new ideas.

When any new alternatives in the plan are accepted as beneficial, and subsequently put into action, the "Adjustment Phase" and the "New Commitment Phase" will in turn be affected. New adjustments and commitments will then need to be made, such as implementing a new language arts program. During the Readiness for Change phase, individuals will begin to change their original ideas and look for new ways to modify their program. They will explore other alternatives. As they grow more confident and feel more secure, they gain insights as to why they initially resisted the new program. They now are less fearful to try new ideas. This type of growth helps people move to the Adjustment phase, where they have longer periods of exploration with new materials and ideas. When people receive more personal rewards from their work, they are more willing to let go of the past and explore their options with others in the project. This new attitude also affects the organization.

An essential aspect of the model is the importance of the many factors that operate within each phase. When an emphasis is placed on the psychological welfare of the individual, a feeling of confidence increases, which encourages growth within the individual, and the project is affected. The individual is now involved in intellectual, emotional, physical, and social adjustments that are recognized and dealt with.

An additional factor to be considered in the model is that of the duration of time that will be needed for the individual to experience each phase. Because each person is unique, the time will be different for everyone.

The Awareness Phase

During the Awareness phase, the individual becomes aware of the need for change, whether this is initiated from within or from without. Individuals tend to intellectualize the need for change while they emotionally are unable or unwilling to let go of their old familiar patterns and ideas. When people develop feelings of self-doubt, their anxiety is increased, they feel a threat to their known patterns of thinking and behaving, and the result is resistance to change. The Awareness phase in most cases is of short duration, and then the individual moves to the next phase.

The New Insights Phase

When individuals begin to focus on the intellectual reasons for why the change needs to take place, they will move into Phase II, New Insights. At this time they are more open to intellectually grasping the need for making self-transformations, and they begin to think about what is needed and why it is needed. However, anxiety over the unknown, frustration regarding the outcome, and fear as to their own role in the new project or plan block them from moving forward. Some individuals will regress back to Phase I and challenge their new awareness of the need for any type of transformation either by rationalizing or denying the validity of the need for changing, while others will move to Phase III, Resistance.

The Resistance Phase

The phase of Resistance is similar to phases experienced during any loss in life, such as the death of a loved one. Individuals experience a sense of loss for their previous ways of behaving and thinking. Their emotions include anger, fear, grief, and despair. They often deny reality and resist any new ideas or plans presented to them. Their sense of loss is so great that in many instances they withdraw and become defensive and even hostile. In cases in which the threat is perceived to be too great, most individuals will regress to methods and procedures that have been safe for them in the past.

It is at the Resistance phase that the greatest amount of support and encouragement must take place. Helping Professionals are essential during this phase, and they need to develop an intervention program if any type of transition is to be continued and eventually is to be successful. Using needs inventories (Chapter 4) will be extremely beneficial at this phase to help individuals learn to identify their unmet emotional, physical, intellectual, and social needs. Also, it is vital at this point to develop support groups where people can talk through their fearful and threatening feelings. Helping people gain insights into what they are experiencing in the transformation process and providing coping strategies that help them learn how they can work through their feelings are critical. Learning to identify unmet needs and practicing new coping strategies to meet their needs will enable individuals eventually to move to Phase IV.

The Readiness for Change Phase

The fourth phase, Readiness for Change, takes place after individuals have worked through their ambivalence and uncertainty and have begun to feel a certain sense of security. They usually begin this phase with an insecure, cautious exploration of ideas and events, and they often feel apprehensive which may lead to some form of regression. However, their desire to look at alternatives is a positive and powerful force that works toward transforming the individual. This positive force helps motivate them toward changing some of the previous ideas and behaviors that they have been hanging onto for a sense of security. Emotionally individuals are experiencing anxiety due to the transformations they are experiencing. To handle the anxiety, a denial of feelings takes place. The defense mechanism of denial works to help them tolerate the intensity of the negative feelings.

Helping Professionals, acting as support agents, who listen and validate the feelings and ideas of the individual are critical components of this phase. They can help individuals feel empowered and capable of handling the transformations they are experiencing as they gain insights into their feelings and behaviors.

Up until this phase, little progress has been made with the project itself. However, results are not to be expected until the transformations within individuals have had time to be worked through. Any evaluations of the project at this point would be misleading, and, if outcomes are expected, would be discouraging.

As individuals are given time to work on their feelings, defense mechanisms, and perceptions of the project, they are more able to progress through the phases, and any transformations taking place will be more successful. It may take some resistant individuals months to move through even one of the phases. In fact, they usually regress to previous phases if they perceive any threat as being too great to handle. This is another reason why support persons and support groups are critical. The support groups, however, must be positive and problem-solving centered, and they must maintain a strong bond of confidentiality (Gold & Roth, 1993). Each phase in the transformation process is critical, and what happens at one phase strongly affects the others.

The Adjustment Phase

The fifth phase, Adjustment, is entered into when individuals become more involved with their interests in the project. They no longer are threatened by the fact that a new project is being adopted. They begin to think more about the project, and they work for longer periods of time on areas that interest them as they explore new ideas and materials. Some of their attitudes toward the project, other people, and even themselves begin to be transformed. They begin to let go of old attitudes and behaviors and they slowly develop new ones. As the personal rewards increase, they are even more highly motivated to change. Personal rewards such as developing new skills, practicing more effective teaching strategies, improving student performance, involvement with other teachers, and a sense of excitement in what they are doing all act as motivators for change. As teachers receive personal rewards, they grow in confidence and are empowered and motivated.

Even though the rewards are greater than previously, there will still be a certain amount of anxiety due to the changing state of things. For these reasons, Helping Professionals are still needed to support and guide teachers through stressful experiences. They will need to continue encouraging the teachers to become strengthened through the challenges.

Collegiality is a strong motivator throughout the transformation process. However, during the first four phases many teachers will withdraw and not receive support from colleagues. When teachers do begin to interact with one another, the success rate of the transformation process is increased. Personal sharing with others will help teachers learn how to adjust to the changes being made and to become more willing to evaluate the desirability of the project itself. When they feel more confident, they are in a better position to know their own strengths and what transformations they need to make. As this type of growth occurs, individuals are more qualified to judge the merits of the project.

Teacher certainty and teacher commitment reinforce one another and are most evident in this phase. Individuals who make a commitment to the project and who are willing to make the necessary changes required in this phase move on to Phase VI, New Commitment.

The New Commitment Phase

Teachers' collaborative work and creative development are most evident in the New Commitment phase. As they work together, deeper forms of interaction, such as joint planning and experimentation, take place. Their sense of belonging is more keenly developed, and the outcomes of their work are greater. Increased confidence is evident as teachers share their ideas and their successes. They are eager to share ideas with others and seek ideas from colleagues. They enjoy small-group interactions where they can test new ideas, solve problems, and assess their own effectiveness and the effectiveness of the project. They are now capable of giving and receiving help. In fact, they welcome new ideas. This is one of the clearest signs that change is taking place and that the project will be successful. Personal satisfaction is received from the transformations being made. Individuals continue to learn new skills as they redefine their roles and their responsibilities. The rewards are greater than the problems when individuals progress to this phase of transformations.

In the phase of New Commitment, the role of the Helping Professional is one of listening and appreciating teachers' ideas and achievements. Encouraging them to develop their ideas and talents is especially important now. Support groups are more focused on higher-level growth processes, and teacher leaders emerge as a natural result of the process that has taken place.

At this stage of growth we see teachers becoming more aware of their own need to improve. Insights are developed through their analysis of their needs and their interests. They are more flexible in receiving new ideas and in trying them in their classrooms. They encourage others to observe what they are doing, and they enjoy visiting other teachers' classrooms for the purposes of sharing ideas and of growing themselves. In fact, they express their need for learning a wide variety of approaches, and they seek information to make lessons more creative and more interesting for their students and for themselves. This is an exciting phase in the transformation process. It is a time of accelerated growth and a time of inquiring as teachers collaborate with one another. Most important in this period of growth is teachers developing their skills of inquiry and reflection. This is truly the center stage of the growth process. It is a time of meaningful transformations when teachers interact with others, analyze "best practice," and make critical evaluations of their teaching.

Loucks-Horsley et al. (1987) developed a list of ten characteristics that they believed were effective for the successful development of teachers. These ideas can be a source of referral for Helping Professionals, especially during the Adjustment and New Commitment phases:

1. Collegiality and collaboration
2. Experimentation and risk taking
3. Incorporation of available knowledge bases
4. Appropriate participant involvement in goal setting, implementation, evaluation, and decision making
5. Time to work on staff development and assimilate new learnings
6. Leadership and sustained administrative support
7. Appropriate incentives and rewards
8. Designs built on principles of adult learning and the change process
9. Integration of individual goals with school and district goals

10. Formal placement of the program within the philosophy and organizational structure of the school and district

The Continuation Phase

The next phase of the transformational process is that of Continuation. This phase continues until the individual needs to begin a new project and starts again at the Readiness phase. The Continuation phase is one of the most vulnerable phases for individuals if the Helping Professional and support groups or support persons are removed. It is essential at this phase of the transformational process that support groups have already been formed and that they are operating independently from the Helping Professional, who can now act as a follow-up support agent when needed. One of the most important functions of the Helping Professional is that of developing and training support groups and support leaders throughout the entire process of transformation. These groups must be able to function successfully on their own when the time comes for the Helping Professional to have a less vital role. When Helping Professionals and other support persons are removed too soon, many individuals in the project will begin to regress to previous phases. This is often the case in projects that appeared to be successful in the later stages of the project and then disintegrated because of the lack of support that was still needed.

When effective support is maintained throughout this phase, individuals do not experience a sense of loss, so they are able to maintain their growth and they develop in new areas. The result will be a strong commitment to the new program and an openness to other new projects and programs. When individuals experience success going through the transformations in the existing program, a sense of confidence in themselves and in others with whom they have worked is created. They also feel more confidence in the process of self-transformation. People become aware of the phases they are experiencing, they know how to identify their unmet needs as they use the needs inventories, and they have learned coping strategies that will assist them throughout all of the phases of the transformation model. They transfer all of this growth to a new project and begin the transformation process again.

Concluding Thoughts

Teachers must be respected, educated, guided, and supported through the many transformations that must take place during the restructuring of any school. When teachers are made aware of the Transformational model, and when they can recognize and relate to what they are experiencing, they are more open to making necessary changes. They are more eager to try new ideas and to evaluate their work. They gain confidence in themselves and in their colleagues. Their creativity is encouraged, they are able to reach higher levels of program planning, and they develop effective materials to enhance the learning of their students.

During periods of anxiety and frustration in any project, teachers must be guided through an understanding of their own needs, and they must be assisted in meeting them. When this takes place, their levels of commitment and productivity increase. With this type of assistance, teachers learn to set goals for their personal and professional growth, they analyze their behavior, and they practice new coping strategies for healthy development. They develop new personal and professional skills as they learn to reflect and solve problems in an environment that encourages a healthy lifestyle.

The Role of the Helping Professional in the Transformational Model

The role of the Helping Professional is a challenging and rewarding one. Participating in a process that enables teachers to mature and develop, as well as creating schools that foster healthier psychological and intellectual environments, is a legacy worth working for.

The following list of guidelines for Helping Professionals has been most profitable for the many mentors, principals, and others with whom we have worked. As Helping Professionals work with teachers who are experiencing changes within their schools, they understand the process of change and they have the knowledge and skills for helping others through it.

Guidelines for Helping Others Make Transformations

Awareness Phase ↔ **New Insights Phase** ↔ **Resistance Phase**

1. Discuss feelings of loss and the difficulties in "letting go" of familiar programs and practices.
2. Become aware of the process of transformation and identify each phase individuals are experiencing.
3. Help individuals understand the grieving process they must go through to let go and go on with new methods and programs.
4. Identify unmet needs (needs inventories) and help individuals plan specific ways they can meet their needs so growth can take place.
5. Develop support groups that are problem solving, action-oriented, and nonjudgmental.
6. Provide stress management education rather than "quick fix" methods.
7. Provide assistance for individuals who are most resistant to change.
8. Focus on the positive benefits of the new project for each person.

↔ **Readiness for Change Phase** ↔ **Adjustment Phase** ↔

1. Work with support groups to develop an open, supportive environment where transformations can take place.
2. Plan sessions to help individuals learn about the transformations expected of them.
3. Focus on the strengths, skills, and interests of each person in the project.

4. Encourage all involved to share their ideas and talents.
5. Help individuals identify the personal rewards for them.
6. Focus on alternative ways to approach problems and issues.
7. Plan ways individuals can expand their skills in support of self-transformation.
8. Work together to plan a new set of expectations.
9. Map out a personal development plan to assist individuals in learning new strategies for coping with the transformations.

New Commitment Phase ↔ **Continuation Phase** ↔

1. Discuss positive aspects of the project for the individuals and the group.
2. Plan ways individuals can use their talents to help others in the project.
3. Develop action groups to plan new programs, materials, and curriculum that is exciting and enhancing for everyone.
4. Provide intellectually stimulating activities.
5. Talk about ways to redefine roles.
6. Continue support groups. Form new interest support groups for those interested.
7. Talk about individuals' excitement for the transformations being made and that will be made.
8. Give extra support to those who need it.
9. Focus on successes and achievements.
10. Plan ways to build resilience through self-empowerment, positive mind set, and creativity.
11. Keep communication open and encouraging.
12. Work to build continued commitment.

Assessing the Helping Professional's Skills throughout the Transformational Process

The instruments in Table 3-1 may assist Helping Professionals in assessing how effectively they are working with others who are experiencing self-transformations. Helping Professionals can use the feedback to develop or enhance their own skills. The scale ranges from 1 to 5. A score of 1 = low effectiveness (I do not see myself practicing this type of behavior), and a score of 5 = high effectiveness (I do see myself practicing this behavior very effectively on a consistent basis). The table allows Helping Professionals to assess their own capabilities in working with people during the transformational process.

Final Thoughts

The role of the Helping Professional is one of challenge and one of tremendous responsibilities. These individuals must have developed the skills and experiences in their own lives to be authentic to others. Effective Helping Professionals

TABLE 3-1 Preparing Individuals for Transformations

	During Times of Transformation ...	Level of Effectiveness
		1 2 3 4 5

1. I communicate easily with others.
2. I am eager to work with others and encourage discussions with them.
3. I work to develop an environment that is safe for individuals to discuss their true feelings and ideas.
4. I plan seminars and discussion groups to help individuals understand the Transformational model and what they can expect during times of change.
5. I help individuals work through their fears and resistances.
6. I have clear communication throughout the project.

Working with Individuals' Resistance during Times of Transformations ...

1. I am aware of the past and its positive aspects and acknowledge these to others.
2. I help individuals recognize the loss they are experiencing and help them work through the process of loss.
3. I work to develop positive relations with everyone.
4. I clarify the phases in the Transformational model and help individuals through the phases, especially the resistance phase.
5. I encourage people to talk about their feelings and concerns about the transitions.
6. I encourage individuals to identify the barriers they could have that block them from changing.
7. I help people identify and deal with the ambiguity involved in making transformations.

Helping Individuals Build Commitment during Times of Transformations ...

1. I help individuals set goals for themselves that provide understanding of what they can accomplish.
2. I assist people in identifying their successes that help promote transformations.
3. I develop support groups and teams that promote transformations.
4. I help people develop their thinking, knowledge, skills, and practices that will help them and the school in the future.
5. I bring teachers together to evaluate how we are doing as a team based on the goals we established together.
6. I offer support and training for teachers who are having difficulty in making necessary commitments for transforming their lives.

are individuals who have grown and matured and developed a desire to assist others who are going through the growth process. They are not "super human beings." They are humble and gracious and desirous of assisting others who are making transitions in their lives. Respect from individuals must be earned as they work with them.

Taking time to evaluate oneself is essential for Helping Professionals' growth. Also, belonging to support groups for Helping Professionals will give the type of feedback necessary to keep a healthy, humble perspective regarding oneself. We encourage support groups for Helping Professionals.

One of the greatest rewards in life is sharing what we have learned with others. Helping Professionals are individuals who want to do this. They are also mature enough to know that they are always in a process of change and growth. They too are always making transformations in their life.

Exercises That Help in Understanding the Transformational Process

1. To check your own resistance, find a partner. Ask your partner to stand in front of you and push against your shoulders with the palms of the hand. Continue for 30 seconds. What do you want to do? Now, change roles—you push against your partner's shoulders for 30 seconds. Discuss how each of you felt and what you wanted to do.

   Remember, to resist a force is a biological reflex. Whenever coercion occurs, resistance increases. The stronger of you most probably could have overcome the resistance. However, the resistance does not disappear when this happens. It is hidden and becomes even more of a problem.

   Discuss how coercive strategies used for change can increase the level of generalized resistance and hinder the probability of successful long-term transformations.

2. We discussed in this chapter how every transformation causes loss for someone. In groups of three, share an experience in your life when you lost something of great value to you or when someone you loved died. After each person has shared, on a large chart list all of the feelings each of you experienced during the time of loss. Share the charts from the small groups with the entire group and brainstorm what teachers going through the transformational process will need from Helping Professionals when they are experiencing loss. Record these ideas for use later on.

3. Using the Transformational model, think of an area of your own life in which you are experiencing some form of transition. Analyze the model and identify what phase you are going through. Write out your own responses to each of the items listed under that phase. Share these with others in the group who are also involved in the same phase.

Closing Remarks

We have looked closely at the process of change and have examined a number of change models. One of the important areas that must be understood and incorporated into your own life is that of identifying your personal and psychological needs if you are to help yourself and others. The next chapter will define these needs and guide you in assessing your own needs through inventories and questionnaires.

References

Bandura, A. (1969). *Principles of behavior modification.* New York: Holt.

Berman, P., & McLaughlin, M. (1978). *Federal programs supporting educational change: Vol. 8. Implementing and sustaining innovations.* Santa Monica, CA: Rand Corporation.

Bloom, B. S. (1980). The new direction in educational research: Alterable variables. *Phi Delta Kappa, 61*(6), 382–385.

Bussis, A., Chittenden, E., & Amarel, M. (1976). *Beyond surface curriculum.* Boulder, CO: Westview Press.

Comte, A. (1875 [1852]). *System of positive polity: Social statics or the abstract theory of human order* (4 vols.). London: Longmans, Green.

Cuban, L. (1988). A fundamental puzzle of school reform. *Phi Delta Kappan, 69*(5), 341–344.

Elder, J. P., McGraw, S. A., Abrams, D. B., Ferreira, A., Lasater, T. M., Longpre, H., Peterson, G. S., Schwertfeger, R., & Corleton, R. A. (1986). Organizational and community approaches to community-wide prevention of heart disease: The first two years of the Pawtucket Heart Health Program. *Preventive Medicine, 15,* 107–117.

Elmore, R. F., & McLaughlin, M. W. (1988). *Steady work: Policy, practice, and the reform of American education.* Santa Monica, CA: RAND Corporation.

Fullan, M. G. (1991). *The new meaning of change.* New York: Teachers College Press.

Fullan, M. G. (1993). *Change forces probing the depths of educational reform.* New York: Falmer Press.

Fullan, M., Miles, M. B., & Taylor, G. (1981). *Organizational development in schools: The state of the art.* Washington, DC: National Institute of Education.

Fullan, M., & Park, P. (1981). *Curriculum implementation: A resource booklet.* Toronto, Canada: Ontario Ministry of Education.

Fullan, M., & Pomfret, A. (1977). Research on curriculum and instruction implementation. *Review of Educational Research, 4*(2), 335–393.

Gold, Y. (1996). Beginning teacher support: Attrition, mentoring and induction. In J. Sikula, T. Buttery, & E. Guyton (Eds.), *Handbook of research on teacher education* (2d ed.). New York: Macmillan.

Gold, Y., & Roth, R. A. (1993). *Teachers managing stress and preventing burnout: The professional health solution.* London: Falmer Press.

Guba, E., & Clark, D. C. (1976). *Research on institutions of teacher education. III: An institutional self-report on knowledge production and utilization activities in schools, colleges and departments of education.* Bloomington, IN: RITE Project.

Hall, G. E., & Hord, S. M. (1987). *Change in schools.* Albany: State University of New York Press.

Harp, L. (1991). States' fiscal woes put education on the defensive. *Education Week, 10*(18), 22–24.

Havelock, R. G. (1971). *Planning for innovation through dissemination and utilization of knowledge.* Ann Arbor: University of Michigan, Institute for Social Research.

Havelock, R. G. (1973a). *The change agent's guide to innovation in education.* Englewood Cliffs, NJ: Educational Technology Publications.

Havelock, R. G. (1973b). *Training for change agents.* Ann Arbor: University of Michigan, Institute for Social Research.

Hawkinshire, F. B., & Liggett, W. A. (1990). Lewin's Paradigm of planned change: Theory and application. In S. A. Wheelan, E. A. Pepitone, & V. Abt (Eds.), *Advances in field theory*. London: Sage.

Huberman, M., & Miles, M. (1984). *Innovation up close*. New York: Plenum.

Kelly, J. G. (1979). Tain't what you do, it's the way you do it. *American Journal of Community Psychology, 7*(3), 239–261.

Kelly, J. G., Snowden, L. R., & Munoz, R. F. (1977). Social and community interventions. *Annual Review of Psychology, 28*, 323–361.

Kirst, Michael W. (1982, September). How to improve schools without spending money. *Phi Delta Kappan, 64*, 6–8.

Lasater, T., Abrams, D., Artz, L., Beaudin, P., Cabrera, L., Elder, J., Ferreira, A., Knistey, P., Peterson, G., Rodrigues, A., Rosenberg, P., Snow, R., & Carleton, R. (1984). Lay volunteer delivery of a community-based cardiovascular risk factor change program: The Pawtucket experiment. In J. D. Matarazzo, S. H. Weiss, J. A. Herd, N. E. Miller, & S. W. Weiss (Eds.), *Behavioral health: A handbook of health enhancement and disease prevention* (pp. 1166–1170). New York: Wiley.

Lewin, K. (1947). Frontiers in group dynamics: Concept, method and reality in social science; social equilibria and social change. *Human Relations, 1*(1), 5–41.

Lewis, A. (1989). *Restructuring America's schools*. Arlington, VA: American Association of School Administrators.

Little, J. W. (1982). Norms of collegiality and experimentation: Workplace conditions of school success. *American Educational Research Journal, 19*(3), 325–340.

Loucks-Horsley, S., Harding, C., Arbuckle, M., Murray, L., Dubea, C., & Williams, M. (1987). *Continuing to learn: A guidebook for teacher development*. Andover, MA: Regional Laboratory for Educational Improvement of the Northeast and Islands and National Staff Development Council.

Marris, P. (1975). *Loss and change*. New York: Anchor Press/Doubleday.

Marx, K., & Engels, F. (1988). *Manifesto of the communist party*. New York: Labor News.

McLaughlin, (1989, September). The Rand Change Agent Study: Ten years later: Macro perspectives and micro realities. Paper presented at the American Educational Research Association meeting in San Francisco.

National Commission on Excellence in Education (1983). *A nation at risk: The imperative for educational reform*. Washington, DC: U.S. Government Printing Office.

Passow, A. H. (1989). Present and future directions in school reform. In T. J. Sergiovanni & J. H. Moore (Eds.), *Schooling for tomorrow* (pp. 13–19). Boston: Allyn and Bacon.

Sashkin, M., & Egermeier, J. (1992, April). School change models and processes: A review of research and practice. Paper presented at the American Educational Research Association (Division), San Francisco.

Schmuck, R. A., Runkel, R. J., Arends, J. H., & Arends, R. I. (1977). *The second handbook of organizational development in schools*. Eugene, OR: Center for Educational Policy and Management.

Timar, T. (1989). The politics of school restructuring. *Phi Delta Kappan, 71*(4), 265–275.

Timar, T. B., & Kirp, D. L. (1989). Educational reform in the 1980's: Lessons from the states. *Phi Delta Kappan, 70*(7), 504–511.

Tyack, D. (1990). "Restructuring" in historical perspective: Tinkering toward utopia. *Teachers College Record, 92*(2), 170–191.

Tye, L. (1990, November 23). Downturn forces deficits in 30 states. *The Boston Globe*, pp. 1, 38–40.

Chapter 4

Personal and Psychological Needs: Domain One

Not everything that is faced can be changed but nothing can be changed until it is faced. —JAMES BALDWIN

Meeting the personal and psychological needs of teachers is an important and vital dimension of teacher preparation and professional development. Unfortunately, these types of needs are not fully recognized or addressed as an integral part of teacher preparation programs or professional development programs.

The major concentration in offering support for teachers is in the areas of subject matter knowledge and technical skills for effective practice. Clearly, these are essential. The profession of teaching, however, also includes a critical component of working with a wide variety of individuals. To accomplish this, teachers must understand the values, needs, interests, and motivations of a wide range of personalities. Therefore, the training of teachers must go beyond just the technical knowledge and skills for effective performance, to knowledge that is more personal or intimate. In this respect, teaching has similarities to professions such as psychology, psychotherapy, and medicine.

To be effective in these more personal roles, individuals must be psychologically stable and in a continuous growth process of professional health (Gold & Roth, 1993). This not only is a necessity in their personal interactions in their professional roles, but also has a significant influence on their ability to use fully the technical knowledge and skills made available to them (Farber, 1991; Ward, 1987). Meeting personal and psychological needs is thus an essential part of the professional life of a teacher. Also, with the increasing demands and pressures placed upon educators today, the necessity to address these needs has become critical. This does not mean that every Helping Professional must be a psychologist or psychotherapist to assist teachers with their personal and psychological growth. It does mean, however, that Helping Professionals understand the essential nature of these needs and that they have learned to recognize and meet them in their own life.

We are beginning to see some recognition of the importance of assisting teachers in the domain of personal and psychological needs. For example, more attention is given in the supervision literature to working with the teacher's personal concerns, and beginning teacher support programs all have a component that focuses on emotional support. However, offering emotional support through strategies such as empathic listening and providing reassurance in difficult situations falls short of providing psychological support to meet personal and psychological needs as long-term, life-changing strategies. What is available at the present time is some recognition, although limited, with very little being done in this extremely important domain of professional preparation.

The lack of a concerted effort to address the domain of personal and psychological needs of teachers may be attributed to several causes. First, there is not a widespread awareness of the relationship of these needs to effective practice. Second, although there is some recognition, the extent or depth of this influence is not well understood by teacher educators and supervising school personnel in spite of the growing literature and empirical base (Farber, 1991; Gold, 1996; Gold & Roth, 1993). Third, educators are not professionally prepared in areas such as psychology and often are uncomfortable with psychologically related responsibilities. This may account for the phenomenon that there is a growing recognition to address this domain, but little has been done. Fourth, educators do not see this as their role. Traditionally it has not been their responsibility. Their charge has been to develop professional skills in curriculum and instruction, and not to be concerned with the personal issues of the teacher. This realm is either of no concern or it is considered to be outside the scope of their training and thus their responsibility.

The Transformational Helping Professional model, as we have described it, is very much concerned with all aspects of the teacher's growth. The value system of the model clearly focuses on the importance of the individual and each person's psychological welfare. Also, all aspects of teachers' needs affect their performance in the classroom and in the professional role over all. We thus have been compelled to explore in depth the nature of personal and psychological needs and how Helping Professionals must address them in their own life as well as assisting teachers in their growth process. For the purpose of the Transformational Helping Professional model, the personal needs include the physical, social, and spiritual, and the psychological needs include the emotional and intellectual.

The critical issue to be considered first is how the personal and psychological needs are identified and addressed. Early attempts made to define and address these needs provide an important base of understanding (Blumberg, 1980; Gold,

1988; Gold, 1990; McDavid, 1990–91; Thies-Sprinthall, 1984). A subsequent phase requires a detailed identification of the needs along with clearly defined coping strategies for addressing them. Considerably deeper insights have emerged recently that address this requirement (Gold, 1992; Gold & Roth, 1993) and are an integral part of a comprehensive program of professional health for teachers. This program has been used extensively with large numbers of beginning teacher support groups, staff development groups, and mentor teacher support groups.

This chapter will focus on identifying and addressing the personal and psychological needs of teachers, presenting specific diagnostic tools for identifying unmet needs, and identifying coping strategies for meeting these needs.

Personal and Psychological Needs of Teachers

Issues of public support and respect are of utmost concern for teachers, as was noted in The Metropolitan Life Survey of the American Teacher that began in 1984 and the Gallup Poll of the Public's Attitudes about public schools beginning in 1969. The results of these surveys highlighted a number of critical areas regarding teachers and the public and their views toward each other. Criticism of teachers increased as the public ranked them low in prestige or status in comparison to other occupational groups in the 1981 Gallup Poll. Although teachers were ranked third in their contributions to the general good of society (after clergy and physicians) and second in terms of the amount of stress or pressure they encounter (after physicians), they were eighth in terms of prestige or status (after physicians, judges, clergy, bankers, lawyers, business executives, and public school principals). Thus, public respect for teachers is not consistent with the understanding of the contributions teachers make or the amount of pressure they encounter (Elam, 1984).

Coupled with the lack of respect for teachers is the absence of appreciation for their efforts. In the 1992 Metropolitan Life Survey of the American Teacher the reason most often cited as a major factor for teachers leaving the profession was "lack of support or help for students from their parents" (Harris et al., 1992, p. 15).

The degenerating morale of teachers is reflected in reports that describe the profession as being in a crisis. Wendt (1980) stated that education is in a sense of crisis, and Farber's (1991) book was aptly titled: *Crisis in Education: Stress and Burnout in the American Teacher*. The Association for Supervision and Curriculum Development conducted a study of its membership to determine critical issues for 1990–1992. The study reported that the status of teaching and related morale was at an all-time low (Hodges, 1990). The 1990 Carnegie Report indicated that "nearly 40 percent of the teachers [in their survey] reported that if they had it to do over, they would not become a public school teacher" (Carnegie Foundation, 1990, p. 3).

These types of reports reflect the slow wearing away of the morale of teachers, and this certainly has serious consequences for them and for the profession. Although teachers, and especially new teachers, demonstrate enthusiasm and excitement about teaching, the public criticism and low morale in many schools leave them discouraged and disillusioned (Gold, 1996). When new teachers become personally insecure, lack confidence, or have a sense of not being in control of themselves or their environment, it is not likely that they can be successful in teaching no matter how strong their instructional preparation was.

When teachers are unable to handle the numerous pressures encountered in the profession, the result often is unsuccessful teaching and a decision to drop out of the profession. The necessity to learn how to handle pressures and to manage stress associated with teaching is now at a critical stage. Teachers need to be given knowledge, skills, and psychological support to assist them during difficult periods throughout their career (Gold, 1996).

One critical need of teachers is to be involved in a program of psychological support (Gold, 1992; Gold & Roth, 1993; Thies-Sprinthall & Gerler, 1990). However, psychological support has been defined in many ways. Some of these are emotional support, positive regard, accurate empathy, empathic listening, and meeting psychological needs (Gold, 1996). It has included an array of skills and strategies such as reinforcing a positive self-esteem, confidence building, guidance in developing a sense of effectiveness, learning how to handle stress, instilling a sense of self-reliance, and psychological assistance. Currently a more comprehensive program of psychological support has included various forms of assessing individual psychological needs, developing a personal plan to aid teachers in gaining insights into their unmet needs, acquiring information and strategies for handling stressors and for managing stress, learning new coping strategies to overcome problems, giving attention to burnout prevention techniques, and utilizing communication skills to enhance personal growth (Gold & Roth, 1993).

This type of psychological support is especially needed for preservice teachers and new teachers. As noted in Chapter 1, it is recommended that induction programs include the encouragement of personal growth as well as the emotional development of the individual, not simply focusing on survival skills (Bolam, 1987; Gold, 1987; Thies-Sprinthall & Gerler, 1990).

Featherstone (1992) stated that self-knowledge is a "major fruit" of the early teaching experience and that the new teachers who are the most strict in their classroom discipline may be struggling to manage their students' behavior due to their own struggle to understand and change themselves. She also pointed out that "teaching calls for different spiritual, social, emotional and intellectual qualities than 'studenting,' and so the attempt to teach shows us ourselves in a somewhat new light" (p. 7). Thus, meeting teachers' psychological needs is an important and vital dimension of preservice and inservice programs. Because the need is evident, it must be fully recognized as an essential element of preparation and professional development programs. Although some induction programs for beginning teachers have used emotional support through empathic listening and attention giving, they have not provided more in-depth support to assess and meet personal and psychological needs.

Teachers are often so involved in their professional responsibilities that they have little time left for taking care of themselves. We often hear them report that they rarely have time to concentrate on their own needs, especially the physical ones. This is especially evident during the times of the year when certain illnesses are more pronounced, such as the month of December. When teachers allow their physical health to be neglected, the results are often noted in illness, a lack of energy, and overall poor physical fitness. Taking time to develop a physical plan that fits their schedule and their needs is essential for a healthy lifestyle.

Another area of neglect is that of meeting their intellectual needs. This is especially true of new teachers. Teachers are individuals who desire intellectual stimulation and have this need met during their years at the university. When demanding teaching schedules and home responsibilities rob them of time to engage in intellectual pursuits, the end result is failure to fulfill their intellectual curiosity and needs for growth.

A program that concentrates on meeting the personal and psychological needs of teachers should include the following areas: (1) physical needs, (2) emotional needs, (3) intellectual needs, (4) social needs, and (5) spiritual needs. Each of these domains will be considered separately.

Physical Needs

Do you want to be physically the best that you can be? We have found that most people quickly answer in the affirmative, yet rarely stop to consider defining what "best" means to them. However, how we define this question is the motivating factor in how we carry it out. For you to become more aware of how you answer the question, it is helpful to take a few minutes to think it through and write out your answer:

What does it mean to me to be physically the best I can be?

_____

_____

After you have written a response to the question, take a few minutes to share your ideas with others. Small groups of three or four are usually effective. After each person has shared his or her response, as a group discuss what you have learned about each other and whether you modified your original ideas. You may want to list the responses of each person in the small group on large poster paper for later discussions with the entire group.

Examine the physical needs listed below and observe whether your written response included any of these needs.

Physical Needs
Energy–stamina
Calmness
Safety
Good health
Physical fitness
Physically rested
Physical strength
Flexibility

After you have discussed your responses, the following questions can be of assistance to you in further evaluation of your needs. Answer each question either "Yes" or "No." For any "No" response, answer the question following your "No" answer.

Physical Needs Analysis

1. Do I get enough exercise to keep my energy level where I need it for my lifestyle?
   Yes _____   No _____
   If no, what do I need to change in my routine? _____

2. Do I have a good balance in my life between excitement and calmness?
   Yes _____   No _____
   If no, what is the overall tempo of my life and what do I need to work on?
   _____

3. Do my work environment and home environment meet my needs for safety?
   Yes _____   No _____
   If no, what kinds of changes do I need to make? _____

4. Do I plan a healthy eating program for myself?
   Yes _____   No _____
   If no, what changes do I need to make? _____

5. Am I taking time to exercise and stay physically fit?
   Yes _____   No _____
   If no, do I need to go to a gym to get the support and instruction I need, or do I need a support person or group to help me stay motivated, such as a walking partner or club, etc.?_____

6. Am I getting enough sleep each evening so that I feel physically rested most of the time?
   Yes _____   No _____
   If no, do I need more sleep in the evening and/or periodic rest periods when I can schedule them? _____

7. Do I have the physical strength to enjoy my personal and professional life?
   Yes _____ No _____
   If no, what do I need to do to improve it? _____

8. Is my body flexible enough to do the things I want to? Yes ____ No ____
   If no, why not?_____

After you have answered each question, circle the number of each question that you answered with a "No" response. After you have circled each question, look at the list of physical needs and identify the needs that you marked "No." The needs are in the same order as the questions. For example, Question 1 is energy-stamina, Question 2 is calmness, and so on.

TABLE 4-1 My Physical Needs Plan

Day	Food Diary	Exercise Plan	Relaxation	Sleep	Other
Monday	*sweet roll* *Hamburger, Coke* *TV dinner*	*0*	*watched TV*	*6 hours*	*put locks on windows for safety*

A Physical Needs Plan

Because most people want to live a healthy life, attending to their physical needs is essential. Evaluating one's needs and beginning a plan to meet them will help to improve in this area. A plan such as the one in Table 4-1 can help an individual gain insights into each category every day. Record what you eat each day, your exercise program, what you do for relaxation, and how much sleep you get. If there is anything you want to add, the last column is available.

Many people share with us that it is difficult for them to find time to keep a log of this type. However, when they do make a commitment to keep it for a week, they are often surprised by their responses. We hear reports like Tony's, who shared his plan with us: "I didn't know I ate so much fast food. I eat fast food rather than taking time to prepare healthy food. I spend most of my relaxing time in front of the TV. I need to start a walking plan and get some exercise," and "No wonder I'm so tired. I only get an average of 6 hours sleep a night. I need at least 8 hours."

What we begin to learn is that we are usually not in touch with our daily habits, and we rarely focus on our physical needs. Paying attention to and exerting as much control as possible over our physical needs will help us stay healthy and will enable us to recover more rapidly when we are ill. Helping Professionals must be aware of their own physical needs if they are to assist others with theirs.

Because our physical well-being and our emotions exert a profound influence upon our life, the emotional needs will be examined next.

Emotional Needs

We all are aware that we have emotions and that we express them throughout every day of our lives in one way or another. We enjoy our pleasurable emotions and we often stop to more fully experience them. A few examples given by teachers in a support group we facilitated were taking time to stop and enjoy a cool spring day, enjoying small children at play, and admiring the beautiful mountains covered with snow during the winter time. These kinds of feelings of joy and pleasure are even increased when we share them with a significant other who also enjoys them.

The various ways that we deal with our emotions have a great deal to do with their effects on us. For those individuals who identify their positive emotions and share the experiences and feelings with others who also enjoy them, the pleasure becomes even greater, and the emotional experiences have a more intense effect upon them. This type of effect was reported in a 30-year study of initially healthy young men. In the study the men who demonstrated the most mature emotions and psychological style such as a sense of humor, an altruistic style, and other positive attitudes were found to be the ones who were the healthiest 30 years later (Vaillant, 1976).

In another study, people with an optimistic explanatory style reported better health. The major factors contributing to their good health included stronger immunity, good social support, and a willingness to stick with better health habits (Seligman, 1991).

An explanatory lifestyle is the way people perceive the events in their lives. It is the habitual way people explain the negative things that happen to them. Another way of defining an explanatory style is to say it is a habit, a way of thinking that a person uses when all other factors are equal and when there are no clear right and wrong answers. An explanatory lifestyle has an extremely powerful influence on one's health and contributes to feelings of wellness. Seligman (1991) believes that this type of lifestyle works like a self-fulfilling prophecy. He states that the way a person "explains events in his life can predict and determine his future," and he further explains that "those who believe they are the masters of their fate are more likely to succeed than those who attribute events to forces beyond their control" (p. 178).

These concepts have powerful implications for Helping Professionals in relation to their own lives and in their interactions with others. Paying specific attention to how individuals perceive the events in their lives, how they view the problems they encounter, and the patterns of thinking they demonstrate is very important in helping people develop a sense of control in their life that will contribute toward a healthier lifestyle.

Developing a concept of control, defined as locus of control, originated several decades ago through the work of Julian Roter, who proposed that having control involves the belief that our own actions will be effective enough to control or master the environment (Rice, 1987). Control includes a deep-seated belief that we can impact a situation by how we look at the problems we encounter. It does not mean that we need to control everything around us such as other people, the environment, or our circumstances, whether they are good or bad. However, it is essential to know that we can choose how we think and how we respond to events and to others. Assisting teachers in gaining a sense of increased control includes helping them understand and develop the following concepts in their life:

1. Acquiring knowledge that leads to feeling an increased sense of control because the situation becomes more predictable and manageable
2. Adopting a more positive view of life; becoming aware when you are pessimistic and changing your negative thinking and behavior
3. Developing new and effective coping strategies
4. Building a positive support system for yourself
5. Developing faith in a power greater than yourself in whom you completely trust
6. Preparing yourself for handling difficulties through believing that you already have the ability to develop control in your life

7. Developing strong convictions in your beliefs, values, and ability to handle the problems you encounter

Helping Professionals are in a good position to assist teachers in acquiring information and strategies that will aid them in handling the daily problems they encounter. Classroom discipline is an example of a high stress area for many teachers (Veenman, 1984). Helping Professionals can assist these teachers in developing a sense of control over their discipline problems. They can provide them with information about discipline techniques that have proven to be successful for other teachers, in becoming more aware of situations in which they were successful in applying what they learned in future situations. Also, learning coping strategies that help them handle their own stress will serve to empower them.

When teachers discuss their successes and failures with support persons and support groups, they begin to develop feelings of self-confidence. As they develop a sense of control in their professional life, they begin to believe that their actions will be effective in handling their problems. Also, they learn that they do not have to control everything and everyone all of the time. As a result, they begin to develop a more effective explanatory lifestyle, which in turn contributes to their emotional and physical well-being.

In contrast, the consequences of not dealing with negative feelings are great. There is a growing body of evidence that points toward the concept that "what is going on in our minds, our hearts, and our spirits may have tremendous impact on what happens to our bodies" (Hafen et al., 1992, p. 5). It has been found that there is a physiological reason why emotions can affect a person's health. Specific emotions are associated with different parts of the brain and with specific hormone patterns. Emotional responses release certain hormones that affect the person's health (Henry, 1986). There has been research, for example, reporting that emotionally induced changes in hormones can lead to chronic disease, such as high blood pressure (Henry, 1986). Too much noradrenaline and adrenaline are secreted when a person is aggressive and anxious, and smooth muscle damage occurs from excess hormones. A gradual rise in blood pressure can result in stroke, hypertension, or even heart failure.

Another problem that results from strong emotions is the weakening of the immune system, which usually causes illness. Pilisuk and Parks (1986) believe that our immunity against disease is affected by the emotions we feel. Hammer (1984) describes the immune system as "a surveillance mechanism that protects the host from disease-causing microorganisms. It regulates susceptibility to cancers, infectious diseases, allergies, and auto immune disorders" (p. 49).

We have known for years that disease can affect the immune system. In a more recent series of studies, ample evidence was given that thoughts and emotions can also impact the immune system. A study of more than 4,000 Vietnam-era army veterans reported that the immune system was affected by emotions such as depression and psychiatric conditions such as schizophrenia (Barrett & Flanders, 1989).

We find in our work with student teachers and beginning teachers that many of them are ill around the fourth week of teaching. Their fears and anxieties associated with whether or not they will be successful are strong contributors to the breakdown of their immune systems. What is necessary to assist them is an understanding of their emotional needs and how their feelings alert them to needs that are not being met. The following list provides a sample of emotional needs.

Emotional Needs

Security
Serenity/harmony
Self-acceptance
Self-confidence
Self-esteem
Emotional stability
Worthwhileness
Love

Learning to identify needs that are not being met will assist teachers in discovering areas that are contributing to many of the negative feelings they are encountering. The following questionnaire will help in identifying emotional needs. Answer each question with a "Yes" or "No" response.

Emotional Questionnaire

Yes   No

_____   _____   1. I like myself most of the time.

_____   _____   2. I feel secure in my personal relationships.

_____   _____   3. I believe in my ability to succeed.

_____   _____   4. I have warm, loving relationships in my life.

_____   _____   5. My life is seldom in a state of turmoil.

_____   _____   6. I am pleased with my personal accomplishments.

_____   _____   7. I am able to handle the pressures in life.

_____   _____   8. My deep personal relationships most often work out for me.

_____   _____   9. I accept criticism without feeling personally attacked.

_____   _____   10. I feel financially secure about my future.

_____   _____   11. I feel I have a great deal to offer in a special relationship.

_____   _____   12. I have a peaceful and harmonious lifestyle.

_____   _____   13. I would not want to be someone else.

_____   _____   14. I feel a sense of stability in my emotional life.

_____   _____   15. I handle the failures in my life most of the time.

_____   _____   16. I feel accepted and of value to others.

After completing the questionnaire, record your scores by placing a "Yes" or "No" next to each number:

Security	2 _____	10 _____
Serenity/harmony	5 _____	12 _____
Worthwhile	16 _____	11 _____
Self-acceptance	1 _____	13 _____
Love	4 _____	8 _____
Emotional stability	7 _____	14 _____
Self-confidence	3 _____	9 _____
Self-esteem	6 _____	15 _____

You have identified your unmet emotional needs. Now, circle each of the needs where you placed at least one "No" response. After identifying these unmet needs, select one at a time to work on. We have found it to be of assistance when working with others to have them write out their understanding of what is taking place in their life regarding the need they selected. An example from one of the teachers in our seminars may be informative.

Tom was a first-year high school teacher in our support group. After answering the questionnaire, he shared the following story with the group:

One of the things I just learned is that I am isolating myself with all of the paperwork I have to do. I so want to be successful that I spend most of my time on school work. When I evaluated my questionnaire, I realized that I have many emotional needs not being met. My needs for serenity/harmony, love, self/confidence, and self-esteem are all being neglected. In fact, I haven't been out on a date for 3 months, and I haven't been out with the guys for at least 2 months. No wonder I feel so lonely.

At this point you may be wondering why it is so important to work on unmet emotional needs. This is an essential question to answer. Because our unmet emotional needs do not vanish, and because they do create stress and negative feelings, it is necessary to identify them and work on meeting them in order to have a more fulfilled lifestyle. Emotional needs have important implications for psychological well-being for your professional performance.

When these needs are not met, they have serious consequences as to how an individual will relate to others. For example, repressed hurt may be manifested in anger projected onto others. Individuals often have expressed to us that they don't know why they become so angry and have conflict with others in their profession or at home. When we ask the individual to share more information with us, we discover repressed feelings that are being expressed in negative behaviors.

TABLE 4-2 Personal Log

Feelings	Behavior	Situation	Unmet Needs	Date
anger *frustration*	*yelled at my students*	*classroom*	*self-esteem*	*5/30*
anxiety	*impatient with spouse*	*home/kitchen*	*serenity/harmony*	*5/31*

Personal Log

Keeping a log like the one in Table 4-2 will help in identifying feelings and behaviors that will assist in this process of self-discovery. The purpose of maintaining the log is to gain insights to assist you. To accomplish this, chart your feelings, behaviors, and situations for 1 week. Comparing your personal log with your needs inventory and identifying your unmet needs will help you discover how specific feelings are connected to needs that are not being met. Knowing your own unmet needs and learning ways to meet them will also help you in assisting others.

The role of emotional needs must be addressed if we are to maintain equilibrium and enjoy our personal and professional lives. William Glasser (1975) discussed the importance of meeting our emotional needs when he stated that helping people to fulfill their "need to love and be loved and the need to feel that we are worthwhile to ourselves and to others" (p. 10) is the basis of his *Reality Therapy* (1975).

Intellectual Needs

A major purpose in helping others is to facilitate their growth toward personal fulfillment. Another area of personal fulfillment is that of meeting intellectual needs. Teachers receive a great deal of intellectual stimulation during their years at the university. One of the major roles of higher education is to develop the intellectual interests and capabilities of those who attend, and in most instances students do experience intellectual challenge and success. After leaving the university, many teachers complain that they seldom are intellectually challenged. They usually deal with the daily requirements of preparation, planning, and paperwork that are seldom stimulating intellectually.

Teachers need assistance in evaluating their intellectual needs and in becoming aware of areas that are being neglected. When Helping Professionals are psychologically mature and when they have met their own intellectual needs, they are better able to act as a stimulus for strengthening the intellectual capacities and curiosities of others. Some intellectual needs are listed here:

Intellectual Needs

Discovery
Intellectual excitement
Generating new knowledge

Expanding the knowledge base
Innovative techniques
Developing new ideas
Intellectual challenges
Intellectual curiosity
Use of creativity
Mental gratification
Aesthetic experiences
Developing techniques of inquiry
Critical thinking
Developing novel ways of thinking
Self-analysis
Intellectual stimulation
Positive thinking
Evaluative thinking
Intellectual fulfillment

The purpose of the following questionnaire is to help individuals assess their intellectual needs. Answer "Yes" or "No" to each question.

Meeting My Intellectual Needs

		Yes	No
1.	Am I taking time to read interesting and stimulating books other than those that are required reading?	___	___
2.	Do I discuss my interests and hobbies with others who encourage and stimulate my thinking?	___	___
3.	Do I investigate subjects outside of my own area of expertise?	___	___
4.	Do I seek people who are stimulating to talk with?	___	___
5.	Am I aware of my own intellectual needs?	___	___
6.	Do I actively seek ways to add excitement to my intellectual endeavors?	___	___
7.	Am I using the information I am acquiring to develop new ideas and new ways of thinking?	___	___
8.	Am I seeking ways to build upon the knowledge I now have?	___	___
9.	Do I develop new and innovative materials and strategies to improve my teaching?	___	___
10.	Do I encourage others to challenge my thinking for my own growth?	___	___
11.	Would I consider myself a positive thinker most of the time?	___	___
12.	Most of the time, do I seek out experiences that are aesthetic and fulfilling for me?	___	___

	Yes	No
13. Do I enjoy discovering new and interesting ideas and concepts?	___	___
14. Am I a person who enjoys using my creativity?	___	___
15. Do I like to think up new and novel ways to improve my teaching?	___	___
16. Most of the time, do I reflect on my teaching and evaluate my ideas?	___	___
17. Do I like to broaden my perspectives through stimulating discussions with other educators who are critical thinkers and who challenge me to think critically?	___	___
18. When I select support and discussion groups, are they highly gratifying for me and do they challenge my thinking?	___	___
19. Do I enjoy colleagues who like to use methods of inquiry to strengthen our thinking?	___	___

Answer the following questions:

1. What did I learn from these questions? _____

_____

_____

_____

2. What do I plan to do that will help me meet my unmet intellectual needs?

_____

_____

_____

3. How often will I evaluate this area of my life? _____

_____

_____

_____

After completing the questionnaire, take time to evaluate how you responded to each question, and identify which of the intellectual needs listed each question represents. Write a brief paragraph discussing what you learned about yourself. When you have written what you learned, check your answers on the questionnaire with the Answer Key. After you have finished, answer the four questions following the answer key. Take time to share what you learned about yourself with others in your group.

Answer Key

1. Intellectual curiosity
2. Intellectual stimulation
3. Generating new knowledge
4. Intellectual fulfillment
5. Self-analysis
6. Intellectual excitement
7. Developing new ideas
8. Expanding the knowledge base
9. Innovative techniques
10. Intellectual challenges
11. Positive thinking
12. Aesthetic experiences
13. Discovery
14. Use of creativity
15. Developing novel ways of thinking
16. Evaluative thinking
17. Critical thinking
18. Mental gratification
19. Developing techniques of inquiry

Questions to Consider

1. What intellectual areas are being neglected in my life?
2. What impact is this having on me?
3. What am I planning to do to meet my intellectual needs?
4. Who will act as my support person(s) to encourage me?

It doesn't matter how long teachers have been in education, when they feel frustrated, bored, or discontented with the intellectual stimulation they are receiving, it is important that they learn what is missing. Taking inventory, as you have just done, will provide insights, and then you can plan a program to meet your needs. Unmet desires for knowledge, discovery, and intellectual gratification can easily affect one's self-esteem. On the other hand, when intellectual needs are met, individuals feel more satisfied with their work, which affects how they perceive themselves and their work situation. In addition, teachers need to share their intellectual interests with others because it can be highly rewarding and stimulating. We will examine sharing interests and other social needs in the following section.

Social Needs

Most researchers would define social support as the degree to which a person's basic social needs are met through interactions with other people. Social involvements can take place in a variety of situations. Some of these situations may relate to tangible areas such as needing a ride to work when one's car breaks down, or they may be in intangible areas such as in the emotional realm of receiving understanding, accepting, and encouragement from another person.

We all need to feel that we have others to count on when we have problems, and we look to our close friends for support during difficult periods in life. Cohen (1990) reports that there are three factors that make up our social resources:

1. Social networks—the size, density, durability, intensity, and frequency of social contacts

2. Social relationships—the existence of relationships, number of relationships, and type of relationships
3. Social support—the type, source, number, and quality of resources

Our social agents may include family, friends, professional associates, neighbors, etcetera. We turn to these people when we have a need. These needs may be for relaxation or for assistance during times of adversity. What we have learned through researchers in the area of social relationships is that people with social ties, regardless of their source, live longer than do people who are isolated. These people also maintain higher levels of health and are more successful in handling life's difficulties (Padus, 1986).

When we are having a great deal of stress in our lives, social support enhances our self-esteem, provides stability, and in many instances encourages feelings of control over the situation. Support can also act as a buffer against stress when we realize we are not facing our problems alone.

According to one researcher (Powell, 1987), long lives depend on strengthening bonds with others. Further, she believes that a rewarding social life can nourish the mind, the emotions, and the spirit. She also reports that people with a number of close friends and confidants and people who are able to openly discuss their deepest feelings are better able to handle stress.

The impact of social support and the ability to cope have been especially relevant to the study of beginning teachers. This was reported in Veenman's (1984) analysis of eighty-three studies over a 20-year period, which revealed that the greater the number of problems new teachers encountered, the more likely they were to leave the profession. This was especially evident when the beginning teachers isolated themselves. More currently, it was reported that high rates of attrition are still being observed among beginning teachers (Harris et al., 1992, 1993), which highlights the pressing need for support during this period of their career.

To assist beginning teachers during these transition years, support has been provided in a variety of forms. This interest in offering support has been increasing steadily over the past decade (Anderson & Shannon, 1988: Gehrke & Kay, 1984; Healy & Welchert, 1990), and some researchers believe that support and assistance should be available from the first days of entering the profession as well as throughout the teacher's entire career (Thomas & Kiley, 1994).

One issue is clear: Teachers need to be more aware of their social needs and the various ways they can meet them. The following social needs have been identified as important to successful functioning:

Social Needs

Close relationships
New acquaintances
Collegiality
Personal interactions
A sense of belonging
Friendships

Intimacy
Friendship love
Relationship security
A sense of success with relationships
Emotional comfort from relationships

It is essential that teachers become acquainted with their social needs and work toward meeting those that are unmet. Answering the following questions will guide individuals in developing insights. Taking time to read each question carefully and writing out a short response to each will be most beneficial.

Social Needs Questionnaire

1. I like to meet people and make new acquaintances.

2. Most of the time, I feel a sense of security in my relationships.

3. My friendships are rewarding and enjoyable most of the time.

4. I interact with my colleagues and feel successful and rewarded in these interactions.

5. I have close loving relationships that are fulfilling for me.

6. My close relationships are rewarding and we share our deep feelings to help us gain insights into ourselves.

7. I have a strong sense of belonging both at school and in my personal life.

8. I have close intimate relationships.

9. I participate in a variety of functions in which I interact with a wide variety of people.

10. I receive enough emotional comfort from my personal relationships.

11. I feel successful in the majority of my personal and professional relationships.

After responding to each of the items, take time to evaluate your social needs that require attention. The following key will help in identifying these needs. The numbers correspond to the numbers in the questionnaire.

1. New acquaintances
2. Relationship security
3. Friendships
4. Collegiality
5. Friendship love
6. Close relationships
7. A sense of belonging
8. Intimacy
9. Personal interactions
10. Emotional comfort from relationships
11. A sense of success with relationships

After evaluating the responses, it is helpful to meet with a partner and share what was learned. After each person has shared, making a commitment as to how each person will meet his or her needs assists in the growth process. This process will help you enhance your growth. After 1 week, meet again and share any progress. Making commitments and taking part in follow-up discussions will help individuals continue the growth they have started.

Most teachers enter the profession because they enjoy interacting with others. They care about people, and they often have strong needs to help others. They enjoy interacting through sharing ideas and experiences with their colleagues. These sharings add significance and meaning to life and are an essential part of the growth process. We all need to give and to receive in order to grow and mature.

When teachers are going through stressful times, their support networks are vital. The size of their network and the frequency of the contacts play an important part in the healing process. When social relationships (the number and type) are lacking, teachers feel isolated and vulnerable. They experience feelings of loneliness and separation when they are isolated in their classrooms. The more severe the social need becomes, the more it will have an impact on teachers' self-esteem and on their ability to function in the classroom. If negative feelings are disregarded for a prolonged period, teachers will manifest symptoms of discouragement and dissatisfaction. Their needs for intimacy, belonging, and emotional support must be attended to.

How then can the social needs of teachers be met professionally? Because the need to interact with colleagues is of great importance to most teachers, opportunities must be provided to meet these needs. Teachers must be made aware of their needs and given information as to how their needs can be met.

One area of great promise is that of support groups made up of lead teachers who are perceived by other teachers as being encouraging, supportive, and trustworthy. How these groups are organized is critical if they are to be successful. Facilitators must be trained in how to give support, and they must know strategies for communicating and for offering encouragement (Gold & Roth, 1993). When members of the group feel accepted, they are more free to openly explore areas of their lives that are difficult and painful for them. The environment must be one of trust and support. When members feel safe, they are more free to learn about themselves and they are more motivated to change.

Jackie is a prime example of a teacher who needed support during a difficult time in her life. She was recently separated from her husband and had no children or relatives living in the area. They had moved to a new area the year before due to her husband's job change. Jackie was able to find a teaching position in a school that needed bilingual teachers because she was bilingual. Six months after moving to the new location, Jackie's husband moved out. She was devastated. Not having close relationships in her new location left Jackie feeling isolated and without the support she needed. She spent her evenings and weekends alone and began using alcohol as a form of escape from the pain. The results of these behaviors were frequent absence from school and a decline in her effectiveness in the classroom. Eventually, Jackie realized she must do something for herself, and she made an appointment to see a therapist. After a few months of individual counseling, she was asked to join a support group that was being organized. The group was composed of individuals who were recently separated from their partners. In the safety of the group, meeting other people who were experiencing similar kinds of pain and learning new coping strategies, Jackie began to take control of her life and to change the destructive coping strategies she had been using.

To meet her social needs, Jackie reached out and asked for help. She became involved in a support group that was caring, encouraging, and accepting of her. The feedback she received from the group enabled her to feel understood, validated, and empowered, which helped her to take control of her life and to make necessary changes. She developed a feeling of companionship with the teachers in the group and is now working on reaching out to others and developing new friendships.

At one of the last meetings of the support group, Jackie said she was going to present the idea of forming support groups at her school. She believed having support groups would be of benefit to all of the teachers. She wanted information about the training of facilitators and the organization of groups so they would be successful.

Jackie was one of the fortunate individuals who turned to professional help during a time in her life that was critical. Fortunately, she did not become one of the dropout statistics. She also gathered valuable information and skills to take back to her school and help other teachers.

To meet our social needs, we must reach out and get involved with people who want to offer support and assistance and who also keep confidentiality. One-on-one support and group support are essential aspects of a teacher's professional life. Self-expression with open and honest sharing of pent-up emotions is important if growth is to take place. Developing feelings of acceptance and genuine worth are necessary in creating healthy work environments. Social needs of companionship, friendship, and collegiality must be addressed within the school environment. As teachers become more aware of their social needs and as they receive assistance in meeting these needs, the rewards for both the teachers and their students are great.

Spiritual Needs

The most neglected area of personal need is in the spiritual domain. One of the reasons for this neglect is because most people are reluctant to discuss their spiritual beliefs for fear of offending others or for fear of criticism. It is important when discussing spiritual needs to clarify one's concepts of religion and spirituality, although spiritual experience is the cornerstone of religion. Most people prefer to share their religious views with others who have similar beliefs and commitments, and most would agree that the spiritual dimension of their life brings into focus the meaning of life.

The exact components of spirituality vary from one person to another. One individual's interpretation of spirituality may be centered on family relationships; for another it may be a deep belief in God; for others it may be a belief in humanitarian efforts. Regardless of the source of the meaning, spiritual beliefs serve as powerful inner drives for personal accomplishment. These beliefs are vital to life because without some type of meaning in life, the will to live is lost. Viktor Frankl experienced a challenge to his own meaning in life while in Auschwitz and other Nazi prisons. Through his struggles to survive, he discovered that "it is man's spiritual freedom—which cannot be taken away—that makes life meaningful and powerful" (Frankl, 1976, p. 106).

The spiritual part of ourselves is often expressed through the deepest sense of belonging and participating. Remen (1988) believes that we all participate in the spiritual at all times, whether we know it or not. She further states that the most important thing in defining spirit is the recognition that spirit is an essential need of human nature. There is something in all of us that seeks the spiritual; however, this yearning varies in strength and commitment from one individual to the next.

The spiritual dimension in our life acts as a unifying force that integrates the other dimensions: physical, emotional, intellectual, and social. It brings into focus a meaning in life for each of us. The spiritual dimension also has the capacity to provide a common bond between individuals. It enables us to demonstrate love, compassion, and unselfish giving toward others, and it empowers us to follow ethical principles and to make a commitment to God or a higher power. These principles are based on individual perceptions, faith, and beliefs. In most cases, our perceptions and our faith bring us pleasure and help us survive the most difficult challenges in life. Through our spiritual beliefs, we are able to discover and develop our own basic purposes in life and assist others in achieving their potential.

One of the strongest ways of meeting our spiritual needs is through our relationships with others and through the types of experiences we share. Chapman (1987) reported that the concept of spirituality implies that we are able to give as well as to receive. He believes that we can receive love, joy, peace, and fulfillment and offer these to others in return. Helping Professionals who have deep spiritual convictions have shared with us their experiences of offering peace to a helpee in need through sharing words of encouragement and in some instances sharing thoughts of self-forgiveness. They have also offered deep feelings of caring through numerous acts of personal sacrifice of time and by listening and being supportive.

Many researchers are beginning to view spirituality with new respect. One who has pioneered this type of research is Kenneth Pelletier, who with his colleagues at the University of California at San Francisco investigated the connection between spirituality and health. Pelletier's (1988) research investigations used a sample of top business executives and other prominent people who achieved what most of them considered to be "success." He reported that most of the professionally successful men and women in the sample had strong spiritual values and beliefs. Interestingly, virtually all of the individuals who reported this had suffered a major psychological or physical trauma early in life. Pelletier suggested that these people now have a more effective style of coping with life crises. It may well be that people who have strong spiritual beliefs handle crises better, partially because they are able to find purpose and meaning in life despite the crises they are experiencing.

People who demonstrate a deep sense of spirituality may see life from a different focal point. They have a strong purpose for living, demonstrate a sense of meaning in life, enjoy helping and giving to others, and most often see experiences from a broader perspective. Their beliefs offer them a buffer against the stressors in life, their faith helps them develop a strong foundation for their existence (their purpose for being), and they do not feel defeated by a crisis. They are able to relax their thinking and their bodies, and so they heal more quickly and more completely. They often interpret a crisis as a growth-producing opportunity and as a result are less vulnerable to stress.

Taking time to identify one's spiritual beliefs and needs will assist in better understanding who you are and how you handle life. The following list of spiritual needs will help in this pursuit.

Spiritual Needs

A relationship with God or higher power
A commitment to God and one's beliefs
Comfort in times of adversity
Trust in a power greater than ourselves
Direction for life/focus
Meaningfulness/hope in life
A purpose for living
Fulfillment in life
Peace and serenity
A foundation for existence
Developing one's spiritual nature to its fullest potential
Giving to others

After reviewing the list, take time to write out a short response to each need or clusters of similar needs. Evaluate how the needs are being met. If they are not being met, think about how you want to meet them and write this down. When you have finished, take time to discuss your spiritual needs with a significant other or a close friend. You may want to record some of the ideas you gained from your discussion for future use.

Meeting Personal and Professional Needs: A Life Process

You have spent time learning about your personal and professional needs, have identified your unmet needs, and have discussed what you are learning with others. It is essential that you continue this journey of self-discovery and personal growth. We find that most people are excited and highly motivated in the beginning. However, to keep the momentum, it is beneficial to find a partner and if possible a small support group of people who also are interested in their personal growth. Choosing to meet regularly, such as twice a month or even weekly if time permits, can prove to be rewarding. The desire to learn and to improve ourselves, coupled with the rewards of learning new and healthier patterns of living, is one of the most gratifying aspects of our life. We encourage you as a Helping Professional to continue this discovery throughout your life.

In the next chapter we will be looking at an individual's instructional and professional needs. These needs are also essential to the growth of a Helping Professional.

References

Anderson, E. M., & Shannon, A. L. (1988). Toward a conceptualization of mentoring. *Journal of Teacher Education, 39*(1), 38–42.

Barrett, D. H., & Flanders, W. D. (1989, April). Immune system function and its relationship to psychiatric conditions. Paper presented at the Annual Meeting of the Society of Behavioral Medicine, San Francisco.

Blumberg, A. (1980). *Supervisors and teachers: A private cold war* (2d ed.). Berkeley, CA: McCutchan.

Bolam, R. (1987). Induction of beginning teachers. In M. J. Dunkin (Ed.), *The international encyclopedia of teaching and teacher education* (pp. 745–757). Oxford, England: Pergamon Press.

Carnegie Foundation for the Advancement of Teaching (1990). *The condition of teaching: A state-by-state analysis.* Princeton, NJ: Author.

Chapman, L. S. (1987). Developing a useful perspective on spiritual health: Love, joy, peace, and fulfillment. *American Journal of Health Promotion,* 13.

Cohen, S. (1990). Social support, and physical illness. *Advances, 7*(1), 35–48.

Elam, S. M. (1984). *The Phi Delta Kappan Gallup Polls of attitudes toward education 1969–1984: A topical summary* (Report no. ISBN-0-87367-792-7). Bloomington, IN: Phi Delta Kappa. (ED 252-573.)

Farber, B. A. (1991). *Crisis in education: Stress and burnout in the American teacher.* San Francisco: Jossey-Bass.

Featherstone, H. (1992). *Learning from the first years of classroom teaching: The journey in, the journey out.* East Lansing: Michigan State University, National Center for Research on Teacher Learning.

Frankl, V. E. (1976). *Man's search for meaning.* New York: Pocket Books.

Gehrke, N. J., & Kay, R. S. (1984). The socialization of beginning teachers through mentor-protege relationships. *Journal of Teacher Education, 35*(3), 21–24.

Glasser, W. (1975). *Reality therapy: A new approach to psychiatry.* New York: Perennial Library.

Gold, Y. (1987). Stress reduction programs to prevent teacher burnout. *Education, 107*(3), 338–340.

Gold, Y. (1988, November). The factor structure of a revised form of the Maslach burnout inventory for university students participating in a teacher-training program. Paper presented at the annual meeting of the California Educational Research Association, San Diego, CA.

Gold, Y. (1990, February). Psychological support systems for beginning teachers: Beyond stress management. Paper presented at the annual meeting of the Association of Teacher Educators, Las Vegas, NV.

Gold, Y. (1992). Psychological support for mentors and beginning teachers: A critical dimension. In T. M. Bey & C. T. Holmes (Eds.), *Mentoring: Contemporary principles and issues* (pp. 25–34). Reston, VA: Association of Teacher Educators.

Gold, Y. (1996). Beginning teacher support: Attrition, mentoring and induction. In J. Sikula, T. Buttery, & E. Guyton (Eds.), *Handbook of research on teacher education* (2d ed.). New York: Macmillan.

Gold, Y., & Roth, R. A. (1993). *Teachers managing stress and preventing burnout: The professional health solution.* London: Falmer Press.

Hafen, B. Q., Frandsen, K. J., Karren, K. J., & Hooker, K. R. (1992). *The health effects of attitudes, emotions, relationships.* Provo, UT: EMS Associates.

Hammer, S. (1984). The mind as healer. *Science Digest, 92*(4), 46–49.

Harris, L., & Associates. (1992). *The Metropolitan Life Survey of the American Teacher. The second year: New teachers' expectations and ideals.* New York: Metropolitan Life Insurance.

Harris, L., & Associates (1993). *The Metropolitan Life Survey of the American Teacher: Violence in America's public schools.* New York: Metropolitan Life Insurance.

Healy, C. C., & Welchert, A. J. (1990). Mentoring relations: A definition to advance research and practice. *Educational Research, 19*(9), 17–21.

Henry, J. P. (1986). Neuroendocrine patterns of response. In R. Plutchik (Ed.), *Biological foundations of emotions* (pp. 37–60). New York: Academic Press.

Hodges, H. (1990). *ASCD's international polling panel: 1990–92, resolutions survey: Executive summary.* Alexandria, VA: Association for Supervision and Curriculum Development.

McDavid, T. A. (1990–91). Supporting first year teachers with professional development specialists. *Teacher Education and Practice, 6*(2), 83–85.

Padus, E. (1986). *The complete guide to your emotions and your health.* Emmaus, PA: Rodale Press.

Pelletier, K. (1988). The spirit of health. *Advances: Journal of the Institute for the Advancement of Health, 5*(4), 4.

Pilisuk, M. & Parks, S. H. (1986). *The healing web.* Hanover, NH: University Press of New England.

Powell, B. (1987). *Good relationships are good medicine.* Emmaus, PA: Rodale Press.

Remen, R. N. (1988, Autumn). On defining spirit. *Noetic Sciences Review, 7.*

Rice, P. L. (1987). *Stress and health.* Monterey, CA: Brooks/Cole.

Seligman, M. E. P. (1991). *Learned optimism.* New York: Knopf.

Thies-Sprinthall, L. M. (1984). Promoting the developmental growth of supervising teachers: Theory, research programs, and implications. *Journal of Teacher Education, 35*(3), 53–60.

Thies-Sprinthall, L. M., & Gerler, E. R., Jr. (1990). Support groups for novice teachers. *Journal of Staff Development, 11*(4), 18–22.

Thomas, B., & Kiley, M. A. (1994, February). Concerns of beginning, middle, and secondary school teachers. Paper presented at the annual meeting of the Eastern Educational Research Association, Sarasota, FL.

Vaillant, G. E. (1976). Natural history of male psychological health: V. The relation of choice of ego mechanisms of defense to adult adjustment. *Archives of General Psychology, 33*(5), 535–545.

Veenman, S. (1984). Perceived problems of beginning teachers. *Review of Educational Research, 54*(2), 143–178.

Ward, B. A. (1987). State and district structures to support initial year of teaching programs. In G. A. Griffin & S. Millies (Eds.), *The first years of teaching: Background papers and a proposal* (pp. 35–64). Chicago: University of Illinois State Board of Education.

Wendt, J. C. (1980). *Coping skills: A goal of professional preparation* (Report no. SP 019 605). Houston, TX: University of Houston, Department of Health, Physical Education and Recreation. (ED 212-604.)

Chapter 5

Instructional and Professional Needs: Domain Two

The return from your work must be the satisfaction which that work brings you and the world's need of that work. With this, life is heaven, or as near heaven as you can get. Without this—with work which you despise, which bores you, and which the world does not need—this life is hell.
—WILLIAM EDWARD AND BURGHARDT DUBOIS

Learning to teach is a complex and often confusing task for most teachers. It requires new teachers to develop their own skills of managing a classroom while they are also attempting to develop a discipline system that is successful for them. They now must begin to focus on their teaching strategies and evaluate materials and resources they have collected throughout their teacher preparation. After a few months, they begin to realize they have little prior experience to draw from. They try to relate the activities they are teaching to what they believe their students should be learning now and for the next few months.

Along with trying to focus on their teaching skills, new teachers also find it difficult to shift the focus from themselves to others and from the subjects they are teaching to what the students need to learn (Feiman-Nemser & Buchmann, 1987). This self-absorption appears to be characteristic of most new teachers. We have found this phenomenon to be a necessary part of the adjustment period. To ignore new professionals' needs to focus on themselves is insensitive and counterproductive to their growth and development.

This initial adjustment period is a time of personal survival as individuals are coping with the demands of learning new responsibilities and of perceiving themselves in a new role. This is not only true for new teachers, but also for experienced teachers who change grade levels and content areas. They too must draw from prior experience and apply it to the new situation while they also focus on new skills and materials. At the same time, this adjustment period can be an opportunity for personal maturity. Thus, the major reason for assisting individuals through this time of growth is to offer them the type of support that enables them to better understand who they are and what they need personally and professionally. This is the main reason for beginning with Domain One, personal and psychological needs, as discussed in the previous chapter.

As new professionals or experienced teachers in new assignments begin to feel more secure in their role, as they learn to identify and handle their feelings, and as they receive support from others, they become more confident and motivated to look outside themselves and focus on the needs of others around them. For teachers, this focus centers on their students, other faculty members, and the subjects they are teaching. They are now better able to make contributions to the welfare of the organization. Thus, the importance of focusing on teachers' personal and psychological needs prior to assisting them with their instructional and professional needs becomes more clear.

We have previously concentrated on the personal and psychological needs of teachers. The purpose of this chapter is to address their instructional and professional needs from the preservice through the inservice periods and to analyze the interactive nature of these two areas of need. The goal here is to examine the categories of the two needs areas and to observe how teachers change as they grow and develop throughout their professional career.

Teachers' Instructional and Professional Development

Knowledge of teachers' instructional and professional growth patterns can provide educators with a foundation from which they can offer assistance to teachers in training and throughout their career. Understanding teachers' instructional and professional needs will greatly assist Helping Professionals in diagnosing strengths and weaknesses and in planning programs to guide the growth and development of the teachers with whom they are working.

To understand teachers' professional development, it is necessary to examine the changes that take place throughout their career. A great deal of information has been published regarding the phases of adult life and adult developmental characteristics. However, it is important to note that the term "adult development" is not yet a completely defined concept. With this limitation in mind, as one examines the research and literature on the developmental phases in the life of a teacher, it will be discovered that teachers demonstrate different professional skills, knowledge, behaviors, attitudes, and concerns that have been categorized into various stages throughout their teaching career.

A survey of the literature regarding teacher career development will first be provided to assist Helping Professionals gain insights into these developmental phases.

Teacher Career Development

One of the early studies of teacher development was conducted by Francis Fuller (1969), who examined the nature of teacher concerns and presented the results of two of her studies. She also reviewed the results of related studies that had been conducted by other researchers. From her conclusions, she recommended a three-stage developmental model of the concerns teachers have when they are in the process of becoming a teacher. These stages were labeled: (1) preteaching phase of no concerns, (2) early teaching phase of concerns, and (3) concerns about pupils. In 1975, Fuller and Bown revised the original phases and called them a developmental sequence of concerns that now included four stages: (1) preteaching concerns, when preservice teachers identify in a realistic way with students but only in fantasy with teachers; (2) survival concerns, when idealized concerns are replaced by concerns about their own survival as teachers, concerns regarding class control, and attempts of mastery of the content to be taught; (3) concerns regarding their teaching performance, the frustrations as well as the limitations of their teaching situation, and the demands being made on them; and (4) concerns about the learning, emotional, and social needs of their students and concerns about their own ability to relate to their students as individuals (Fuller & Bown, 1975). These stages were mainly described in terms of what teachers are concerned about, not according to what they actually accomplished. It was not established whether the stages were distinct or overlapping.

Fuller and her associates' theories have been investigated in a number of other studies. One of these investigators, Adams (1982), conducted a 5-year longitudinal study that generally supported Fuller's early stages of concern about self and instructional tasks, but Adams suggested that there may have been an error in her theory regarding pupil concerns. His research indicated no significant differences in impact concerns across years of experience. Sitter and Lanier's (1982) research on student teachers supported Fuller's work regarding "commonalities" of concern expressed by individuals learning to teach. However, they found that the commonalities did not occur in clusters and did not occur sequentially. They perceived the student teaching period as a time to consolidate and integrate the concerns into a whole, a time to "put it all together."

A number of other studies on the process of becoming a teacher identified stages of development. Sacks and Harrington (1982) reported six stages as students prepare for and move through student teaching. These stages are: (1) anticipation, (2) entry, (3) orientation, (4) trial and error, (5) integration/consolidation, and (6) mastery. They recommended intervention strategies appropriate to each stage. Burden (1980a, 1980b) reported three stages in teaching careers. He labeled these as: (1) a survival stage during the first year of teaching, (2) an adjustment stage occurring the second through fourth year, and (3) the mature stage of the fifth and subsequent years of teaching. Other studies were reported by Feiman and Floden (1980a, 1980b, 1981), Field (1979), Floden and Feiman (1980, 1981a, 1981b), Gregorc (1973), Newman (1979), Peterson (1979), Yarger and Mertens (1980), Katz (1972), and McDonald (1982), which provide interesting comparisons for Helping Professionals who wish to read them.

There are many ways to use these theories of teacher development. Two ways were suggested by Floden and Feiman (1981a), who recommended that teacher educators could use the theory when arranging instructional content and sequence. Another way they suggested that the theory could be useful was by providing a description of the changes individuals must go through as well as the mechanism by which change occurs.

Developmental stage theory appears to hold promise for better preparing preservice teachers, for offering information to better assist beginning teachers, for improving the support offered in staff development programs, and eventually for providing a longitudinal framework for teachers' decision making regarding their careers at various stages of their life. However, additional research needs to be conducted to define and to clarify many aspects of teacher development. Burden (1990) suggested that "research efforts should focus on (1) changes teachers experience; (2) influences on teacher changes; and (3) ways to promote development" (p. 324).

Promoting Teachers' Instructional Growth

In order to assist teachers with their instructional needs, Helping Professionals need to consider various aspects of instruction. They also need to investigate the types of changes teachers are experiencing in their thinking and in their understanding of the content they are teaching as they make various instructional decisions throughout their career.

Effective teachers today not only manage their students and the learning environment, but they also know and manage the subject matter they are teaching. They have learned to identify constructs, understandings, knowledge, skills, and dispositions and to promote learning for all students. The emphasis today has shifted away from what teachers do in their teaching, to an understanding of how they inquire about the knowledge they teach. Teachers organize the knowledge, and, according to Shulman (1987), they construct their own ideas of the topics they teach and generate representations to make these ideas meaningful to their students. From this type of learning, students create their own meaning from what has been taught. In turn, new understandings are gained by both the students and the teacher.

In the next section, teachers' thought processes will be examined.

Developing Teachers' Thought Processes

Society is in a major transition as we progress out of the Industrial Age into a new era that is dependent on technology and service. The need for analytical, creative, secure learners is essential. The ability to think critically and creatively, to have developed skills of brainstorming with others, to synthesize, to organize, and to think abstractly are of greater importance today than ever before.

Because most information today can be accessed easily with technology, the need for organizing, synthesizing, and understanding concepts is a high priority. Demonstrating a breadth of knowledge, integrating disciplines with a clear understanding of the structure of thinking, and gaining insights into the interrelatedness among subjects are all essential for the educated.

With these types of needs, today's teachers must be prepared to develop their own thinking skills so they are able to assist their students with the learning process. As teachers learn to teach, the psychological context of their teaching includes the thinking, planning, and decision making they must learn and effectively perform. In order to successfully accomplish these tasks, the quality of their thought processes will determine the quality of their teaching. Thus, the importance of assisting teachers in developing their thought processes is a challenge for all Helping Professionals.

Background Research on Teachers' Thought Processes
Philip Jackson (1968) in his early book *Life in Classrooms* attempted to describe and to understand the mental processes and constructs underlying teacher behavior. His greatest contributions to the research on teaching were his ideas on the complexity of the teacher's task. He made conceptual distinctions that fit the teacher's frame of reference, such as that between the preactive and the interactive phases of teaching. He also alerted the educational research community to the importance of describing the thinking and the planning of teachers so as to more fully understand the classroom process.

In 1970, Dahllof and Lundgren of Sweden were conducting studies of the structure of the teaching process as an expression of organizational constraints. These studies revealed some of the mental categories that teachers in their sample used to organize and make sense of their professional experiences.

In June of 1974, the National Institute of Education sponsored a week-long National Conference on Studies in Teaching. Their purpose was to create an agenda for future research on teaching. Their report (National Institute of Education, 1975) produced a rationale for and defined the assumptions and the domain of a proposed program of research on teachers' thought processes. They felt strongly that research on teacher thinking is necessary if we are to understand what is uniquely human in the process of teaching. They believed that researchers must study the psychological processes by which teachers perceive and define their professional situations and responsibilities. They viewed the teacher as a clinician and carefully defined their perceptions of this image of the teacher.

This type of classification identified the teacher as a professional and had a profound effect on guiding the research on teacher thinking. An outcome was the establishment of an Institute for Research on Teaching located at Michigan State University in 1976. This organization initiated the first large program of research on the thought processes of teachers.

A Model of Teacher Thought and Action

To assist in understanding the various parts of the research literature on teacher thought processes and how they relate to one another and how research on teacher thought processes complements the larger body of research on teaching effectiveness, Clark and Peterson (1986) developed a model of teacher thought and action. Their model presents two domains involved in the process of teaching: (1) teachers' thought processes and (2) teachers' actions and their observable effects. The first domain, teachers' thought processes, occurs "inside teachers' heads" (p. 267) and, according to the authors, is not observable. In contrast, the second domain, teachers' actions and their observable effects, includes teacher behavior, student behavior, and student achievement scores and comprises observable phenomena that are more easily measured.

There are three categories of teachers' thought processes in the Clark and Peterson (1986) model. These are: (1) "teacher planning [preactive and postactive thoughts]; (2) teachers' interactive thoughts and decisions; and (3) teachers' theories and beliefs" (p. 257). Teacher planning includes all of the thought processes that a teacher is involved in prior to any classroom interactions, as well as the thought processes or reflections she or he engages in after classroom interactions. These thought processes guide thinking and projections for future classroom interactions. For example, a teacher evaluates the lessons at the end of the teaching day and, while reflecting on the lesson, plans specific concepts and activities for the following day. Clark and Peterson (1986) argue that the distinction between preactive and postactive thoughts become blurred because the process is cyclical.

The second category, teachers' interactive thoughts and decisions, is the thought processes that occur during classroom interactions, which appear to be qualitatively different from the kind of thinking teachers do when they are not interacting with their students. The third category, teachers' theories and beliefs, represents the rich store of knowledge teachers bring to their teaching that affects their planning, as well as their interactive thoughts and decisions.

These three categories of teachers' thought processes reflect the research and literature in this area. However, the research in this area is new and there is little available that could be considered a systematic and cumulative body of study. Even though to date no single study has documented every aspect of teachers' thought processes, we can begin to develop our understanding of the teacher as a reflective professional who initiates thinking patterns about instruction during teacher education and continues developing into a more thoughtful professional.

Teachers' theories and beliefs regarding their students, curriculum, subject matter, and the role of the teacher grow and develop. Much of teachers' interactive teaching includes their reflections on learners, the content they are teaching, and future plans and actions to make the learning more understandable for their students.

The extent to which teachers will mature in their thought processes depends largely on how successfully they have progressed through the phases of change presented in a previous chapter. These changes include awareness, resistance, and eventually accepting new methods of thinking. Teachers who have made the necessary changes demonstrate growth and maturity in their thinking processes and in their interactions with their students.

The Relationship between Teacher Thought and Action and the Role of the Helping Professional

Assisting teachers toward greater understanding of how they think and why they behave as they do will help them toward improved teaching effectiveness and improved evaluation of their performance as a teacher. Because teachers' actions are greatly affected by their thought processes, it is essential to assist them with identifying, analyzing, and evaluating how they think.

The research on teachers' thought processes has depended heavily on a variety of forms of self-report by teachers, as well as methods to elicit and interpret reliable and valid self-reports of their thinking processes. It has been argued that verbal reports will be most reliable and valid as data when an individual reports within the context of short-term memory. Reporting on what one is currently focusing on will be more reliable and valid (Ericcson & Simon, 1980).

Therefore, Helping Professionals need to avoid discussing information that is vague and general or that would require teachers to discuss partially remembered information. In fact, combining a number of methods of inquiry will yield more accurate data. Clark and Peterson (1986) recommend five methods of inquiry. These include: "thinking aloud, stimulated recall, policy capturing, journal keeping, and the repertory grid technique" (p. 259). The authors also recommended that these methods need to be "supplemented by interviews, field observations, and narrative descriptions of the task, the content, and the visible behavior of the participants" (p. 259). These five methods of inquiring will be examined in Chapter 12 and will assist Helping Professionals toward more effective use of them.

In addition to these five methods of inquiry about teachers' thought processes and how their thoughts affect their behaviors, researchers have also included teacher planning (Clark & Yinger, 1987) as an essential area to be considered.

Teacher Planning

In the area of teacher planning, researchers have mainly focused on a single type of planning and have largely studied teachers at the elementary level (Borko et al., 1988). The most obvious type of planning in American schools has been to transform and modify the curriculum to fit the unique needs of each teaching situation. Teacher planning is an important area to be considered because it has been one of the major topics of research on teacher thinking. Researchers of teacher thinking have mainly concentrated on, and attempted to describe, the lives of teachers. Clark and Yinger (1987) explain that researchers in this area "hope to understand and explain how and why the behaviorally observable activities of teachers' professional lives take on the forms and functions that they do" (p. 84).

Within the body of research on teacher thinking, planning has been defined in two major ways. First, planning has been defined as a set of basic psychological processes whereby the teacher visualizes the future, inventories what she or he perceives to be the means and ends, and constructs a framework that will guide her or his future actions. This concept of planning borrows from the theories and methods of cognitive psychology. Second, planning has been defined as "the things that teachers do when they say that they are planning" (Clark & Yinger, 1987, p. 86). This definition suggests a descriptive approach to research on teacher planning.

Some of the areas that a Helping Professional may wish to investigate are: (1) what are the types and functions of teacher planning, (2) what models have been used to describe the process of planning, and (3) what is the relationship between teacher planning and subsequent action in the classroom? Two informative sources for reference are Clark and Peterson (1986) and Clark and Yinger (1987).

Concluding Ideas on Teacher Thought

Helping teachers organize their thinking about teaching by providing them with various means to articulate explanations and to construct understandings of their teaching is a vital function of the Helping Professional. Teachers need social support to help them as they develop their thinking patterns through their interactions with others. As they share their thinking about teaching, first as students and later as teachers, their ideas are developed and changed. Their shared knowledge can be reshaped by their newly learned understandings. In these ways, teachers are active participants with a wide variety of thinking strategies to incorporate into their teaching. They must be guided and encouraged to integrate a large amount of information learned as a student, to combine this with their own beliefs and goals, to make critical decisions, and to anticipate the consequences of their actions. It is through understanding how teachers develop their thought processes that Helping Professionals may begin to provide the guidance and support necessary to facilitate this type of growth throughout a teacher's career.

Teacher Content Knowledge

Researchers for a number of years have investigated how teachers think about their teaching for the purpose of improving the practice of teaching. Through extensive study, the emphasis has shifted from what teachers do in their teaching to inquiries about the knowledge they hold, how they organize the knowledge, and how various knowledge sources affect their teaching. One of the leaders in this movement is Lee Shulman at Stanford University. He and his associates have been studying ways in which teachers' understandings of both their disciplines and pedagogy combine to create what Shulman identifies as the content-specific pedagogy demonstrated in their teaching decisions (Shulman, 1987; Shulman & Ringstaff, 1986; Wilson, Shulman, & Richert, 1987).

In his earlier work, Shulman (1987) discussed the need for a more coherent theoretical framework of content knowledge and proposed three categories:

(1) subject matter content knowledge, (2) pedagogical content knowledge, and (3) curricular knowledge.

Shulman's subject matter content knowledge refers to the amount and organization of knowledge in the mind of the teacher. He proposed, "To think properly about content knowledge requires going beyond knowledge of the facts or concepts of a domain" (p. 9). Shulman argued that the teacher needs to "not only understand that something is so, [but] the teacher must further understand why it is so" (p. 9).

His second category, pedagogical content knowledge, goes beyond knowledge of the subject matter to the dimension of subject matter knowledge for teaching. One of the key concepts here is the challenge to teachers to take what they already know and understand and prepare it in a way that leads to effective instruction. Shulman labels these "the most powerful analogies, illustrations, examples, explanations, and demonstrations, . . . of representing and formulating the subject that makes it comprehensible to others" (1986, p. 9).

The pedagogical knowledge that teachers must know and understand includes a body of general knowledge, beliefs, and skills related to teaching, as well as knowledge and beliefs concerning learning and learners; knowledge of general principles of instruction such as academic learning time (Carroll, 1963) and wait time (Rowe, 1974); knowledge and skills related to classroom management (Doyle, 1986); and knowledge and beliefs about the aims and purposes of education. Helping teachers remake their understandings in these areas will undoubtedly require a great deal from Helping Professionals both in preservice and inservice programs.

The last category, curricular knowledge, according to Shulman (1987) includes "the full range of programs designed for the teaching of particular subjects and topics at a given level, the variety of instructional materials available in relation to those programs, and the set of characteristics that serve as both the indications and contraindications for the use of particular curriculum or program materials in particular circumstances" (p. 10).

Helping Professionals can guide inexperienced teachers and other teachers who need help in going beyond knowledge of the facts or concepts of a domain, preparing key concepts in ways that are ready for effective instruction, and designing a variety of instructional materials. Offering workshops, training sessions, and opportunities to observe experienced teachers who model these skills and materials is useful. Developing support groups to share ideas and to discuss various ways of developing materials to enhance learning can be highly successful. These types of groups give teachers an opportunity to ask questions, design new materials, and later experiment with new knowledge and materials in their own classrooms. They can later discuss what they learned with members of the support group, which gives them an opportunity to receive encouraging feedback. The Helping Professional can act as a guide to bring about constructive discussions that are problem-solving oriented.

What is necessary today if teachers are to make educated decisions is for them to understand all of the elements that interact in a teaching situation. The subject matter, learning, learners, and teaching must all be given special attention.

Teachers must be able to understand the connections among ideas. They must also understand how content and pedagogy interact to influence what they are teaching and what students are learning. Thus, in order to teach subject matter, teachers must know what concepts, ideas, and principles are involved in the primary content of the discipline. Furthermore, teachers need to know how the discourse within a discipline relates to the teaching of school subjects. They must be aware of fundamental ideas and principles and transform them in understandable ways for their students. They must be familiar with what is of value for their students.

This type of understanding will enable the teacher to evaluate more critically the types of insights students are acquiring as well as to help students add to their insights. In fact, Barnes (1989) argues that "understandings of the relationships among the various domains and how such knowledge informs teachers' judgment and actions must be the ultimate goal of teacher education" (p. 17).

The challenges facing student teachers and beginning teachers center around the transformation of their subject matter knowledge learned in preservice education into a form of knowledge that is appropriate and comprehensible for their students. They must also possess knowledge of learners and learning, of curriculum and context, of goals and objectives, of general pedagogy, and of subject-specific pedagogy. Helping Professionals can assist them in drawing from a number of different types of knowledge and skills and in translating their knowledge of subject matter into instructional representations.

Central to organizing the knowledge and mental representations of the learner is the view of the constructivist, which is addressed in the next section of the chapter.

A Constructivist View

We hear a great deal today about the *constructivist* view of learning and its application to teaching and to teacher preparation. To understand the basic tenants of constructivism, one can review Von Glasersfeld (1984) for an historical account. The constructivist perspective is not entirely new, for it has very old philosophical roots and draws much of its development from the work of Piaget (1968/1970, 1970, 1975, 1977) and his colleagues of the Genevan tradition.

According to Fosnot (1989), constructivism can be defined by the following four principles:

1. *Knowledge consists of past constructions.* Constructivists take the position that people can never know the world in a "true," objective sense, separate from themselves and their experiences. They can only know it through their logical framework, which transforms, organizes, and interprets their perceptions. This logic is constructed and evolves through a process of development as they interact with their environment and attempt to make sense of their experiences.

2. *Constructions come about through assimilation and accommodation.* This principle was borrowed from Piaget. Self-regulation is divided into two polar processes of assimilation and accommodation. Assimilation refers to the logical framework or scheme that people use to interpret or organize information. When their assimilatory scheme is found to be insufficient or contradicted, they accommodate, or develop a higher-level theory or logic to encompass the information. Old concepts are adapted and altered.
3. *Learning is an organic process of intervention*, rather than a mechanical process of accumulation. For the constructivist model it is believed that structural leaps in cognition are made throughout development, producing qualitatively different frameworks of understanding, rather than learning as an accumulation of facts and associations as viewed by the empiricist/reductionist approaches. Constructivists believe that the learner must have experiences with hypothesizing and predicting, questioning, researching answers, manipulating objects, imagining, inventing, and investigating so that new constructions can be developed. Thus, the learner must construct the knowledge, while the teacher's role is one of mediating the process
4. *Meaningful learning occurs through reflection and resolution of cognitive conflict* and thus serves to negate earlier, incomplete levels of understanding. Whatever scheme the learner constructs must be a contradiction to an earlier one in order to bring about disequilibrium, which leads to learning.

Classrooms using a constructivism model would include a great deal of reflection, inquiry, and action by the learners. Teachers would be engaged in questioning, hypothesizing, investigating, imagining, and debating with their students. A learner-centered, active instructional model would be demonstrated. Sundar's classroom is an example of this philosophical orientation.

To help his 2nd grade students better understand the role of community agencies, Sundar planned a unit on the fire department. He sat down to think about the needs of his students, and to write the following sequence: (1) students will discuss their understanding of the fire department as the teacher assesses their prior knowledge; (2) as a class, concepts from the children's past experiences and knowledge will be recorded on large chart paper; (3) students will be engaged in active participation with books, objects, and materials to organize their perceptions of the role of the fireman and the role of the fire department; (4) a wide variety of books, materials, and objects will be provided for students to explore and share with one another; (5) students will interact with one another as they are learning new concepts; (6) groups will be developed to explore specific aspects of the fire department (cooperative learning groups); (7) students will be encouraged to question, imagine, problem solve, investigate, and invent as they construct the knowledge they are acquiring through group interactions; (8) the teacher will mediate the process; (9) murals, diagrams, charts and booklets will be constructed to demonstrate students' learning; (10) creative projects such as role play, drama, readers' theater, etc. will be provided; and (11) a field trip to the fire department will be planned so students will experience what a real fire department is like.

Sundar sat back and evaluated his ideas. He liked planning a variety of activities for his students so they could interact with one another and with the environment to make sense of their experiences. Sundar also looked to see if he had included enough experiences with questioning, manipulating objects, inventing, and investigating. Sundar wants his students to create their own understandings. He also reviewed his plan to see that he had included many activities and experiences where social interactions take place. Sundar knows that these social interactions are essential for development of students' thinking tools and of their understandings of how they can use them. Sundar was pleased with his plan. Learning will be meaningful and applicable to each learner.

In summarizing the essence of the constructivist perspective, Lerman (1989) proposed two assertions: (1) that knowledge is actively created by the knower and not passively received in an unmodified form from the environment; and (2) that the process of knowing and learning does not reveal an increasingly accurate, objective, or true understanding of "an independent, pre-existing world outside the mind of the knower" (p. 211).

The constructivists' perspective borrows from Piaget (1975) when stating that "intelligence organizes the world by organizing itself" (p. 275). There is an ordering and organization of a world constituted by our experience. This is demonstrated by teachers as they assist their students in constructing their own worlds so that learning results in a meaningful form from which they can function adequately.

For constructivist teachers, knowing is created, as we saw in Sundar's class, rather than imparted or transferred to their students. Therefore, teachers continuously integrate each experience with everything they understand that can enable their students to create their own understandings. Because every student is unique and has his or her own complete perceptions of the experience, teachers must understand each student, know the content they are teaching, and possess specific strategies to make the learning interesting and meaningful for their students. This is also true for Helping Professionals who work with new teachers in integrating their teaching experiences with their teacher preparation to create their own understandings of teaching, as well as create their role as teacher.

Teachers' Instructional Needs: Learning to Teach

Teachers must be prepared to engage learners in inquiry about content areas and help then in reflection on pedagogy. In order to accomplish these goals, teachers must be taught how to critically reflect on and interpret the subject matter and to think critically and creatively about pedagogy. They must find multiple ways to represent the information to students using a variety of techniques, such as analogies, examples, metaphors, demonstrations, discussions, problems, and classroom activities. They also must adapt the material to meet the needs of each student's preconceptions, prior knowledge, and cultural background, as well as provide a social context in which interpersonal interactions occur. Teachers also must reflect on their own judgments and actions and become empowered, thinking individuals.

The Role of the Helping Professional

Learning to teach presents tremendous challenges for new teachers as they struggle personally to survive their first few years of teaching. The expertise of the Helping Professional is critical during this stage of development as new teachers are imprinting their ideas and feelings regarding teaching and their role as a teacher (Gold, 1996).

Many experienced teachers also need assistance in understanding teaching and learning in specific contexts with specific students so that students are able to construct useful understandings in that given context. Teachers also need assistance in understanding their students' abilities, attitudes, learning strategies, ages, developmental levels, prior conceptions of the subject they are learning, and motivational patterns. An additional area of need is that of helping teachers understand the social, political, cultural, and physical environmental contexts that shape the teaching and learning process. From the constructivist perspective, helping teachers' understand that learning must be created from the students' perceptions and that it must be built upon the students' understandings is essential.

Guiding teachers in evaluating how all of these areas affect learning and when they come into play is critical to teachers' growth. Empowering them to make the types of evaluations discussed here will contribute to their success, for they are the ones who select the content to be learned and the strategies to be used within the social context. Assisting teachers in evaluating their abilities in the areas of subject matter knowledge, knowledge of pedagogy, environmental contexts to be selected, and understanding of their students will empower them as they plan programs to meet the needs of their students.

New teachers and many experienced teachers must be guided in understanding the knowledge of the curriculum they are teaching and in developing educational goals and purposes so they are viable for them. Helping Professionals will be most effective here as they help teachers observe and reflect on their own teaching and assist them in planning many opportunities for follow-up, reflection, and feedback. This can be accomplished through the use of case studies, cooperative classroom methods, micro teaching, and team teaching, as well as guidance from the Helping Professional.

Many teachers need assistance in making sense of their teaching situations by comparing them to other teaching experiences they have encountered. The insights gained must be generated from their own perceptions and personal experiences. Teachers need assistance in drawing from their prior knowledge and reflecting on and critically analyzing their previous experiences. Helping Professionals can be an essential part of their learning as they offer interpretations of situations the teachers are sharing. Teachers need skills to help them reflect upon their teaching experiences and for revising their prior understandings.

When teachers are encouraged to reflect on their own judgments and actions, to acknowledge their own potential for learning and teaching, and to acquire confidence in their ability to make evaluations, they begin to grow professionally and mature personally. This growth is not only in knowledge about teaching and the expertise needed, but in personal confidence as they believe they can become the successful teacher they envision themselves to be, a professional educator.

TABLE 5-1 Teachers' Instructional Needs

Knowledge of Learners:
    characteristics: child growth and development
    students' background knowledge and experiences
    learning styles of students, individual differences
Knowledge of discipline models
Knowledge of discipline strategies and application of strategies
Knowledge of classroom management strategies and application of strategies
Time management strategies and practical applications
Logistical procedures
Knowledge of motivational theories
Knowledge of motivational strategies and application of strategies
Organizational techniques (knowledge and application)
Planning (preactive and postactive thoughts)
Goals and objectives of lessons
Pacing lessons (thinking processes)
Knowledge of and application of instructional strategies
Subject matter content knowledge
    content of subject areas
    organizing knowledge
    organizing concepts
    syntactic structures
    creative use of content
    understanding "why"
Pedagogical content knowledge
    blending of content and pedagogy
    reflection of pedagogy
    use of analogies, examples, illustrations, demonstrations, explanations
Circular knowledge
    varieties of instructional materials
    uses of curriculum in particular circumstances
    wide range of programs
Structuring of knowledge
Identifying constructs
Gaining understandings of content and pedagogy
Developing new comprehensions
Creative use of content
Developing students' thought processes
Making application of concepts learned
Interactive thoughts and decisions regarding teaching
Developing theories and beliefs
Gaining insights
Critical analysis of previous teaching experiences
Revising prior understandings
Developing thinking skills of self and students:
    problem solving
    abstract thinking
    inquiry
    creative thinking
    critical thinking

TABLE 5-1 *Continued*

           analytical thinking
           synthesizing
           organizational thinking
           insightful thinking
           evaluative thinking
           reshaping thinking
Methods of inquiring:
           thinking aloud
           stimulated recall
           making relationships
           content analysis
Knowledge of various paradigms in a field
Knowledge of relationships between discourse and subjects taught
Knowledge of significant events, people, places, procedures
Knowledge of evaluation procedures for teaching and planning
Creating evaluation strategies appropriate for students
Skill in assessing individual students
Development of higher-level observation techniques
Development of schemata to connect the theoretical and practical knowledge
        into teaching
Reasons soundly about his/her teaching
Performs skillfully in his/her teaching
Understands and practices diversity and equity in the classroom

Teachers' Instructional Needs Inventory

The Instructional Needs Inventory in Table 5-1 provides a list of instructional needs derived from research and literature. Helping Professionals may use the list as a resource to assess instructional needs of teachers. To assist you, check the areas that need attention. With the teacher, plan specific ways to meet each instructional need. As you plan together, review the section of this chapter that focuses on teachers' thoughts and actions. Guide the teacher in thinking through how she or he will focus on a specific instructional need. When the teacher has used the specific instructional need in a lesson, help the teacher think through his or her behaviors and the students. Encourage the teacher to become an active participant in the thinking process.

Meeting Teachers' Professional Needs

In order to fully understand teacher development, both the instructional and professional needs of teachers must be addressed. We have found that categorizing the needs into these two areas more fully describes the needs that teachers have throughout their careers.

Examining Kohlberg's (1973) writings, we find that he proposes the idea that developmental sequences involve changes in quality, competence, and form as the individual moves from one stage to another, rather than changes in performance, quantity, and content. He views adult development in a person as a definite progression from concrete, undifferentiating, simple, unstructured patterns of thought to more abstract, differentiating, and complex patterns of thought. Kohlberg (1969) emphasizes moral development as people change in their orientations toward authority, others, and self when making decisions.

Loevinger (1966) described how as adults try to understand themselves, they pass through stages. They move from conformity to emotional independence and, lastly, to a state in which they are able to reconcile inner conflicts, to renounce the unattainable, appreciate their individuality, and more clearly define their identity.

Based on Perry's (1970) work, it was noted that in stages of intellectual and ethical development, individuals move from dualistic thinking in which they view things from a right-or-wrong perspective, to relativistic thinking in which the world of knowledge is viewed as relativistic, and uncertainty becomes legitimate. Finally, they move to a point where they make choices to define their identity.

Using a cognitive stage model, Harvey, Hunt, and Schroeder (1961) presented a pattern of beliefs, attitudes, and values by which individuals interpret their experience. They included four conceptual stages in which individuals: (1) are perceived as basically self-centered and have an orientation toward external causality and the primacy of concrete rules, (2) are able to examine themselves apart from external standards and conditions, (3) achieve even greater personal introspection, and (4) develop a more integrated and independent set of internal standards that may or may not be consistent with external pressures and cultural norms.

Teachers' professional development encompasses many of the aspects presented by the researchers cited here. As teachers mature through years of teaching and personal growth, they experience changes in the quality of their competence. They begin their career with little or no confidence in their ability to teach and handle their students, and they move to levels of competence as they experience a sense of efficacy in using basic skills of instruction and in understanding and handling their students.

As teachers begin to experiment more, they try new techniques and strategies, demonstrate growth in their development of critical judgment, and begin to seek opportunities for professional development. This is the time when many teachers want to share what they have learned with new teachers, and they may desire to take on the role of a Helping Professional. This last level is similar to what Kohlberg (1973) describes as the definite progression from concrete, unstructured patterns of thought to more abstract, differentiating, and complex patterns of thought. This is a time of emotional independence, and the more professionally mature teachers are now able to appreciate their individuality (Loevinger, 1966).

Beginning teachers often view their teaching from a right-or-wrong perspective and lack the experience to feel secure with experimentation in their teaching. This is similar to Perry's (1970) view of intellectual and ethical development in which individuals move from dualistic thinking to relativistic thinking. Teachers who are more professionally mature are more secure in their world of knowledge so that uncertainty becomes a reality for them. They demonstrate considerable depth in most every phase of their professional life, and they are very secure in their performance as a professional educator. They are able to accept change as a dominant part of life and are eager to work with other teachers.

Teachers' Professional Needs Inventory

The inventory in Table 5-2 will assist Helping Professionals as they diagnose the professional needs of the teachers with whom they work. Checking the needs that are not evident in a teacher's professional life can be helpful. Discuss the needs with the teacher and together plan ways to meet them. Responding to these needs not only benefits the teacher, but the students and the schools in which the teacher works as well.

The instructional and professional needs we identify here provide a focus for the assessment, diagnosis, guidance, and support foundation of the Helping Professional. In Chapter 11 we also provide specific types of instructional and instructional-related expectations of teachers that form another element of the content of helping.

TABLE 5-2 Teacher's Professional Needs

Reflecting on teaching
Making changes in the quality of teaching
Making changes in the form and competence of teaching
Interpret own teaching experiences
Demonstrate a sense of efficacy
Experiment with new techniques and strategies
Develop emotional independence
Reconcile inner conflicts
Define own identity
Demonstrate self-examination
Achieve personal introspection
Develop an integrated and independent set of internal standards
Share ideas, values, and beliefs with colleagues in support groups
Develop the skills of critical judgment
Seek opportunities for professional development
Move to more abstract, differentiating, and complex patterns of thought
Practice experimentation
Demonstrate consistency and structure
Demonstrate flexibility: make new choices and strengthen existing ones
Practice concrete, unstructured patterns of thought
Demonstrate growth in the use of techniques and perspectives of inquiry
Manage programs

Continued

TABLE 5-2 *Continued*

> Demonstrate knowledge of educational contexts:
> > group work
> > governance of schools and districts
> > governance of communities and cultures
>
> Expand thinking and knowledge base
> Knowledge of educational ends, purposes, values, philosophical and
> > historical grounds
>
> Assess the knowledge already possessed
> Communicate effectively with parents
> Seek deeper and more abstract questions
> Develop new awareness at higher levels
> Demonstrate confidence
> Actively participate in professional organizations, seminars, journals, degree programs
> Develop a vision
> Participates in meaningful intellectual, social, and emotional engagement with colleagues in
> > and out of teaching
>
> Engage in focused study groups and similar modes of professional development
> Participate in teacher collaboratives and long-term partnerships
> Provide leadership and assistance roles in schools and districts

Teacher Socialization: A Complex Process

A major question to consider when exploring the concept of professional development is what role does teachers' socialization play throughout their career.

Teacher socialization is a complex process that begins with the preservice teacher education period and continues throughout the professional career. During this time, individuals make adjustments to their new role, make many changes in their perceptions of the profession and of their own roles, and learn new interpersonal skills. All of this takes place as a variety of changes occur. Teachers entering the profession bring from their preparation period an understanding of the institutional context, their teaching philosophy, knowledge of the subject matter, and a variety of teaching strategies. Over a period of time, teachers' interpersonal and instructional skills are modified and changed as they face the vast demands placed upon them. They begin to reshape their thinking about their students, evaluate their responses to contextual constraints, and reformulate their perceptions of their role as a teacher.

Lisa is an example of a beginning teacher in her first month of teaching. She shared her insights about how her thinking was undergoing changes:

> *I'm beginning to really take a look at my teaching. When I started last month I felt so excited to have my own classroom and spent long hours getting the room ready for the first day of school. I had taught 6th grade during student teaching so I felt prepared. When the students first came in I was so happy to see them and had lessons prepared that really went well in student teaching. I just couldn't believe my ears when they*

were disrespectful and did not want to do the activities I had for them. My class in student teaching liked my lessons. These students are different. I didn't expect this kind of response. I keep trying my fun lessons but they aren't working. Also, the teachers in the school are different from the ones in student teaching. They are all very nice; they just don't share ideas. I miss the sharing of ideas and the fun we had at the other school. These teachers are more businesslike. Being a teacher isn't anything like I thought it would be. It's not like my other school.

The group leader encouraged Lisa to share what she had liked at her other school and then encouraged the group to share their experiences and how they are different from student teaching. As the group leader guided them, she helped them see how they needed to change some of the perceptions of teaching they had developed during student teaching. As the beginning teachers began to evaluate their responses, they were better prepared to discuss how they needed to adjust to their new role and their new teaching situation. Over the period of a few weeks and meeting once a week, the beginning teachers began to reshape their thinking about teaching and about teachers. They not only discussed their role as a teacher, but also looked at their personal and psychological needs as an individual. Lisa shared that she wanted to feel more secure as a person and as a teacher. This opened the discussion of developing new interpersonal skills and how they could relate more positively and successfully with other teachers on the faculty. Challenging their beliefs and evaluating their behavior helped these beginning teachers grow in maturity and develop a sense of security. Communicating their concerns with other beginning teachers and the group leader assisted these teachers through their own socialization process. The role of the group leader or Helping Professional is critical in helping beginning teachers to understand the socialization process and the changes they need to make.

Stanton and Hunt's (1992) review indicated that the changes a person experiences during the socialization process occur through the interaction among internally held beliefs, the forces of the context as communicated through agents, and the actions an individual takes in consideration of these forces. They found that although biography is a strong influence at the outset of teaching, teachers' instructional and interpersonal approaches change. They also believed that we still do not have a clear picture of the "actual communication patterns, the communication strategies, the language used, the speech situations, and the meaning of communication events for prospective/beginning teachers and agents" (p. 131).

The socialization process, according to Stanton and Hunt (1992), "includes not only the influence of agents on prospective/beginning teachers, but the reciprocal, mutual influence, as well" (p. 132). Thus, the role of Helping Professionals becomes even more important as they interact with teachers.

The research and literature on teacher socialization offers a great deal to Helping Professionals in the process of assisting teachers at all levels of their career. Preservice teachers need to clarify for themselves the role of a teacher and how this compares with the perceptions they have formulated prior to and during their preparation. This is a time to help individuals gain insights into themselves, into the role of the teacher, and into why they selected teaching as a career. The purpose of helping preservice teachers clarify each of these areas is so they can become better prepared to make necessary changes in their perceptions of teachers and of teaching. Students enter any learning situation with their previously formed ideas, knowledge, and beliefs, along with the capabilities they have acquired through their prior experiences. All of these affect the ways in which they interpret and use new information gained during their preparation period and their first few years of teaching. The Helping Professional can help teachers gain insights into their perceptions by asking them to write down their understandings of teachers, learning, and teaching. During group discussions or individually, the teachers can discuss how they initially formulated their ideas and developed the perceptions they now have and how these beliefs and perceptions affect their teaching.

In his very influential work on the sociology of teaching, Dan Lortie (1975) took the position that students' predispositions stand at the center of becoming a teacher, and that they exert a much more powerful socializing influence over them than either preservice training or later socialization in the workplace. If we accept this position, then it is essential that Helping Professionals assist preservice teachers in training, new teachers, and experienced teachers to become aware of and to clarify their perceptions of the teachers they have had during their school years and during their preservice training. They also need an understanding of the educational process that they acquired throughout their lifetime. Insight into how these predispositions affect the new perceptions they have been acquiring throughout their preparation will help to clarify how they have been affected by the socialization process.

From a psychoanalytic perspective, it has been reported that teacher socialization is affected to a great extent by the quality of relationships teachers had as children with important adults like parents and teachers. Thus, becoming a teacher is to some extent a process of becoming like significant others in one's childhood, or in trying to replicate early childhood relationships (Gold, 1996; Wright, 1959; Wright & Tuska, 1967). This perspective points out that early relationships with significant others are the prototypes of subsequent relationships throughout life. Therefore, the kinds of teachers that education students become are greatly influenced by the effects of the early childhood modeling on their personalities.

The psychoanalytic perspective may be more difficult for most Helping Professionals to deal with when working with teachers. We have found this to be true during our own training of Helping Professionals because in most instances they do not have the background that psychotherapists have. There are, however, perspectives to be learned from this approach that are useful to Helping Professionals.

In our own model, using a psychotherapeutic approach (Gold & Roth, 1993), we have discussed the use of early memories to help individuals gain understanding of the socialization process. One of the strategies that we have found to be most helpful in gaining insights into the early experiences of teachers is for the individual teachers to recall their early elementary years. Writing down memories of their parents, teachers, and significant others who were most influential during this time can lead to insights. Keeping a journal or a log titled "My Early Memories of My

Dad," "Early Memories of Mother," and "The Teachers I Remember from My Early Elementary Years" will help teachers become aware of relationship issues, values learned, and beliefs acquired during these most influential years. After they have recorded the memories that are most significant for them, ask them to read the situations they have recorded. As they read, they may gain insight into how these early relationships influenced their perceptions and behaviors now when they teach and interact with others. Utilizing group discussions of what the members learned will enhance insights about positive and negative role models in their lives. Also, discussing memories they recalled that influenced negative socialization and how their present teaching is influenced by these early negative memories will be beneficial. The next step is to discuss how they can change any current behaviors in their teaching that need changing. The Transformational Change model in Chapter 3 is a useful context for any attempts to alter behavior.

Follow-up assignments and discussions of journals and logs are good vehicles for discovering the socializing influences that individuals bring to teacher education programs and to teaching. Other methodologies that can be used are biographical and life history writings, which aids in understanding the development of teachers' knowledge. A number of studies have employed a variety of these methodologies, including: autobiography (Grumet, 1981; Pinar, 1988); collaborative autobiography (Butt, Raymond, & Yamagishi, 1988); narrative inquiry (Connelly & Clandinin, 1987); repertory grid techniques (Ingvarson & Greenway, 1984); diary interviews (Burgess, 1988); and the combined use of biographical and ethnographic methods in the same study (Raymond & Surprenant, 1988). These interpretive and critical studies have provided us with information that can be especially useful for gaining insights into the ways in which teachers' perspectives have their beginnings in a variety of personal, familial, religious, political, and cultural experiences, and that these experiences and perceptions are brought with them into teaching.

In the literature on socialization in the workplace there is some evidence that supports the view that pupils, the ecology of the classroom, colleagues, and institutional characteristics of schools all play essential roles in the socialization of teachers. Helping Professionals who take each of these areas into consideration when working with teachers will be of greater assistance in helping teachers change old patterns.

It is extremely important that Helping Professionals be aware of the literature on teacher socialization. Also, they must work to bring about institutional and social changes that are necessary within their professional environment if our hope for the welfare and professional development of teachers is to be realized.

Professional Development Programs

One of the challenges of inservice education is to meet the professional needs of teachers, and one of the major goals of professional development is to expand the individual repertoires of each teacher and provide appropriate opportunities for application of the new information. An additional goal is that of providing classroom consultations and guidance as teachers learn to apply the new ideas they have learned.

Assisting teachers with their professional growth has become more challenging due to reforms that have taken place in subject matter standards, curriculum content, and pedagogy that now require more rigorous student outcomes. Today's reforms require teachers to develop more skill in integrating subject content and in organizing opportunities for students to learn. Focus also has centered on challenges of diversity and equity in classrooms across the nation. Teachers have needed additional training to identify and modify their classroom practices that often may have contributed to the failure of some of their students and may even have undermined equal opportunity to learn.

Little (1993) recommended specific principles that she believed could contribute to the professional development of teachers, encourage discussion or even debate, and enhance the growth and enrichment of teachers. This growth can be directed toward their intellectual development, which is enhanced by both individual and group support. It can encourage teachers to expand their thinking and their knowledge base.

Opportunities for active involvement with other teachers and Helping Professionals also will contribute to a teacher's emotional growth. Providing focused study groups, teacher collaboratives, and long-term partnerships in which trust and collegiality are built will encourage the sharing of ideas, as well as the discussion of differences in values and beliefs. Teachers need opportunities to share ideas and to gain support, which will assist them in challenging their own underlying assumptions. This type of professional development leads toward strengthening individual and group beliefs, encouraging teachers to make new choices and strengthening existing ones, and broadening the perspectives and connections within the profession. It can promote healthier organizations. According to one author, there is a "quiet revolution" in teacher development that focuses on teacher mentoring and collaboration (Darling-Hammond, 1996). Outcomes of this type of social support will be the preparation and development of teachers not only to improve their knowledge and pedagogy skills, but to provide leadership roles in schools and in districts.

Through the development of professional support groups, teachers' intellectual curiosities and capacities can be enhanced. As they discuss innovative approaches, they will expand their learning, their knowledge will be stimulated, and they will have opportunities to assess the knowledge they possess and that of their colleagues. As teachers apply the knowledge they are learning, they will expand their use of techniques and their skills of inquiry. Individuals will feel a sense of respect and trust for each other, which in turn will encourage them to challenge their own beliefs and their instructional patterns. From these types of discussions, teachers become active learners who welcome change and initiate research to assist them in improving their teaching and in improving their schools.

This type of professional development program encourages teachers to meet their individual needs and to focus on the welfare of the overall faculty. It helps to create healthy, productive individuals along with organizations that demonstrate a healthy psychological climate.

The professional development of teachers proposed in our Transformational model includes not only the teachers' intellectual development to meet their intellectual needs; it also includes the development of strong social support groups to meet the social needs of teachers. In these groups their choices, beliefs, and underlying assumptions are clarified and strengthened.

Another area of attention prescribed in this model is that of teachers' emotional needs. These needs are met through meaningful intellectual stimulation and through enthusiastic and growth-producing social support that enhances their emotional health. This type of program stimulates intellectual, motivational, and attitudinal well-being of individuals and of organizations.

The instructional and professional needs of teachers are closely linked with their personal and psychological needs. Both must be addressed in any teacher preparation or professional development program.

Meeting Teachers' Needs

The most promising models for preservice and professional development provide teachers with opportunities to investigate the problems, issues, and challenges that are meaningful for them and to apply what they learn in ways that will have an impact on them personally and professionally. These types of opportunities encourage teachers to become more productive, inquiring, and responsible members of their profession. These models are in direct contrast to other models that place teachers in passive roles in which they are consumers of knowledge that is selected for them, where the opportunities for integrating the knowledge acquired and organizing opportunities for students' learning are lacking. The philosophy of the Transformational model values active teacher learning, in which teachers fully participate in self-analysis and self-directed growth.

Encouraging teachers to develop their intellectual capacities and curiosities while acknowledging their contributions to their teaching will improve professional practice. This type of professional development produces enthusiastic teachers who in turn develop students with greater excitement for learning.

When teachers are aware of their needs and are working on meeting them, they are less likely to look to others for solutions. These teachers will be healthier, more confident, and more successful in their work. The follow excerpt describes how the precepts discussed here can apply in an individual situation.

> *Rose is an example of a teacher who identified her unmet needs and began a planned program to meet them. She discovered from her Needs Inventory that her need for security was unmet. As she became more aware of how much she needed others to reassure her that she was an effective teacher, Rose realized how vulnerable she was to others on her faculty. She had been afraid to say "No" to certain assignments and would not confront other teachers who at times took advantage of her inability to refuse others' requests. As Rose concentrated on becoming more secure and worked with the Helping Professional in her school, she began to appreciate her own teaching and looked within*

herself for positive feedback. When other teachers complimented her teaching, she would enjoy the statement for what it was, rather than needing it. Rose also began to say "No" to some of the assignments she was asked to take and felt more respect for herself. Over a period of time she began to receive more respectful statements from other teachers. Rose is now more secure, enjoys her teaching more, and said that she is a healthier person. Her last statement to us was, "I feel so good now that I'm not so needy. I feel stronger and I know that I have more to offer others."

Preparation programs for preservice teachers, as well as professional development programs that use a diagnostic and prescriptive approach with therapeutic methods of the types presented here, will produce teachers who are more intellectually challenged and psychologically mature. These teachers will demonstrate more meaningful intellectual development that challenges their thinking and expands their knowledge base. Also, when Helping Professionals concentrate on meeting the needs of teachers, they will be better able to help teachers broaden their perspectives and strengthen their connections with others. They then will be challenged and encouraged to work in collaborative ways to improve themselves, their practice, and their school environment.

Another important outcome centers on the students who have teachers with this type of preparation. They too demonstrate active involvement with others, which strengthens their attitudes toward learning and their motivation for working together. As students expand their knowledge base and develop into problem solvers who accept the challenges offered them in the classroom, they also will use these skills as they interact in society, and society will reap the benefits.

References

Adams, R. D. (1982, March). Teacher development: A look at changes in teacher perceptions across time. Paper presented at the meeting of the American Educational Research Association, New York. (ED 214-926.)

Barnes, H. (1989). Structuring knowledge for beginning teaching. In M. C. Reynolds (Ed.), *Knowledge base for the beginning teacher* (pp. 13–22). New York: Pergamon Press.

Borko, H., Livingston, C., McCaleb, J., & Mauro, L. (1988). Student teachers' planning and postlesson reflections: Patterns and implications for teacher preparation. In J. Calderhead (Ed.), *Teachers' professional learning* (pp. 65–83). London: Falmer Press.

Burden, P. R. (1980a). Teachers' perceptions of the characteristics and influences on their personal and professional development (Doctoral dissertation, The Ohio State University, 1979). *Dissertation Abstracts International, 40,* 5404A.

Burden, P. R. (1980b). *Teachers' perceptions of the characteristics and influences on their personal and professional development.* Manhattan, KS: Author. (ERIC Document Reproduction Service No. ED 198-087.)

Burden, P. R. (1990). Teacher development. In W. R. Houston (Ed.), *Handbook of research on teacher education* (pp. 311–328). New York: Macmillan.

Burgess, R. G. (1988). Examining classroom practice using diaries and diary interviews. In P. Woods & A. Pollard (Eds.), *Sociology and teaching.* New York: Croom Helm.

Butt, R., & Raymond, D. (1987). Arguments for using qualitative approaches in understanding teacher thinking: The case for biography. *Journal of Curriculum Theorizing, 7*(1), 62–93.

Butt, R., Raymond, D., & Yamagishi, L. (1988). Autobiographic praxis: Studying the formation of teachers' knowledge. *Journal of Curriculum Theorizing, 7*(4).

Calderhead, J. (1981). A psychological approach to research on teachers' classroom decision making. *British Educational Research Journal, 7*, 51–57.

Calderhead, J. (1991). The nature and growth of knowledge in student teaching. *Teaching and Teacher Education, 7*(5/6), 531–539.

Carroll, J. B. (1963). A model of school learning. *Teachers College Record, 64*(8), 723–733.

Carter, K. (1990). Teachers' knowledge and learning to teach. In W. R. Houston (Ed.), *Handbook of research on teacher education* (pp. 291–310). New York: Macmillan.

Clark, C. M., & Peterson, P. L. (1986). Teachers' thought processes. In M. C. Wittrock (Ed.), *Handbook of research on teaching* (3d ed.) (pp. 255–295). New York: Macmillan.

Clark, C. M., & Yinger, R. J. (1987). Teacher planning. In J. Calderhead (Ed.), *Exploring teachers' thinking* (pp. 84–103). London: Cassell Educational Limited.

Cochran-Smith, M., & Lytle, S. L. (1990). Research on teaching and teacher research: The issues that divide. *Educational Researcher, 19*(2), 2–10.

Connelly, F. M., & Clandinin, D. J. (1986). On narrative method, personal philosophy and narrative unities in the study of teaching. *Journal of Research in Science Teaching, 23*(3), 15–32.

Connelly, F. M., & Clandinin, D. J. (1987). On narrative method, biography and narrative unities in the study of teaching. *Journal of Educational Thought, 21*(3), 130–139.

Dahllof, U. S., & Lundgren, U. P. (1970). *Macro and micro approaches combined for curriculum process analysis: A Swedish educational field project*. Goteborg, Sweden: University of Gothenburg, Institute of Education. (ED 044-435.)

Darling-Hammond, L. (1996). The quiet revolution: Rethinking teacher development. *Educational Leadership, 53*(6), 4–10.

Doyle, D. P. (1986). Who should teach the teachers? *Teacher Education Quarterly, 13*(1) 19–21.

Elbaz, F. (1988). Critical reflection on teaching: Insights from Freire. *Journal of Education for Teaching, 14*(2), 171–181.

Elbaz, F. (1990). Knowledge and discourse: The evolution of research on teacher thinking. In C. Day, M. Pope, & P. Denicolo (Eds.), *Insights into teachers' thinking and practice* (pp. 15–42). New York: Falmer Press.

Ericcson, K. A., & Simon, H. A. (1980). Verbal reports as data. *Psychological Review, 87*(3), 215–251.

Feiman, S., & Floden, R. E. (1980a, April). Approaches to staff development from conceptions of teacher development. Paper presented at the meeting of the American Educational Research Association, Boston.

Feiman, S., & Floden, R. E. (1980b). *What's all this talk about teacher development?* (Research Series No. 70). East Lansing: Michigan State University, Institute for Research on Teaching. (ERIC Document Reproduction Service No. ED 189-088.)

Feiman, S., & Floden, R. E. (1981). *A consumer's guide to teacher development* (Research Series No. 94). East Lansing: Michigan State University, Institute for Research on Teaching. (ERIC Document Reproduction Service No. ED 207-970.)

Feiman-Nemser, S., & Buchmann, M. (1987). When is student teaching teacher education? *Teaching and Teacher Education, 3*(4), 255–273.

Field, K. (1979). *Teacher development: A study of the stages in development of teachers*. Brookline, MA: Brookline Teacher Center.

Floden, R. E., & Feiman, S. (1980, April). Basing effectiveness criteria on theories of teacher development. Paper presented at the meeting of the American Educational Research Association, Boston. (ED 196-890.)

Floden, R. E., & Feiman, S. (1981a, February). *A development approach to the study of teacher change: What's to be gained?* (Research Series No. 93). East Lansing: Michigan State University, Institute for Research on Teaching.

Floden, R. E., & Feiman, S. (1981b, July). *Problems of equity in developmental approaches* (Research Series No. 91). East Lansing: Michigan State University, Institute for Research on Teaching.

Fosnot, C. T. (1989). *Enquiring teachers, enquiring learners: A constructivist approach for teaching*. New York: Teachers College, Columbia University.

Fuller, F. F. (1969). Concerns of teachers: A developmental conceptualization. *American Educational Research Journal, 6*(2), 207–226.

Fuller, F. F., & Bown, O. H. (1975). Becoming a teacher. In K. Ryan (Ed.), *Teacher education* (74th yearbook of the National Society for the Study of Education, Part II) (pp. 25–52). Chicago: University of Chicago Press.

Gold, Y., & Roth, R. (1993). *Teachers managing stress and preventing burnout: The professional health solution.* London: Falmer Press.

Gold, Y. (1996). Beginning teacher support: Attrition, mentoring and induction. In J. Sikula, T. Buttery, & E. Guyton (Eds.), *Handbook of research on teacher education* (2d ed.). New York: Macmillan.

Gregorc, A. F. (1973). Developing plans for professional growth. *NASSP Bulletin, 57*(377), 1–8.

Grossman, P. L. (1990). *The making of a teacher: Teacher knowledge and teacher education.* New York: Teachers College Press.

Grumet, M. (1981). Pedagogy for patriarchy: The teminization of teaching. *Interchange on Educational Policy, 12*(2), 165–184.

Harvey, O. J., Hunt, D. E., & Schroeder, H. (1961). *Conceptual systems and personality organization.* New York: Wiley.

Ingvarson, L., & Greenway, P. (1984). Portrayals of teacher development. *The Australian Journal of Education, 28*(1), 45–65.

Jackson, P. W. (1968). *Life in classrooms.* New York: Holt, Rinehart & Winston.

Katz, L. G. (1972). Developmental stages of preschool teachers. *The Elementary School Journal, 73*(1), 50–54.

Kirst, Michael W. (1982, September). How to improve schools without spending more money. *Phi Delta Kappan, 64*(1), 6–8.

Kohlberg, L. (1969). Stage and sequence: The cognitive developmental approach to socialization. In D. Croslin (Ed.), *Handbook of socialization theory and research* (pp. 347–380). New York: Rand McNally.

Kohlberg, L. (1973). Continuities in childhood and adult moral development revisited. In P. B. Baltes & K. W. Schaie (Eds.), *Life-span developmental psychology: Personality and socialization* (pp. 179–204). New York: Academic Press.

Lerman, S. (1989). Constructivism, mathematics and mathematics education. *Educational Studies in Mathematics, 20*(2), 211–223.

Little, J. W. (1993). Teachers' professional development in a climate of educational reform. *Educational Evaluation and Policy Analysis, 15*(2), 129–151.

Loevinger, J. (1966). The meaning and measurement of ego development. *American Psychologist, 21*(3), 195–206.

Lortie, D. C. (1975). *School teacher: A socialization study.* Chicago: University of Chicago Press.

McDonald, F. J. (1982, March). A theory of the professional development of teachers. Paper presented at the meeting of the American Educational Research Association, New York.

The National Institute of Education (1975). *Journal of Educational Communication, 1*(2), 20–25.

Newman, K. K. (1979). Middle-aged experienced teachers' perceptions of their career development. Paper presented at the annual meeting of the American Educational Research Association, San Francisco. (ED 171-697.)

Perry, W. (1970). *Forms of intellectual and ethical development during the college years.* New York: Holt, Rinehart & Winston.

Peterson, A. R. (1979). Career patterns of secondary school teachers: An exploratory interview study of retired teachers (Doctoral dissertation, The Ohio State University, 1978). *Dissertation Abstracts International, 39,* 4888A.

Peterson, P. L., Marx, R. W., & Clark, C. M. (1978). Teacher planning, teacher behavior, and student achievement. *American Educational Research Journal, 15*(3), 417–432.

Piaget, J. (1968/1970). *Structuralism.* New York: Basic Books.

Piaget, J. (1970). *Genetic epistemology.* New York: Columbia University Press.

Piaget, J. (1975). The construction of reality in the child. In H. E. Gruber & J. J. Voneche (Eds.), *The essential Piaget* (pp. 250–294). New York: Basic Books. Original from J. Piaget (1937/1954), *The construction of reality in the child* (Margaret Cook, Trans.). New York: Basic Books.

Piaget, J. (1977). Problems of equilibration. In M. Appel & L. Goldberg (Eds.), *Topics in cognitive development: Vol. 1. Equilibration: Theory,* research, and application (pp. 3–13). New York: Plenum Press.

Pinar, W. F. (1988). The reconceptualization of curriculum studies, 1987: A personal retrospective. *Journal of Curriculum and Supervision, 3*(2), 157–167.

Raymond, D., & Surprenant, M. (1988, April). Investigating teachers' knowledge through ethnographic and biographical approaches: A case study. Paper presented at the American Educational Research Association, New Orleans, LA. (ED 294-874.)

Rowe, M. B. (1974). Relation of wait-time and rewards to the development of language, logic, and fate control: Part II—Rewards. *Journal of Research in Science Teaching, 11*(4), 291–308.

Russell, T. (1988). From preservice teacher education to first year of teaching: A study of theory and practice. In J. Calderhead (Ed.), *Teachers' professional learning* (pp. 13–35). London: Falmer Press.

Sacks, S. R., & Harrington, G. (1982, April). Student to teacher: The process of role transition. Paper presented at the meeting of the American Educational Research Association, New York.

Shulman, L. (1987). Knowledge and teaching: Foundations of the new reform. *Harvard Educational Review, 57*(1), 1–22.

Shulman, L. S., & Ringstaff, C. (1986). Current research in the psychology of learning and teaching. In H. Weinstack (Ed.), *Learning physics and mathematics via computers* (pp. 1–31). Berlin: Springer.

Sitter, J. P., & Lanier, P. E. (1982, March). Student teaching: A stage in the development of teacher or a period of consolidation? Paper presented at the meeting of the American Educational Research Association, New York.

Stanton, A. Q., & Hunt, S. L. (1992). Teacher socialization: Review and conceptualization. *Communication Education, 41*(2), 109–137.

Tierney, R. J. (1990). Redefining reading comprehension. *Educational Leadership, 47*(3), 37–42.

Tripp, D. H. (1987). Teachers, journals and collaborative research. In J. Smyth (Ed.), *Educating teachers: Changing the nature of pedagogical knowledge*. Philadelphia: Falmer Press.

Von Glasersfeld, E. (1984). An introduction to radical constructivism. In P. Watzlawick (Ed.), *The invented reality* (pp. 17–40). New York: Norton.

Vygotsky, L. S. (1986). *Thought and language* (A. Kozulin, Ed.). Cambridge, MA: MIT Press.

Wilson, S. M., Shulman, L. S., & Richert, A. E. (1987). 150 different ways of knowing: Representations of knowledge in teaching. In J. Calderhead (Ed.), *Exploring teachers' thinking* (pp. 104–125). London: Cassell.

Woods, P. (1987). Life histories and teacher knowledge. In J. Smyth (Ed.), *Educating teachers: Changing the nature of pedagogical knowledge*. New York: Falmer Press.

Wright, B. (1959). Identification and becoming a teacher. *Elementary School Journal, 59*(7), 361–374.

Wright, B., & Tuska, S. (1967). The childhood romance theory of teacher development. *School Review, 75*(2), 123–154.

Wright, B., & Tuska, S. (1986). From dream to life in the psychology of becoming a teacher. *School Review, 76*(3), 253–293.

Yarger, S. J., & Mertens, S. K. (1980). Testing the waters of school-based teacher education. In D. C. Corrigan & K. R. Howey (Eds.), *Concepts to guide the education of experienced teachers*. Reston, VA: Council for Exceptional Children.

Chapter 6

The Five Dimensions of Helping

The philosophical framework underlying the Transformational Helping Professional model provides a conceptualization of the helping role. It suggests that the role is multifunctional and is concerned with two broad domains of need: personal-psychological and instructional-professional. The way the role descriptions relate to current needs and contemporary practice illustrates the rationale for an emphasis on helping as the primary component of mentoring and supervising. The premises described in Chapter 2 provide a basis for determining the principles of practice for, and the personal characteristics of, the Helping Professional. The basic areas of practice will be categorized and described in this chapter.

In reviewing the research on effective school supervision, mentoring, student teaching supervision, and helping professions, certain key attributes and functions are found consistently across these roles. In order to make a difference, professionals in these roles must consciously work to bring about their own personal and professional growth and to assist others in enhancing their personal and professional lives. That is, they must have developed the skills and strategies for healthy living before they can be effective with others. Without having developed their own skills in their own lives, helpers cannot provide sufficient support to enable teachers or other professionals to function at their maximum potential level.

Furthermore, when one looks at the dynamics of today's schools and classrooms, it becomes clear that in order to perform at an accomplished level, a teacher needs a combination of a wide range of personal and professional skills. These go beyond the technical aspects of teaching. Consistent with this, the Helping Professional must be able to assist teachers in acquiring these skills and meeting their varied needs. Helping Professionals also must be proficient in these areas in order to more fully understand the teachers' needs and to be able to model skills related to them.

Based on research, and consistent with the characteristics and responsibilities embedded in the Helping Professional philosophy, the role and functions of helping are envisioned as having five basic dimensions. These dimensions provide for the categorization of the techniques and skills necessary for functioning as a professional helper. They are found to be a convenient way of viewing the competencies needed. They also serve as a framework for both conceptualizing the role and designing preparation for it.

The Five Dimensions of Helping are as follows: (1) self-enhancement of the Helping Professional, (2) interpersonal effectiveness—communication and helping strategies, (3) assessing and diagnosing, (4) guidance and support, and (5) revitalizing the Helping Professional. The rationale for each of these dimensions, why they are essential to helping in contemporary education, and how they emanate from the philosophy of the Transformational Helping Professional model will be explored. These dimensions and their components will be treated in more depth in the subsequent chapters devoted to each. An overview of each dimension is provided here as an introduction.

Self-Enhancement for Helping Professionals: Dimension One

The self-enhancement dimension deals with the critical area of increasing the effectiveness of the Helping Professional through personal and professional growth. The process of giving is often emotionally and physically draining, and the most frequently neglected aspect in mentoring and supervising is recognizing the importance of providing nurturing, enrichment, and support for the Helping Professional. This includes identifying distinguishing characteristics of a healthy individual, strategies for bringing about self-enhancement, and techniques for maintaining a high degree of energy and motivation in the role of the Helping Professional.

The Helping Professional philosophy contains a number of elements that require that attention be given to self-enhancement. A fundamental premise of the helping philosophy is that in order to help others, one must first be emotionally and physically healthy. A realistic and positive self-concept is extremely important and relates to a high regard for self-worth. In order to strengthen and enhance their own positive characteristics, Helping Professionals find it necessary to engage in self-enhancement in order to achieve higher levels of competence, maintain their vision, and sustain their spiritual strength.

The Helping Professional has a clear set of beliefs and values, lives consistent with them, and evaluates them periodically. This process of introspection related to beliefs and values is within the self-enhancement dimension. Similarly, the notion of ongoing personal and professional growth of the Helping Professional is a vital part of this dimension. An important concept identified in this philosophy is that Helping Professionals must recognize their own immediate and long-term needs and develop strategies to meet them, if they are to be effective in working with others. This also clearly suggests that an important dimension of being a

Helping Professional is to engage in self-enhancement. Helping Professionals are constantly growing. They are committed to the process of growth and engage in concomitant growth with the individuals with whom they are working. They are able to experience feelings of identification with others, be supportive of others' ideas, and develop trust and rapport that encourages confidence and stimulates growth. These are essential elements of the self-enhancement process.

The U.S. educational system is under intense criticism. There is constant pressure to reform and achieve the objectives of the system. Goals 2000, the 1996 Education Summit, and the comprehensive movement for standards in K–12 education are putting additional pressure on the system and calling for higher degrees of accountability. Thus, not only are teachers required to function at high levels of effectiveness, but mentors and other support personnel are expected to assist teachers in meeting the levels necessary to achieve the institutional objectives. This requires a constant search for growth and accurate, realistic views of one's assets and strengths on the part of the Helping Professional in today's schools.

There are more complex issues, greater demands, and increased pressures, both personally and professionally, in today's classrooms. The Helping Professional must engage in self-enhancement in order to hone skills, acquire new strategies, and maintain a sense of personal balance. Meeting one's personal and professional needs truly is the foundation of successful helping. The models of mentoring and supervising that currently are in practice focus exclusively on the process of supervising and assisting, or on the needs of the teachers in the programs. The needs of the mentor have been neglected or virtually omitted in these programs and philosophies. An effective program can no longer function without a self-enhancement dimension for helpers.

Interpersonal Effectiveness—Communication and Helping Strategies: Dimension Two

Helping Professionals cannot adequately fulfill their functions unless they are competent in the interpersonal effectiveness dimension. They must be able to establish working relationships that are productive, mutually satisfying, and rewarding. This is a consistent theme in the Transformational Helping model. The areas of interpersonal effectiveness include conferencing skills, helping skills, creating positive working relationships, building and maintaining trust, developing rapport, and using effective communication skills. An entire chapter (Chapter 8) is devoted to helping skills, and a separate chapter (Chapter 9) addresses communication skills in order to provide a comprehensive description and analysis of the interpersonal effectiveness dimension.

The Helping Professional philosophy strongly supports the need for interpersonal skills, such as the development of rapport and trust. The Helping Professional is designated as a leader in the growth of others, which is more readily accomplished when she or he has the necessary skills for relationships. The process of change is embedded in the Helping Professional model, and it is through interpersonal skills that the teacher is guided and supported throughout the change process. Helping Professionals have a strong commitment to helping others. They experience deep feelings of identification with others. Therefore, it is imperative that an interpersonal effectiveness dimension be part of the helping model.

In today's classrooms there is greater insecurity because of the extreme pressures and stresses experienced by teachers. These have reached significantly high levels, as noted by several studies and documented in a number of publications (Farber, 1991; Gold & Roth, 1993). Some of these studies have indicated a loss of up to 50 percent of new teachers within the first 3 years of teaching (Schlecty & Vance, 1983). Under these conditions it is imperative that a Helping Professional have effective interpersonal skills to develop trust and rapport critical to assisting teachers through these difficult times.

It is noted again that both the personal-psychological and instructional-professional domains require strong interpersonal skills on the part of the Helping Professional. Using interpersonal skills in both of these critical domains is absent from or insufficiently dealt with in current mentoring and supervising models. The Transformational model incorporates both communication and helping skills within the context of interpersonal relations. The Helping Professional approach thus offers a unique system for the application of interpersonal skills.

Assessing and Diagnosing: Dimension Three

In order to assist colleagues, student teachers, or beginning teachers, it is necessary to know what their current level of functioning is and what their needs are in the different domains. Growth is a personal process that obviously must be related to where one currently stands in one's development. In the philosophy of the Transformational Helping Professional model, a realistic view of oneself is of vital importance. Often one is not able to provide an accurate self-assessment of one's skills, abilities, or the ways in which one relates to others. It is particularly important to understand how one is viewed by others in the classroom and while performing one's professional responsibilities within the school and community. However, self-analysis can be misleading, as individuals view their demeanor and performance through their own filters, such as their own perceptions of what they want to see, what they hope to see, and what they do not want to see. Therefore, another trained pair of eyes and ears can be extremely valuable—and may even be absolutely necessary to receive a realistic picture of their behaviors and performance.

A Helping Professional must know the individual with whom she or he is working in order to be effective in assisting the other person in growth. One of the most useful things one can do to assist another is to provide information or reflect back the ways in which the other is functioning. Earlier, a distinction between assessment and evaluation was made, suggesting that assessment does not make judgments about one's worth, but provides an analysis that is primarily descriptive, although somewhat analytical. This is part of the feedback process.

A characteristic of the Helping Professional is that the professional should be an expert observer of the classroom and people. The reason for this skill is to provide the appropriate assessment and diagnosis required in the Transformational Helping Professional model. This enables the Helping Professional to provide a clear and accurate description of the teacher's work, which is an essential foundation if the teacher is to develop further.

In today's classrooms the role of the teacher is very complex, much more so than in previous decades. With changing demographics and increasing cultural and linguistic diversity, the challenges within the classroom continue to increase. As a result of this, as well as recognition of advances in research, the required level of instructional competence far exceeds prior expectations.

Teachers need assistance in knowing how well they are doing in relation to the range of classroom variables. They must have a clear picture of their skills, behaviors, and classroom effects in these complex settings. It is quite difficult to keep track of or be aware of the multitude of elements necessary for teacher effectiveness. In today's classrooms, diagnosis and assessment are particularly needed.

It should be noted that one of the unique aspects of the Helping Professional approach is that assessment and diagnosis must address both the personal-psychological needs and the instructional-professional needs. Teachers need feedback on their level of functioning in both of these areas, and the assessment and diagnosis process integrates these domains in a way quite dissimilar from other approaches. With changing conditions in the classroom and the more complex nature of responsibilities, levels of stress are exceedingly high in today's schools. Teachers need to understand how they are responding to these pressures and what symptoms they may be manifesting. Assessing and diagnosing the teacher's needs in both of these domains is critical to increasing knowledge of self. Therefore, feedback is an essential component. This is provided through the dimension of assessment and diagnosis in the Transformational Helping Professional model.

The skills of assessing and diagnosing are primarily related to observation and interpretation strategies. Assessment provides for the collection of data regarding the teacher's activities, level of knowledge, technical expertise in instruction, and psychological needs. In diagnosing, one provides an analysis of the information collected and looks for trends, anomalies, or missing competencies. The diagnosis is based on the Helping Professional's experience, background, and expertise related to the instructional processes or the professional role. The diagnosis includes relationships, understandings, and insights inferred from the information in order to assist the teacher in understanding his or her behavior or psychological state.

In the assessing and diagnosing dimension, areas that one might address include the following: effective instruction, classroom management, instructional planning, new teacher needs and phases, student personal problems, parent relations, motivating students, individual differences, evaluating students, coping strategies, and individual psychological needs. The focus or content of assessing and diagnosing was reviewed more thoroughly in the chapters on needs (Chapters 4 and 5) and also will be addressed in the chapter on content (Chapter 11).

Guidance and Support: Dimension Four

Guidance and support provide for actively engaging in the process of helping. They involve using nonevaluative styles for advising, encouraging, and enhancing the growth of the teacher. Of particular importance are conferencing skills and individual consultation on personal needs and growth plans. Among the strategies are coaching, modeling, establishing outcomes, setting priorities, and mutually developing plans for achieving goals. Assisting the teacher in reflective conversations and gaining personal insights are related strategies. A wide range of support skills is used to assist and guide.

In guidance and support the Helping Professional is using the information gathered through the assessing and diagnosing dimension, incorporating interpersonal skills to provide expert guidance and support. The focus of guidance and support is on the individual personal and professional needs of the teacher. These relate to instructional effectiveness, personal needs, and organizational goals. In many instances the objective is to develop an individual plan for professional development and to provide support in the process of implementing the plan.

Guidance and support are embedded in several elements of the Helping Professional philosophy. The premise of focusing on the individual requires a plan of guidance and support based on individual needs. Related to this is the concept of psychological and personal needs as motivating factors. Guidance and support are intended to assist the teacher in addressing these needs, thus enhancing the individual's motivation and increasing the effectiveness of the professional.

A key area is professional competence and technical proficiency required by teachers in the instructional process. Guidance and support are intended to enhance directly this area of competence. Another important element in the Helping Professional philosophy is that of increasing capacity for growth. This is one of the major functions of guidance and support. Guidance is not intended to always provide answers and solutions, but rather to assist and guide individuals to arrive at their own insights and gain the capability for managing their own growth. This support process provides the necessary conducive conditions for continuing growth through difficult periods of change and in the process of acquiring new skills and strategies. In essence, the Helping Professional guides and supports teachers through their transformation.

Change also is a fundamental issue within the Transformational Helping Professional philosophy. Initiation of productive change is facilitated by the guidance and support process, as well as encouraged throughout the change period. Teacher efficacy is an objective of the philosophy that is significantly aided through the guidance and support process by providing feedback and validation of accomplishment.

Developing a strong knowledge base is integral to both personal and professional competence. The guidance and support process is intended to lead teachers to acquiring deeper levels of knowledge, as well as greater insights into its use.

An essential element in the Helping Professional philosophy is the commitment to help others. The guidance and support process is precisely the means by which this commitment is put into action. The Helping Professional also appreciates the moral, ethical, and theoretical issues in the educational process. The Helping Professional and teacher collaborate on these important dilemmas of education within the context of guidance and support.

One of the most significant components of the Transformational Helping Professional model is assisting teachers in the search for personal and professional fulfillment. The guidance and support process encompasses all of the strategies and techniques intended to aid the teacher in this critical search for professional meaning. The Helping Professional approach calls for a shared vision of both the teaching and learning process and individual growth. The shared vision is created through the process of guidance and support. Also, it is noted that personal meaning is best learned and accepted through situations in which resolutions to problems can be achieved. The guidance and support dimension is intended to provide the framework, processes, and strategies for this to occur.

In today's schools, guidance and support are particularly relevant. Complex technology, more sophisticated teaching strategies, and new curricular frameworks are constantly emerging. These require ongoing support through the help of a professional who is knowledgeable and who has the skills to assist teachers in this quest for growth. Many of today's classes are still isolated, and teaching is a lonely profession. The mechanism for providing assistance to teachers and a framework for guidance and support are even more urgent today. As classrooms become increasingly complex in contemporary schools, guidance and support become even more essential for effectively dealing with these situations.

It also is noted that many teachers today have limited preparation. This is due to the number of states that either limit the professional component in teacher education or provide for quick-entry or limited-preparation programs. These include alternative routes and emergency credentials, which continue to be issued in large numbers throughout the United States. In these particular situations, guidance and support are critical if teachers are to succeed.

It is also known that self-help is not as effective as the support provided by those prepared for this role. With increasing responsibilities and lack of support from traditional agencies, such as the home or church, teachers have an increasingly complex and difficult responsibility. This dictates that there must be a system of guidance and support in order to encourage and retain teachers who are capable of making important contributions to the classroom. This is particularly notable when it is recognized that guidance and support are needed in both the technical and psychological domains. Support groups, for example, are one means of providing support in the psychological domain in order that teachers need not "go it alone." Programs for preparing supervisors do not address both of these domains. In addition, the instructional component of guidance and support is viewed from a much broader perspective in the Helping Professional model.

Revitalizing the Helping Professional: Dimension Five

One of the greatest problems for Helping Professionals is not knowing when they have given too much to others. Giving of one's emotional energy over a long period of time to a variety of individuals can be physically and emotionally draining.

Recognizing the risks involved in helping and taking time to meet one's needs will prevent burnout and dropout. The risks for each helper may be somewhat different; however, there are a number of risks common to all helpers. These will be explored in more detail in Chapters 14 and 15.

In the Transformational Helping Professional model, one of the core values is the worth of the individual. Thus, the worth of the Helping Professional is a critical concern. Too often the focus of helping is on the helpee while the needs of the helper are ignored. Helpers must become aware of their own needs and develop a plan to meet them if they are to achieve healthy growth and help others to grow.

Helpers also need assistance in identifying their needs. They must have a realistic view of themselves and their skills to be effective. To accomplish this, it is important that they assess their own risk areas and begin to change what they can. The Risk Inventory in Chapter 15 will help them gain insight into these areas. A major concern for helpers is recognizing the consequences of helping too much. Becoming aware of the consequences and learning how to eliminate them will contribute to their revitalization.

Developing a clear understanding of the types of things that bring them fulfillment can assist helpers in developing a balanced lifestyle. Also, in order to have the energy to participate in the enjoyable activities, helpers must work to maintain good health, emotional stability, intellectual challenge, and a strong spiritual belief system that provides hope and encouragement for them. Too often helpers become so involved in assisting others that they neglect the balance in their own life. They must take time to evaluate how they are doing. They must know themselves and their current state or condition. In order to assist helpers in finding more fulfillment in their life, inventories are provided and specific types of activities are included in Chapter 15 to help bring about specific types of changes.

One of the critical aspects of the Transformational Helping Professional model is that of supporting the helper during the process of personal growth. Just as helpees need support as they are changing old patterns of thinking and behaving, so do helpers. Support groups made up of helpers are an excellent means for providing feedback and encouragement.

Two major strategies are presented in Chapter 15 to assist helpers in achieving the growth they desire. The first strategy focuses on individual growth, with the major emphasis on developing one's potential. The other strategy is one of social consciousness and change, in which helpers find fulfillment through discovering ways to bring about change in organizations such as the school, family, and home. The first strategy includes the deep inner exploration of oneself and contributes to the development of a healthier and more knowledgeable individual. The result is a person who is better prepared to assist others in enhancing their quality of life, which affects the organization as well. The second strategy focuses on encouraging and bringing about growth in others.

The first strategy has been criticized as being selfish. The Transformational Philosophy separates selfish from "selfness." Samples (1977) defines selfness as the exploitation of oneself for the benefit of others, while selfish is the exploitation of others for the benefit of oneself. The philosophy of this model focuses on the welfare of others. Because growth is a choice, it cannot be forced on anyone. Helpers who are healthy, well-adjusted individuals are in a better position to encourage and model these characteristics for others. In contrast, helpers who are unable to evaluate their own needs and who lack healthy coping strategies are hindered in assisting others toward positive growth.

The Helping Professional model provides specific assessment instruments to help people become aware of their personal and professional needs. It also provides coping strategies to change old patterns of thinking and behaving. Helping Professionals must be models of healthy growth to motivate those they help to change their own life.

Specific areas that are addressed in the revitalizing dimension include: (1) recognizing the risks of helping: stress and burnout, (2) becoming aware of the consequences of helping too much, (3) developing a clear view of oneself, (4) finding personal fulfillment, (5) becoming aware of resistances that hinder one's growth, (6) knowing when to take a break from helping, (7) discovering specific techniques to revitalize oneself, and (8) learning about the rewards that come from revitalizing oneself.

The end result for helpers who do work on revitalizing themselves is well worth the time and commitment. They learn to enjoy themselves more fully, and they reach new levels of personal growth and satisfaction.

Summary

The Five Dimensions of Helping have been devised to provide a comprehensive framework for the implementation of the roles and functions of the helping process. Collectively, they create an operational vision of the philosophy. The remainder of this book will focus on the dimensions and their respective elements. Each makes a critical contribution to the overall process of helping, and an in-depth analysis of the research, theory, and practical applications for each will be provided.

References

Farber, B. A. (1991). *Crisis in education: Stress and burnout in the American teacher*. San Francisco: Jossey-Bass.

Gold, Y., & Roth, R. A. (1993). *Teachers managing stress and preventing burnout: The professional health (PH) solution*. London: Falmer Press.

Samples, B. (1977, May). Selfness: Seeds of transformation. *AHP Newsletter, 1*, 1–2.

Schlecty, P. C., & Vance, V. S. (1983). Recruitment, selection and retention: The shape of the teaching force. *Elementary School Journal, 83*(4), 469–487.

Related Readings

Feistritzer, C. E., & Chester, D. T. (1993). *Alternative teacher certification: A state-by-state analysis 1993–94.* Washington, DC: National Center for Education Information.

Kalliopuska, M. (1986). Empathy, its measurement and application. *British Journal of Projective Psychology, 31*(20), 10–18.

Chapter 7

Self-Enhancement for Helping Professionals (Dimension One)

*Every good thought you think
is contributing its share to the
result of your life.* —GRENVILLE KLEISER

In most instances, people are working toward personal fulfillment virtually every minute of their lives. In fact, the majority of people wish to be healthy and happy and to fulfill their potential as they interact in both their personal and their professional lives. The greatest motivation for Helping Professionals in assisting others is to observe their growth as they search for personal and professional fulfillment. In order to be effective in assisting others, helpers must consciously work to bring about their own growth and to develop their own potential.

This chapter on the first of the five Dimensions of Helping is based on several fundamental premises: (1) Self-enhancement is an essential part of the Helping Professional's growth, (2) developing a positive view of one's self is of utmost importance in helping others, (3) self-esteem is a vital part of the helping relationship and must be a high priority, (4) developing empathy with others is critical for any helping relationship, (5) meeting teachers' personal and psychological needs is the foundation of support, and (6) identifying characteristics of mature Helping Professionals will help to facilitate growth in all helpers. Each of these fundamental premises will be examined separately.

Self-Enhancement: An Essential Aspect of Growth

People who are in the helping role have many demands made on their time, emotions, and intellect. As a consequence, they often give so much that they become physically and emotionally drained. Not recognizing their limitations can lead to diminished productivity and even to personal disillusionment. To counteract these problems, Helping Professionals must concentrate on identifying and meeting their own immediate and long-term needs.

Perhaps one of the most important concepts of self-enhancement is the belief that there is a wide variety of possibilities for enhancement. When individuals truly believe this, their attitudes and energies are more creative and more clearly focused; thus, their chances of success are greater. The following suggestions will assist in this exploration. In using these ideas with Helping Professionals, we have found them to be highly effective and thought-provoking in the quest for self-enhancement.

1. Find pleasure and meaning in your life. Concentrate on your successes and learn from your failures. Identify aspects of your life that bring you personal rewards.
2. Recognize and acknowledge your abilities, and evaluate how you are using them both professionally and personally.
3. Seek opportunities to enrich your life that are not connected to helping others.
4. Develop new interests and talents—risk in new areas where you do not have a record of success.
5. Nurture new relationships in which you are involved in activities different from those with which you are familiar.
6. Monitor your physical health—plan exercise and eating programs that are healthy for you.
7. Concentrate on developing new intellectual interests. Identify as many intellectual areas as possible.
8. List areas of life that are of greatest value to you, and evaluate whether you are living in a way that is consistent with these values.

The temptation for helpers is to continue giving to others and to neglect themselves. Suggestions like these act as stimuli for self-enhancement. Applying the various suggestions on the list will take time, creativity, and commitment, as well as support from others. The rewards of following through on these suggestions are significant, while neglecting to apply them in one's life can have grave consequences.

It is a recognized principle that we can offer help to others only in direct proportion to the growth and insights we have obtained in our own life. It is also true that the helper grows and develops as a result of the interactions with those being helped. Thus, it is essential for the helper to be open to growth and to actively seek it.

Healthy Self-Valuing: The Fundamental Purpose of Helping

One of the most essential characteristics of psychologically healthy people is that they have a high degree of self-worth. They perceive themselves in essentially positive ways so that they confront the world openly and with certainty, and they are open to experiences. Having a positive view of self affects their efficiency and freedom to confront new situations and circumstances. They are able to deal with the problems of life with security and confidence, they believe they are people of dignity and worth, and their behavior reflects their beliefs.

View of Self

How we view ourselves, whether positive or negative, colors our life. When we see ourselves in a positive light, we approach life with an openness and freedom, and we are more willing to explore ourselves and our environment. We take risks and enjoy using our creativity. We develop trust in ourselves and in our ideas, and we are eager to learn and to grow. We have a clear understanding of our values and beliefs, and our behavior is consistent with them, which produces a sense of trustworthiness and confidence. Others know we are dependable because they observe it in our behavior. We are open to ourselves and others, and we have a clear understanding of the interdependency necessary in life regarding our relationships with others. This type of confidence insulates us and empowers us to be able to confront emergencies in life. Having a strong belief in self and a desire to fully experience life contributes to the development of positive attitudes about self and others.

On the other hand, people who approach life with negative views of self tend to deal with life through a narrow and distorted lens. They approach problems with a negative outlook that often produces fear and hopelessness. Negativism undermines a person's confidence and produces feelings of inadequacy and even despair. Negative people are usually inflexible, which hinders them from changing and growing and limits their ability to handle emergency situations. Viewing life from a negative perspective results in a negative self-esteem and robs an individual of spontaneity, appreciation, creativity, trust, love of self and others, and openness to people and experiences. Thus, these individuals are not able to experience life in positive and rewarding ways. Instead, they confront their world with suspicion and fear. The loss of their creativity and spontaneity is great to them and to society. In most situations these types of people are closed to growth and they resist the assistance of others. Thus, Helping Professionals need to remind themselves that they will make little progress with these types of personalities until they are motivated to make changes.

Because emotionally healthy people nurture a positive belief in self, are open to experiences, and demonstrate confidence in themselves and others, they develop a healthy self-esteem. These types of people are enjoyable to be with.

Therefore, it is essential that Helping Professionals continuously assess their own perceptions of themselves. The following questionnaire will assist with this process.

My View of Me

Directions: Answer each of the statements either "Yes" or "No" as you see yourself. Respond in terms of how you view yourself <u>most of the time</u>:

Yes	No	Most of the time...
___	___	1. I am a positive person.
___	___	2. I trust my ideas and my perceptions.
___	___	3. I enjoy the process of learning.
___	___	4. I have a clear understanding of what I value.
___	___	5. My behavior is consistent with my values.
___	___	6. I am a dependable person.
___	___	7. I have a healthy confidence in myself.
___	___	8. I enjoy most of the things I do.
___	___	9. I am flexible and adaptable.
___	___	10. People enjoy being with me.

After completing the questionnaire, take time to look over your responses. Writing a paragraph describing yourself can help to clarify your interests, values, and perceptions.

Identification with Others

How we relate to others is of great significance because people are the sources of our deepest satisfactions and our greatest frustrations. The nature of our relationships determines to a great extent how we feel and think about ourselves. Much of our self-fulfillment depends upon how successful we are in working out our relationships with others. When we are successful, we have a sense of oneness with the other person and we feel good about ourselves. In contrast, when we lack the necessary skills to interact successfully, or when we are unable to resolve conflict with others, we have feelings of frustration and we experience a sense of disequilibrium. Therefore, it is essential that Helping Professionals continually assess their relationships with others and examine the effects of the relationships on themselves.

Psychologically mature people experience deep feelings of identification with others. They enjoy interacting with others to explore and strengthen their existing beliefs. Meaningful interactions help them think through areas that need redefining and clarifying. As they grow and mature in these areas, they also are better prepared to help others with their own ideas and beliefs. They are supportive of others' ideas and other people feel enhanced by the transactions. In return, people respond to them openly and warmly.

Because psychologically mature people expect to be successful in their interactions with others, they develop warm, accepting relationships that permit all involved to grow and mature. They approach relationships in a compassionate, understanding way that creates a nonthreatening environment. Therefore, trust in oneself and others encourages confidence and stimulates the exploration of ideas and beliefs. Where there is little fear, people are better able to commit themselves to problem solving and growth. Psychologically mature individuals commit themselves wholeheartedly to their interactions with others, and they are highly successful in the role of helper.

Promoting Self-Esteem in Self and Others

Much is being written today about self-esteem. We hear about the necessity to develop self-esteem in students, in families, and in the general public (Braucht & Weime, 1992). However, little is being written about the enhancement of teachers' self-esteem. If Helping Professionals are to assist teachers in this area, it is essential that they understand what self-esteem is and that they are able to evaluate their own self-esteem. This point was clearly made by Dewhurst, who argued that "there is a difference between making a correct estimate of oneself and possessing self-esteem" (1991, p. 4). We all are aware that positive feelings about oneself help to increase involvement with others, and these types of feelings contribute to successful performance. Promoting self-esteem is a basic component of any helping relationship and therefore an essential theme of this chapter.

An individual is not born with positive or negative self-esteem. People develop ideas of being good or bad, lovable or unlovable, and smart or stupid. These ideas and images are developed as individuals interact with significant people. According to Lackovic-Grgin and Dekovic (1990), the term " 'significant others' refers to persons who occupy high rank on an 'importance' continuum and whose opinions are considered meaningful" (p. 839).

How we view ourselves is not exactly the same as our self-esteem. We can define self-esteem as being the "content" of our view of our self, that is, the perceptions and opinions we hold about ourselves. The positive or negative attitudes and values by which we view ourselves, along with our evaluations or judgments about these attitudes and values, form our self-esteem. Thus, self-esteem is the content of our evaluations or judgments about our attitudes and beliefs that we bring with us as we face the world. It includes our beliefs as to whether we can expect success or failure, how much effort we think we should put forth, whether or not we will feel hurt if we fail a task, or whether we will become more capable as a result of difficult experiences. Nozick (1974) believed that self-esteem is a commodity that is not and cannot be equally distributed throughout the population. He believed that self-esteem is essentially a comparative: We evaluate how well we do something by comparing our attitudes about our performance to others and to what others can do. Therefore, we can say that self-esteem provides a mental set that prepares us to respond according to expectations of success, acceptance, and personal strength.

Self-esteem is a vital part of the helping relationship for both the helper and the helpee. Helpers who feel good about themselves and their abilities function more successfully in their role. Therefore, developing a positive self-esteem in helpers will greatly affect how they interact with their helpees, as well as how they will encourage helpees to grow. Although self-esteem refers to the evaluation an individual makes and customarily maintains with regard to her- or himself, it certainly affects others. Self-esteem expresses an attitude of approval or disapproval and is an indication of the extent to which a person believes her- or himself to be capable, successful, significant, and worthy.

In summary, people's self-esteem is a judgment of worthiness that is expressed by the attitudes and feelings they hold toward themselves. It is a subjective experience conveyed to others by verbal reports and other overt expressive behaviors. A positive self-esteem on the part of the helper will therefore have a positive effect on the helpee, while a negative self-esteem will have an adverse effect. A teacher's self-esteem has a similar influence on the students in the classroom.

Because attitudes and judgments about one's self may be either conscious or unconscious, people are not always aware of their impact upon others. Thus, helpers may not be aware of their attitudes toward themselves and how they are impacting their helpees. Therefore, analysis of their own self-esteem is essential before helpers can truly be effective with others.

The following questionnaire was developed to help people understand themselves better. Below is a list of statements about your feelings and beliefs about yourself. If the statement describes how you <u>most often feel</u>, put an X in the column "Like Me." If a statement does not describe how you <u>most often feel</u>, put an X in the column "Unlike Me." There are no right or wrong answers. Mark all of the statements.

Like Me	Unlike Me	How I most often feel:
____	____	1. People I live with understand me.
____	____	2. I'm a lot of fun to be with.
____	____	3. Things are all mixed up in my life.
____	____	4. I'm not as good-looking as most people are.
____	____	5. I get discouraged with the things I am doing.
____	____	6. I do not allow others to dominate me.
____	____	7. I easily get upset at work.
____	____	8. I do not allow others to hurt me or put me down.
____	____	9. I wish I were another person.
____	____	10. Most people are better liked than I am.
____	____	11. Things usually don't bother or upset me.
____	____	12. The people I live with usually are considerate of my feelings.

Like Me	Unlike Me	How I most often feel:
____	____	13. It is difficult to be me.
____	____	14. I often feel upset with situations at home.
____	____	15. It is very difficult for me to talk in front of a group.
____	____	16. I do not take responsibility for my feelings and emotions; I often blame others when I get upset or angry.
____	____	17. I am responsible for changing what I don't like in my life.
____	____	18. People most often follow my ideas.
____	____	19. I can't be depended upon.
____	____	20. There are a lot of things about me that I'd like to change.
____	____	21. It takes me a long time to become comfortable with anything new.
____	____	22. I make up my mind without too much trouble.
____	____	23. I have a low opinion of myself.
____	____	24. I give in too easily.
____	____	25. If I have something to say, I most often say it.

Scoring

A. Score the following items one point if they have been answered "Unlike Me."

3 ____   8 ____   15 ____   23 ____
4 ____   9 ____   16 ____   24 ____
5 ____   10 ____ 19 ____
6 ____   13 ____ 20 ____
7 ____   14 ____ 21 ____

Total ____

B. Score the following items one point if they have been answered "Like Me."

1 ____   17 ____
2 ____   18 ____
11 ____ 22 ____
12 ____ 25 ____

Total ____

C. Total the scores from "Unlike Me" and "Like Me" and multiply by 4.

Example: "Unlike Me" = 15 points   21 total points
          "Like Me"   = 6 points   ×4
                       21 total points   84 raw score

Caution is exercised when interpreting any raw score. However, we may say that a raw score of 50 to about 75 could describe people who feel good about themselves, while a raw score of about 76 to 100 most probably describes people who are very confident in themselves and feel especially good about themselves and what they do.

A raw score of 25 to 49 may describe people who have a number of negative feelings and beliefs about themselves and would benefit greatly from concentrating on developing a more positive self-esteem. A score of 0–24 would describe people who need a considerable amount of work on their attitudes, beliefs, and feelings toward themselves and how they interact with others.

It is beneficial for Helping Professionals to take the inventory and to analyze their responses. The next step is to decide on any areas that they will need to concentrate on to enhance their own self-esteem.

A mentor teacher in one of our workshops examined her responses and shared these insights with us.

Mary is a 29-year-old mentor teacher in a middle school in an urban community. She learned that her needs were mainly in the area of personal appearance. She marked items 4, 9, 10, 20, and 23 "Like Me." After gaining insights into these areas, she planned specifically how she would change her beliefs and attitudes about herself, and how she would develop a personal plan to improve her physical appearance (diet and exercise). She believed that these changes would help her feel more positive about herself, and she realized how these areas affected her interactions with others. Mary expressed these feelings to the support group at a future meeting: "I now feel a little more confident in myself and believe I can accomplish my goals."

Developing a personal plan helped guide Mary in a positive direction, as well as helped her to feel empowered. Sharing her personal plan with a "buddy" was also beneficial, because she needed encouragement and support during the time she was changing old behaviors. Evaluating her attitudes about herself and working on feeling more capable, worthy, and significant regarding her personal appearance all had positive effects on Mary's self-esteem. As she became more successful in these areas, she was better prepared for helping others gain awareness about their own self-esteem and for helping them learn new methods to enhance attitudes and beliefs about themselves.

Believing ourselves to be capable, successful, significant, and worthy is essential for developing a positive self-esteem. As Helping Professionals gain insights into their own beliefs and feelings toward themselves, they can improve their mental set, which in turn prepares them to respond in a more positive and encouraging manner toward others. Therefore, self-esteem issues are a vital part of the helping relationship.

Developing Empathy: A Feeling of Oneness

Sensitivity is a crucial part of any helping relationship, and it is an essential characteristic of Helping Professionals. Caring individuals desire to demonstrate sensitivity to other people, and they are genuinely interested in how others perceive themselves and their experiences. When an individual is sensitive to how another person perceives the world, it provides valuable information for understanding the other person and for offering help. Helping Professionals need accurate perceptions of the ways in which the other person is thinking, feeling, and perceiving her- or himself and the world if they are to be understanding and to be of assistance. This way of relating was defined by Berger (1987) as the technical meaning of empathy. He described it as "the capacity to experientially comprehend the thoughts and feelings of the patient" (p. 16). Thus, it is essential that Helping Professionals continually grow in their sensitivity toward others. This is especially true when they are interacting with individuals who feel threatened when they are offered suggestions for improvement. It takes more time and encouragement to develop rapport with these types of personalities.

Sensitive people are aware that how another person perceives situations and events creates a reality for that person. It then is more difficult for understanding to occur when the perceptions of the other person are contrary to their own, as is evident in the following example.

> Andrea, a teacher in one of our support seminars, discussed a problem she was having with her principal. She described how her principal wanted her to change her methods for disciplining the students. The principal said that Andrea was too critical and that she should use more positive support statements and eliminate the negative ones. One of the men in the group, Bob, spoke up and said that the principal was right and teachers shouldn't use negative statements when disciplining students. Andrea immediately withdrew emotionally and became very quiet. Her nonverbal communication reflected her hurt and anger. The group leader stated, "Andrea, you expressed that your methods of discipline are familiar to you and you felt your principal was not accepting you nor your methods of disciplining your class." Andrea immediately looked up, smiled, and said, "Yes, I need her to understand my methods of disciplining rather than saying I have to change." The Helping Professional asked Andrea to tell the group what she needed from her principal. After this discussion, communication skills were practiced that included examples of feedback techniques. The purpose of using the skills was so that the group would become more comfortable with ways they could communicate with their principals and other teachers when there was a difference in perceptions of situations. After the practice session in which feedback skills were used, Bob looked over at Andrea and said, "I feel like I didn't try to understand you and how you felt about your situation. I was quick to judge you and to support your principal because I agreed with her. I owe you an apology." This was one of those special moments in support groups. A new bond developed between Andrea and Bob. This carried over into future sessions, in which there were more demonstrations of sensitivity and concern for each other.

This is a good example of an individual (Bob) who is focused on how situations look to him rather then on how things look to the other person (Andrea) and demonstrates an ineffective method of interacting with another person.

Book's method of testing whether or not a helper is effective when giving empathic responses was reviewed by Raines (1990). Book suggested that the extent to which the response stimulates and deepens the flow of a helpee's message will be demonstrated through the helpee's behavior. She or he will "look away, stop talking, or change the topic" when the empathetic response is incorrect in its timing or administration (p. 68). Sensitivity toward another is essential, and many counselors and therapists rank empathy as the first quality for effective helping relationships.

Empathy is a deep and subjective understanding of one person about another. It is personal identification with another individual without losing separateness of one's own identity. For these reasons, Helping Professionals especially need accurate conceptions of the ways they think, feel, and perceive themselves and their world if they are to truly understand and assist others. If helpers are unaware of their own feelings, thoughts, and perceptions, it is doubtful they will be sensitive toward others. Without a high level of understanding about oneself and a genuine desire to understand the other person, there is no real basis for helping. Therefore, according to Carkhuff and Anthony (1991), empathy is a key ingredient in any helping relationship.

When Helping Professionals demonstrate empathy, they are letting the helpees know that their feelings and content are important and that they are of value. This facilitates self-exploration. Kalliopuska (1986) expressed it well by saying that "for a flashing moment, one experiences the life and experiential world from another's viewpoint" (p. 14). Even though acceptance of feelings and content is essential, the integrity of the support person is a vital aspect of the relationship because trust and integrity go hand in hand. Without trust there will be little or no self-disclosure.

It is essential that Helping Professionals examine their behavior and assess whether they are demonstrating empathy to the helpee. The purpose of examining one's role is not to look at techniques being used, but to assess one's ability to demonstrate empathy and to model authenticity. This was reported in a study by Godley, Wilson, and Klug (1986) in which mentors listed empathy as one of the important aspects of their role with beginning teachers.

The following list provides guidance in the process of assessing one's ability to use empathy with others.

Helpers Demonstrate Empathy When They:

1. Concentrate intensely on both the verbal and the nonverbal communication of the other person
2. Respond to feelings and content
3. Use the language of the helpee
4. Use voice tone congruent with the helpee
5. Are active in the process
6. Are a positive model

7. Help the other individual understand
8. Adjust when necessary
9. Value and believe in the other
10. Are nonevaluative
11. Encourage the other person's free expression
12. Are genuine and spontaneous
13. Focus on the needs of the other
14. Demonstrate respect and problem solving
15. Look for surface and underlying feelings
16. Use content to complement and add deeper meaning to the communication

Using the list as a guide to grow and to develop in their own responding with empathy has been very helpful for mentors in our workshops and seminars. Reviewing the list before conferencing with a helpee can assist helpers in focusing on key areas that are needed in the session. Reviewing the list as a means of self-evaluation after the conference will aid Helping Professionals in becoming more aware of areas that they need to work on to help others and to enhance themselves. This fits very well into the conferencing issues discussed in Chapter 13, on guidance and support dimension.

It is also important that Helping Professionals receive empathy from other helpers. We find that many Helping Professionals need someone who will listen to them and offer them support. One of the ways to meet this need is through the use of support groups composed of Helping Professionals. These support groups are formed specifically for the purpose of working on self-enhancement areas. Under the guidance of an experienced leader, discussions will be growth-producing and highly rewarding.

Meeting Personal and Psychological Needs: The Foundation for Helping

Identifying personal and psychological needs as well as learning coping strategies for meeting one's needs were discussed in Chapter 4. A quick review of that information will be beneficial at this point to reacquaint you with these important domains.

The focus of this chapter is on how Helping Professionals can meet their own needs and in turn assist others. It has been accepted in the field of mental health that Helping Professionals must become well acquainted with their own needs and that they must develop coping strategies for handling difficulties before they are competent in assisting others. Many university programs in psychology and counseling include the requirement that students in training have their own psychotherapy prior to working with others. These university programs recognize that it is essential for Helping Professionals to know their own needs and to practice healthy coping strategies so as not to have any dysfunctional perceptions and behaviors that would be projected onto those with whom they work.

Identifying your needs and practicing healthy coping strategies will enable you to lead a healthier and more rewarding life—a rather significant benefit! Reviewing your responses to the inventories in the needs chapters (Chapters 4 and 5), and evaluating how you have been working on meeting them is essential for your continued growth. We often hear from individuals in the therapy room and from people in workshops and seminars that they do not have enough time to spend on their own needs. They often list all of the demands in their life and they share that there is little time left for them. This comment is characteristic of individuals in the helping professions, and it is one of the major reasons for burnout, which we will discuss in detail in another chapter.

An example of someone who experienced this growth process illustrates the concept. Tom is a Helping Professional in a high school located in a metropolitan area. He joined our support group because he felt he might need to stop helping others. Tom said that when he got home at night he had little energy or desire to spend time with his family (two small children and a wife). He found himself withdrawing from others and going to bed early. After a few months, Tom's wife asked him to seek help from a counselor or someone who could advise him as to what was happening to him. Tom heard about our support group from another teacher and came to the next meeting.

During one of our sessions on meeting the needs of the helper, Tom shared that he could identify with the statement that helpers often postpone their own immediate needs for fulfillment. He discovered that he had been gaining a great deal of personal enjoyment in helping other teachers until this year. For the past 9 months he had been helping a teacher who was especially needy. Tom had been staying late most evenings and listening to the teacher discuss personal problems. At first Tom experienced a great deal of personal satisfaction from listening to her and encouraging her. However, over the past few months he felt inadequate in helping her resolve the conflicts in her personal life. Tom also became aware that he was postponing his own immediate needs for relaxation and companionship with his family. This neglect resulted in fatigue and negative feelings toward himself. Tom began to realize that he was attempting to help the teacher in an area in which he was not qualified, and he had been unable to accept this fact. This was an important insight for Tom. He is now learning how to help others in areas in which he is qualified, and he is also learning to set limits with his time.

Helpers do not have to be perfect and help others solve all of their problems. What they do need is an accurate, realistic view of themselves, their assets, and their limitations. Effective helpers do not attempt to exceed their areas and levels of competence. Tom had been trying to help in an area where he lacked the necessary skills. He was not accepting his limitations. Because of his new insights, Tom recommended that the teacher he had been trying to help get assistance from a trained counselor who could help her in her personal relationships. Tom took the needs inventories in Chapter 4 and assessed his own needs. At the last support meeting, he reported that identification of unmet needs helped him isolate the problem behavior. He indicated having a much healthier relationship with his family.

Changing oneself includes gaining knowledge and acquiring feedback from others. People discover who they are as they receive feedback from their interactions with others and through the exploration of their personal meanings. Examining your needs and how you feel about yourself, working to meet your needs, and acquiring new coping strategies are all essential parts of the growth process.

It is important to remember that self-examination in and of itself is of limited value. Our self-concept cannot be changed by simply deciding to be different or deciding to concentrate on certain behaviors. We discover who we are from the feedback we receive in our interactions with others and from what we choose to do with this information. Tom found this to be true as his wife gave him feedback about his behavior at home and the support group gave him feedback about his feelings and ideas. As Tom analyzed the needs in his life that were not being met (insight from the inventories), discussed his ideas with others, gained new insights, thought about what he values and cares about, and acted in new ways toward others, he began to feel better about himself. Tom is gaining a clearer understanding of himself, his talents, and his limitations, and he is learning to be more consistent in all of these. He is discovering a unity and harmony that exist in his own feelings and thoughts, rather than trying to be someone he thinks he should be. Tom is learning to be comfortable with himself. He is gradually and sometimes painfully exploring himself and learning who he truly is. He is discovering new insights through his relationship with his wife and through the encouragement and safety of the support group.

Strategies for Self-Realization

In order to change, we first must be motivated to examine our life, to honestly take a look at ourselves, and we must have a strong desire to mature and grow. When we add to this initial step an atmosphere that is free for exploring and one in which we feel safe, we can go deeper into this journey. Helping Professionals and support groups are essential at this stage of development. To be accepted for who we are and to be encouraged to explore areas in our life that we have the power to change will significantly enhance our growth. In this type of atmosphere we can explore our thoughts and feelings and allow ourselves the freedom to let go of masks or facades that we have developed.

Statements from a helper in one of our support groups who had been involved in 4 months of personal exploration revealed the struggles of getting to know herself better.

> *As I look at myself now, I realize I was peeling off layer after layer of defenses that I'd built up over 35 years. I didn't know how far I had to go, I just knew I had to get to the "real me." At times I was afraid to find out; however, I had to keep trying. At first I was afraid the group would criticize me for my defenses, like needing to help others in order to feel important and powerful. Soon I learned that others in the group had similar kinds of feelings. I began to see how all of us were beginning to explore our experiences and to examine our contradictions. I learned that I lived my life by what I*

thought should be, and by what others thought about me. I had to have others think I was important to feel good about myself. I now realize the deepest responsibility I have in life is to get to know me and to be who I am. A new pattern of living is emerging for me as I discover what I want and what I have to contribute. I feel very fortunate to be part of a group of people who want to drop defensive masks and discover and experience our hidden parts. I am growing in trusting myself and others. I can accept the fearsome responsibility of being a unique individual, and I am learning to accept others. I know I have so much more to give to myself and to other people. I no longer need to help others to feel "important" or "powerful." These are very freeing feelings and insights. I know that I am now in the process of growing healthier.

It may be that this individual has taken her growth process more intensely than many Helping Professionals may wish to. The important fact is that she wanted to, and she is. The decision is always within each of us. However, learning to identify our needs and working to meet them can be motivated by healthy or selfish interests. When we concentrate on our own growth so that we may enjoy our own life and contribute to the growth in others, we know we are making healthy choices. When people desire to meet their own needs and they care little about other people or how they affect others, the motivation is a selfish one and does not lead to healthy growth.

Growth refers to personal development in a desired direction. A person is considered to show growth when she or he becomes more competent, capable, creative, productive, insightful, understanding, knowledgeable, prudent, and/or discerning. However, what we consider to be growth for one individual may not be the same for another, and we need to be careful not to evaluate one another. Each of us possesses certain capabilities that we develop as we mature and grow. However, we can never really know our own growth capacities until we test them. As we become open to new experiences and expand our ideas, we open ourselves to growth. We can more fully obtain this growth as we interact with others who confirm our progress, encourage us, and even challenge us to be more than we are or think we can be. This is one of the main reasons why Helping Professionals need to interact with others who can encourage and nurture them.

Growth Assessment Tools

Practically speaking, assessing your own personal growth can provide insights into your own needs. One means of engaging in this assessment is to answer the following statements and questions and discuss them with other Helping Professionals. You may choose to take one item at a time and explore it in depth, rather than concentrating on too many items in one group session.

Personal Discovery

1. To what extent are you growing and realizing your potential?
2. Recall an experience in your life when you felt creative and growing.
3. In what ways have you changed in the past few years? Explain whether these changes are toward positive growth or not.

4. What kind of future personal growth would you consider desirable in yourself?

Small Group Interaction

1. All members in the group take turns enumerating their personal strengths as they see them. Members of the group orally respond to what the person has said and add any other strengths they know in the person. Share insights rather than offering advice.
2. All group members share what prevents them from fully developing their strengths. Group members discuss ways an individual may overcome barriers in life.
3. All members share a time in their life when they made rapid progress in some area. They also share the impact on their life now.

Growth has always been fascinating to most people. It is letting go of experiencing something that is known and then reorganizing it and developing it in new ways that are often not familiar. We may not always be aware of the changes taking place in us at the time we are reorganizing thoughts and behaviors. This time of reorganization can be frustrating and frightening, as was described in Chapter 3 on change. Thus, support is essential. When we help each other we aid and confirm one another's growth.

Characteristics of a Mature Helping Professional

Most individuals enter programs for the helping professions with high motivation and a quest for knowledge. These are important strengths to bring to the role of helper. However, they are only part of what a professional helper needs. Whatever knowledge an individual possesses, and whatever method she or he uses must be well understood and deeply personal so the quality of belief is felt by the helpee. A clear understanding of one's values and beliefs with true conviction in living them earns respect from others.

We reviewed characteristics of the Helping Professional in Chapter 2. In addition to those, examining the following profile of an effective helper will be of assistance in evaluating your own values and beliefs in relation to self-enhancement.

Mature Helping Professionals Demonstrate:

1. A clear understanding of their beliefs and values and behaviors that are consistent with them
2. A strong commitment to self to maintain honesty and integrity
3. An understanding that information affects behavior in direct proportion to its personal meaning for each individual
4. That learning is facilitated by challenge and can be thwarted by threat
5. Knowledge of the concept that the greater the meaning of an event to the individuals involved, the stronger the emotions experienced
6. That learning is a social activity that is deeply affected by feelings of belonging

7. An understanding that learning is most effective when accompanied by feedback that is enhancing and meaningful
8. That personal meaning is best learned and accepted through situations that can be problem-solved such as seeking appropriate resolutions, questions, and events, as well as confronting dilemmas
9. A commitment to group support to enhance personal growth
10. Understanding that helping relationships often require helpers to postpone their own immediate needs for fulfillment
11. Acquiring self-discipline through continued understanding of their thoughts and actions
12. Acceptance that helpers do not have to be perfect, and what is essential is an accurate, realistic view of themselves, their assets, and their limitations
13. A variety of methods and strategies to adapt to many different types of helpees
14. Acceptance that effective helpers are human beings, that they experience problems and frustrations like all people, and they work to sufficiently resolve their own problems so as not to interfere in their helping others
15. A broad understanding of different styles of practice; an understanding of the practical principles that underly practice; and an appreciation of the moral, political, and theoretical issues underlying educational practice (Maynard & Furlong, 1994)
16. Growth in cognitive complexity and development through their interactions with others
17. A continued reflection on their beliefs and practice, and a desire for personal growth

One of the cautions that must be considered after reading a list of this type is not to feel overly discouraged. Many inexperienced helpers assume that they must demonstrate all of the characteristics listed or they fall short of being successful. To assume that helpers must be superior people who demonstrate extraordinary character at all times is unrealistic.

We all have problems, frustrations, and failures. An effective helper does not live a life free of problems. The important consideration is that helpers sufficiently resolve their problems so they don't interfere with helping others. Growth is a continuous process, and learning how to handle personal problems can result in new insights and understanding.

Continuing to remind oneself of the difference between personal self and professional role is essential. Our personal selves consist of our personal belief system, our ways of viewing ourselves, and feedback from our interactions with others and our world. Our professional roles define our responsibilities and our appropriate ways of behaving toward others in professional settings. Even though these roles are related to each other, they are not identical. We must be authentic in our professional role, but this role does not have to carry over into our private life. In our personal life we can live the philosophy of being helpful to others.

We can apply our values and beliefs to our entire life, yet we are not Helping Professionals to the people with whom we live. In fact, a note of caution is in order: Our personal relationships will become contaminated if we try to apply our professional helping role to them. Helping a person who has not asked for assistance most always communicates a lack of acceptance of the individual and robs the relationship of choices and of the necessary comfortableness. The intense concentration of effort that takes place when we help another person can become exhausting. Also, the rigorous self-discipline necessary to help others requires a certain amount of self-denial. This is why the helper must take time away from the Helping Professional role. It is important to remember that the most effective helpers do not work at their professional roles all of the time.

Finally, growing entails being open to our experiences and to other people. When we function effectively in the world, our concepts are confirmed and we feel good about ourselves and others. When we meet impasses and failure in the pursuit of our goals, our habits, concepts, and expectations are challenged. As we face these challenges and incorporate new ideas and new experiences, we grow. We all have choices at these times. We can emerge from difficulties and challenges as stronger and wiser individuals who are better able to handle the next set of difficulties and are better prepared to assist others who are facing their own times of adversity. These experiences and choices all design our "profile of self."

Adding to Our Life Plan: Self-Enhancement

Now that you have a clearer understanding of the importance of working on personal fulfillment for a healthier life, it is necessary that you apply what you have learned in the chapter to the life plan you began in Chapters 4 and 5. Adding a section to your plan will assist you in continuing your growth and in developing your own personal profile. The addition to your plan may read as in Table 7-1.

Select examples from the various concepts presented in the chapter that you feel are important for you to work on. Remember to record the date and the concept. When you know you have accomplished some growth, be certain to take time to record the date and your accomplishments as soon as you become aware of them. The sample profile in Table 7-2 was shared at a support meeting

Keep your Self-Enhancement Profile in mind as you interact each day, and record your specific insights as soon as you have time. You will discover a great deal about yourself and your growth, and you will also nurture your self-esteem. We believe one of the most exciting and rewarding experiences in life is that of helping others grow. This is especially true when the growth is in familiar areas in which we ourselves have met challenges in our lives and have matured through

TABLE 7-1 Self-Enhancement Profile

Date	Concept to Work On	Accomplishments	Date

TABLE 7-2 Self-Enhancement Profile

Date	Concept to work on	Accomplishments	Date
4/16	Recognize and acknowledge my abilities, evaluate how I am using them both personally and professionally.	I recognized that I am an excellent listener. I am able to truly focus on another and listen to both their content and feelings. The other person feels accepted and cared for. I like this about me.	5/10
4/30	Helpers are not perfect people and are always in search of growth.	I learned that I want to be perfect to avoid criticism from others. If I'm going to really grow, I need to begin to admit areas in my life where I am not perfect. This is frightening right now for me, but I'll try.	5/20

them. This type of assistance can be exciting and fulfilling for you. To not take time for personal growth is to deny your right as an individual to grow and to mature. A resistant attitude toward self-growth also will hinder one's effectiveness as a helper.

Summary

In summary, self-enhancement of the Helping Professional is an essential part of the preparation and the continuing career of any helper. Learning how to grow and mature, as well as actively seeking one's own enhancement, is critical to the effectiveness of all helpers. Learning to value oneself, concentrating on one's self-esteem, and interacting with other professionals who are actively involved in their own growth make for an exciting journey and will encourage the Helping Professional toward a healthier and more rewarding life.

References

Berger, D. M. (1987). *Clinical empathy*. Northvale, NJ: Aronson.

Braucht, S., & Weime, B. (1992). The school counselor as consultant on self-esteem: An example. *Elementary School Guidance and Counseling, 26*(3), 229–236.

Carkhuff, R. R., & Anthony, W. A. (1991). *The skills of helping*. Amherst, MA: Human Resource Development.

Dewhurst, D. W. (1991). Should teachers enhance their pupils' self-esteem? *Journal of Moral Education, 20*(1), 3–11.

Godley, L. B., Wilson, D. R., & Klug, B. J. (1986, February). The teacher consultant role: Impact on the profession. Paper presented at the annual meeting of the American Association of Colleges for Teacher Education. Chicago.

Kalliopuska, M. (1986). Empathy, its measurement and application. *British Journal of Projective Psychology, 31*(2), 10–18.

Lackovic-Grgin, K., & Dekovic, M. (1990). The contribution of significant others to adolescents' self-esteem. *Adolescence, 25*(100), 839–846.

Maynard, T., & Furlong, J. (1994). Learning to teach and models of mentoring. In D. McIntyre, H. Hagger, & M. Wilkin (Eds.), *Mentoring: Perspectives on school-based teacher education.* London: Kogan Page.

Nozick, R. (1974). *Anarchy, state and utopia.* Oxford, England: Blackwell.

Raines, J. C. (1990). Empathy in clinical social work. *Clinical Social Work Journal, 18*(1), 57–72.

Chapter 8

Interpersonal Effectiveness — Helping Strategies (Dimension Two)

> *A friend is one
> to whom one may pour
> out all the contents
> of one's heart,
> chaff and grain together
> knowing that the
> gentlest of hands
> will take and sift it,
> keep what is worth keeping
> and with a breath of kindness
> blow the rest away.*
> — ARABIAN PROVERB

Most people in education would agree that effective, rewarding teaching is dependent upon teachers having a reasonably positive self-esteem, adequate academic preparation, a sense of community, a desire to help students, decision-making ability, teaching skills, and a commitment to their own personal and professional growth.

In the past, professional growth for teachers has largely been left to principals and lead teachers. To assist teachers, workshops and professional development programs have been planned to address their instructional needs and in some instances their areas of special interest. Many principals and lead teachers have had special training to develop helping strategies that assist them in working with others. Some, however, are expected to help colleagues while having little or no specialized training in the area of helping.

Helping strategies are necessary to assist teachers' instructional and personal growth. In our work with mentors and supervisors we consistently find an eagerness and excitement as they approach the learning of helping strategies. They often ask us how they can acquire additional skills for helping. These helpers are extremely receptive to the information and enthusiastically practice the skills provided.

The personal development of teachers, in comparison with the instructional development, has been greatly neglected. As was noted earlier in the book, most educators have had little preparation in helping others with their personal-psychological needs, and this area has been left to counselors and ministers. This is unfortunate because there is a great deal that educators can do to help teachers in their personal-psychological development, as we have described throughout the book. We find that teachers, mentors, and administrators demonstrate great curiosity about personal-psychological growth. What is lacking is not interest, but rather the specific knowledge and skills to provide psychological support. The feedback we receive from those who have learned to help teachers with their personal needs is extremely gratifying.

The focus of this chapter is on how Helping Professionals can: (1) examine interpersonal support and develop positive relationships characterized by rapport and trust, (2) evaluate specific types of helping strategies that are effective in working with others, (3) acquire insights through group processes, (4) understand diversity, and (5) examine accountability for themselves and other Helping Professionals.

Interpersonal Support

Interpersonal relationships can be one of life's greatest rewards. When people are asked, "What would you say makes your life meaningful," the answer is usually friends, siblings, spouse, children, and valued colleagues. For most people their primary sources of happiness are the people they love and their feelings of being loved and valued by others who are important to them. When most people stop and think about what makes them the happiest, their response most often is, "My valued relationships."

Our personal relationships help to shape our lives and to give life meaning. We are influenced by our meaningful personal relationships and somewhat by our friendships. We benefit from successful relationships and we grow and mature through the encouragement and guidance from people we respect. Our psychological health depends on our ability to build and maintain interdependent, cooperative relationships with others. The supportive relationships in our life help us to reduce our psychological distress and to cope more effectively with stressful situations. We develop more resilience to handle problems in life, and we become more self-reliant through the encouragement and support given by others. Paradoxically, through healthy relationships we learn how to become more autonomous, and we are better able to internalize the love, support, and acceptance people offer us. Johnson stated it well when he said, "It is within our most meaningful relationships that we autonomously live in the present to actualize the person we have the potential to be" (1993, p. 11).

We all need other people to interact with and to give us feedback. Our relationships are essential to our forming an identity, finding meaning in our lives, coping with adversity, achieving success in our profession, maintaining psychological and physical health, and developing our potential. To not have significant others in our lives leaves us feeling lonely and unfulfilled. Thus, it is essential that we form caring and committed relationships.

Learning how to connect with others can be difficult for some individuals. Interpersonal skills are needed in order to develop and keep positive relationships. They also are essential for developing rapport, trust, and confidentiality. Helping Professionals who understand the essential elements of a relationship and have developed their own effective interpersonal relationships are more successful in guiding and assisting others who have not developed these skills.

Developing and Maintaining Positive Relationships

The effectiveness of our behavior depends to a great extent on how aware we are of ourselves, of other people, and of what others need. Being effective also depends on our being able to evaluate the consequences of our behavior and to assess how well our actions match our intentions.

Our interaction with others arouses their impressions and observations. We also stimulate ideas and trigger certain feelings and behaviors within other people. Our effectiveness, when we interact with others, depends to a great extent on our feelings of security and self-confidence, as well as on our ability to develop rapport and communicate clearly the messages we wish to convey.

Developing Rapport

Relationships begin when one person chooses to reach out to another. To accomplish this, we must have a desire to meet the other person and be willing to be open and accepting of the other individual. We do this through sharing common interests, goals, values, and activities. Another aspect of sharing with others is the willingness to disclose parts of ourselves. This self-disclosure is most often cautious in the beginning until we learn whether the other individual is also willing to be open with us. This initial stage of the relationship is always the most vulnerable part because trust and rapport have not been developed. Helping Professionals need to understand this initial stage of a relationship and handle it slowly and carefully as trust and rapport are developed. Rapport must be established so that the two individuals feel comfortable with one another and feel that they have enough common elements in the relationship to move into another stage of development.

When two people have developed rapport, they begin to explore other areas of common interest. The Helping Professional can initiate this through self-disclosure in safe areas of interest to both parties, such as sharing experiences they have had in working with students. Self-disclosure in a professional relationship does not mean revealing intimate details of one's life. Self-disclosure is effective when it helps the other person get to know and understand you through sharing experiences in which you both have a common interest. However, self-disclosure does carry an element of risk. Knowing too much about another person's personal issues may detract from the professional relationship. Sharing areas of one's professional life that will assist another in gaining insights into his or her own situation can be beneficial. When a helpee learns how a more experienced person handled a situation, it can help to build rapport and eventually a bond of trust between the two people.

An example of healthy disclosure took place between Joan, the Helping Professional, and Leslie, the beginning teacher. Leslie was experiencing anxiety over her difficulty managing her sixth-grade students. Joan had been offering support and encouragement along with some strategies for class management. One day Leslie broke down and cried and said she just couldn't get it together for herself. She just couldn't be like the other beginning teachers in her school who were more confident and successful with discipline. Joan sensed the importance of sharing herself with Leslie at this stage of their relationship. She told Leslie how she felt as a beginning teacher.

> *I lacked confidence in my ability to handle all of my students. I wanted each of them to behave and follow my directions. I just couldn't get some of them to try. I would go home at night and feel exhausted. I would often cry myself to sleep. Other teachers talked about their great lessons and how much fun they were having. I felt like a failure. One evening when I felt I just couldn't go back the next day, I got a phone call from a friend who was teaching in another state. We talked a long time and she told me she had problems too. However, she concentrated on the students who would follow directions and she enjoyed her interactions with them. I thought about this for a long time. I realized that I was permitting those three or four students to rob me from enjoying all of the others. The next day I tried very hard to refocus my attention and thinking from the negative students to the ones who were willing to learn and enjoy my lessons. In time, I could laugh more and have fun with my class. I still tried to reach the difficult students, but I didn't allow them to take all of my time and energy.*

Leslie shared that she had no idea that Joan had ever struggled with discipline problems. She said that she felt encouraged and would practice focusing on the positive and try not to think about the negative so much of the time. This is an example of how effective self-disclosure can be when one person shares an experience common to the other so that she can gain insights into herself and her situation.

If we are to build meaningful relationships, we must disclose parts of ourselves to another. However, there is always an element of risk that the other person may choose to reject us rather than accept us. Experienced Helping Professionals will carefully select areas of their life to share that are both professional and growth-producing for others. Without risk, trust cannot be established and relationships remain at a very low level of functioning. Self-disclosure must be relevant to the relationship as well as appropriate to the situation in which we are developing the relationship.

Building Trust

Another essential area in building a relationship is that of trust. Getting to know another person and encouraging the person to know you involves trusting each other to interact in ways that do not hurt one another. Trust is essential if relationships are to grow and develop. A climate of trust must reduce each person's fears of betrayal and rejection as well as promote the hope of acceptance, understanding, and support. Also, trust is constantly changing. Everything people do in a relationship either increases or decreases the trust level they have developed. Trust is difficult to build and easy to destroy. Once it has been destroyed, it takes years to develop a new trust, and one destructive act can destroy it again.

Trust is difficult to define. One of the more useful explanations was proposed by Deutsch (1962) and includes the following elements:

- You are in a situation in which a choice to trust another person can lead to either beneficial or harmful consequences for your needs and goals. Thus, you realize there is a risk involved in trusting.
- You realize that whether beneficial consequences or harmful consequences result depends on the actions of another person.
- You expect to suffer more if the harmful consequences result than you will gain if the beneficial consequences result.
- You feel relatively confident that the other person will behave in such a way that the beneficial consequences will result.

Even though there are risks in trusting, most people find that the majority of their relationships are worth the risks they have taken. Unfortunately, trust is not something that, once built, is forever there. The level of trust in any relationship continually changes as individuals are willing to trust and to be trusted. We are always vulnerable when we allow ourselves to trust another because we risk being hurt. When we risk sharing ourselves in a group, we risk the possibility of having the group laugh at us or criticize us. We feel good when people appreciate our ideas, and we usually feel hurt when they reject us. Therefore, acceptance is most often the first condition we are looking for in a relationship. When we feel accepted by others we are usually willing to disclose more of ourselves. What is needed, then, is a willingness to trust and a commitment from ourselves to be trustworthy in our relationships with others.

Helping Professionals can encourage helpees by accepting their disclosures as they also demonstrate a willingness to trust. This is especially important when the Helping Professionals do not agree with everything the helpees are communicating. We can express different ideas and opposing points of view at the same time that we are accepting the other persons and providing support for them.

To understand better how trust can be maintained, it also is important to be aware of behaviors that will damage it. Some of these destructive behaviors are rejection, ridicule, betrayal, or disrespect in responding to a person's openness. Laughing at people, moralizing about their behavior, or evaluating them are all forms of rejection that destroy some form of trust in the relationship.

Another negative behavior is refusing to reciprocate to the other person's openness. People will not trust the person who is closed when they are open, because conversely they feel vulnerable. Refusing to share feelings, thoughts, and reactions with others decreases the level of trust that has developed.

Helping Professionals need to be aware of and avoid these negative behaviors. As we noted, once trust is broken, it is extremely difficult to develop again because distrust is highly resistant to change. The other person is most often fearful that betrayal will occur again. When trust has been broken, it is essential that it be reestablished. The following principles have proven to be beneficial for reestablishing trust: (1) Explore the factor(s) contributing to loss of trust; (2) work to establish new goals in the relationship that are highly attractive to the other person, and ones they are extremely motivated to work on; (3) openly and consistently discuss fears and concerns of each person; (4) reestablish trust by being certain all actions on the part of the one who broke the trust are consistent with his or her word; (5) be consistently trustworthy in your interactions; (6) seek to understand the other person's feelings and perceptions immediately and sincerely whenever you see signs of doubt; (7) apologize immediately when you have said or done something to cause the other person pain or mistrust; and (8) evaluate your own motives and behaviors to see that you are consistent in your thoughts and actions not only when you are with the other person, but also when you are away from him or her.

Evaluate Your Integrity

The following exercise will be insightful as you examine your trustworthiness. Respond to each statement as objectively as you can, answering the question "To what extent is this true of me?" It is most helpful to write your response because this will help you think through your own beliefs and actions.

1. I take risks and express my ideas and feelings with another.
2. I accept and support other people who take risks and who share their thoughts and feelings.
3. I am highly supportive of other people who have difficulty expressing their ideas and emotions.
4. I feel strongly that trust is essential for any relationship.
5. I firmly believe that consistency between my words and behaviors determines whether other people will learn to trust me and continue to do so.
6. If I did something to break trust with another person, I would do all I could to regain his or her confidence in me.

After you have responded to each of the statements, meet in groups of three or four and share something that you learned about yourself. Also share what you learned about the importance of trust in a relationship. You may want to review the previous section on building trust.

Helping Strategies: Essential Tools for Groups

Many people enjoy and prefer relationships in which there are only two people interacting. They find these experiences safe and also believe they meet many of their needs for intimacy. There are other people who prefer groups for receiving guidance and support. Both types of interacting can be helpful and growth-producing because each has different purposes and functions. An examination of specific components that contribute to the success of support groups will be examined first, and a discussion regarding working with individuals will follow.

There are a number of strategies that Helping Professionals can use in assisting others to gain insight into their problems, sharing information about specific topics, offering support, promoting helpees' growth, developing rapport and trust, and learning and practicing new coping skills. A number of strategies will be described in view of their effectiveness in working with others in groups

Elements for Group Success

As we learned in Chapter 3, changing oneself is a complicated process that takes place through numerous interactions that must be guided rather than left to occur at random. Being able to identify and analyze elements that enhance the success of the group process will contribute to a higher rate of success. There are numerous components involved in working with groups. We have selected for analysis the elements that we find are essential:

1. Commonality
2. Commitment and trust
3. Group cohesiveness
4. Genuine caring for others
5. Sharing information and insights
6. Catharsis
7. Modeling
8. Offering hope
9. Gaining insight
10. Developing communication skills
11. Dealing with diversity

Most of these elements will be examined separately even though they are interdependent and do not function in isolation. (Developing communication skills is covered thoroughly in the next chapter and will not be examined here.) Each of the elements will have varying degrees of usefulness for different individuals depending to a great extent on where they are in the change process.

Commonality

Every group needs to have something in common for the members to be motivated to be part of the group. People usually join a group because they have needs, interests, and purposes similar to those of other individuals in the group. This is evident in weight loss groups, those that are working on controlling an addiction, religious groups, and many others.

Teachers are a group of individuals who have many common interests and needs. Subject matter groups, beginning teacher groups, and mentor teacher groups, to name a few, are becoming common. One area of need that has been slow to develop is that of forming groups to meet teachers' personal and professional needs (Gold & Roth, 1993). Helping Professionals can make a tremendous contribution in this neglected area by forming groups to help teachers grow and mature both personally and professionally.

Commitment and Trust

The most essential ingredient in making any group successful is that of commitment. If an individual is to stay with a group and develop healthier skills in life, whether these skills are personal or professional, the person must be committed to the program. Learning about oneself can be highly threatening, and some people who fear risking will drop out. Being willing to look at oneself and being open to growth are essential and involve courage and commitment. A person who lacks commitment seldom will be successful in staying with the group.

Helping Professionals will need to discuss the importance of members making a commitment to the group and to the group meetings. Committed members who are willing to work on themselves and to work with others in the group through regular attendance and sharing of feelings and ideas will be rewarded through their growth and the growth of others.

Another critical element is that of developing trust within the group. This chapter has already discussed the importance of trust and the consequences of trust that has been broken.

Developing Group Cohesiveness

It is essential that a feeling of unity (cohesiveness) among group members emerges during the first few meetings. The members who develop cohesiveness will value the group more highly and be more interested in the welfare of the group. This is important if trust and commitment are to be developed. Cohesiveness is not always consistent, nor is it continuously held by the group even after it has been established. In fact, it fluctuates the entire time the group is together.

It is especially important for the Helping Professional to focus on developing group cohesiveness early in the formation of the group. When this takes place, there will be greater levels of self-disclosure among the members, and the relationships will be more satisfying. Other related outcomes are that attendance will be more consistent, the interactions of group members will be of a higher level, and there will be more follow-through.

Genuine Caring for Others

Developing an atmosphere of acceptance is a major ingredient for helping people change. When individuals feel accepted, the feeling of threat is reduced and self-exploration is greater. Helping Professionals who demonstrate sensitivity toward others will create a climate in which people feel accepted and cared for.

Relationships begin with someone initiating some type of social interaction. Each person perceives what the other person is doing and decides how to respond. The Helping Professional can facilitate this process so that it will be successful by initially selecting topics that are nonthreatening to group members. As the Helping Professional models genuine caring for each person in the group, an atmosphere of acceptance will more easily be developed.

Relationships are the key to our development socially and cognitively. They help us form our own identity and find meaning in our lives. An example of this occurred during a support group meeting of teachers. We had met for six sessions of 2 hours each. The facilitator asked, "What are you most afraid of?" The group members individually listed their fears. Then they shared their fears with a partner. After sharing with a partner, as a group we listed the fears on a chart titled "Our Greatest Fears." Individuals were asked to volunteer anything they wanted to share. A number of teachers responded. Some of their responses were: "I'm afraid I will die alone," "I'm afraid I won't get married and have children," "I'm afraid I will fall out of love with my wife," and "I'm afraid I'll spend all of my time working and I won't have time to develop a lasting relationship." A discussion followed in which they talked about what they could do to handle the fears and to make necessary changes in their life. When an atmosphere of genuine caring is established, people feel free to explore themselves and to look at areas that are most fearful for them. They also are more willing to begin to make necessary changes in their life, as these teachers did. Some of the teachers are taking time to develop new relationships, and a few are beginning to share what is important to them. Others are looking at their defense mechanisms and learning how their fears keep them from trying new experiences.

The Helping Professional can be a guide who develops an atmosphere of caring in which teachers are willing to look at their greatest needs and then begin to change areas of their lives that need changing. This type of growth is rewarding for the members and for the Helping Professional.

Sharing Information

When trust and rapport are established in a group, people are more willing to share complex areas of their lives. When group members offer support, reassurance, and information that leads to insights, people begin to feel that they can handle their problems and that they can change. The important consideration here is that the Helping Professional must guide the group toward problem solving rather than just an airing of individual problems.

When teachers in the group begin to problem-solve specific areas of their life that need attention, growth will begin to take place. The Helping Professional needs to guide them through this type of process. Problem solving is encouraged; advice giving is discouraged. Communication techniques for listening and validating (discussed in Chapter 9) are especially important here.

Catharsis: A Therapeutic Process

We have found that catharsis plays an important part in the therapeutic process. When group members have established cohesiveness and commitment along with a bond of trust, catharsis can be most helpful. When individuals feel free to express their hurt feelings and negative thoughts, catharsis takes place. As they are able to explore their areas of concern and release their negative feelings, they move forward in their growth process.

Catharsis is especially important as people are going through change. They need to express their fears and concerns in order to deal with them. Being able to share negative feelings can help people acquire understanding of the problems they are facing. They then can venture forward into new, uncharted areas of their personal and professional life.

Modeling: A Most Helpful Technique

Teachers look up to people they admire and wish to be like. We often hear teachers comment that they wish they could be like their Helping Professional. This is extremely important if growth is to take place. Bandura's research, discussed in Chapter 3, supports this type of thinking.

Modeling ourselves after individuals who demonstrate characteristics we wish to develop in ourselves is a powerful tool for change. Helping Professionals can play a significant part in this process by themselves being models who are trustworthy, caring individuals.

Offering Hope to Others

If groups are to be successful, members must feel that they can develop enough hope in themselves as a result of their interactions with members in the group to solve the problems in their life. A teacher in one of our support groups stated that she felt encouraged when other members shared their own difficulties as first-year teachers. She said, "I don't feel all alone now. I hear that others have the same kinds of problems. I feel encouraged—there is hope for me." She felt accepted and cared for by the group, which helped her gain the strength in herself to try new ways of interacting with her students.

Helping Professionals can play a major part in guiding group members toward encouraging one another and looking for areas of similarity when they are discussing major issues. Most people feel a connection with others who have similar kinds of problems. When groups problem-solve issues together, and when they look for possible solutions, individuals within the group feel genuinely accepted and cared for. All of these factors contribute toward people feeling a greater sense of hope. Most often, hope is developed or even renewed when these types of interactions take place.

Gaining Insight

Often, when we are struggling with problems and issues in our life, we find it difficult to grasp the important aspects of the situation. We are too involved with just trying to survive the situation and are unable to focus on new insights that could be learned. It usually is during a discussion with others who listen to and affirm us that we gain some of our most helpful insights.

These new learnings help us to become motivated to read and acquire new understandings that will then clarify what we were trying to resolve. New realizations take place. We begin to recognize what had been missing in our thinking and what had hindered us from solving the problem. These new insights help us to more effectively problem-solve the situation.

We often are blocked in our understanding of how to work through a personal issue. Our defense mechanisms frequently will keep us from seeing new and creative ways to solve the situation. Discussing the problem with others who offer support and feedback, without giving advice, can help us gain knowledge about the issue and can lead to acquiring new ideas that can be applied to solving the problem.

When we are aware of the importance of gaining insights into our problems, we are more motivated to seek help and to try new ideas and methods. We have found the following steps to be very helpful for groups and for individuals in learning to gain insights into issues they want to resolve. Discussing them in your support groups will prove to be beneficial.

Steps to Acquire Insights through Group Processes

1. Clearly identify the problem/issue.
2. Seek information about the problem/issue.
3. Discuss the problem with others in your support group.
4. Be open to new ideas and concepts.
5. Verbalize the insights you are gaining.
6. Identify what you will do as you apply the new insights and the new knowledge you have gained.
7. Make a verbal commitment to the group about what you will work on.
8. Begin to change what you have the power to change.
9. Report your progress to the group for accountability and renewed commitment.

Understanding Diversity

Interacting effectively with other individuals necessitates having knowledge about people from different cultures, ethnic groups, social classes, historical backgrounds, special needs, et cetera. If we are to interact successfully with others, we need to first accept ourselves and be interested in building relationships with diverse peers. As we interact with people, we need to be open and willing to clarify misunderstandings, to define mutual goals, and to work together cooperatively. Support groups are an excellent resource for learning about ourselves and other people.

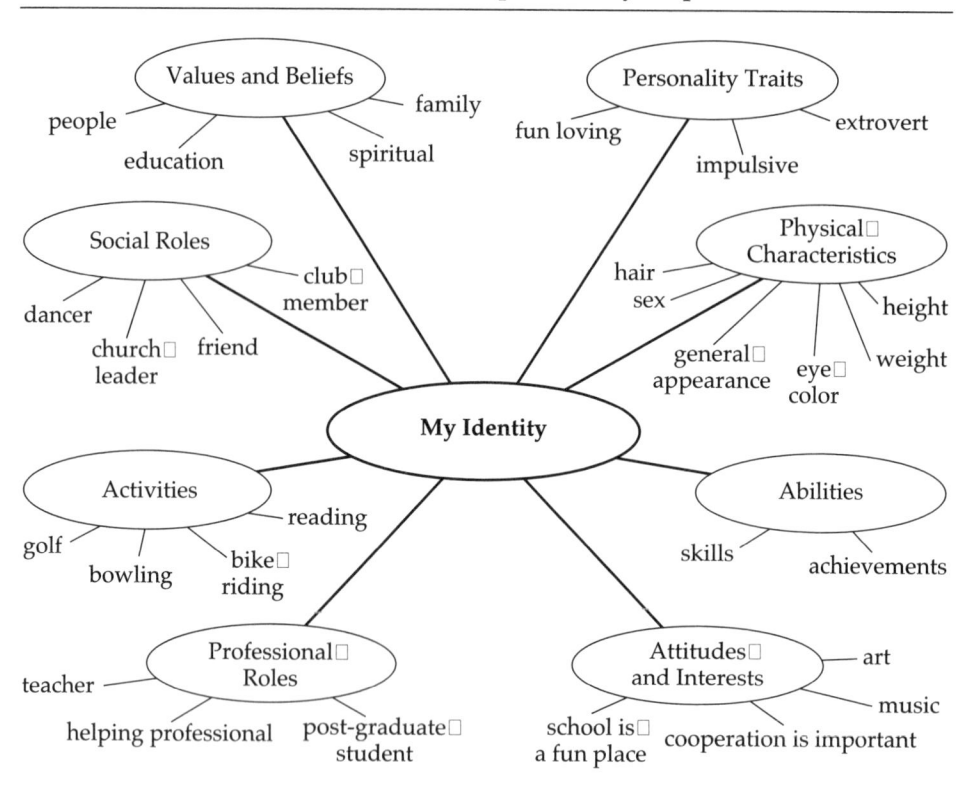

FIGURE 8-1 Sample Identity Map

Identity map showing "My Identity" at center, connected to: Values and Beliefs (people, education, spiritual, family); Personality Traits (fun loving, impulsive, extrovert); Social Roles (dancer, church leader, friend, club member); Physical Characteristics (hair, sex, general appearance, eye color, weight, height); Activities (golf, bowling, bike riding, reading); Abilities (skills, achievements); Professional Roles (teacher, helping professional, post-graduate student); Attitudes and Interests (school is a fun place, cooperation is important, art, music).

Before we can successfully appreciate others, we must first appreciate ourselves for who we are and accept the unique kind of person we are. The more we accept ourselves, the more secure and integrated we will become. We need to view ourselves as unique individuals, separate and autonomous from others. As we grow in our own understanding of ourselves, we are better prepared to develop constructive relationships with diverse peers.

Our identity is a consistent set of attitudes that define who we are. We may call this identity a self-schema that involves the total of who we are today, made up from all of our past experiences. We all have multiple identities and multiple schemas that include our physical characteristics, our social roles, the many activities we participate in, our attitudes and interests, our abilities, and our general personality traits. Our ethnic identity is our sense of belonging to one particular ethnic group, and our gender identity is our fundamental sense of our femaleness or maleness. Our identity also is made up of the parts that we would like to be, or even imagine ourselves to be. We have both positive and negative views of our self-schemas.

We have designed an exercise to help people become better acquainted with their identity. First, brainstorm all of your different schemas (values and beliefs, personality traits, etc.) as "mapped" in Figure 8.1. You will need to change the items under each schema to specifically describe you (e.g., under Personality Traits change "fun loving," "impulsive," "extrovert" to words that specifically describe you). You may add more if you want to. This creates your own "identity map."

It is helpful to have all in the group do their own identity map and then share what they feel comfortable discussing with others. After the group members have shared their identity maps, make a group identity map, to which everyone contributes, and observe how the people in the group are similar and how they are different. With this type of information we can become more aware of ourselves and of others and learn to appreciate one another. We can learn to value and respect fundamental differences among people.

Groups can be highly rewarding for everyone involved, and a great deal of change can take place in individuals as a result of group support and the many individual insights that are shared. There are specific goals and activities that need to be established with groups to derive maximum benefit. We will examine reasons for using groups for growth, and will look at specific types of activities to use that will encourage individual insights.

Working with Groups

The popularity of structured exercises used in groups began in the 1950s during the T or Training Group movement (Yalom, 1985). Several authors have recommended the use of exercises in a group setting to stimulate discussion, insight, and awareness (Corey, 1982; Dyer & Vriend, 1980). Jacobs, Harvill, and Masson (1988) cite a number of reasons for using structured exercises in groups:

1. To generate discussion and participation
2. To get the group focused on a common topic or issue
3. To shift or deepen the focus
4. To provide an opportunity for experiential learning
5. To provide the leader with useful information
6. To increase the comfort level
7. To provide fun and relaxation

Structured exercises are usually carried out with the entire group in order to accomplish one or more of these specific purposes. The group leader usually selects, introduces, and conducts the exercise and then closes by having members discuss what was learned or gained as a result of the exercise. This final step is essential in helping individuals evaluate their own growth.

A number of group exercises have been published. (A useful source is Johnson and Johnson, 1994.) Each group leader will need to evaluate them as to their value for the group with which she or he is working. Some guidelines for selection of activities are (Kees & Jacobs, 1990):

1. Make certain the exercise meets the needs of the group.
2. Check on the amount of time needed for the exercise so as to adapt it to meet the goals and objectives for the session.
3. Evaluate the purpose of the activity and determine whether it is primarily educational, for discussion, to accomplish a task, for support, for personal growth, or some combination of these.
4. Formulate your questions in connection with your purpose. Questions need to be written out.
5. Write out the desired outcomes.
6. Examine the time frame and the size of the group.

Other important considerations for the group leader are thinking through the trust level of the group at the time the exercise is to be used, the ability level of the group, and the communication skills of the members.

The group leader is the key to the success of any exercise. All leaders must evaluate their own skills and level of experience when selecting any exercise. We have found structured exercises to be highly effective in working with groups, and we encourage Helping Professionals to develop their own collection of activities that fit their purposes and personality.

The Helping Professional: Personal Qualities

One of the rewarding aspects of offering support to others is that of observing their growth and their acquisition of new coping strategies to enhance their life. Assisting Helping Professionals to develop additional effective support skills is one goal of this text. High-functioning Helping Professionals are able to integrate and synthesize large amounts of data. They are able to differentiate between relevant and irrelevant factors while interacting with teachers, are independent and competent, are less influenced by external cues that would distract them, are objective and flexible in their thinking, and hold themselves accountable. They demonstrate empathic understanding with a wide variety of personalities with whom they work.

Qualities that have been identified throughout the text as essential for helpers are: (1) the ability to be a good listener, (2) the ability to express themselves effectively in words, (3) demonstrating understanding and support, (4) being warm, and (5) being objective (Patten & Walker, 1990). Other helper characteristics that affect the nature of the relationship are: (1) awareness of self and values, (2) awareness of culture and experiences, and (3) a strong sense of ethics and responsibility (Brammer & Macdonald, 1996). Helpers also use a wide variety of skills such as nonverbal communication, questioning, reflecting, listening, self-disclosure, reinforcement, opening, and closing. Personal characteristics of Helping Professionals must also include integrity, honesty, and the potential to develop high levels of trust with others. Helpees must feel that the interaction between themselves and the helper is confidential. "Confidentiality is both an ethical and legal issue" (Parsons, 1995, p. 197). Being able to maintain confidentiality requires professional judgment.

It is important for helpers to gain feedback about their interacting with others. Support groups made up of Helping Professionals provide an opportunity for continued professional and personal growth. These types of groups may be the only available avenue for feedback on helping performance (Cloud, 1986; Greenburg, Lewis, & Johnson, 1985; Remley, Benshoff, & Mowbray, 1987).

Support groups for Helping Professionals can be most successful when specific guidelines are followed. This is necessary in order to prevent peers from becoming overly supportive or from offering advice. The following guidelines have been found to be most helpful for these peer groups: (1) All group members need to be involved; (2) all members need help in giving focused, objective feedback; (3) all members need to give particular attention to the feedback they are receiving; (4) all groups need to be adaptable for both novice and/or experienced helpers; (5) all groups need to provide an approach that helpers can internalize for self-monitoring; and (6) all members must be held accountable for their actions.

Critical to the success of any support group is the ability of participants to give honest and constructive feedback. In this type of environment helpers can become aware of their own "blind spots" and they can discuss ways to overcome them. Usually small groups of three to six members and one lead helper are most productive. Monthly meetings from 1 to 2 hours are sufficient to accomplish the established goal or goals.

Support groups for Helping Professionals are essential sources for growth throughout their professional years. Insights learned through interactions with colleagues contribute to personal and professional development, thus making the helpers more effective in their interpersonal relationships.

Summary

The chapter has focused on helping strategies and the effectiveness of the Helping Professional. Interpersonal support for Helping Professionals is a key area of the chapter because it is essential to the effectiveness of every helper. Also, the important role of group support was examined. Rapport, empathy, and trust are critical aspects of all relationships and were discussed along with activities to assist in evaluating one's effectiveness in these areas. A final area of consideration is that of the personal qualities and accountability of the Helping Professional.

Relationships can be a blessing or a curse. However, every relationship mirrors a great deal about ourselves. As the Arabian proverb at the beginning of the chapter stated, "The gentlest of hands will take and sift it, keep what is worth keeping and with a breath of kindness blow the rest away."

References

Brammer, L. M., & Macdonald, G. (1996). *The helping relationship*. Boston: Allyn and Bacon.

Cloud, J. (1986). Supervision for the counselor in private practice. *Michigan Journal of Counseling and Development, 17*(2), 37–40.

Corey, G. (1982). *Theory and practice of counseling and psychotherapy*. Monterey, CA: Brooks/Cole.

Deutsch, M. (1970). Trust, trustworthiness, and the F scale. In K. J. Gergen & D. Marlowe (Eds.), *Personality and social behavior*. Menlo Park, CA: Addison-Wesley.

Dyer, W., & Vriend, J. (1980). *Group counseling for personal mastery*. New York: Sovereign Books.

Gold, Y., & Roth, R. A. (1993). *Teachers managing stress and preventing burnout: The professional health solution*. Washington, DC: Falmer Press.

Greenburg, S. L., Lewis, G. J., & Johnson, M. (1985). Peer consultation groups for private practitioners. *Professional Psychology: Research and Practice, 16*(3), 437–447.

Jacobs, E., Harvill, R., & Masson, R. (1988). *Group counseling: Strategies and skills*. Monterey, CA: Brooks/Cole.

Johnson, D. W. (1993). *Reading out*. Boston: Allyn and Bacon.

Johnson, D. W., & Johnson, F. P. (1994). *Joining together*. Boston: Allyn and Bacon.

Kees, N. L., & Jacobs, E. (1990). Conducting more effective groups: How to select and process group exercises. *The Journal for Specialists in Group Work, 15*(1), 21–29.

Patten, M. I., & Walker, L. G. (1990). Marriage guidance counselling: What clients think will help. *British Journal of Guidance and Counselling, 18*(1), 28–39.

Parsons, R. D. (1995). *The skills of helping*. Boston: Allyn and Bacon.

Remley, T. P., Jr., Benshoff, J. M., & Mowbray, C. A. (1987). A proposed model for peer supervision. *Counselor Education and Supervision, 27*(1), 53–60.

Yalom, I. (1985). *The theory and practice of group psychotherapy* (3d ed.). New York: Basic Books.

Related Readings

Brammer, L. M. (1993). *The helping relationship: Process and skills* (5th ed.). Boston: Allyn and Bacon.

Burn, D. (1992). Ethical implications in cross-cultural counseling and training. *Journal of Counseling and Development, 70*, 578–583.

Corey, G., Corey, M., & Callanan, P. (1988). *Issues and ethics in the helping professions* (3d ed.). Monterey, CA: Brooks/Cole.

Cormier, W. H., & Cormier, L. S. (1991). *Interviewing strategies for helpers* (3d ed.). Monterey, CA: Brooks/Cole.

Egan, G. (1990). *The skilled helper* (4th ed.). Monterey, CA: Brooks/Cole.

Goodlad, J. (1990). *The moral dimensions of teaching*. San Francisco: Jossey-Bass.

Kanfer, F., & Goldstein, A. (1986). *Helping people change* (3d ed.). New York: Pergamon Press.

Karoly, P., & Kanfer, F. H. (1982). *Self-management and behavior change*. New York: Pergamon Press.

Locke, D. C. (1992). *Increasing multicultural understanding: A comprehensive model. Multicultural Aspects of Counseling Series 1*. Newbury Park, CA: Sage.

Parsons, R., & Wicks, R. (1994). *Counseling strategies and intervention techniques for the human services*. Boston: Allyn and Bacon.

Chapter 9

Interpersonal Skills and Communication

The role of the Helping Professional cannot be performed effectively without significant expertise in communication skills. The Helping Professional interacts with the teacher in the continual processes of assessing, diagnosing, guiding, and supporting. It is essential, therefore, that the Helping Professional be aware of communication styles and conditions that must be present in order to achieve the desired results with the teacher being helped.

Application and Scope

Awareness of appropriate communication style and characteristics, such as warmth and rapport, is necessary but not sufficient. Awareness and understanding must be extended to practical application. For this reason, our focus here will be on identification of specific skills and interpersonal processes that the Helping Professional needs to make operational. The Helping Professional must learn and practice the skills in order to be able to use them in actual settings.

The traditional approach to supervision places great emphasis on conferencing skills for technical assistance with instruction. Models addressing mentoring also place considerable emphasis on this particular area. The Helping Professional, however, has a broader scope of vision addressing all needs of the teacher to provide a more balanced and comprehensive system of support. In the Transformational Helping Professional model, the role is expanded to deal with the personal-psychological as well as the instructional-professional needs of individuals that were discussed in Chapters 4 and 5. The emphasis is on a variety of areas of teacher growth, including promoting reflection, enhancing cognitive complexity, gaining personal insights, and meeting particular needs.

Skills and Artistry

In order to achieve the desired growth outcomes, communication skills are used, not in isolation, but rather in combinations that frame the style and approach to a particular situation with a given individual. Communication in helping, as in teaching, supervision, and mentoring, is a process that requires both skills and artistry. Although we identify a number of specific skills in this chapter, we must emphasize that the real effectiveness of these skills is when the Helping Professional weaves them together artistically. This requires understanding the individual, reading the situation, and having a clear idea of the purpose or objectives of the interaction.

Objectives of Communication

In functioning as a Helping Professional, one strives for several key conditions. Two of the major objectives in exercising communication skills are to establish rapport and trust, which were discussed in the previous chapter. Helping Professionals cannot be optimally effective unless they are able to establish these conditions in their relationship with the person being assisted. Communication that is open and honest and actions that are congruent with the communication contribute to the establishment of a condition of trust.

Another goal of communication skills is to enhance the teacher's self-esteem. Self-esteem is related to each of the domains of the Helping Professional model, instructional-professional and personal-psychological. Meaningful communication can contribute in many ways to the establishment or the reinforcement of the teacher's self-esteem.

The area of collegiality is also important in helping relationships. Communication with respect, being nonevaluative, and possessing effective communication strategies contribute to this important condition.

Because the Transformational Helping Professional model emphasizes teacher thought processes, communication skills also are used to engage teachers in reflection on and analysis of their own thinking and teaching. An essential element of the process of conferencing with teachers is to assist them in reflecting on practice, increasing their cognitive complexity, and thinking through much of what they do as part of professional practice.

It should be noted that communication skills are strongly linked to and embedded in helping skills. Communication is part of the helping skills strategies, described in the previous chapter. Our focus here will be on selected communication skills of particular relevance to assessing, diagnosing, guiding, and supporting.

Approaches and Strategies

The strategies, behaviors, and skills of Helping Professionals have been viewed from varied perspectives and organized in several ways. Analysis of their specific responsibilities provides for the identification of three levels or ways of describing the approaches and competencies of Helping Professionals. These are: (1) the style or general approach, (2) the conditions that are to be created or characteristics demonstrated by the Helping Professional, and (3) the specific processes or behaviors of the Helping Professional.

Professional Styles

An early example of supervisory styles is that of Blumberg (1980). His classification of styles includes the following: (1) high-direct, high-indirect—the supervisor tells and criticizes and also asks and listens; (2) high-direct, low-indirect—the supervisor tells and criticizes more than asking and listening; (3) low-direct, high-indirect—the supervisor rarely uses direct methods such as telling or criticizing and gives significant emphasis to listening and reflecting the teacher's ideas; and (4) low-direct, low-indirect—the supervisor is passive, with few discernible behaviors.

Mosher and Purpel (1972) refer to a counseling style that is focused on ego development. It consists of phases such as analysis, synthesis, and action. This is a client-centered style. Glickman, Gordon, and Ross-Gordon (1995) refer to styles as clusters of behaviors, as follows: nondirective, collaborative, directive-informational, and directive-controlling. We will review these styles in more detail in Chapter 14.

This first level of description provides a general overview of one's approach as a Helping Professional. It is general in nature and sets the tone for the kinds of skills that may be needed.

Conditions and Characteristics

A second level to be considered is the type of conditions that should exist or be created by the Helping Professional, or characteristics that should be demonstrated. Most of the texts on mentoring, supervising, or helping identify a variety of conditions for which one should strive as a Helping Professional. The noted psychologist Carl Rogers, for example, described three conditions that provide for quality in the interpersonal relationship. These include congruence (the sense of genuineness felt by and displayed by the Helping Professional), empathy (sensing the other person's personal meanings), and unconditional positive regard (respect for the other person; accepting the person, but not necessarily approving all that the person does) (Rogers, 1962).

Shostrum (1967) identified the following characteristics: warm, sensitive, dependent, supportive, controlling, critical, strong, and aggressive. Obviously, one may link the conditions or characteristics to the varied styles. For example, an indirect style would be more warm and supportive, whereas a more direct style would be controlling and directing.

Processes and Behaviors

The third category is the processes or process behaviors in which the Helping Professional engages. These provide information about what one does in order to establish the conditions that are congruent with a particular style. These are descriptions of categories of behavior that guide the Helping Professional as to the tone, demeanor, and types of specific skills that may be used.

Various models incorporate a variety of these types of process behaviors. One of the earlier approaches was described by Carkhuff (1980), who identified the following helping behaviors: attending, responding, personalizing, initiating, and helping. Later Burke (1984) identified three such categories: attending, responding, and facilitating. More recently, Glickman, Gordon, and Ross-Gordon (1995) provide the following: listening, clarifying, encouraging, reflecting, presenting, problem-solving, negotiating, directing, standardizing, and reinforcing. In relation to the styles, Blumberg (1980) associated some of these process behaviors with his direct and indirect styles. For example, direct categories include process behaviors such as criticizing, giving opinions, telling, or suggesting. Indirect behaviors include accepting, clarifying, praising, and discussing feelings.

These categories of behaviors provide an excellent framework for defining the communication function of the Helping Professional. They provide insight into effective styles, conditions, and behavioral processes. Helping Professionals may work their way through these levels and find congruent strands. As an example, one may select the indirect style or nondirective approach and identify the preferred conditions, such as sincerity, warmth, and support. A subsequent step is to identify the groups of behaviors that would be consistent with those approaches, such as clarifying, supporting, encouraging, etcetera, versus directing, lecturing, controlling, or criticizing. It may be necessary to adapt one's style depending on the state or needs of the individual being helped.

Acquiring the Strategies

The essential question then becomes: "How does one specifically make operational a particular style, set of characteristics, and process behaviors?" Knowing what one's objectives are does not translate directly into being able to know how to achieve them. One may approach it intuitively, based on expertise and experience accumulated through the years.

What we will discuss here is how one can specifically address particular behaviors. For example, if you wish to be nondirective and encouraging, or if you wish to achieve congruence through attending, what are the specific skills you can use to effectively implement this into the interpersonal interactions in the helping situation? We will describe here the specific skills and provide examples of their use. It again is important to recognize that these are not implemented in isolation.

We suggest that Helping Professionals will need to follow three steps in order to utilize skills effectively. First, they will need to think about their philosophical approach to helping, the intended style, and the desired characteristics. This provides the rationale and forms a part of the Helping Professionals' philosophy of approach to assisting, guiding, and supporting.

It is then necessary to identify specific skills that fit into a matrix of behaviors that emanate from the desired style. Having a repertoire of skills at one's disposal, one can respond to a given situation in terms of particular needs of the individual and context. This again is where the artistic element enters into the process.

In addition, knowledge of these skills is necessary but not sufficient. Acquisition of skills takes practice, particularly with feedback. This is the third step. There are a variety of ways that the Helping Professional can practice these skills. You might first try these on your own, practicing in the privacy of your office or home. Some individuals like to tape themselves while practicing. In reviewing the playback, determine the degree of proficiency with the skill, as well as related aspects such as tone of voice, emphasis, and the general feeling conveyed.

Practicing with others, of course, is more productive. One means is to select a particular skill for a period of time, perhaps 1 week, and to consciously use that skill whenever the situation presents itself. This process moves from skill to skill until several skills have been acquired. Subsequently these skills can be integrated in appropriate situations as part of one's practice.

A more structured approach is to practice these skills in training sessions in which there is a sender, receiver, and observer. The receiver and observer, or receiver alone, can give feedback as to how well the skills are being implemented. An essential point here is that it takes practice to actually acquire skills at a highly proficient level.

Essential to skill development is practice, particularly with feedback. A variety of ways of practicing skills have been described. Develop your personal plan for enhancing skill acquisition and refinement. Describe the specific activities in which you will engage, identify frequency and length of practice, and specify others who might work with you. Discuss class activities that might be conducted to provide practice.

An example is as follows:

Skill	*Activity*	*Frequency/Length*	*Others*
Listening	Identify two or three elements of effective listening (e.g., pause before responding, acknowledging, paraphrasing)	Each listening opportunity; 2 weeks (or until a habit)	School administrator (check with and support each other); ask teachers for feedback

Specific Communication Skills

There is a wide range and large number of specific communication skills that can be identified and developed. Our discussion will be limited to those that are particularly relevant to the helping process. The skills addressed are listening, nonverbal communication, questioning, paraphrasing and acknowledgment, and validating.

In order to select the most appropriate skills and provide insights as to how they can be used, they have been placed into categories that reflect the responsibilities and functions of the Helping Professional. The six categories are (1) interactive attending, (2) reflecting understanding, (3) validating, (4) facilitating, (5) clarifying, and (6) promoting reflection.

Interactive attending skills consist of active listening, responding, and nonverbal attentiveness. Types of listening and responding are identified within this category.

Reflecting understanding includes the skill of paraphrasing. A variety of types of paraphrasing are included.

The third category is that of validating. The purpose of this skill is to establish rapport. It includes the skill of using specific types of support statements. Also involved are the specific skills of verifying, confirming, recognizing, or acknowledging. Interpretive paraphrasing also is used here.

Facilitating is another category of skills that the Helping Professional needs to use frequently. Its purpose is to facilitate learning, harmony, growth, or change. This includes the use of appropriate questioning strategies and support statements. It avoids the use of negative statements. Facilitating involves questions that support thinking, assist in gaining personal insight, and illuminates the teacher's instructional practice. Use of support statements for validation and feedback are elements of facilitating.

Category 5 is that of clarifying. This includes the use of paraphrase and clarifying questions.

Promoting reflection (Category 6) is the process of helping the teacher to think through the instructional process. This includes open-ended questions, reflective verbs, and other types of questioning strategies. The processes of the six categories are composites of skills. In general, these skills involve listening, communicating nonverbally, questioning, paraphrasing, and validating.

The Helper As Listener

A common perception of the role of the Helping Professional is that it involves conveying information, advising, encouraging, questioning, and in other ways directing communication toward assisting the teacher. Perhaps the most critical skill in the area of communication is that of receiving rather than sending. This is the act of listening.

One of the essential points about listening is that it is an active as well as passive process. Focusing, clearing your input channels, making a conscious effort to be receptive, and processing the meaning of the speaker's communication are important ways of attending. In addition, there are the behavioral aspects of listening, which are important to recognize, understand, and use effectively.

Much of the literature refers to "active listening." The active listener engages in behaviors that reflect participation in the communication process and receiving the message, particularly through nonverbal communication. The most effective listening, however, goes beyond this. This has led to the development of the term "interactive listening" (Gold & Roth, 1993). In effect, this suggests that listening is truly interacting with the other person, rather than just receiving the message. Active listening involves participation with body and head movements, such as moving forward and nodding acknowledgment. Interactive means that the receiver not only takes in the information, but also responds in order to reflect understanding, encourage the speaker, clarify communication, probe, or interpret. The various types of behaviors that are involved in the full interactive listening will be described in the following paragraphs. The sum total of these behaviors constitute active-interactive listening.

Listening Attitudes
Perhaps the most difficult part of listening is trying to pay attention. The difficulty with paying attention can be countered with two strategies. The most obvious one is to remind yourself during the listening process that you are to fully and intently concentrate. You need to catch yourself drifting or engaging in one of the distracting behaviors or mental processes that interfere with proper receiving.

A second strategy to enhance focusing is perhaps the most important. It involves approaching the listening situation with a positive attitude about receiving the other person's message. It is the willingness to cast aside preconceived notions, one's own needs (such as conveying one's own message in response), and emotional factors (yours or those conveyed by the other person) that could interfere with the listening process.

Focus of Listening
Another component in the mix of listening variables is our own filters. We bring with us to communication our values, interests, beliefs, and attitudes toward issues, people, and situations. These screen out, filter, or modify the messages we receive. Messages are filtered through these perceptual screens and are thus altered in some way.

One of the ways to deal with filters is to be aware of them. The more that Helping Professionals can recognize their own filters and those of others and be aware of them prior to a listening encounter, as well as during the encounter, the better they will be able to receive an unbiased, objective message. This does not mean, however, that in all instances we discount the context, person, or situation.

One of the implications of listening filters is that they guide the areas in which we will focus our attention during the listening process. As an example, researchers into this phenomenon have determined that we have different content orientations in our listening habits. One set of studies revealed that we may be either people-oriented listeners, action-oriented listeners, content-oriented listeners, or time-oriented listeners (Watson & Barker, 1995).

How can you determine your listening style? The simplest way is to just think about the kinds of things that interest you. Another quick guide is to recognize that listening with an emphasis on the relationship is more people-oriented. When the emphasis is less on listening and more toward actions or getting the task done, it is action-oriented. A more comprehensive mode is to use Watson and Barker's instrument, The Listening Styles Profile (1995).

Another strategy is to adapt your listening style to the needs of the situation. What you are focusing on in the interaction may depend upon the individual, the situation in which you find yourself, or an understanding of the needs that the other person (teacher) is trying to communicate.

Verbal Component of Listening

The nonverbal signals one sends during the listening interaction create an active listening approach. This can be extended through certain verbal strategies as well, which creates an interactive listening process. As you use the verbal interactive strategies, note the response that you get from the speaker. If he or she makes some sort of positive acknowledgment, then, of course, your strategies may be working.

One of the functions of the verbal strategies is clarification. Clarification may be achieved through asking questions, requesting clarification from the speaker, or restating the speaker's message in your own way (paraphrasing). Requesting clarification can take many forms, such as asking that the speaker define a term or make a statement in another way, or conveying to the speaker your interpretation of the message in order to check for understanding.

Using questions is another way to enhance understanding of the message in the listening process. Questions may be used to request the speaker to clarify or expand upon comments. They may be used to help separate the content and feeling part of the message. For example, the listener might ask, "How did you feel about that incident?" This encourages the speaker to expand, as well as to identify the emotional part of the message.

An important part of the listening function is to offer encouragement to the speaker to continue or expand by noting that you are attentive and the message is being received. There are several short, quick statements that can be used for this purpose, such as "Interesting," "Really," "Tell me more," "Go on," and "How?"

Summary of Listening Skills

The following listening strategies and skills can guide your professional development in listening:

1. Approach with a positive listening attitude.
2. Be interactive.
3. Understand why you are there to listen.
4. Know your listening style(s).
5. Maintain concentration, avoid mind wandering, and diminish effects of distractions.
6. Identify both content and feeling of the message.
7. Seek clarification when necessary.
8. Use verbal and nonverbal interactive skills.
9. Keep an open mind; avoid letting your knowledge of the speaker filter or bias the message you receive.
10. Encourage the speaker with feedback and cues.
11. Avoid being distracted by the speaker's delivery, such as a style contrary to yours.
12. Use silence and give attention to timing and duration of silence.

13. Pause before responding.
14. Share your understanding of the speaker's message (paraphrase, summarize).
15. Strive to continually improve your listening: Analyze it, request feedback, seek new skills, practice changing poor habits, and acquire new ones.

Practicing these skills will enhance a helper's effectiveness.

Listening Exercise
Arrange the class or group in pairs, facing each other. Person A may talk about anything, personal or professional (but not lewd or offensive). Person B is to totally ignore A, making no eye contact—not even looking at A. Person B may look in other directions, doodle, fidget, and so on, but remain seated across from A. Continue this for about 2 minutes. Stop, but say nothing about the experience. Reverse roles for another 2 minutes.

Discuss how each of you felt or what went through your mind as the speaker. What effect would these feelings have on the helping relationship? What does the listener's behavior say about how the listener values each individual? What could a helper do to improve listening skills? Discuss what was going on in the listener's mind and emotions.

Nonverbal Communication

Nonverbal communication is a silent but powerful form of communication. We communicate nonverbally virtually all of the time. The importance and magnitude of nonverbal communication has been documented in a number of studies (Burgoon, Buller, & Woodall, 1989; Miller, 1986; Nievenberg & Calero, 1973).

Types of Nonverbal Messages
The nonverbal messages we send may be deliberate, spontaneous, inadvertent, or unintended. Inadvertent messages are those that we send but are not aware of, although they may reflect the sentiment or opinion we have. For example, a listener's eyes may be darting around the room and the feet or body is partly turned away from the speaker out of disinterest. However, the listener certainly does not want to deliberately offend the other person by conveying disinterest.

Unintended communication can be defined as messages we do not intend to send that do *not* actually reflect our sentiments at the time. The receiver may have misinterpreted the behavior, or the speaker may have used expressions or nonverbal behaviors that are commonly identified with a particular disposition or specific feeling.

Range of Nonverbal Behavior
Nonverbal communication includes a range of behaviors. These messages may be sent by the face, head movements, hand gestures, body position, position of arms or legs, manner of dress, voice, timing of behaviors, and relationship of nonverbal to verbal behaviors.

Facial expressions are the most frequently used form of nonverbal communication. They can be easy to read and often are the most meaningful. The eyes, the mouth, and overall facial expressions constitute facial messages. The eyes have been identified as the "windows of the soul." Enlarged pupils (dilated) suggest excitement or deep interest.

The Helping Professional should watch for a variety of body movements that may convey messages. These range from the more obvious, such as nodding "yes" or "no," and shrugging one's shoulders to indicate not knowing or caring, to more subtle cues such as tenseness in the shoulders, slightly quivering lip, or fidgeting.

Congruency and Clusters
There are two important factors about reading nonverbal behavior. These are the factors of congruence and clusters of behaviors. Congruence means that our nonverbal and verbal messages must be consistent with each other. If you say, "I really want to know how you feel about your lesson today" and you are looking down or your eyes are darting around the room, the receiver is not sure that you really mean what you say. This message will confuse the other person, who may be frustrated or uneasy about the relationship. Congruence adds to a sense of sincerity and trust. In the helping relationship these are critical factors.

One of the mistakes frequently made by individuals is that they see a behavior and assume that it reflects the attitudes or feelings of the person. At times this may be true, but not necessarily always. We strongly suggest that Helping Professionals take note of the *cluster* of behaviors being demonstrated.

Interpretation of nonverbal behaviors is aided by reading clusters. It also should be noted that there may be differences in interpretation of particular nonverbal expressions in differing social groups. The meaning placed on certain behaviors by cultural groups may be vastly different. Standing close can be a sign of warmth, necessary for everyday interpersonal communication, or it can convey a threat or warning. Individual differences, contextual factors, clusters of behaviors, and cultural differences are all variables that need to be taken into account in understanding nonverbal communication and being effective in using it.

Summary of Nonverbal Skills
The following guidelines are useful in the quest for more effective nonverbal communication:

1. Recognize the potential individual nature of nonverbal communication.
2. Learn the other's idiosyncrasies and mannerisms.
3. Recognize that nonverbal communication is related to feelings and preferences.
4. Be perceptive and focused during interactions to identify any cues and be ever aware of nonverbal communication.
5. Seek congruency between the nonverbal and verbal.
6. Look for clusters of behaviors including precedent and simultaneous and antecedent events.

7. Account for contextual influences and cultural variations.
8. Think about the less obvious nonverbal signals, such as timing, dress, and space.
9. Become more aware of your own nonverbal expressions.
10. Seek feedback on your nonverbal communication and how it is being interpreted.
11. Seek to improve your nonverbal skills through practice with feedback.

Discussing ways to use these skills will enhance a helper's effectiveness.

Nonverbal Communication Exercise
In groups of two, take turns saying, "I really do care about communicating with you." Use different nonverbal cues each time you say the statement, such as smiling, looking away, looking intently, or other behaviors. Discuss the relative effect of the verbal and nonverbal communication. Discuss how you felt when the speaker smiled, looked away, looked intently, and so on. Share ways the Helping Professional could use nonverbal communication to develop rapport with a helpee.

Questioning

Questioning is one of the most frequently used skills and can be one of the most effective means of communicating and creating a supportive environment. It also is a powerful tool for stimulating thinking. Questioning receives considerable attention in the clinical supervision models and among mentors, as it is particularly effective in the process of conferencing with teachers. Understanding the variety, types, and uses of questioning is an essential part of the repertoire of the Helping Professional's skills.

Types of Questions
Among the various purposes of questions one might use in the helping process are the following: seeking initial information, probing for more information, requesting clarity, stimulating thinking or reflective analysis (expanding on ideas, creating or pondering alternatives, considering consequences, reflecting on practice and metacognition, thinking about decision making, and other thought processes), application, and seeking a decision or closure.

Eliciting Thinking
Eliciting thinking is a broad category of questioning that has several specific intents. These include promoting reflection on teacher or student behaviors, guiding the teacher to think about his or her own thinking or cognitive processes (metacognition), generating alternative ways of approaching an issue or lesson, or thinking through the underlying rationale or belief system.

Reflective Analysis Questions
One of the objectives of guidance and support is to promote an intellectual autonomy and teachers who are role models as intellectually independent learners

(Cook, 1993). Several studies have been conducted and analyses made on the process of preparing reflective teachers, as summarized by Pultorak (1993) and Sparks-Langer and Colton (1991). One conclusion is that teachers should be able to reflect on their own actions, their students, and the context of teaching in order to make appropriate decisions (Guyton & McIntyre, 1990; Murry, 1986; Smyth, 1992; Zeichner & Liston, 1987).

An important aspect of the process of acquiring reflective skills is the conditions that lead to or foster the skills, including behaviors of the Helping Professional. These include the complexity and difficulty of looking back and learning from one's practice (Buchmann & Schwille, 1983; Feiman-Nemser & Buchmann, 1985; Shulman, 1988), lack of time (Jackson, 1968; Richert, 1990), insufficient insight and support from supervisors (Killen, 1989), lack of structured opportunities for reflection (Wedman, Martin, & Mahlios, 1990), and demanding workloads of university supervisors who influence teacher reflection (Rudney & Guillaume, 1990; Zeichner & Liston, 1987).

In order to enhance the reflective process, Helping Professionals need to use reflective questions. Pultorak (1993) suggests the following (p. 290):

- What were essential strengths of the lesson?
- What, if anything, would you change about the lesson?
- Do you think the lesson was successful? Why?
- Which conditions were important to the outcome?
- What, if any, unanticipated learning outcomes resulted from the lesson?
- Can you think of another way you might have taught this lesson?
- Can you think of other alternative pedagogical approaches to teaching this lesson that might improve the learning process?
- Do you think the content covered was important to students? Why?
- Did any moral or ethical concerns occur as a result of the lesson?

Reflective questions are very important in terms of their potential effect on the teacher's thought processes and, ultimately, his or her behavior in the classroom. These questions ask that the teacher evaluate what has occurred by thinking back about the processes used and resultant behaviors of students. Their initial intent is to influence the cognitive processes of the teacher that ultimately are realized in terms of different and, optimally, improved behaviors on the part of the teacher and students. Influencing teacher thought processes is a major objective of the Helping Professional model and was discussed in Chapter 5.

Reflective questions promote higher-level thinking. These usually relate to the processes of application, analysis, synthesis and evaluation. In other words, the Helping Professional might ask the teacher to apply a concept or skill to a new situation or might ask the teacher to review a teaching vignette, a lesson that the Helping Professional demonstrates, or a transcript/tape script of another teacher's lesson and analyze it for patterns, concerns, and the like. Synthesis requires pulling together various strategies into new patterns, new lesson designs, or instructional procedures. In evaluating, the teacher may be asked to create his or her own criteria for evaluating a lesson, curriculum, student behaviors, or other component, and then to apply the criteria to determine the effectiveness of the particular episode or product. The following are some verbs that might be used in posing questions related to these functions: *compare and contrast, hypothesize, imagine, project, analyze, evaluate, apply, select with rationale, create,* or *consider.*

Metacognitive Questions

Metacognitive questions are a class of reflective questions, but they have a specific purpose. These questions ask that the teacher think through his or her practice and engage in higher-level thinking. In these respects, they are reflective questions. The specific focus of metacognitive questions, however, is that they ask teachers to think through their own thinking processes. It helps teachers discover how they make decisions, what they think about in the planning process, and what they use as the basis of their planning, such as assumptions and values. They promote reflection on what teachers think about during the act of instruction and what they think about during the evaluation process when looking at their own instruction.

The intent of thinking about thinking is to help one to not only analyze what one does, but also to better understand the thought processes behind it. It thus leads to greater insight about why one behaves in a particular way in the instructional process or in other professional activities. These are some of the most powerful types of activities one can engage in to learn more about one's practice.

Some examples of questions that stimulate metacognition-cognition are:

- What goes on in your mind when you are planning this type of lesson?
- What are some of the most common things you consider during the course of teaching your lesson?
- What changes would you make in the way you think about your planning for instruction?
- What are the most critical factors in thinking about the instructional process?
- What has this conferencing caused you to reflect on?

Questioning Skills Exercise

Divide the class into groups of three. Each group is assigned one of the questioning types. Each group prepares a description of how the question type is used in a helping relationship and develops four examples of this type of question that could be applied in conferencing with a teacher. Some of these may be role-played before the entire class. The class identifies the type of questions demonstrated after the role playing.

Paraphrasing

The skill of paraphrasing is often mentioned but is frequently not used appropriately. Also, it is usually used in a limited way, which is to restate another person's words. Paraphrasing has a variety of forms and uses. Understanding these increases the effectiveness of the skill.

There are several important purposes of paraphrase, each with its attendant benefits. First and foremost, paraphrase provides for greater understanding in the communication process. It enhances clarity of meaning, interpretation, and the precision of communication. Paraphrasing communicates to the sender that we understand the message sent. This is an extremely important purpose because often a great deal of miscommunication occurs when the parties involved believe they understand each other when actually they may have different interpretations. In essence, paraphrasing communicates *your* understanding of the message being sent.

The most important purpose of paraphrase is to convey the message to the sender that you truly want to understand the sender's message. You want to understand the other person's ideas and feelings. Paraphrasing is another way of communicating that you are more interested in the other's ideas than in expressing your own.

Types of Paraphrase
Johnson (1990) points out that there are four types of attempts at paraphrasing, not all of which are appropriate. These are the following:

1. Identical Content. This is an attempt at clarifying understanding that repeats the same words. It is not very helpful in clarifying understanding other than being used as a literal paraphrase to ensure the right words were heard.
2. Paraphrasing Content. This is rephrasing in fresh words the gist of the sender's expression without changing the meaning or feeling tone.
3. Shallow or Partial Meaning. This is referring to only a part of the message or by watering down the feeling tone. It is an incomplete interpretation.
4. Additional Meanings. This is a response that goes beyond the meaning of the sender and adds meaning or feeling not expressed. This is inappropriate in that it takes liberties and becomes more than a paraphrase.

These four types reflect the use and misuse of paraphrase. As noted, there are other types of paraphrase as well. Practice will help one gain mastery of these skills.

Paraphrasing Exercise
Identify a partner for this exercise. Person A makes a few statements about a topic he or she chooses. Focus on ideas, situations, opinions, understandings, and the like, not on emotion or feeling. Person B uses some of Person A's own words to convey understanding of the message. Use one of the suggested lead-ins provided in this section. Discuss the accuracy of the interpretation. Reverse roles and again discuss.

In a second round, begin with person B. In this instance, person B should make several statements that reflect emotions or feelings about a situation, relationship, or idea. Person A then reflects back the message received. Discuss accuracy and then reverse roles. Also, discuss what you learned about the importance of paraphrasing.

Validating

One of the most powerful forms of communication, particularly in helping relationships, is that of validating. Validating is a means of showing others that you understand their point of view by confirming the emotions they are experiencing or ideas that they are expressing. In validating you convey that you recognize that something is painful, that an idea or part of an idea has merit, and you indicate that the other person has a right to his or her feelings. Validating is not giving advice, nor is it evaluating. Rather, it is indicating that you understand, recognize, and accept the feeling or idea and the person's right to experience or express it.

Validating is a process of confirming. It also helps to put one in sync with the other individual, since it demonstrates that one understands the dilemma, situation, or perspective of the other person. The following are some statements that can be used to introduce validating statements:

- It really is painful for you to . . .
- You really must be . . .
- What you are experiencing is . . .
- I can see your (frustration, pain, gratification) . . .

Support Statements

Related to validation is the use of support statements. The purpose of support statements is to find some way of being positive and, of course, supportive. When you appear to be supportive in a helping relationship, you will be more effective as a Helping Professional. Support leads to building rapport, which we have seen as one of the essential objectives of the helping relationship.

One can praise to a point of diminishing returns, when such praise becomes meaningless. It is important to note that we are not actually talking about praise here. We are talking about areas of agreement and support.

Validating Exercise

Divide the class into triads. Person A expresses an opinion on an issue of importance to education. Take no more than 1 minute. Person B validates A's statements. Person C provides feedback on B's statement as validation. Discuss as a triad. Reverse roles until each has a turn at validating. Share why you believe validation is such a powerful communication skill.

Summary

This chapter has provided you with goals of communication and many specific skills to deal with varying situations. The communication skills are used in conjunction with helping skills and should be compatible with the particular helping style that you are developing. It again is important to recognize that the most important and effective way of acquiring these skills is through practice. We suggest that you begin with the skills for which you have the greatest need right now.

Once you have these reasonably in command and are comfortable with them for your values and goals in working with others, you can begin to practice another skill. It is important to periodically revisit these skills to reinforce their development, as well as to increase your effectiveness. Over time, you also will learn how to better integrate these into your own particular artistic style.

Competence in communication skills is essential for the implementation of the Helping Professional's philosophy and style. These skills empower the helper to be more effective in assisting others. Communication skills are a critical link in the chain of helping skills that will significantly enhance the relationship.

Issues and Questions for Review and Reflection

1. Communication skills are essential in helping relationships. Discuss the purposes of using these skills, such as the conditions and outcomes to be achieved.

2. Identify three areas of communication skills in which you would like to develop your skills further. Design a plan that provides for practice and feedback for each skill over the next 3-week period. Share with a partner to get feedback.

3. Six communication functions were described. What are the key specific skills needed to implement each?

4. Identify, compare, and contrast the various types of questioning skills.

5. What are some of the advantages and dangers of paraphrase? What are specific pitfalls to watch for in reflecting back a person's message? How can these pitfalls be avoided?

6. Discuss the meaning and power of validating. How can it be used in helping?

References

Blumberg, A. (1980). *Supervisors and teachers: A private cold war.* Berkeley, CA: McCutchan.

Buchmann, M., & Schwille, J. (1983). Education: The overcoming of experience. *American Journal of Education, 92*(1), 30–51.

Burgoon, J. K., Buller, D. B., & Woodall, W. G. (1989). *Nonverbal communication: The unspoken dialogue.* New York: Harper & Row.

Burke, J. B. (1984). Interpersonal communication. In J. Cooper (Ed.), *Developing skills for instructional supervision.* New York: Longman.

Carkhuff, R. R. (1980). *The art of helping* (vol. 4). Amherst, MA: Human Resource Development Press.

Cook, P. (1993). Defining reflective teaching: How has it been done for research? Paper presented at the annual meeting of the Association of Teacher Educators, Los Angeles.

Feiman-Nemser, S., & Buchmann, M. (1985). Pitfalls of experience in teacher preparation. *Teachers College Record, 81*(1), 53–65.

Glickman, C. D., Gordon, S. P., & Ross-Gordon, J. M. (1995). *Supervision of instruction: A development approach* (3d ed.). Boston: Allyn and Bacon.

Gold, Y., & Roth, R. A. (1993). *Teachers managing stress and preventing burnout: The professional health (PH) solution.* London: Falmer Press.

Guyton, E., & McIntyre, J. (1990). Student teaching and school experiences. In W. R. Houston

(Ed.), *Handbook of research on teacher education: A project of the Association of Teacher Educators.* (pp. 514–534). New York: Macmillan.

Jackson, P. (1968). *Life in classrooms.* New York: Holt, Rinehart & Winston.

Johnson, D. W. (1990). *Reaching out: Interpersonal effectiveness and self actualization* (4th ed.). Englewood Cliffs, NJ: Prentice-Hall.

Killen, L. (1989). Reflecting on reflective teaching: A response. *Journal of Teacher Education, 40*(2), 49–52.

Miller, P. W. (1986). *Nonverbal communication.* Washington, DC: National Education Association.

Mosher, R., & Purpel, D. (1972). *Supervision: The reluctant profession.* Boston: Houghton Mifflin.

Murry, F. (1986). Goals for the reform of teacher education: An executive summary of the Holmes Group report. *Phi Delta Kappan, 68*(1), 28–32.

Nievenberg, G. I., & Calero, H. (1973). *How to read a person like a book.* New York: Hawthorn.

Pultorak, E. G. (1993). Facilitating reflective thought in novice teachers. *Journal of Teacher Education, 44*(4), 288–295.

Richert, A. (1990). Teaching teachers to reflect: A consideration of programme structure. *Journal of Curriculum Studies, 22*(6), 49–52.

Rogers, C. R. (1962). The interpersonal relationship: The core of guidance. *Harvard Educational View, 32*(4), 416–429.

Roth, R. A. (1989). Preparing the reflective practitioner: Transforming the apprentice through the dialectic. *Journal of Teacher Education, 40*(2), 31–35.

Rudney, G., & Guillaume, A. (1990). Reflective teaching for student teachers. *The Teacher Educator, 25*(3), 13–20.

Schön, D. A. (1983). *The reflective practitioner.* New York: Basic Books.

Schön, D. A. (1987). *Educating the reflective practitioners.* San Francisco: Jossey-Bass.

Shostrum, E. L. (1967). *Man, the manipulator.* Nashville, TN: Abingdon.

Shulman, L. (1988). Teaching alone, learning together: Needed agendas for new reform. In T. J. Sergiovanni & J. H. Moore (Eds.), *Schooling for tomorrow: Directing reform to issues that count.* Boston: Allyn and Bacon.

Smyth, J. (1992). Teachers' work and the politics of reflection. *American Educational Research Journal, 29*(2), 267–300.

Sparks-Langer, G. M., & Colton, A. B. (1991). Synthesis of research on teachers' reflective thinking. *Educational Leadership 48*(6), 37–44.

Watson, K. W., & Barker, L. L. (1995). *Listening style profile: Facilitator's guide.* San Diego, CA: Pfeiffer.

Wedman, J., Martin, M., & Mahlios, M. (1990). Effect of orientation, pedagogy and time on selected student teaching outcomes. *Action in Teacher Education, 12*(2), 15–23.

Zeichner, K., & Liston, D. (1987). Teaching student teachers to reflect. *Harvard Educational Review, 57*(1), 23–48.

Related Readings

Borrisoff, B., & Victor, D. A. (1989). *Conflict management: A communication skills approach.* Englewood Cliffs, NJ: Prentice-Hall.

Bramson, R. M. (1981). *Coping with difficult people . . . in business and in life.* New York: Ballantine Books.

Brooks, M. (1989). *Instant rapport.* New York: Warner Books.

Delmar, K. (1984). *Winning moves: The body language of selling.* New York: Warner Books.

DeVito, J. A. (1989). *The interpersonal communication book* (5th ed.). New York: Harper & Row.

Ekman, P., & Friesen, W. V. (1975). *Unmasking the face.* Palo Alto, CA: Consulting Psychologists Press.

Elgin, S. H. (1980). *The gentle art of verbal self defense.* Englewood Cliffs, NJ: Prentice-Hall.

Fisher, R., & Ury, W. (1980). *Getting to yes: Negotiating agreement without giving in.* New York: Penguin Books.

Gordon, T. (1974). *Teacher effectiveness training (T.E.T.).* New York: McKay.

Gordon, T. (1977). *Leader effectiveness training (L.E.T.). The no-lose way to release the productive potential of people.* New York: Ballantine Books.

Nierenberg, G. I. (1981). *The art of negotiating.* New York: Simon and Schuster.

Phillips, G. M., & Wood, J. T. (1983). *Communication and human relationships: The study of interpersonal communication.* New York: Macmillan.

Richmond, V. P., McCroskey, J. C., & Payne, S. K. (1987). *Nonverbal behavior in interpersonal relations.* Englewood Cliffs, NJ: Prentice-Hall.

Stark, P. B. (1994). *It's negotiable: The how-to handbook of win/win tactics.* San Diego, CA: Pfeiffer.

Tanner, D. (1986). *That's not what I meant! How conversational style makes or breaks relationships.* New York: Ballantine Books.

Tanner, D. (1990). *You just don't understand: Women and men in conversation.* New York: Ballantine Books.

Ury, W. (1993). *Getting past no: Negotiating your way from confrontation to cooperation.* New York: Bantam Books.

Chapter 10

Models for Assessing, Diagnosing, Guiding, and Supporting

In this chapter the nature and operational elements of models will be examined for the purpose of assisting the Helping Professional in assessing, diagnosing, guiding, and supporting. Observation is practiced to help assess the scope of assistance needed and how best to enhance a helpee's insights into and comfort in the role of the teacher.

The chapter will provide an overview of the Transformational Helping Professional model to place it in comparison with other models that have been developed in the history of mentoring and supervising. Lastly, a framework for analyzing models and understanding their essential components will be provided as a template. This template will provide essential characteristics of various models in order to assist helpers in designing a model for helping that addresses the dimensions of assessing, diagnosing, guiding and supporting.

The Nature of Models

The concept of model is somewhat elusive, and the term is used interchangeably with other words such as approach, philosophy, and theory. The central issue is the function of a model. Models provide organizational or interpretive frameworks for viewing interrelationships, processes, operations, and structures. They describe components, characteristics, and dynamics. Intellectual models (in contrast with physical models) are abstractions that represent reality.

Models have both a focus and a screening dimension. They enable us to organize what we view so that particular aspects stand out while others become less noticeable. This has both a binding and an enlightening effect. It is enlightening in that it enhances our perception of critical elements by illuminating certain aspects of the model. The model draws our attention to significant features that warrant our attention based on the underlying premises of the model.

Conversely, a model may be limiting in that there is a tendency not to look beyond its walls. We may become so focused on the areas of emphasis in the model that we fail to see other significant events or players. Thus, the model is a template or a lens that provides the frame or focus of our inquiry. For example, a model may guide us to focus on overt actions and neglect to account for the role of context. This separating of field from ground has both benefits and liabilities.

A perceptual model may be characterized as a paradigm. A paradigm is the way we view a part of the world associated with the domain of the paradigm. By understanding the concept of a paradigm, we gain greater insight into why we interpret, infer, and come to understand in the ways we do. The world is understood in terms of our own frame of reference. Recognizing that there are varied and contrasting paradigms helps us gain insights into other individuals' ways of understanding and thinking. Understanding our own paradigm and comparing and contrasting it with others' opens up new ways of perceiving, learning, communicating, and interacting with others. It also enables us to engage in paradigm shifts in which we can then change our perceptual models based on learning and insight. We thus use models in our daily living and they greatly influence the ways in which we conduct our lives. In this sense models may not only be useful, but essential for learning. As powerful tools, they not only help us to understand, but also help us to reconstruct and grow.

In our study of mentoring and supervising, we are thus compelled to look at the models that have been constructed as representations of the helping process. This in turn allows us to devise a new paradigm or vision of the role and relationships of the Helping Professional.

Underlying a model are the values, beliefs, and assumptions that provide the groundwork for the design of the model. Collectively these constitute the philosophy or orientation of the model. The various approaches one takes, strategies used, and outcomes sought reflect the underlying set of philosophical premises. Although not always explicitly stated, the philosophy is manifest in the way the model is designed and operationalized.

To explore the diverse nature of models themselves, Joyce and Weil developed a framework for analyzing models. In their classic work, *Models of Teaching* (1986), they identify seven concepts for describing models. These include the following: (1) orientation or focus of the model (aspects that are most emphasized), (2) syntax or phasing (activities that typify the model), (3) principles of reaction (reactions or responses, such as to supervisees), (4) social system characteristics (roles, relationships, and norms), (5) support systems (conditions necessary for this model's existence), (6) theoretical assumptions (understandings and hypotheses), and (7) principles and major concepts (the big ideas of the model).

These are useful in analyzing, comparing, contrasting, and constructing models. Our concern here is more with the operational implications than with the conceptual elements, although attention is and must be given to both. This template will not be used for in-depth analyses of models for observation, but the reader may find it useful to refer to these concepts as part of one's own inquiry into models.

It also is useful to consider the function of a model as a predictor. In this realm the model projects what outcomes, consequences, or conditions will result from engaging in the syntax, reactions, and social systems of the model. In a sense, this is the sine qua non of the model. Without these, why participate in it? These are the promises it holds to those who embrace it.

Realistically, of course, there is no perfect model in the human realm, and hence no perfect predictor of outcomes. In teaching and mentoring, the application of models is within a fluid context (McGill, 1991), the empirical validity is shallow, and the technical means of application often are somewhat obtuse.

Operational Elements of Clinical Models

In order to approach the process of observing teachers in classrooms and conferring about the observation, at least three areas must be addressed. These include the content, structure, and process of the approach.

The Element of Content

In order for a mentor or helping model to be substantive, it must be based on underlying beliefs about the nature of teaching and learning. The specifics of the process of teaching and learning and the content to be learned are derived from these principles. These frame the substance of the observation and related discussion with the teacher regarding the teacher's instructional performance. These also become the factors that the Helping Professional is looking for in assisting the teacher in the instructional-professional domain. They are used as the basis for the professional development plan and the professional growth of the teacher involved in the process.

The content to be observed in the particular clinical model may be derived from a variety of sources. Recently the models have turned to the development of a research basis as the foundation for their focus of the observation. The Praxis/Pathwise developed by Educational Testing Service is one example. The Florida Beginning Teacher Assessment Program is another. Each of these has a comprehensive set of research information that supports the particular areas of content to be assessed during the observation and is part of the overall observation process.

In order to have a complete model, it is necessary to have some understanding of what one is looking for in the classroom. Mentors must have content described in a model or their own set of constructs, biases, understandings, and expectations of what should occur in the classroom in order to conduct effective observations. Thus, a basic component of observation is to have a clear conception of what one is assessing in the classroom. This will range from a general framework to a description of the instructional practices, knowledge, and specific competencies that the teacher is to demonstrate. When this content is specifically described, the model provides for an observation focus. This is thus referred to as a focused observation approach.

Structure of Models

Once one knows what is to be addressed, a second step is to construct the procedures to be followed when engaging in the processes of observation. These procedures form a structure for a particular approach. There are two basic approaches to defining procedures in a helping model. These are to specify the steps or structure, or to not impose a structure at all. In general, we can refer to structured or unstructured approaches, although there are varying degrees of structure. Obviously, the greater the specificity in defining steps to be taken, the more structured the approach.

As an example, the Goldhammer, Anderson, and Krajewski model (1993) for supervision consists of five steps: pre-observation conference, observation, data analysis, post-observation conference, and post-conference analysis. There are a variety of systems that have fewer steps or more steps in their structure. Some eliminate the pre-observation conference and move directly into the observation. Sometimes this varies with the individual with whom one is working. Clearly a minimum would be an observation of the teacher and subsequent conferral regarding the information collected in the observation. These steps may be formal or informal, structured or unstructured, required or optional. Thus, a model may have specific steps that one follows in order to implement the program. The more steps involved in the model, the more prescriptive, and the more it falls into the category of a structured system.

The Process Component of Models

The third area is the processes that one uses in the mentoring procedure. Once one has identified the specific areas of interest to be observed and a set of procedural steps has been defined, the actual implementation still needs to be conceptualized, clarified, and made operational. For example, one may decide that it would be appropriate to have a pre-observation conference with the teacher. This might be an initial step in the structure of the particular observational system. The question then is how does one go about conducting this pre-observation conference? What are the appropriate skills and strategies to effectively set the stage for the subsequent observation? How can a Helping Professional conduct this type of session in order to make it most productive and conducive for the continuation of the helping process? These and a variety of other operational questions are included in the processes defined for the particular system.

Some systems approach the process from an intuitive perspective, suggesting that helpers draw upon their expertise and function within the pre-observation conference as needed, adjusting to the needs, interests, and direction of the conversation. This would reflect an open system. Other systems approach this more systematically and identify specific kinds of objectives that should be achieved. These then provide for a number of different skills and strategies that one may use, and they reflect a more closed system.

One may also perceive the process to be such that there are certain skills and techniques that are helpful as a resource for the helper to draw from as needed, but are not prescribed. Whether the pre-observation conference is structured and well defined, or whether it is left to the expertise of the observer, the skills are useful and may be used appropriately by the Helping Professional. The process component thus includes the ways and means of enhancing the helping relationship during the observation activity and reflects the philosophy of the model being used and that of the helper.

In summary, as the Helping Professional functions as a mentor, supervisor, or administrator, it is necessary to identify the means by which classroom observations will be conducted. This means that decisions need to be made about the content or what needs to be observed. This includes instructional processes and content of teaching and learning. In addition, there should be some definition of the procedures that will be followed during the observation. This entails the steps that the observer and teacher may follow as they interact during the observation cycle. Finally, the helper must have command of the requisite skills, strategies, and knowledge in order to effectively implement an observation cycle and provide the supportive environment needed to enhance the growth of the teacher. These are the processes of the model and reflect its philosophy.

Helping Professionals can adopt one of the contemporary models, synthesize them into their own pattern, or develop a new approach based on a set of principles, such as those underlying the Transformational Helping Professional model.

In the Transformational Helping Professional model, a key component is assessment and diagnosis as a way to identify the personal and professional needs of the helpee. The helping process includes assessing and diagnosing the individual's needs, so that plans can be made to assist and enhance the teacher's growth. Also, a variety of strategies will fit well into the Helping Professional approach, as long as they are consistent with the philosophy, are appropriate to helping the individual meet identified needs, and further the supportive relationship between the Helping Professional and the teacher.

The Role of Observation and Assistance

Observation is not viewed as an end in itself. It is part of a broader process of providing assistance and supporting the teacher's personal and professional growth that occurs throughout the helping relationship. It is an essential element in the role of the mentor, school supervisor, student teaching supervisor, and the other curriculum and instructional specialists within the schools. Observing the teacher in actual practice is essential if one is to obtain a true determination of the teacher's level of expertise and related areas of need.

Assistance implies more of a supportive role, rather than one of evaluating. The purpose of assistance is to provide information that guides and supports the teacher in his or her personal and professional growth. This is consistent with the purpose of the Transformational Helping Professional model, which is to assist the teacher in all aspects of growth, with an emphasis on professional-related development.

A positive environment created through a program of professional help provides the context and foundation for productive and professionally healthy observations. Much of the groundwork for providing a positive observation and related interaction is established throughout the professional helping relationship. Using the skills described in the Transformational model, the helper takes considerable time to develop a nurturing relationship in which trust and openness are readily achieved. These are exactly the kinds of conditions that must exist in order to engage in a productive observation and assistance program.

Scope of Assistance

The Helping Professional must have an array of information about the individual gained through a variety of assessment techniques. Perhaps the most fundamental of these assessment sources is that of observation; however, it is only one part of the assistance process. The process also includes conferring with the teacher about the fundamental rationale of the observation and its activities, understanding any changes made during the lesson, providing means for self-assessment, and assisting in analysis of needs in order to design a professional development plan.

It is important again to note the relationship between observation for assistance and for teacher evaluation. There are times when the observation is used as part of an evaluation procedure. For our purposes, the observation is considered to be a necessary strategy for assessing personal and professional development. In most situations, growth and development are the ultimate purposes. Those who function as mentors or Helping Professionals with no evaluative role find that professional development is the exclusive purpose for which the observation is eventually used. School supervisors and administrators may find themselves in a position in which the information will be used as part of an overall evaluation. In either event, it is the personal and professional development functions that are of relevance.

Observation is not the goal of the process, but only part of it. The Helping Professional must look at the various dimensions of the teacher's professional life, as well as personal aspects that influence how the teacher functions as a professional. The primary focus of the teacher's activities, of course, is his or her instruction in the classroom. There are other roles of the teacher that are important to becoming a fully functioning professional. These relate to peer interactions, parent relationships, personal growth and development, and obligations to the school and community.

Most models would identify performance in the classroom as the Helping Professional's hub or center of assistance and basis for enhancing professional growth. In the Helping Professional model, it is proposed that the focus is on the teacher's personal and professional needs. Observation is one vehicle in the assessment of these needs. There thus is a cyclical pattern or arrangement that involves the analysis of instructional performance, addressing the broad scope of the teacher's personal and psychological needs and how these affect performance, the subsequent improvement of performance in the classroom, and the growth of the teacher as a professional.

It is found that addressing the scope of a teacher's personal and professional needs provides much greater leverage for professional improvement. Indeed, there is wisdom in observing the teacher's classroom performance and developing ways to improve that performance by examining strengths and weaknesses. This is a necessary part of professional development and integral to the Helping Professional model. However, to limit needs assessment to classroom observation data is insufficient. Assistance set in a context of support and encouragement provides for the enhancement of technical proficiency as well as personal satisfaction, intellectual growth, and personal development.

Role of the Teacher

Consistent with the premises of the philosophy of the Transformational Helping Professional model, observation is not perceived as a tool to "fix" teachers, making them better in the classroom by telling them what to do. Growth must come from within the teachers themselves. The Helping Professional is not perceived as one who changes or transforms others, but rather as one who provides the guidance, support, and assistance necessary to enable teachers to make necessary changes for themselves. Observation thus can be viewed as another opportunity to encourage change and to guide the transformation of teachers.

One of the contributions of the observation process is that it provides diagnostic information that assists teachers in gaining insights about their practice and level of professional competence. The observation process, in one sense, is a mutual exploration of the teacher's needs. Although the process entails an important mutual cooperative relationship, the primary emphasis and impetus for change are in the hands of the individual teacher because the change process requires individual commitment to growth.

As an example, the teacher must be willing to participate in the process for change in the first place. The helper may guide the teacher in the process of identifying concerns, but it is considerably less valuable if the helper directly advises the teacher of his or her areas of need. Furthermore, the teacher must be willing to make the necessary changes once the areas have been identified, as was discussed in Chapter 3, A Process of Transformations.

In each of these instances the Helping Professional may provide encouragement, support, and guidance, always being aware that changing is a personal choice of the individual teacher. For these reasons, the philosophy of the Transformational Helping Professional model contains a strong commitment to the principle of a personalized approach.

The Transformational Helping Professional Model

The essential elements of the Transformational model were described in some detail in Chapter 2. This approach to mentoring focuses on the role of the Helping Professional. The major purpose of the Helping Professional is to assist individual teachers in achieving their highest personal and professional potential in order to enhance professional effectiveness and subsequently impact the learning and growth of their students. The needs addressed are in both the instructional-professional and personal-psychological domains (discussed in Chapters 4 and 5), and they are highly interactive. Focusing only on classroom behaviors or thought processes related to instructional decisions would thus be quite limiting. As noted, the focus of the Helping Professional philosophy is characterized as being person-centered, needs-based, and achievement-focused. It is a search for significance, both personally and professionally.

The fundamental basis for the Transformational Helping Professional model is a psychotherapeutic approach. A basic starting point in this approach is a diagnosis of the individual's needs. Without an understanding of one's personal set of needs, professional assisting strategies may be inefficient or misdirected.

Consistent with this is the central component of the Helping Professional philosophy. It is essential for helpers to know themselves as well as knowing the teachers with whom they are working. This self-diagnosis and knowing how to assist others with their own self-diagnosis are critical to establishing the groundwork for enhancing the growth and development of both the individuals and helpers throughout the helping process.

An appropriate follow-up to the diagnosis phase is the "prescription" phase. This is not intended to imply that specific directions are given to individuals on how to change and modify their practice. Prescription is a design for coaching, guiding, and supporting individuals through their own assessments, self-evaluations, and insights that lead to personal and professional growth. The prescriptive phase leads to the development of strategies and the use of assistance for guiding individuals in achieving their plans and objectives. Reassessment is part of the cycle in which individuals are re-diagnosed based on ongoing data collection, and plans for growth and development are modified as necessary.

As one reviews the history and development of the mentoring and supervising process, the need for a new perspective is evident in the literature. Some of the elements of the Transformational Helping Professional model are embedded in a variety of different approaches. The basic premise of collegiality and support is inherent in the various forms of mentoring and supervising; however, these elements are given differential emphasis in the several models. It is of interest to note that this type of model has been of interest and the elements have been pursued over time, but no specific model has yet been devised to focus on it in quite this way. There are some models that focus more on the technical aspects of mentoring and supervising and seem to be devoid of any interest in working with the individual needs of the teacher outside the realm of the instructional-technical. There also are models that are more humanistic, dealing with interpersonal relations, but have not found ways of specifically identifying fundamental needs relating to improved practice on the part of the individual based on better understanding and acceptance of him- or herself.

These goals, although highly valued and sought out, are not fully developed in any one of the models, nor could one be developed from a collective analysis of the models. What is needed is a new perspective capitalizing on the strengths of existing models and adding new dimensions as a fundamental context for instructional and personal analysis and subsequent professional improvement and personal growth.

An interesting example of the changing attitudes toward the necessary recognition of personal and professional issues for teachers is that of Acheson and Gall in their most recent text (1992). Acheson and Gall state they had advised in previous editions of their book that supervisors avoid the counseling role with teachers. They felt supervisors need to spend time on improving instructional efforts, rather than attempting to function as "amateur psychiatrists," which could potentially cause considerable harm. Recently, however, they stated: "In the case of serious problems, we still feel this way, but we have modified our position somewhat" (1992, p. 203). Acheson and Gall indicate that as they continue to work with supervisors, they have recognized that it is impossible to separate teachers' instructional problems from their personal problems. Acheson and Gall thus suggest that an approach is needed that avoids having one acting as an amateur therapist, yet deals directly with personal problems that impact the teacher's classroom performance. Interestingly, they note: "It is conceivable that a conscientious supervisor might perform all the tasks of planning, observing, and giving feedback . . . and still not be regarded as helpful to the teacher" (1992, p. 204). Acheson and Gall thus find that the technical approach to improvement of skills may be a valued and necessary function, but it is not sufficient in fully dealing with the broad range of the teacher's needs.

In an analysis of research and knowledge on successful teaching, Zimpher and Howey (1987) identified four major types of teaching competence: technical, clinical, personal, and critical. *Technical* refers to basic instructional practice. In *clinical* competence the teacher acts as a problem solver and clinician who identifies problems and appropriate solutions. *Personal* competence relates to the teacher's understanding of his or her own teaching methods that provide meaning and significance. The helper assists the teacher with personal competence by enhancing the teacher's self-awareness, professional practice, and interpretive capacity. *Critical* competence focuses on issues of values, importance, and meaning that underlie one's teaching practice. Teaching is an ethical practice concerned with worth and purpose.

These models express the need to extend beyond technical competence and deal with a variety of aspects of the teacher's abilities and functions. The model teacher is a technically competent, clinical problem solver who is a socially conscious change agent and is self-actualized. This requires dealing with the teacher's underlying needs, particularly his or her psychological needs as they relate to performance in all of these areas. Sergiovanni and Starratt (1993) suggest that teaching is more than just a job and more than a profession. In effect, much of it is an extension of the teacher. Teaching reveals many of the personal aspects of the teacher. Much of the teacher's characteristics, moral fiber, and psychological make-up are expressed in his or her interactions as a professional in the classroom and in other capacities as a teacher. Teaching is a personal expression of the teacher. The technical and personal dimensions of the teacher are inextricably tied to and manifested in the process of functioning as a professional.

In the Transformational Helping Professional model it is necessary for the mentor to make a diagnosis of teachers' needs in order to effectively provide a program to assist in their practice and their personal growth. For example, Duke (1987) believes the successful helper should be able to diagnose the differential needs and potential of each teacher and thus develop an understanding of each person's current skills and knowledge base. Thus, the pre-observation phase should be characterized as more than planning for the observation. An extended initial phase of our model has to do with the diagnosis of the teacher's personal and professional needs (as covered in Chapters 4 and 5). This includes, but is not limited to, a pre-observation conference dealing specifically with instructional practice and the upcoming observation, as well as the emotional, physical, and social needs of teachers as outlined in the needs inventories.

Given the personal nature of teaching, the role of helper may be one of both interpersonal intervention and the helper's own self-intervention. One of the characteristics of the teaching profession is the psychological overload experienced by teachers (Glickman, Gordon, & Ross-Gordon, 1995). Psychological needs thus become of greater importance, although they are often overlooked in the observation process. As noted by Sergiovanni and Starratt: "Readiness for change is a critical point in the process of clinical supervision. It is at this point that an appropriate support system needs to be provided. Part of the support system will be psychological..." (1993, p. 234).

As a response to these various insights about the need for assistance to teachers in our contemporary schools, the Transformational Helping Professional model was devised around the concept of psychological needs. It also helps teachers meet their personal and professional needs as a means of achieving healthy growth, which in turn affects those with whom they work (teachers, students, and others in a school setting).

A Template for Review of Models

With the variety of models available, it may be quite confusing which to select and which might be most appropriate for the supervisor. One way of approaching the selection process is to look at the essential elements of the models. This also provides a mechanism for individuals to construct their own model from the various

Models for Assessing, Diagnosing, Guiding, and Supporting 193

theories, factors, and approaches. One way to construct a framework is to provide key elements. These key elements includes the following characteristics:

1. *Purpose/Outcomes*: Improve instructional skill, improve curriculum, promote professional growth, promote personal psychological growth, and improve decision-making capacity.
2. *Beliefs, Values, and Assumptions*: Teacher must be self-motivated, needs fulfillment is the driving force, individual satisfaction is a key element, supervisor must have inherent interest in helping, etc.
3. *Nature of the Relationship*: Interpersonal, collaborative, professional helper–oriented, supervisor-oriented, consultative, nonpersonal.
4. *Focus of the Process:*
   - Teacher Focus: Teacher behaviors, thinking processes, sensitivities, psychological needs, teaching style.

FIGURE 10-1   Essential Elements of Various Models

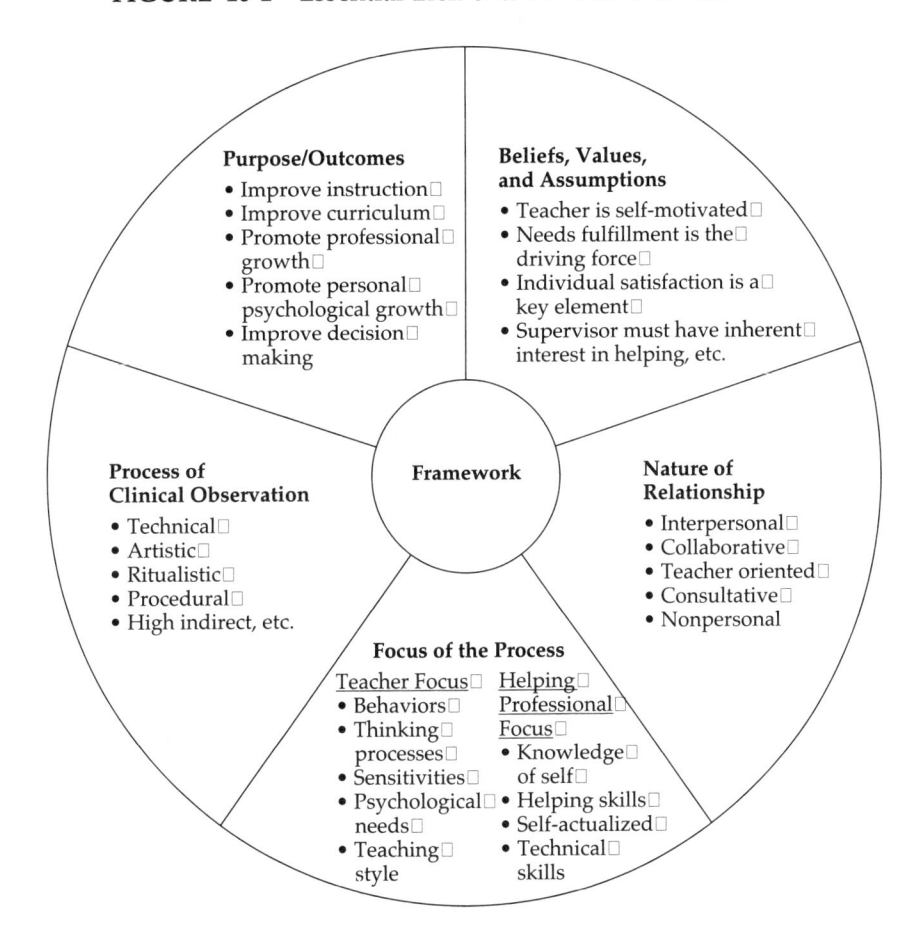

Framework

Purpose/Outcomes
- Improve instruction
- Improve curriculum
- Promote professional growth
- Promote personal psychological growth
- Improve decision making

Beliefs, Values, and Assumptions
- Teacher is self-motivated
- Needs fulfillment is the driving force
- Individual satisfaction is a key element
- Supervisor must have inherent interest in helping, etc.

Process of Clinical Observation
- Technical
- Artistic
- Ritualistic
- Procedural
- High indirect, etc.

Nature of Relationship
- Interpersonal
- Collaborative
- Teacher oriented
- Consultative
- Nonpersonal

Focus of the Process

Teacher Focus
- Behaviors
- Thinking processes
- Sensitivities
- Psychological needs
- Teaching style

Helping Professional Focus
- Knowledge of self
- Helping skills
- Self-actualized
- Technical skills

- Mentor or Helping Professional Focus: knowledge of self, helping skills, self-actualized, technical skills.
5. *Process of Clinical Observation*: Technical, artistic, ritualistic, procedural, high indirect, etc.

Another view of the elements can be seen in Figure 10-1.

Closing Thoughts

This framework is one means of developing and constructing one's own approach, but the central characteristic is to analyze one's own values and beliefs. A system of beliefs is fundamental to the process of helping, and the elements selected for one's model must be consistent with the values and beliefs. A number of questions could be asked, such as: What is the ultimate purpose of the process? What kind of relationship needs to be established with the individual? What are the areas of personal and professional needs that must be addressed? By clarifying these and other questions, one can develop a framework based on one's philosophy and design the best approach in terms of structure, process, and content.

Issues and Questions for Review and Reflection

1. There are three areas to consider in reviewing observation systems: structure, content, and process. Discuss the importance of each.

2. In terms of content, there are basic underlying principles that define its focus. Describe principles of the teaching-learning process that guide what you would look for in teacher observation.

3. Identify which approach you prefer. Write a one- to two-page description of your observation model.

4. In the Transformational model, emphasis is placed on the role of the Helping Professional. How would you describe this role?

References

Acheson, K. A., & Gall, M. D. (1992). *Techniques in the clinical supervision of teachers: Preservice and inservice applications* (3d ed.). New York: Longman.

Anderson, C. J., Barr, A. S., & Bush, M. G. (1925). *Visiting the teacher at work*. New York: Appleton-Century.

Blumberg, A. (1980). *Supervisors and teachers: A private cold war* (2d ed.). Berkeley, CA: McCutchan.

Cogan, M. (1973). *Clinical supervision*. Boston: Houghton Mifflin.

Costa, A. L., & Garmston, R. J. (1985). Supervision for intelligent teaching. *Educational Leadership, 42*(5), 70–80.

Costa, A. L., & Garmston, R. J. (1994). *Cognitive coaching: A foundation for renaissance schools*. Norwood, MA: Christopher-Gordon.

Duke, D. L. (1987). *School leadership and instructional improvement*. New York: Random House.

Eisner, E. W. (1982). An artistic approach to supervision. In T. J. Sergiovanni (Ed.). *Supervision of teaching: 1982 yearbook* (pp. 53–66). Alexandria, VA: Association for Supervision and Curriculum Development.

Glickman, C. D., Gordon, S. P., & Ross-Gordon, J. M. (1995). *Supervision of instruction: A developmental approach* (3d ed.). Boston: Allyn and Bacon.

Goldhammer, R., Anderson, R. H., & Krajewski, R. J. (1993). *Clinical supervision: Special methods for the supervision of teachers* (3d ed.). New York: Harcourt Brace.

Hunter, M., & Russell, D. (1990). *Mastering coaching and supervision: Principles of Learning series.* Thousand Oaks, CA: Corwin Press.

Joyce, B., & Weil, M. (1986). *Models of teaching.* Englewood Cliffs, NJ: Prentice-Hall.

McGill, M. V. (1991). The changing face of supervision: A developmental art. *Journal of Curriculum and Supervision, 6*(3), 255–264.

Pajak, E. (1993). *Approaches to clinical supervision: Alternatives for improving instruction.* Norwood, MA: Christopher-Gordon.

Schön, D.A. (1987). *Educating the reflective practitioners.* San Francisco: Jossey-Bass.

Sergiovanni, T. J., & Starratt, R. J., (1993). *Supervision: A redefinition* (5th ed.). New York: McGraw-Hill.

Zimpher, N. Z., & Howey, K. R. (1987). Adapting supervisory practice to different orientations of teaching competence. *Journal of Curriculum and Supervision, 2*(1), 101–127.

Related Readings

Adams, A., & Glickman, C. D. (1984). Does clinical supervision work?: A review of research. *Tennessee Educational Leadership, 11*(11), 38–40.

Black, L., Daiker, D., Sommers, J., & Stygall, G. (1994). *New directions in portfolio assessment.* Portsmouth, NH: Boynton/Cook.

Bowers, C. A., & Flinders, D. J. (1991). *Culturally responsive supervision: A handbook for staff development.* New York: Teachers College Press.

Flinders, D. J. (1991). Supervision as cultural inquiry. *Journal of Curriculum and Supervision, 6*(2), 87–106.

Garman, H. (1990). Theories embedded in the events of clinical supervision: A hermeneutic approach. *Journal of Curriculum and Supervision, 5,* 201–213.

Glatthorn, A. (1983). *Differentiated supervision.* Alexandria, VA: Association for Supervision and Curriculum Development.

Glickman, C. D., & Bey, T. M. (1990). Supervision. In W. R. Houston (Ed.), *Handbook of research on teacher education.* New York: Macmillan.

Henson, K. T. (1995). *Curriculum development for education reform.* New York: Harper Collins.

Holland, P. E., Veal, M. L., Clift, R., & Johnson, M. (1991, April). A structural analysis of supervision. Paper presented at the annual meeting of the American Educational Research Association, Chicago.

McCoombe, M. (1984). Clinical supervision from the inside. In W. J. Smyth (Ed.), *Case studies in clinical supervision* (pp. 45–57). Victoria, Australia: Deakin University Press.

Oliva, P. F. (1989). *Supervision for today's schools* (3d ed.). New York: Longman.

Smyth, J. (Ed.) (1985). Developing a critical practice of clinical supervision. *Journal of Curriculum Studies, 17*(1), 1–15.

Stalling, J. (1987). For whom and how long is the Hunter-based model appropriate? Response to Robbins and Wolfe. *Educational Leadership, 44*(5), 62–63.

St. Maurice, H. (1987). Clinical supervision and power: Regimes of instructional management. In T. S. Popkewitz (Ed.), *Critical studies in teacher education: Its folklore, theory and practice* (pp. 242–264). London: Falmer Press.

Waite, D. (1995). *Rethinking instructional supervision: Notes on its language and culture.* London: Falmer Press.

Chapter 11

A Focus on Content

In the previous chapter we identified three basic components of assisting that warrant consideration. These are the content, structure, and processes in the system. The content is the focus of the observation, consisting of the expectations of teacher competence. This is what the Helping Professional seeks to obtain information about and to diagnose. The Helping Professional then provides guidance to assist the teacher in acquiring the content.

In this chapter we will review the substance or content of observation that can be of assistance to helpers. Essentially, the content consists of teachers' thought processes or cognitive development and the behaviors teachers demonstrate in the process of performing their instructional and other professional responsibilities.

Setting the Stage

The basic issue to be addressed here is what to look for in observing the teacher's instructional practice in the classroom or during instructional-related activities. The focus is on what is known about teaching and learning, what the research or best practice has revealed about effective performance in the classroom. The specific content of instruction is not prescribed in the Transformational Helping Professional model, although Chapter 5 outlines the instructional areas in which teachers must be proficient. These areas were derived from research and our experiences in working with teachers.

The Transformational model, however, holds to strong beliefs about the nature of the content, such as focusing on thought processes of teachers and structure of disciplines in the curriculum. A purpose of guidance and support is enhancing thought processes for improved professional practice, so the Helping Professional needs to help teachers toward greater understanding of how they think and why they behave the way they do. Because teachers' actions are greatly affected by their thought processes, helpers can assist them in identifying, analyzing, and evaluating how they think. Methods of inquiry that a helper could use are provided in Chapter 5.

When we think about what to look for in observing teachers, such as classroom behaviors or planning activities, these actions may be viewed as reflecting teacher beliefs. The Helping Professional can assist teachers in identifying their beliefs and how they are demonstrated in practice, as well as identifying incongruities in their beliefs as compared to their practice. These perspectives of thought processes and beliefs form a significant area of content as the focus of assistance and observation of teachers' behaviors and instructional approaches.

We view the various categorizations of instructional practice as frameworks. They provide insights on practice that are helpful when placed within the context of the subject, the nature of the students, prior learning of the students, subsequent lessons, evaluation by the instructor of her or his teaching, and so forth.

We will focus here primarily on instructional practice. We will look at the research and standards that have been developed from the research as means of assisting the Helping Professional in looking at what happens in classrooms. The emphasis in this chapter is on the instructional-professional area, although the influence of the personal-psychological domain on instruction must be kept in mind.

In order to provide a balanced approach to the content of classroom observation or instructional practice, we will look at the cognitive elements as well as the behavioral. We previously gave some attention to the issue of cognitive development in Chapter 5 on instructional and professional needs. We also will focus a great deal on cognitive issues in the chapter on diagnosing and assessing (Chapter 12) and the chapter on guidance and support (Chapter 13). We thus do not need to deal with the issue of cognitive functioning as content in any depth in this chapter. We will, however, give greater emphasis to instructional behaviors and those areas of instructional practice reflected in the various sets of standards developed by state agencies and professional organizations.

Content As Meaning

We believe it is important to describe the actual events that are occurring in the classroom as data for teachers to analyze and from which they gain insights about their own instructional practice. The content of the observation should not be limited to actual events or behaviors observed, but should include the attitudes, meanings, and climate that appear to exist or are reflected during the process of teaching in the classroom. The content thus is not limited to literal descriptions, but should be expanded to provide interpretations through rich descriptions of what seems to be occurring and what the teacher appears to be demonstrating and producing.

The distinction between picturing versus disclosure as models of classrooms is of value here (Ramsey, 1964; Mann, 1967). The differences have been expanded by Sergiovanni and Starratt (1993), who suggest that picturing involves describing the teaching phenomena as exactly as possible, whereas disclosure is interpreting the phenomena to illuminate issues, meanings, hypotheses, and agendas. As they note, picturing as accurately as possible is useful for certain times and purposes, such as an overall description of what occurred for the teacher and Helping Professional to analyze. The disclosure approach to viewing content is more appropriate for other purposes, such as when the mentor functions as connoisseur or the helping relationship provides for an interpretive analysis of the classroom.

One issue of content the Helping Professional should inquire into is the teacher's professional style, which reflects the teacher's beliefs and attitudes. Describing the teacher's style and understanding it are more important than, and are distinctly different from, evaluating it. The intent here is to provide feedback on what that style and belief system seems to be as it is manifested in the way the teacher approaches planning and instruction. In fact, one of the objectives of the helping process is to assist teachers in identifying their model of instruction so that they then can begin to examine their model and a variety of others (Joyce & Weil, 1986).

Teaching is characterized as a process of decision making, so part of the content of the observation is determining what kinds of decisions are made within the particular context. In the instructional-professional domain the content of the helping process might include both the process and content of instruction itself. We will not delve much into the issue of content of instruction, as this is determined by the particular goals of local school districts. In order to address this question, however, the Helping Professional must understand the school's belief system related to issues such as the purposes of education, the nature of the learner, the learning process, and the substance of content to be delivered.

Teachers' approach to instruction, including the curriculum, instructional processes, and evaluation, is part of the content of diagnosis and assessment. It is necessary for the Helping Professional to assess this in order to assist teachers in understanding these elements of their education platform, assist them in reflecting upon these, and to identify any discrepancies between beliefs and behaviors.

Glickman, Gordon, and Ross-Gordon (1995) offer a series of questions that assist teachers in identifying their own education platform. This, in turn, forms part of the content the Helping Professional must be concerned with during the diagnosing and guidance processes. These questions include the following concepts: (1) the purpose of education, (2) the content of the school curriculum, (3) control of the learning environment, (4) the relationship of teacher and students, (5) conditions that make student learning most successful, (6) what motivates students to do their best, (7) a teacher's definition of effective teaching, (8) personal characteristics of a successful teacher, (9) how a teacher assesses student learning, and (10) your definition of a good school. Beliefs about issues such as these, whether they are implicit or explicit, form the foundation of practice.

Cognitive Complexity

The Transformational Helping model places considerable emphasis on the issue of cognitive development of teachers and the complexity of their cognitive processing as a means of understanding their instructional practice. This too becomes part of the content of the observation and guidance processes. Although the cognitive function is not directly observed, there may be manifestations of it that allow one to infer cognitive processes. Teacher behaviors also provide opportunities for discussion within which the Helping Professional and teacher can delve into the teacher's cognitive processing.

As we noted, higher levels of cognitive complexities are characterized by ability to apply or integrate a variety of concepts to the particular topic of the lesson, by demonstrating interconnections among concepts, and by ability to understand, identify, and deal with the various cues and subtle events in the classroom. Helping Professionals look for these kinds of characteristics in the teacher's instructional repertoire as they observe in the classroom. This is an important part of content as well.

Providing information on the way teachers appear to be thinking and determining the extent to which they engage in reflecting about their own thinking (metacognition) are important parts of the content of diagnosis and observation. As noted by Clark and Peterson (1986), three categories of thought processes form part of the foundation of content, as follows: (1) Pre-active and post-active thoughts in planning, (2) interactive thoughts and decisions, and (3) teachers' theories and beliefs. Sergiovanni and Starratt (1993) indicate that cognitive complexity is concerned with both content and structure, but particularly with structure. The cognitive structure or frameworks have been defined with terms such as dialectical thought (Kramer, 1983; Riegel, 1973), integrative thought (Kramer, 1987), and epistemic cognition (Taranto, 1987).

A related area of the content of diagnosis and support is teacher knowledge. Shulman (1986) proposed three categories of content knowledge: (1) subject matter content knowledge, (2) pedagogical content knowledge, and (3) curriculum knowledge. We thus suggest that another area of the content of observation guidance is to determine the teacher's grasp of these various types of knowledge.

In Chapter 5 we provided a very extensive matrix on teachers' instructional needs. These serve as a framework for identifying the content of the observation and diagnosis process. For example, among the things the Helping Professional should learn about teachers are their levels of knowledge within the instructional needs categories, such as the following: knowledge of learners, knowledge of discipline strategies, knowledge of motivation theories, planning, subject matter knowledge, curricular knowledge, knowledge of developing thinking skills, methods of inquiry, and so forth. The processes of guidance and support are intended to assist the teacher in the development of these knowledge areas. Before commencing the guidance and support function, the Helping Professional must determine the status of the individual's knowledge in each of these categories. The focus or content of these processes thus includes examining these instructional needs.

We also identified in Chapter 5 a wide range of professional needs. The content of assessment and diagnosis includes professional needs, such as the following: reflecting on teaching; changes in quality of teaching; interpreting teaching experiences; demonstrating a sense of efficacy; defining professional identity; developing the skills of critical judgment; engaging in more abstract or complex patterns of thought; demonstrating flexibility; demonstrating growth and inquiry; communicating effectively with parents; actively participating in professional associations; and engaging in meaningful, intellectual, and social dialogues with colleagues.

Collectively, these form an extensive base of content to be assessed, diagnosed, and guided throughout the helping process. These are some of the factors that one looks for as part of the process of assisting teachers to engage in more complex thinking patterns and to consider issues of greater significance in the instructional process.

Consistent with this is the Holmes Group conception of tomorrow's teachers. Their vision of teaching is drawn from what they refer to as "time-tested conceptions of teacher qualities and responsibilities, and of recent understandings about role requirements" (Holmes Group, 1986, p. 28). They assert that central to their vision "are competent teachers empowered to make principled judgments and decisions on their students' behalf.... They exemplify the critical thinking they strive to develop in students, combining tough-minded instruction with penchant for inquiry" (pp. 28–29).

Curriculum and Planning

There are a variety of different areas on which one can focus in looking at the overall set of teacher practices. These relate not only to the actual instruction, but also to the curriculum, the way students are accommodated, views of student intelligence and types of intelligence, and other related issues. We do not intend to provide an exhaustive treatment of these at this point, but rather will provide a few examples to guide readers in broadening their perspective on the nature and extent of content of assessment and diagnosis.

Multiple Intelligences

An area of current interest is that of multiple intelligences. There are a variety of similar such concepts that might be looked at, and this is used as an example of how to view content. Howard Gardner's book *Frames of Mind: The Theory of Multiple Intelligences* (1983) provides a foundation for much of the current work on multiple intelligences and how it is applied to the classroom. One objective of the Helping Professional might be to identify the activities in the classroom that incorporate a concept such as multiple intelligences. Two recent publications by Gardner further expand this concept. These include *Multiple Intelligences: The Theory and Practice* (1993b) and *Creating Minds* (1993a). Treatments of how to teach for multiple intelligences are provided by Lazear (1992) and Armstrong (1994).

The basic premise of the theory is that intelligence has to do with the capacity for solving problems and fashioning products in a context-rich and naturalistic setting. Based on this, seven intelligences are described as follow (Armstrong, 1994):

1. *Linguistic intelligence*: The capacity to use words effectively

2. *Logical-mathematical intelligence*: The capacity to use numbers effectively
3. *Spatial intelligence*: The ability to perceive the visual spatial world accurately
4. *Bodily-kinesthetic intelligence*: Experiencing using one's whole body to express ideas and feelings
5. *Musical intelligence*: The capacity to perceive, discriminate, transform, and express musical forms
6. *Interpersonal intelligence*: The ability to perceive and make distinctions in moods, intentions, motivations and feelings of other people
7. *Intra-personal intelligence*: Self-knowledge and the ability to act adaptively on the basis of that knowledge

There are four major points that develop from these categories. These are that: (1) each person possesses all seven intelligences, (2) most people can develop each intelligence to an adequate level of competency, (3) intelligence is usually worked together in complex ways, and (4) there are many ways to be intelligent within each category (Armstrong, 1994).

If the Helping Professional is expected to look for evidence of addressing the multiple intelligence concept as part of the content of the observation, then there are a variety of aspects that might be noted.

Assessing Students' Multiple Intelligences

Assessment of multiple intelligences can be accomplished through checklists or observations of students in order to gather data about the ways in which they interact with their environment and with each other. Other approaches include collecting documents (such as products of students' work), looking at school records, talking with other teachers, talking with parents, asking students selected questions, and setting up special activities (Armstrong, 1994).

Developing Multiple Intelligences

There are several ways to approach the development of multiple intelligences. In essence, these are the collective activities described within this section. These include analysis and diagnosis of the student, including instructional and curricular strategies; providing a conducive environment; administering appropriate assessment; and so on. An important point is that one attempts to develop a balance in each student, and also recognizes and encourages the development of a particularly strong area.

Multiple Intelligences Curriculum

A variety of techniques can be used to incorporate the range of multiple intelligences in curriculum materials. A basic strategy is to take a given objective of the lesson and identify the ways in which the various multiple intelligences can be addressed. Armstrong (1994) suggests asking questions such as: "How can I involve the whole body or use hands-on experiences for the bodily-kinesthetic intelligence?" "How can I bring in numbers or calculations for critical thinking for the logical-mathematical intelligence?" (p. 58).

Teaching for Multiple Intelligences

As with curriculum, a variety of teaching strategies can be used that specifically enhance or relate to particular types of intelligence. The premise is that students have preferences or proclivities for one or more of the intelligences. It is important for the teacher to use those modalities in their instructional practice. Armstrong (1994), for example, presents thirty-five teaching strategies, five for each of the seven intelligences. The teacher interested in addressing the range of multiple intelligences then must provide for a variety of instructional strategies in the classroom. The role of the Helping Professional is to help identify these in the planning process, to assist in determining the extent to which these are made operational during the lessons, and to participate in assessing their degree of effectiveness.

Multiple Intelligences and Assessment

The multiple intelligences approach suggests there is a wide range of means by which to assess an individual's achievement or levels of competence. Obviously this is a move away from a single mode such as a written test. The multiple intelligences model is more amenable to the authentic assessment approach. As noted by Gardner (1983, 1993b) one can best assess students' multiple intelligences by observing them and manipulating the symbol system of each intelligence. Assessment thus calls for using work samples, anecdotal records, observations and tapes, informal assessment, and criterion-referenced assessment. Portfolios, of course, can be of particular importance in the multiple intelligences system.

Multiple Intelligences and Cognitive Skills

Supporters of multiple intelligences indicate that memory, for example, is a variable that depends upon one's intelligence preference. Thus, memory is intelligence-specific, as individuals may have better memories in certain areas than in others. The philosophy of multiple intelligences suggests that the teacher must help students gain better access to their more functional type of memory. Thus, memory work should be taught in a way that uses all memories. In addition to memory, multiple intelligences in the cognitive skills can be applied to problem solving and Bloom's cognitive complexity.

Integrated (Thematic) Curriculum

In discussing multiple intelligences, we noted that use of curriculum was one essential vehicle for responding to multiple intelligences. A central strategy within that is the use of thematic curriculum development. Approaching the design of integrated (thematic) curriculum is another example of an area that might serve as content of observation, diagnosis, and guidance by the Helping Professional. Other areas are multidisciplinary, interdisciplinary, and transdisciplinary approaches.

In a multidisciplinary approach, a specific theme is identified. Relevant concepts, strategies, and knowledge from the various disciplines that impinge on the theme are then brought together to form the curriculum. One outcome is to illustrate that the disciplines are not isolated and that they have interrelated functions in particular areas of study.

In the interdisciplinary skills approach the purpose is to find skills that cross discipline boundaries. For example, literature, history and science have the common skills of literacy, collaborative learning, thinking skills, numeracy, and research skills, among others (Drake, 1993). The Helping Professional might ask if appropriate competencies have been identified, if the commonalties are truly across the disciplines, and if the critical skills in each of the disciplines are included in the lesson or unit plan.

The transdisciplinary approach is one in which study is focused on real-life situations. The purpose is to help students become more productive citizens. The Helping Professional may ask which skills of the real world for productive citizenship have been identified, and if these components of the various disciplines were brought to bear in this particular curriculum development.

The areas of multiple intelligences and the integrated curriculum provide examples of how the focus of guidance and observation can be developed depending upon the particular interests of the school and that specific classroom. A variety of other topics might be identified as an area of emphasis for a given period of support. It is important that these be identified mutually so that they are recognized as priorities, particularly for the teacher. Other areas of interest, for example, are: technology in the classroom, global education, multicultural perspectives, whole language–phonics relationships, and the democratic classroom.

Standards for Teachers

A number of groups have developed standards that identify the knowledge, skills, competencies, and attitudes required of teachers in order to be successful in today's classrooms. As we noted earlier, these provide a framework with which to observe and assess teachers in their classrooms. They are not intended to be prescriptive, but rather informative. They also provide varied perspectives in a wide range of specific areas that might be included as part of the content of the assessment, diagnosis, and support.

There are a number of ways in which the knowledge base might be divided and characterized. Hunter and Russell (1990), for example, suggest that there is research-based propositional knowledge, procedural knowledge that translates psychological and educational propositions (how to do it), and conditional knowledge of when, why, and how to do it (p. 7).

In the following sections we will look at national standards, state standards, and standards developed by other agencies.

National Learned Societies

A number of national professional organizations have developed standards for their respective areas. Many of these focus on standards for student learning. Organizations such as the National Council of Teachers of Mathematics (NCTM), the National Council of Teachers of English (NCTE), and a large number of others have created these standards in order to guide the curriculum for K–12 schools. In addition to these, a number of learned societies have developed standards for the preparation of teachers for their specific disciplines. This is an effort that is being conducted in cooperation with the National Council for Accreditation of Teacher Education (NCATE). These standards are used to approve the subject area professional preparation programs at the colleges and universities that seek NCATE accreditation. At the time of this writing there are eighteen such sets of standards developed for specific teacher preparation areas by the respective professional associations.

In general, these sets of standards describe the basic areas of knowledge that one needs in order to teach that discipline. Some of these are quite detailed, specifying the specific knowledge base. The standards also delve into the area of instructional competency that one needs and relate to the kinds of curriculum that the candidate should be able to develop.

National Standards and Accreditation Efforts

Other national organizations have begun to develop guidelines that they seek to apply across state lines.

The National Board for Professional Teaching Standards

In 1987, the National Board for Professional Teaching Standards (NBPTS) was created. Its mission is to establish high and rigorous standards for what teachers should know and be able to do, to certify teachers who meet those standards, and to advance related educational reforms for the purpose of improving student learning in America (National Board). There are five central policy positions being pursued. These include: (1) what teachers should know and be able to do, (2) prerequisites for National Board certification, (3) the initial framework of National Board certificates, (4) principles to guide the development of assessment, and (5) education policy and reform priorities.

It is the intent of the National Board to develop certificates in over thirty fields, ranging from early childhood/generalists, to early adolescent, to young adulthood/vocational education. The Board identified four overlapping student development levels: early childhood, ages 3–8; middle childhood, ages 7–12; early adolescence, ages 11–15; and adolescence and young adulthood, ages 14–18.

For further information and copies of standards write to: National Board for Professional Teaching Standards, 300 River Place, Suite 3600, Detroit, MI 48207.

National Council for Accreditation of Teacher Education

The National Council for Accreditation of Teacher Education (NCATE) establishes standards for the accreditation of teacher preparation programs in the United States. Included in these standards are a number of statements regarding the necessary competencies that teachers need to demonstrate. These standards are periodically reviewed and revised to reflect current research and perspectives of the teaching profession. The most recent standards were developed in 1995.

For information write to: National Council for Accreditation of Teacher Education, 2010 Massachusetts Avenue NW, Suite 500, Washington, DC 20036-1023.

Interstate New Teacher Assessment and Support Consortium
In 1987, the Interstate New Teacher Support and Assessment Consortium (INTASC) was established to enhance collaboration among states interested in rethinking teacher assessment for initial licensing, as well as for the preparation and induction into the profession. INTASC currently is sponsored by the Council of Chief State School Officers (CCSSO). "These are standards that embody the kinds of knowledge, skills, and dispositions that teachers need to practice responsibly when they enter teaching, and that prepare them for eventual success as Board-certified teachers later in their careers" (INTASC, 1992, p. 1).

These standards are divided into three categories: knowledge, dispositions, and performances. The knowledge and dispositions categories are very broadly stated and are not that functional for our purposes here.

The standards being developed by INTASC are still in a developmental stage. If you are interested in viewing the full text of these standards or receiving updated versions as they are developed, write to the following address: INTASC, Council of Chief State School Officers, One Massachusetts Avenue NW, Suite 700, Washington, DC 20001-1431.

The National Association of State Directors of Teacher Education and Certification
Teacher preparation programs are approved by their respective state agencies in order to recommend candidates for a state license. Whereas NCATE accreditation is voluntary, state program approval is mandatory. States thus develop program approval standards (and sometimes state certification or licensing standards as well) for the purpose of reviewing teacher education programs at colleges and universities.

The National Association of State Directors of Teacher Education and Certification (NASDTEC) is an organization of state directors of teacher education program approval and certification whose responsibility is to provide for the development of standards that reflect expectations and teacher competencies. NASDTEC thus develops model standards that are often used by individual states to guide the standards development for that state. NASDTEC standards are adapted or sometimes fully adopted by state agencies.

For more information about the NASDTEC standards and programs, as well as updated versions of the standards, write to the following: NASDTEC Office, Attention: Donald Hair, Executive Director, 3600 Whitman Avenue N., Suite 105, Seattle, WA 98103.

State Standards

Individual states determine the expectations and education requirements of those who teach in their systems. Only a few are reviewed here, as examples.

State of California Standards
The document "California Standards of Program Quality and Effectiveness" has a specific category that identifies the required level of candidate competence and performance. There are ten basic competencies. For each of these there is a rationale and a list of factors to consider to determine whether or not the candidate meets the particular standard of competence. There are from three to five specific factors identified for each of the competencies.

For further information write: Commission on Teacher Credentialing, 1812 9th Street, Sacramento, CA, 95814-7000.

The State of California has also developed a statewide program for the support of beginning teachers. It is the Beginning Teacher Support and Assessment Program (BTSA). Its function is to provide observation of levels of beginning teacher competency through assessment instruments and to integrate this assessment information with an extensive program of support. The state has developed the "California Standards for the Teaching Profession" (July 1997).

Entry-Level Standards for Michigan Teachers
The Michigan document for beginning teacher competency contains six standards.

For further information write to the State of Michigan: Michigan State Department of Education, Department of Teacher Education, P.O. Box 30008, Lansing, MI 48909.

The Florida Performance Measurement System
The State of Florida has developed a comprehensive system for evaluating teachers in their initial years in the profession. The validity of this system is based on extensive analysis of the research. The content that is observed is contained in the domains of the Florida Performance Measurement System. These domains are research-based and are made up of several concepts each. Each concept also has indicators of performance. These are much too extensive to even summarize.

For further information and additional documents contact the following: Panhandle Area Education Cooperative, 411 West Blvd., Chipley, FL 32428.

Other Instruments of Teacher Assessment

Educational Testing Service: Pathwise and Praxis
The Educational Testing Service has also developed an extensive system for assessing teacher performance. This system includes a set of criteria organized into four domains. The first three domains have five criteria and the fourth domain has four. Each domain has scoring rules that provide for the rating of the teacher on a scale from 1.0 to 3.5, with 3.5 being the highest.

For further information write to: Educational Testing Service, Princeton, NJ, 08541.

Teacher Expectations and Student Achievement (TESA)
TESA is a program sponsored by Phi Delta Kappa. It relates to issues of equity in

the classroom. There are fifteen categories of teacher behaviors that make up the TESA system. The first has to do with equitable distribution of response opportunities to provide for equal involvement by gender, ethnicity, or other factors.

Information on the TESA model can be obtained from: Phi Delta Kappa, P.O. Box 789, Eighth & Union Streets, Bloomington, IN 47402-0789.

Closing Remarks

There are a significant number and variety of types of classifications of teacher behaviors and competencies. These provide the observer with a wide selection of areas to look for and to assess, diagnose, and guide. How and what the Helping Professional selects for the content will depend on the needs of the teacher, the philosophical orientation and the style of the Helping Professional, as well as the school district's expectations or standards.

Whether Helping Professionals use one of these systems, integrate the various approaches, or create their own, it is important to involve the person being assessed in the selection of the content. In many instances the content is specified by the school or other kinds of regulations. Sometimes these are broadly stated; some of the specific items provided by the various systems described here can be used to further delineate the broader statements if desired. In any event, the Helping Professional has a rich resource of options to use to assist and guide the teacher.

References

Armstrong, T. (1994). *Multiple intelligences in the classroom*. Alexandria, VA. Association for Supervision and Curriculum Development.

Association for Childhood Education International (1993). *Basic elementary education guidelines*. In the *NCATE approved curriculum guidelines* (pp. 65–82). Washington, DC: National Council for Accreditation of Teacher Educators.

California State Department and Commission on Teacher Credentialing (1995). *Beginning teaching in California: Expectations for teacher development*. Sacramento, CA: Author.

Clark, C., & Peterson, P. (1986). Teachers' thought processes. In M. C. Wittrock (Ed.), *Handbook of research on teaching* (3d ed.), (pp. 255–296). New York: Macmillan.

Commission on Teacher Credentialing and California Department of Education (1995). *Draft framework of expectations for beginning teachers.* Sacramento, CA: Author.

Commission on Teacher Credentialing (1992). *Standards of program quality and effectiveness for professional teacher preparation programs for multiple and single subject teaching credentials with a (bilingual) crosscultural, language and academic development emphasis.* Sacramento, CA: Commission on Teacher Credentialing.

Drake, S. M. (1993). *Planning integrated curriculum: The call to adventure.* Alexandria, VA: Association for Supervision and Curriculum Development.

Educational Testing Service (1995). *Teacher performance assessments: Assessment criteria.* Princeton, NJ: Author.

Florida Performance Measurement System (1983). *Knowledge base: Domains of the Florida Coalition for the Development of a Performance Evaluation System.* Tallahassee, FL: Florida Department of Education.

Gardner, H. (1983). *Frames of mind: The theory of multiple intelligences.* New York: Basic Books.

Gardner, H. (1993a). *Creating minds.* New York: Basic Books.

Gardner, H. (1993b). *Multiple intelligences: The theory of practice.* New York: Basic Books.

Glickman, C. D., Gordon, S. P., & Ross-Gordon, J. M. (1995). *Supervision of instruction: A developmental approach* (3d ed.). Boston: Allyn and Bacon.

Holmes Group (1986). *Tomorrow's teachers: A report of the Holmes Group.* East Lansing, MI: Author.

Hunter, M., & Russell, D. (1990). *Mastering coaching and supervision: Principles of Learning series.* Thousand Oaks, CA: Corwin Press.

Interstate New Teacher Assessment and Support Consortium (INTASC) (1992). *Model standards for beginning teacher licensing and development: A resource for state dialogue.* Washington, DC: Council of Chief State School Officers.

Joyce, B., & Weil, M. (1986). *Models of teaching.* Englewood Cliffs, NJ: Prentice-Hall.

Kramer, D. A. (1983). Post-formal operations: A need for further conceptualization. *Human Development 26*(2), 91–105.

Kramer, D. A. (1987, May). Age-relevance of content material on relativistic and dialectical reasoning. Paper presented at the annual symposium of the Jean Piaget Society, Philadelphia.

Lazear, D. G. (1992). *Teaching for multiple intelligences.* Bloomington, IN: Phi Delta Kappa Educational Foundation.

Mann, J. S. (1967). Curriculum criticism. *The Teachers College Record, 71*(1), 27–40.

Michigan State Board of Education (1993). *Entry level standards for Michigan teachers.* Lansing, MI: Department of Teacher Education.

National Association of State Directors of Teacher Education and Certification (1994). *Outcome-based standards and portfolio assessment: Outcome-based teacher education standards for the elementary, middle, and high school levels* (2d ed.). Dubuque, IA: Kendall/Hunt.

National Board for Professional Teaching Standards (1991). *Toward high and rigorous standards for the teaching profession* (2d ed.). Washington, DC: Author.

National Board for Professional Teaching Standards (1994, September). *Early adolescence/generalist standards for National Board certification.* Washington, DC: Author.

National Board for Professional Teaching Standards (1996, January). *Middle childhood/generalist standards for National Board certification.* Washington, DC: Author.

National Council for Accreditation of Teacher Education (1995). *Standards, procedures, and policies for the accreditation of professional education units.* Washington, DC: Author.

National Council of Teachers of Mathematics (1993). Basic K–4, 5–8, and 7–12 guidelines. In the *NCATE approved curriculum guidelines* (pp. 268–287). Washington, DC: Author.

Phi Delta Kappa (1993). *Teacher Expectations and Student Achievement (TESA).* Bloomington, IN: Author.

Ramsey, I. (1964). *Models and mystery.* London: Oxford University Press.

Riegel, K. (1973). Dialectical operations: The final period of cognitive development. *Human Development, 16:* 346–370.

Sergiovanni, T. J., & Starratt, R. J. (1993). *Supervision: A redefinition* (5th ed.). New York: McGraw-Hill.

Shulman, L. (1986). Those who understand: Knowledge growth in teaching. *Educational Researcher, 15*(2), 8–9.

Taranto, M. (1987, May). *Wisdom and logic.* Paper presented at the annual symposium of the Jean Piaget Society, Philadelphia. (ERIC ED 282 099.)

Chapter 12

Assessing and Diagnosing (Dimension Three)

This chapter will describe and analyze three aspects of the assessing and diagnosing dimension. These aspects are why one needs to assess and diagnose, what should be assessed and diagnosed, and how it should be done.

Purpose of Assessing and Diagnosing

Growth is greatly facilitated through knowledge of self. The more individuals know about their personal attributes, skills, and professional competencies, the better position they will be in to grow. This self-knowledge relates to strengths, weaknesses, and needs. It is acquired through various types of assessments. The assessment for teachers is most valuable when it deals with the two domains of need: personal-psychological and instructional-professional.

It is generally accepted that feedback is essential for improved practice and personal functioning (Joyce & Showers, 1983.) In order to provide feedback that is relevant and accurate, an assessment must be made and diagnostic information provided. Assessment provides for the collection of information, and diagnosis involves an interpretation or analysis. The intent is to develop a realistic picture. This is a necessary first step in building a basis for professional development.

In the helping professions, it is recognized that intervention requires learning about the individual. Medicine and psychology make assessments through intakes on patients to acquire baseline data that assists in diagnoses. Observation also is a standard procedure in mentoring and supervising. For Helping Professionals in any profession, this is deemed sound practice.

The philosophy of the Transformational Helping Professional model centers around meeting the needs of individuals so they can function more productively in both personal and professional areas. Meeting needs is a prime source of motivation in the model. It assists in developing positive self-esteem and coping with stress and burnout. A necessary and logical starting point is needs analysis. This is the function of the assessing and diagnosing dimension. Diagnosis is one of the most important skills of highly effective people. If there is no confidence in the diagnosis, there is no confidence in the prescription (Covey, 1990).

The Focus of Assessing and Diagnosing

What is one looking for in observation and assessment? As described in earlier chapters, it is essential that needs in both the personal-psychological and instructional-professional domain be the focus of assessment and diagnosis. Teachers have critical needs in each of these areas that must be addressed in order to work with the whole teacher. These will be examined in some detail here.

The Process of Assessing and Diagnosing

It may be useful to recall the distinction between assessment and evaluation. In this dimension of the Transformational model, assessment is a data collection process and may involve comparison with norms, standards, or other criteria for descriptive purposes only. It is not intended to make judgments of worth, but to provide information for analysis, inference, and diagnosis. The diagnostic function is to discern discrepancies, inconsistencies, and patterns, as well as positive practices and activities when compared to expectations or outcomes. It also should be made clear that assessing and diagnosing are ongoing processes. In some models, it is assumed that information is collected once or twice and the remainder of the time is spent on providing assistance. Monitoring of changes, improvements, and the current level of functioning is necessary to determine effectiveness of interventions and the helping process. This ongoing process is not an accountability check or inspection; rather, it should be viewed as an objective inquiry.

In the Transformational Helping Professional model, often what transpires between the Helping Professional and the teacher is quite different than in traditional interactions. This is a psychoanalytic model; hence, much of the process is focused on the needs of the teacher. Assessment and diagnosis take on a different tone and emphasis in this approach.

The strategies and techniques for assessing and diagnosing vary to some extent in relation to the nature of information being collected. When determining behaviors, observation techniques are the best means of obtaining the needed information. If the focus is on development of products, such as lesson plans and evaluation instruments, a portfolio is more appropriate. It should not be assumed that all information can be collected in the same way or from the same source. A variety of perspectives or data types collected from a variety of sources, even on the same issue, typically is more informative and more accurate. It provides a more balanced and comprehensive description of the area of need.

Those who are experiencing difficulty need more frequent status checks and assessments of where they are and how they are progressing. A more in-depth analysis is appropriate. For experienced teachers who are doing well and wish to strengthen particular areas of interest or need, only a limited or very focused assessment would be in order. One of the guiding principles of the Transformational Helping Professional model is flexibility and adaptation. Because it is highly individualized and personalized, set protocols that apply to everyone are not used.

Personal-Psychological Needs

Meeting the needs of individual teachers is the prime focus of the Helping Professional. In the personal-psychological domain, this must be done with great care. Helping Professionals must know the limitations of their expertise and education. The limits on inquiry into personal and psychological needs also must be clear. In order to function in the role of Helping Professional, it is not necessary to have preparation as a psychotherapist or psychologist. It should not be interpreted that the Helping Professional will be dealing with deep psychological issues. This is beyond the purview and scope of the role of mentor or supervisor.

The personal-psychological needs described in Chapter 4 are those that can be readily assessed. They are needs with which the Helping Professional is qualified to provide assistance. The processes and skills for extending this support are provided in this book. If the Helping Professional does not address these personal-psychological issues, the support rests only in the technical domain and can become somewhat sterile and depersonalized. This is counterproductive to the role of the Helping Professional.

When considering personal-psychological needs, the degree of anxiety may be greatly magnified. Identifying areas for improvement in one's technical skills is one thing, but to reveal personal and psychological needs is quite a different matter. It is a revealing of one's inner self. To some this is a private matter, and there is a reluctance to discuss, yet alone reveal, information in this personal realm.

In view of this hesitancy in the personal-psychological domain, the issues of rapport and trust become even more critical. This domain must be approached very carefully. The stronger the relationship between the helper and the teacher, the more the teacher will be interested in participating. This is where the helping and communication skills are of significant value.

Conducting an assessment is not to be treated casually and without sensitivity. The stage must be set. Most treatments of the mentoring process focus on the importance of establishing a positive setting before the helper confers with the teacher about the teacher's performance. This is the guidance and assistance phase of the helping process. Understanding personal-psychological needs is important for successfully setting the stage for observation and for subsequent guidance.

The Personal-Psychological Needs Areas and Instruments

Chapter 4 introduced the domain of the personal-psychological needs of teachers. It has been an area neglected in the past, one that has become increasingly important for enhancing one's professional development and increasing professional effectiveness. It is necessary for Helping Professionals to understand clearly these needs, to have experience in using the instruments, and to have acquired insights about their own needs before assisting others and using the instruments as an assessment tool. For these reasons, the Helping Professional was provided an opportunity to personally take them in Chapter 4. One of the principles emphasized throughout the program is that the more one is able to identify and work on one's own needs, the better one will be able to help others work on theirs.

In this chapter the way the instruments can be used to collect information consistent with the assessment and diagnosis dimension will be examined. The instruments provide significant information on the personal and psychological needs of the teacher, which is not accessible through traditional observation systems and processes. This domain is almost always overlooked in the assessment phase of mentoring and supervising because it is not perceived to be within the purview of educators. This often creates a degree of discomfort. So it is important to learn these skills and put them into practice. Commitment to this effort must be made, as these skills are indispensable to the role of the Helping Professional.

When helping, the first step is to have the teacher complete the questionnaires in Chapter 4. We suggest beginning with a review of the physical needs and proceeding in the order they are presented in the chapter. This process needs to take place over a period of a few weeks. The instruments are not intended for one sitting. The questions in the instruments are intended to help teachers gain insights into their respective needs.

Physical Needs

Questions may arise about the purpose for beginning the inventory process with assessment of physical needs. The Helping Professional must understand the rationale for this activity and clearly articulate this to the teacher. The concern is for the well-being of all aspects of teachers that affect their performance as professional educators. This goes beyond assessment of technical-instructional proficiency alone.

There is a considerable body of research that links one's physical state to emotions, behavior, and level of performance (Hafen et al., 1992; Pelletier, 1993). When our physical condition is out of balance, we simply cannot function at our best, or even normal, level of performance. We feel out of sync, or just "not with it" for that day or period of time. When this unease is chronic, it has a definite and significant impact on one's personal as well as professional life. It is essential that both the Helping Professional and teacher understand the role of physical needs and are able to identify their needs in order to ascertain ways of addressing them more effectively and completely. One of the purposes of the needs instruments is to raise teachers' consciousness levels and prepare them for guidance and assistance in this area.

The Helping Professional's Responsibilities and Influence in the Physical Area.
As a Helping Professional, one cannot assume responsibility for another's behavior. Self-responsibility is a key concept in this model of helping. All individuals, including Helping Professionals, must take responsibility for their own growth. The process of change discussed in Chapter 3 incorporates this approach as a fundamental premise. Helping Professionals' responsibility is to assist, encourage, guide, and support teachers in the process of becoming aware of their unmet needs and meeting them, which will also affect their professional growth.

It is through the assessment and support process that Helping Professionals have a significant influence on teachers' attending to their own needs, be they physical, emotional, or other. In fact, the function of Helping Professionals is to exercise their knowledge and skills to assist teachers in bringing about personal change and growth.

In the physical area there are six needs that the teacher is to address. The important question becomes "What do the instruments and the responses reveal about physical needs?" The first area relating to physical needs is that of energy, and exercise is identified as one vehicle for assisting with energy levels. The diagnosis might reveal that the teacher is greatly depleted of energy, and that the lack of energy has significantly interfered with the teaching process. This is a common problem. Many teachers indicate how tired they are throughout the day and that they have little time for social activity, let alone intellectual engagement. It is valuable to work with the teacher in determining how much of a problem this really is, noting whether or not it requires medical attention. Related to this is what changes should be made in order to accommodate this issue of insufficient energy. A plan of action is thus needed to help the teacher follow through.

A Case Example. The following actual case study illustrates how this physical need and assessment can impact the teacher's professional functioning. Gwen is a third grade teacher in her fourth year of teaching. She has taught second grade, as well as third, and feels she basically has her routines down to a comfortable level. She is concerned, however, that her teaching is not at the level she expects of herself or has been capable of in the past. "I just can't seem to get with it. I can't keep up. I'm motivated, I really want to do well, but it just isn't happening the way it should."

In doing an analysis of her workday and needs, she realized that she had been extremely tired lately. Although she was aware of being tired, she had not realized the extent to which it had increased in her life. After some discussion, she realized that it had become serious enough to require significant attention. She kept a log of the amount of sleep she was getting, the type of exercise she was involved in, and the degree of physical energy she exerted during the day.

Her teaching strategies, classroom management plans, and approach to lesson planning had not changed to any great extent, but her teaching was not as effective. The critical factor was that she was not implementing her skills to the extent that she was capable of or that she had done in the past. Efforts to work with her on classroom organization and planning did not seem to help because there were no serious problems in these areas. Her teaching was suffering because she was physically not able to conduct herself in the ways that she was capable of and expected of herself.

By concentrating only on the professional and instructional level, the supervisor and the teacher together were not able to pinpoint the problem. With this new insight about her life, Gwen was able to plan on how to gain increased energy levels and to feel better about herself, as well as about her teaching.

Factors of Physical Assessment. The calmness factor in the instrument relates to the degree of balance in the teacher's life. Assessment determines whether the daily experience is sufficiently serene. In diagnosing the calmness factor, one determines the impact it is having on the teacher's life. It is important to note how significant it is to the teacher at this point in time. Also of interest is discerning what elements are related to the hectic nature of the day, and which are the most critical factors related to this feeling of lack of balance.

The safety factor can be clearly determined. The assessment should seek to determine whether or not it is of genuine concern. Further, is it a critical barrier to the normal functioning of the individual's life? The diagnosis should relate to determining how it affects the individual's professional role. This, in turn, would lead to ideas about what changes should be made.

Another area of assessment is general health, including nutrition. Assessing the individual's general health status often reveals important information regarding the ability to function in the teacher role. Is there a chronic illness? Are there frequent illnesses? Is the diet putting the teacher on energy highs and lows?

Exercise is related to energy levels, but physical fitness in general needs to be looked at in terms of its impact on the variety of areas of one's personal life. The assessment should determine whether or not the physical state of the individual is adequate. As a diagnostic perspective, the teacher needs to come to recognize how physical fitness appears to be affecting his or her life, both personally and professionally.

Sleep patterns also are relevant to the overall physical well-being of the individual. The assessment is to help the teacher determine what the sleep pattern reveals for him or her. The diagnosis should determine whether or not this is sufficient. The sleep pattern may be one's regular habit and not necessarily abnormal for that person. However, the question is "Does it fit the person's current demand for rest?"

Emotional Needs
Unmet emotional needs can have devastating effects. One may be well aware of physical needs as these have more noticeable symptoms and consequences.

However, the emotional area can be even more telling on one's lifestyle. The emotional questionnaire reveals a wealth of information that leads to significant insights. Each of the emotional needs can have a profound effect on the way we function. It is essential to understand the degree to which each of these needs is being met.

The security need relates to how confident and emotionally safe we feel. Financial concerns fit into this area as well. Personal relations quite frequently are the source of difficulty that may put one out of sync. Looking with the teacher at the responses to the questions about personal relationships and financial security may help the teacher become aware of the degree to which this need is being met.

Serenity and harmony are emotional factors that one needs to be aware of, because they can have an effect even in subtle ways. Turmoil and pressures result from hectic schedules, people conflicts, and time constraints. These are all common factors in the lives of teachers. Part of the assessment here is to understand these elements in the teacher's life. One question to ask is "How fast is your pace?" Ultimately, one needs to determine whether or not this area needs attention.

Self-acceptance, self-esteem, and self-confidence are independent factors, yet they have some relationship. Much of what one does is helped or hindered by one's perception of self—how well one accepts and is comfortable with one's self. Insight about one's self is needed as a reality check. One subsequently needs to face the reality of self-perceptions. Most teachers do not realize these needs and deal more with surface issues than with fundamental areas. As seen in the questions, there are various dimensions in these areas of self-understanding, each of which provides different insights to the teacher. They form an important part of the assessment of the teacher's emotional needs.

In Chapter 4 the significance of emotional needs in one's personal and professional lives was described. Emotional stability has been increasingly related to effective performance in the teaching profession. One purpose of assessment in this area is to raise teachers' consciousness level of this need, help them understand how well it is being met, determine what influence it is having on them, and understand in what ways it is having an influence. The diagnosis of its influence helps to determine ways to deal with it.

Having no warm, loving relationships in one's life can leave a significant void. It is even more devastating if the individual feels that he or she is not capable of having strong personal relationships, as identified in Question 8. Having significant others in one's life provides a foundation from which one can develop positive coping skills. It provides an area for retreating when one needs comfort or validation of worth. One may not realize that the lack of these kinds of relationships may be influencing one's professional functioning.

Intellectual Needs
The intellectual needs of teachers is an area frequently misunderstood. Teachers may not realize that their lives throughout their training had been focused around intellectual issues. Teaching is an intellectual enterprise and profession that requires thought processes as its basis. Yet, teachers get tied up with the daily grind

and paperload and neglect much of their need for intellectual stimulation. Teachers may be caught in an activity trap where they are busy doing required things, rather than having time to stop and reflect on ideas or their practice.

This area of psychological need relates closely to the instructional-professional area as well. Important questions to ask the teacher after taking the instrument are: "What is the extent of your intellectual stimulation?" "Are you sufficiently stimulated in relation to your instructional practice?" Once the teacher thinks about it, ask, "Is it an area you find lacking in your life?" There are a variety of ways to deal with this, and these will be examined in the next chapter on guidance and support.

Social Needs
In the social needs questionnaire there are eleven areas of needs identified. Teachers often are surprised to note the variety and complexity of social needs. In assessing these, look at each item and discuss its influence on the teachers' professional work and on themselves personally. Also, take an overall perspective of the social needs area to obtain a feel for how well the teacher is functioning in general. Sometimes one looks at the specifics and loses a feel for the general.

Spiritual Needs
The area of spiritual needs has been considered taboo in that it has been linked to religious dogma or even the zealous imposition of other people's ideas. Spirituality, broadly characterized in Chapter 4, includes issues such as religion, family, and a sense of being. Spirituality may be centered on family relationships, a deep belief in a higher being, or a belief in humanitarian efforts. The important point is that it provides a source of meaning, a driving force for personal accomplishment. It helps provide purpose, meaningfulness, vision, and, for many, the essence of life. Teachers need to assess their needs in this area by reviewing the list of spiritual needs identified in Chapter 4. They need to ask which of these are of particular importance to them. If there is a sense of emptiness or a vacuum, particularly with the lack of purpose, then these spiritual needs might be carefully reviewed to determine which can be of assistance in providing more significance to the teachers' life.

Professional Health
Assessment of the personal-psychological needs can be one of the most productive and effective ways of assisting teachers and improving their professional life. No matter how strong one's instructional-professional skills are, without a firm foundation of healthy emotional, personal-psychological needs, the skills will not be as accessible or usable by the teacher.

A first step is understanding what these areas of needs are. A subsequent step is to then determine, through this assessment process, one's status relative to the particular needs. Identification of unmet needs in this personal-psychological area can be an extremely enlightening process. It also provides an opportunity to build a program of guidance and support to assist the helpee in meeting these needs. Teachers must be healthy, productive individuals who have a firm personal foundation and possess technical-professional skills. Together these form a condition of professional health (Gold & Roth, 1993).

Psychological Needs Summary

We have reviewed a wide range of personal-psychological needs. The purpose of assessment and diagnosis in this domain is to lay the groundwork for the guidance and support process that follows. The principle upon which this is based is that a mature, psychologically balanced individual has a strong foundation for building competence in the instructional-professional domain. These two domains go hand in hand, with each supporting the other. The more teachers' personal-psychological needs are met, the better they will be able to use the instructional skills they already have, and the better they will be able to learn, acquire new skills, and grow professionally. Similarly, the more proficient teachers are in their practice, the better they will feel about themselves, which contributes to meeting certain personal-psychological needs.

The next section will focus on the instructional-professional domain. In focusing on a single domain, one may see clear links to the other. Problems in managing classroom discipline, for example, may have roots in a teacher's emotional areas such as unmet self-esteem needs. This interaction of the needs and classroom performance takes time to discern and understand, but awareness is the first step.

Instructional-Professional Needs

Assessment and diagnosis of instructional-professional needs must address a variety of areas and teacher functions. These include areas such as planning, classroom discipline, delivery of instruction, student evaluation, thought processes, and self-analysis or reflection. A more complete specification of instructional needs was provided in Chapter 5. The focus here is on the process of assessing and diagnosing instructional-professional needs. Although process and content are not isolated from each other, the process of assessing and diagnosing will be more closely examined in this section.

Assessing Teacher Thinking

In Chapter 5 the instructional-professional needs of teachers and how these needs influence their professional practice were reviewed. Various theories were examined to provide a context for understanding the ways in which teachers develop. These also provided implications for understanding the changes individuals must go through, as well as the mechanisms by which change occurs. Chapter 3 also provided insights into the process teachers must go through to change. A critical factor presented in Chapter 5 was that Helping Professionals need to consider the thought processes that guide teachers' thinking before, during, and after a lesson and to understand the type of thinking they are doing. The helper also needs to be aware of teachers' understanding of the content being taught, as well as the various instructional decisions they must make during their teaching. These types of thinking will develop and change throughout their career.

As noted, the research emphasis has shifted from what teachers do to inquiries about what teachers think and how this influences their performance. In view of the complexities of today's classrooms, the current emphasis on constructivist approaches to teaching and the increase in teachers' roles in decision making in the instructional process make it even more imperative that the helper assess teachers' needs in these areas. This section of the chapter will thus identify the mechanisms that are available to the Helping Professional in assisting teachers to assess the extent of their needs and implications for their instructional practice.

As an advance organizer, it may be noted that the methods for assessing teacher thought processes can be organized into three categories, as proposed by Clark and Peterson (1986). These include planning (pre-active and post-active thoughts), interactive thoughts and decisions, and theories and beliefs. The distinction among categories is particularly important in view of the perspective that teachers' interactive thoughts and decisions appear to be qualitatively different from the kind of thinking they do when they are not interacting with students. It is of interest to note that teacher thought processes significantly affect teacher performance, and teacher performance is used as a means of feedback to modify thought processes. This thought process–performance dynamic is an important principle in the Transformational Helping Professional model.

The five processes of inquiry proposed by Clark and Peterson (1986) and referred to in Chapter 5 will be applied here. These are thinking aloud, stimulated recall, policy capturing, journal keeping, and the repertory grid technique. Each of these can be related to the content areas deemed essential for effective practice in contemporary classrooms. The content areas include subject matter knowledge, pedagogical content knowledge, and curricular knowledge, as identified by Shulman (1986). All of these techniques need to be focused on teachers' thought processes, and the Helping Professional assists in developing this focus.

Thinking Aloud Technique
One way to assess teachers' thought processes related to subject matter, curriculum development, instructional practice, or other associated areas of teaching is to have teachers verbalize their understandings. This process of "thinking aloud" is a means of capturing what the teacher believes about curriculum and instruction. What makes this of particular interest is that it is done in conjunction with the actual practice in which the teacher is engaged.

In the process of thinking aloud, the Helping Professional would assist the teacher in recording what is occurring. It is the Helping Professional's responsibility to provide as accurate a record as possible to be shared with the teacher at a later time.

If the data are collected and shared positively with the teacher in the guidance and support phase, the teacher will be encouraged and more willing to participate in the future. Furthermore, the more useful the teacher finds this record to be, the more enthusiastically she or he will participate in this process.

Stimulated Recall Technique

The stimulated recall method was developed to deal more directly with teachers' thought processes during the actual teaching act. This process involves an audio or video recording of the teacher instructing in the classroom. Stimulated recall can be quite challenging, as it often is difficult to remember what one was thinking at the time of instruction. Thus, it should be noted that the process is not completely accurate and is somewhat imprecise as a methodology.

Each of the concerns regarding the participation of the teacher in the thinking aloud strategy applies to stimulated recall as well.

Policy Capturing Technique

In the policy capturing strategy a series of student descriptions or hypothetical teaching situations are presented to the teacher. The teacher is asked to make decisions about these, thus revealing decision-making strategies. It is useful in assessing this component of teacher thinking, but the strategy has several disadvantages. The student descriptions and teaching situations must be developed, as well as tested for feasibility related to eliciting decision-making strategies. The time and effort required for development can be quite restrictive.

Journal Keeping Technique

Journal keeping also is a very effective tool in the assessment process. Although journal keeping research related to teacher thinking has mainly been used in the study of planning, it also can be used for investing several aspects of the teaching role and process. Journaling thought processes prior to teaching and after teaching often is very productive. There are a variety of ways to construct journals and to identify the elements that need to be recorded. To some extent this will depend upon the level of the teacher's experience.

Journal writing need not be limited to any set areas because it is a broadly applicable process. Teachers may record in their journals reflections on planning, interactive thoughts and decisions, and their theories and beliefs. On the other hand, the journal might be used to focus on specific areas of teacher need.

A teacher may wish to examine in more detail a lesson design, thinking through not only the basis for its development, but its effectiveness and implications for future planning. This type of reflection will lend insights into the thinking process of the teacher, and the Helping Professional can encourage ways of developing the thinking into new areas of thought.

Repertory Grid Technique

The repertory grid strategy also is one that is more appropriate for teacher preparation or for professional development situations. This strategy may be somewhat contrived and thus less valuable in assessing the teacher's areas of instructional need. It should be noted, however, that the process could reveal some very fundamental issues that may explain much of the teacher's thinking that influences instructional behaviors. The purpose is to assist in defining the individual's personal constructs as related to the teaching process.

Subject Matter Knowledge

A first step in the assessment of subject matter is to realize that there are basically at least three components to look at: subject matter knowledge, pedagogical content knowledge, and curricular knowledge. The Helping Professional assists teachers in assessing their subject matter knowledge by engaging in a mutual analysis of the discipline. The discussion might include a description of the fundamental ideas and concepts. Teachers might be asked to identify what aspects of the subject they feel are important for the students to learn.

In terms of pedagogical content knowledge, the question of importance is to determine whether or not teachers understand ways of transforming the content into useful representations for the level and background of the students with whom they are working.

An assessment of curricular issues might be made of teachers' understanding of the structure of the curriculum in terms of both breadth and depth and what is the most appropriate mixture of the two in the development of classroom curriculum. Knowledge of curricular programs, instructional materials, and criteria for selection and use of these materials specific to the discipline are useful elements of the assessment and diagnosis of subject matter knowledge.

Assessment and Diagnosis in the Instructional-Professional Domain

The emphasis of assessment and diagnosis in the instructional domain is on the actual delivery of instruction. This is an area of primary interest to Helping Profesionals.

In addition to observations, assessment and diagnosis must extend to documents and activities related to pre- and post-instruction events. When analyzing a teacher's planning, for example, a review of lesson plans is necessary. Other approaches are needed depending upon the nature of information desired, the type of activity being reviewed, and the source of information. In addition to formal classroom observation, the assessment and diagnosis processes may include casual/informal observation, interviews, questionnaires and checklists, analysis of teacher-developed documents such as portfolios, student-developed documents (could also use portfolios), critical event documentation, student performance documents (standardized and teacher-made tests), and records of teacher preparation or performance (prior teaching, examinations).

Interviews

The purpose of the interview (or conference) is to collect information directly from the teacher in a manner that may be more personal than through a survey or questionnaire. The interview also may provide opportunities to pursue issues that arise during the discussion, depending upon the type of interview procedure being employed. The interview or conference is a data-collection process that contributes to the diagnosis and the subsequent processes of guidance and support.

Conferences are an integral part of advising, preparing for some types of observations, and for post-observation reviews. A Helping Professional may meet with a beginning teacher to provide feedback on classroom management. A student teacher supervisor or master teacher may review a lesson plan with a student teacher, or a school supervisor may discuss teacher-developed student assessment practices with an experienced teacher. These are examples of conferences in which feedback is given or analysis is made of a teacher's skills or activities. They provide perspectives on how well the teacher is doing.

There are several ways to conduct interviews, and selection of the approach must be given careful consideration. The method selected will depend upon the kinds of information being sought, the nature of the inquiry, the setting one intends to establish, the approach one is using, the type of relationship one has with the teacher, and the characteristics of the teacher involved. All of these factors considered collectively determine how one will structure and engage in the interview process.

The most flexible approach is an open style, a general inquiry without a specific structure. The process is not tightly designed. The Helping Professional might begin by asking what topics or issues the teacher would like to discuss, and then move in whatever direction appears useful. No particular procedure is specified in advance. The disadvantage of this very open approach is that it may not yield information essential to the needs analysis. If the Helping Professional allows the teacher to go off on tangents, the discussion might only address some critical concerns and neglect others. The pros and cons of this approach thus need to be weighed against the purpose of the interview and the expertise of the interviewer.

Another approach to the interview is to have a clear and specific goal in mind. This is a more focused approach both in terms of the questions asked and the sequence of questions.

An even more structured approach to the interview uses a previously developed script that the Helping Professional adheres to closely. The information recorded is limited to the responses to the predetermined questions. There may be a coding system to record or score responses.

A variety of ways to conduct interviews has been described. Selecting the right approach will depend upon one's purpose and information needs. It is not necessary to select only one strategy. Combinations of these interview types are quite effective. As one prepares for interviews or pre-observation conferences, one will review what each approach might offer in terms of the information needed.

Questionnaires

Questionnaires are written forms of data collection and serve the same purposes as interviews. Interviews have the advantage of allowing the interviewer to pursue responses in more depth or take the interviewee in different directions.

In using questionnaires, the data needs are clearly established. As an assessment tool a questionnaire may be focused on the needs of the teacher. In this instance there is particular concern with the instructional-professional area. In essence, a questionnaire can be a needs-assessment instrument.

Documents for Assessment: Portfolios

One way of organizing documents that has gained popularity in recent years is the portfolio. A portfolio is seen as being a more authentic assessment of abilities. It is intended to be a meaningful collection of the teacher's work through documents that represent the teacher's efforts, expertise, thinking, and outcomes. These documents are used to assess the teacher's level of skill or understanding in particular areas.

Portfolios are very helpful when used in conjunction with other assessment strategies. For example, during an interview, teachers may illustrate their questions or concerns by providing a sample of work from their portfolio. The Helping Professional could follow up with questions about the documents to ascertain the thinking and planning that went into their development.

An important principle of portfolios particularly relevant to assessment is that portfolios require teachers to learn about their own work, competency status, or level of understanding. They may consider factors such as what they do as a teacher, how they approach their tasks, how well they do it, and what their strengths and weaknesses might be. Portfolios should be used to encourage reflection.

Purposes and Types

There are different types of portfolios, varied purposes for their development and use, a range of formats for their construction, and extensive choices of content. Each of these components requires careful review in order to make a portfolio an effective tool for needs assessment and diagnosis.

Portfolios serve two basic functions. The first is to provide a basis for evaluation of competence and performance. This is a summative evaluation function; decisions regarding effectiveness, retention, or tenure may be made from the evidence provided in the portfolio. Portfolios for K–12 students are being used in this way at an increasing rate. The authentic assessment movement is a major focus of conferences and literature on today's schools. Some states are developing portfolio assessments as a means of granting state teaching licenses (Darling-Hammond, Wise, & Klein, 1995).

A second major purpose of portfolios is formative assessment. In this instance the documents are reviewed as a means of identifying areas of need.

Content

It should be noted that a particular document may be used for more than one category, depending upon how the portfolio is organized. The content will vary with the nature of the developmental stage and type of teacher. Student teachers, for example, will have different types of artifacts than experienced teachers will have.

The documents selected should reflect the objectives of the program, the district, and the individual teacher. One should always bear in mind the purpose of the portfolio. The information must be of value in assessing the needs, interests, and competencies of the teacher. If it is not helpful, do not include it.

In relation to guidance and support, a criterion would be the extent to which the document enhances teacher reflection and growth. Attention to details of this nature makes portfolios meaningful in this domain.

Observation of Teaching

The most common method of assessing and diagnosing is to observe the teacher's performance. This provides firsthand knowledge of how the teacher is functioning in the classroom.

The observation of classroom performance is not an isolated activity. It is part of a procedure with a series of steps. The focus of the observation is usually derived from preceding events. These events may be prior experience with the teacher, a teacher's indication of what he or she is seeking assistance with, a pre-observation conference, or combination of these. In any event, these precedent experiences help formulate the focus of the observation. This does not mean that all classroom observations are formal, based on specific objectives. Even when the observation is spur of the moment, the observer usually brings to it information or biases that influence what he or she is looking for and how the observation will be conducted.

It is important to keep in mind the issue of assessment or evaluation. The purpose here, of course, is to collect information to assess needs in order to assist the teacher. An observation for evaluation purposes may not be all that different as an information-gathering exercise. The evaluation aspect might take place later when the data are analyzed.

Types of Observations

A variety of forms of observation have been developed. It is estimated that over a hundred observation instruments have been tested and used in the classroom, and these are only the objective type instruments (Goldhammer, Anderson, & Krajeweski, 1993). There are certain basic approaches to the observation process, and a number of specific ways to record classroom events. Each of these will be reviewed in the context of the assessment's purpose and the kind of information being sought.

One way of organizing the basic approaches is to classify them as structured or unstructured, and general or specific in focus. A matrix can be constructed to illustrate these factors. (See Figure 12-1.)

A *structured* approach has a well-defined system for data collection. It is specific in terms of its procedures and methods. An example would be an approach that has particular procedures to follow, such as how often to sample classroom events. Usually a form is developed that defines the parameters of the observation process and the content as well. The structured approaches also specify the manner in which data will be recorded. These include checklists, event sampling, time sampling, coding of events, scripting, et cetera.

FIGURE 12-1　Matrix of Observation Approaches

	Specific Focus	General Observation
Structured System	Specific Structured	General Structured
Unstructured Approach	Specific Unstructured	General Unstructured

An *unstructured* approach allows for flexibility on the part of the observer. There is no predetermined way to collect data or observe the classroom. The observer is free to decide on whatever means she or he wishes to use to record classroom events and activities. The observer exercises professional judgment as to how best to construct a record of the classroom. This is consistent with the artistic approach described by Eisner (1982) and Blumberg (1980).

The specific focus versus general observation approaches concern the content or substance of the observation. A *specific focus* approach to observation identifies in advance particular elements that will be given attention during the observation. The fundamental issue is that there are specific things that are identified in advance that the individual is looking for and recording in the process of observation.

A *general observation* consists of analyzing the classroom to identify what is significant to the observer. One is not looking for particular types of interactions, activities, or events, but rather noting those events that occur that appear to be significant.

By combining the two elements of structure and focus of an observation approach, one can construct an observation model that is consistent with one's educational and personal philosophy. The similarities and contrast among these also offer opportunities to see how they might best be used for specific purposes. A Helping Professional may decide to use one approach at one time or with a given individual, and another approach at a different time with the same individual or with another teacher. The important consideration is to know why you selected a specific approach and why it is of greatest advantage for the situation or person.

Specific Focus Structured Systems. A structured system with a specific focus is perhaps the most common observation type being used. It maintains that there are specific issues and factors of importance that must be included in the observation process, such as essential elements of instruction or research-based strategies. This model is suited to evaluation because it is more readily adapted to reliability and validity analysis. Some of the concerns with this approach are that it could be somewhat sterile in that it may attend to a narrower range of areas in the classroom, and could lock in the observer to one mode of collecting data that may not always be appropriate.

General Observation Structured Systems. The general observation approach that is conducted through a structured process uses some type of standard technique, but does not look for specific kinds of activities or events. The system for collecting the data, such as time sampling, is well defined. The specific focus of the observation using the structured system is more open to the discretion of the observer. This approach can be summarized by stating that these observers have no particular inclination as to what they are looking for; however, they are very clear about how they will go about collecting the information.

Specific Focus Unstructured Approach. In the specific focus unstructured approach the observer is very clear about the kinds of information he or she wishes to collect; however, there is no specific means identified for collecting this information. The observer may be looking for specific instructional strategies, such as questioning techniques, but will have no particular way of coding the kinds of questions or the question-answer interaction between the teacher and the student. The observer may use a combination of approaches, such as scripting or critical event recording, as she or he deems appropriate for the particular type of interaction.

General Observation Unstructured Approach. The general observation unstructured approach provides the greatest flexibility. In this instance the observation has no particular focus in terms of what is being looked for in the classroom. In addition, there is no specific data-collection system, strategy, or instrument that is used. The informal observation fits this category very well. The helper visits the classroom and attempts to acquire a sense of what is happening. The observer will look for instances of positive and negative instructional behaviors, student behaviors, and student learning activities. There is no particular agenda, rather just a visit with the teacher and the classroom. If anything should be noted, then that may be of value to the supervisory process, but nothing specific is sought out.

Informal Observation. At times it may be of value to drop in for a classroom visit—an informal opportunity to observe class dynamics and offer assistance. This process is helpful in picking up important and obvious issues in a classroom, such as students not on task or safety concerns. On the other hand, this type of observation also may reveal some nuance of the teacher's instruction that the teacher is unaware of (such as often turning to the chalkboard or overhead projector when speaking). This type of observation also increases the sampling of the teacher's classroom work. Whether a big or small issue, this informal assessment process can contribute information to the guidance and support process and the growth of the teacher.

Means of Collecting Observation Data
There is a wide range of options for ways of actually collecting information and providing a description of the classroom. These include event sampling, time sampling, checklists, general scripting, and focused scripting. Prior to the actual implementation, however, it is important to review how to select an appropriate process and how to establish conditions that set the stage for a productive observation.

In selecting the process or processes that one will use, it is important first to establish the purpose of the observation. A second step is to clarify the content of the observation, which will also aid in selecting the process. The content and process often are inextricably linked. The content thus will provide important direction to the selection of the process to be used for collecting information. As noted previously, one may use different approaches at different times with different purposes and with different individuals.

One of the criteria used in selecting an assessment or observation system is the objective of the observation. If one is attempting to construct a profile of the teacher's instructional skills, for example, then it is more common to use a set of criteria that identify performance and levels of competence. In this situation the objective leads to the use of a more focused and structured instrument that yields data that may be tabulated for the categories of interest. When the objectives call for more comprehensive, systematic, or detailed analyses, a specific and structured instrument is used.

Determining the instrument or observation approach to be selected also depends upon the information to be gathered. More specifically, it has to do with the content to be assessed during this process. If one were interested in knowing about the nature of the student interactions in the classroom, then a sociogram type of analysis would be in order. If one were interested in the relationship between teacher talk and student talk and the overall verbal interaction patterns, then an instrument such as the Flanders Interaction Analysis System would be more appropriate.

A number of different systems and procedures have been used to collect data in the observation process. There are two broad domains that can be used to categorize these various systems. These are the global and focused observation processes. The global approach is a process to record all possible information that occurs in the classroom. It is comprehensive and all-inclusive. It does not select or focus on any particular area, but rather is intended to provide a full description of all activities that occur. It is, of course, a rather ambitious approach, but its value is that it is all-inclusive as a description of the entire classroom. This is sometimes referred to as an anecdotal record approach.

The focused domain includes those systems that have particular content areas of emphasis that are the focus of the observation. In these procedures the observer is looking for particular events, interactions, or activities that are recorded in various ways. The distinction between the global and focused approach is primarily that the specific approach does not attempt to record everything in the classroom, only particular areas of interest, whereas the global approach does not discern among varied events nor does it have predisposed categories of observation.

Preparing for the Observation

Unless one is casually entering the classroom for an informal observation, it is beneficial to prepare oneself as well as the teacher for the observation. There are a number of factors to be considered in ensuring that the observation will be productive and efficient and be accepted and mutually beneficial to both the teacher and the Helping Professional. In most instances a pre-observation conference is held between the helper and teacher in order to prepare for the upcoming visit. In many respects this is part of the guidance and support process. It is important to be aware, however, that such a conference is extremely valuable in establishing the stage and climate for the subsequent observation.

Another issue of importance is to have insight into the teacher's degree of acceptance of the observation. Sometimes teachers accept the fact that it will be done and it is helpful, but nevertheless are very apprehensive about the process. Gaining understanding of the teacher's openness and true feelings about the process will aid significantly in determining how it should be approached.

A related issue is the tone the helper wishes to establish prior to and during the observation. Knowing the teacher, knowing the purpose, and understanding the context or openness to the observation allows one to formulate strategies for the appropriate tone.

After an observation, teachers are most anxious to learn about their performance, both in terms of positive aspects as well as areas of need. In view of this, it helps to prepare for the observation by thinking ahead to the type of feedback that might be given to teachers afterward.

A related issue is how soon feedback should be given. Initially, general statements may be provided immediately after the observation, but a more in-depth review may be provided within a specified period of time. Thinking through the nature of information, the sequence, and the timing of the feedback prior to the observation would be most helpful.

Examples of Observation Methods
Script Taping. Perhaps the most frequent method used to develop a description of a classroom is script taping, which means recording everything that the observed teacher says. Script taping is not a structured approach, in that it does not have a specific process or system of recording. It can be used with either a general or focused observation system. When it is focused, it has specific behaviors to be observed. The more specifically these areas of interest are identified, the more focused is the obervation instrument.

Because script taping can be arduous, observers often look for ways of streamlining the process. One way is to develop a type of shorthand or notation system, abbreviating some of the activities often expected to occur. Using key words or phrases rather than entire sentences allows for reconstructing the verbal behavior on the observation record. Madeline Hunter (1983) identified seven advantages of this script taping process.

The focus of script taping is usually on the verbal interaction of the classroom. While attempting to record everything that transpires verbally, the observer may neglect some of the nonverbal aspects that can provide important clues as to what is happening in the classroom. Making notations on the nonverbal dimension of the classroom interaction is one way to compensate for this.

The Flanders System. Perhaps the most frequently used structured observation system is the Flanders Interaction Analysis Category (FIAC) system (Flanders, 1960). This is described as a social/psychological system for recording student and teacher classroom verbal interaction in ten categories. They address what are referred to as Indirect Teacher Influence, Direct Teacher Influence, Student Talk, and Silence or Confusion. In this system the observer records the event occurring in the classroom every 3 seconds.

The Flanders Interaction Analysis Category system is one way of systematically assessing the situation through a focused and structured observation instrument. It provides a great deal of information that may be useful when directed at particular objectives. It is noted that when using any one system, it often is valuable also to use a complementary system to collect additional information.

The Pathwise System. Another approach is the recently developed Pathwise system from Educational Testing Service (1995). In this system the observers undergo an intense 5-day training to ensure a clear understanding of the categories and respective subcategories that define the scoring rules for each system. There are four broad domains, and within each of these specific competencies are identified, usually five per domain. These are the specific assessment criteria for the framework for the observation. The observers attempt to recognize, interpret, and appropriately classify behaviors into the appropriate categories. A number of video tapes are used in order to train the observers and ensure the reliability of observations. During the actual observation the observer is required to label each of the behaviors according to the appropriate categories in order to develop a record of classroom activities.

The Helping Professional provides specific examples that are related to a particular level of competency. Whether positive or negative, teachers are given not only a clear picture of their level of competence or performance, but also very specific indications of areas that can be improved. Examples from the evidence make the feedback very real for the teachers, enabling them to interpret the information in their own way, as well as in consultation with the Helping Professional. It is extremely valuable for the feedback to be very specific and supported by examples in order to be of most assistance to teachers. Pathwise is a structured observation system, focusing on specific criteria derived from research. It can be used for initial observations to provide a baseline for teachers and also can be adapted to focus on particular domains of performance.

Assessment Approaches Matrix

There are a variety of ways to develop a record of teachers' performance and to provide an assessment of their needs at a particular time. The range of needs is quite extensive, and the types of needs vary considerably. The focus here has been on both the personal-psychological as well as the instructional-professional domains.

It is clear that no one observation is going to collect all the necessary information. This is quite obvious when looking at the significant differences between the two major domains. The domains are significantly different and require different approaches. Within each of the domains, one may use different approaches at different times. This would depend on the time of observation and how specific it is. The approach used for general observation to get a database would be different from the approach to provide specific information, such as about classroom management or teacher questioning practices. By clearly understanding one's purpose, one will be able to select from the wide array of approaches identified and described in these chapters.

As an overview of the approaches, a matrix identifying the basic ways of assessing and developing a profile for the individual has been constructed (Table 12-1). In the left column of the matrix, examples of content areas of focus have been

TABLE 12-1 Content-Assessment Approach Sample Matrix

Content	Observation	Portfolio	Interview	Checklists	Diagnostic Instrument	Third Party Input
Classroom instructional behaviors						
Expressed needs analysis						
Psychological needs						
Personal needs						
Instructional products (plans, evaluations)						
Parent relations						
School personnel relations						

identified. Across the top of the matrix, the broad areas of approaches for assessment are listed. Specific examples for each of these have been described throughout this and the previous chapter.

Assessing Teachers' Professional Needs

In Chapter 5 a variety of ways of understanding teacher stages and developmental processes were identified. A simplistic way of approaching this is to get some basic perspective of the teachers' needs by sharing the models and determining the teachers' perception of their stage in accordance with the description provided. For example, related to the cognitive stage level (Harvey, Hunt, & Schroeder, 1961), teachers may be asked to engage in introspection regarding whether or not they are able to examine themselves in terms of their own expectations rather than external standards and conditions (the second stage identified by Harvey, Hunt, & Schroeder). Further study of the references for these various models would provide additional information if the reader is interested in assessing this in more depth.

As noted in Chapter 5, the psychoanalytic approach provides for the teacher to get in touch with earlier experiences in life. Again, Helping Professionals are not expected to be psychotherapists; however, there is much to be gained by helping teachers look at their past experiences in school and determine how these experiences might have influenced their current feelings, attitudes, and behaviors. In support groups this type of discussion is found to be highly effective. This works well both with mentor teachers and beginning teachers. It is important to ensure confidentiality in these discussions so that people will be more willing to volunteer ideas, share experiences, and take risks in order to grow. The methodologies identified as useful in this assessment process include journals, logs, and life histories. It also has been found to be of value for teachers to assess the impact of contextual factors on their socialization in the profession, the school, and even their own classroom. This includes the dynamics of the classroom, peers in the school, the culture of the school, and both the written and unwritten understandings and procedures.

Finally, there is the issue of teachers' professional development with an emphasis on personal components. Of importance here is for teachers to express where they think they are in their own professional development. This can be done first in terms of general feelings about where they are and how much they need to grow at this point in time. Another approach is through an understanding of the total set of data collected about teachers' knowledge and performance. The various classroom observations, interviews, questionnaires, or other instruments used form a rich database from which teachers can draw inferences about their needs and professional development. Teacher and Helping Professionals might review the six principles recommended by Little (1983), described in Chapter 5, as a basis for needs assessment. Further analysis would be conducted as part of the guidance and support process in which a well-conceived plan is designed for an individual teacher's professional-personal growth.

Issues and Questions for Review and Reflection

1. The helping professions such as medicine, psychiatry, and psychology perform some type of assessment and subsequent diagnosis. How does this compare with assessment and diagnosis as a Helping Professional? Why is it important?

2. Discuss the relationship between one's physical needs and effective professional performance.

3. Why is it difficult for school personnel to deal with teachers' physical needs? Why is it difficult for them to deal with teachers' emotional needs?

4. Discuss the use of portfolios, addressing the following issues:
    a. Purpose
    b. Format
    c. Criteria for selection of entries
    d. Content
    e. Limitations

5. What factors are used in selecting a classroom observation approach?

6. Review the instruments in Chapter 4 on personal-psychological needs. How can these be used in assessing and diagnosing a teacher's needs in this domain?

7. Review the instruments in Chapter 5. How can these be used and integrated into observation data to assist a teacher in this domain?

References

Blumberg, A. (1980). *Supervisors and teachers: A private cold war* (2d ed.). Berkeley, CA: McCutchan.

Clark, C., & Peterson, P. (1986). Teachers' thought processes. In M. C. Wittrock (Ed.), *Handbook of research on teaching* (3d ed.), (pp. 255–296). New York: Macmillan.

Commission on Teacher Credentialing (1989). *Standards of program quality and effectiveness, factors to consider and preconditions in the evaluation of professional teacher preparation programs for multiple and single subject credentials*. Sacramento, CA: Author.

Connelly, F. M., & Clandinin, D. J. (1987). On narrative method, biography and narrative unities in the study of teaching. *Journal of Educational Thought, 21*(3), 130–139.

Covey, S. R. (1990). *The 7 habits of highly effective people*. New York: Simon & Schuster.

Darling-Hammond, L., Wise, A. E., & Klein, S. P. (1995). *A license to teach: Building a profession for 21st-century schools*. San Francisco: Westview Press.

Dwyer, C. A. (1994). *Development of the knowledge base for the Praxis III: Classroom performance assessments criteria*. Princeton, NJ: Educational Testing Service.

Educational Testing Service (1995). *Pathwise orientation guide*. Princeton, NJ: Author.

Eisner, E. W. (1982). An artistic approach to supervision. In T. J. Sergiovanni (Ed.), *Supervision of teaching, 1982 yearbook*. Alexandria, VA: Association for Supervision and Curriculum Development.

Flanders, N. A. (1960). *Teacher influence: Pupil attitudes and achievement*. Minneapolis: University of Minnesota.

Gold, Y., & Roth, R. A. (1993). *Teachers managing stress and preventing burnout: The professional health (PH) solution*. London: Falmer Press.

Goldhammer, R., Anderson, R. H., & Krajewski, R. J. (1993). *Clinical supervision: Special methods for the supervision of teachers* (3d ed.). New York: Harcourt Brace.

Hafen, B. Q., Frandsen, K. J., Karren, K. J., & Hooker, K. R. (1992). *The health effects of attitudes, emotions, relationships*. Utah: EMS Associates.

Harvey, O. J., Hunt, D. E., & Schroeder, H. (1961). *Conceptual systems and personality organization*. New York: Wiley.

Hunter, M. (1983). Script-taping: An essential supervisory tool. *Educational Leadership, 41*(3), 43.

Joyce, B. R., & Showers, B. (1983). *Power: In staff development through research on training*. Alexandria, VA: Association for Supervision and Curriculum Development.

Little, J. W. (1993). Teachers' professional development in a climate of educational reform. *Educational Evaluation and Policy Analysis, 15*(2), 129–151.

Lucas, C. (1992). Writing portfolios—changes and challenges. In K. B. Yancey (Ed.), *Portfolios in the writing classroom*. Urbana, IL: National Council of Teachers of English.

Pelletier, K. R. (1993). "Between mind and body: Stress, emotions, and health." In D. Goldman & J. Gurin (Eds.), *Mind body medicine*. New York: Consumer Reports Books.

Phi Delta Kappa (1993). *Teacher expectations and student achievement (TESA)*. Bloomington, IN: Author.

Shulman, L. S. (1986). Paradigms and research programs in the study of teaching: A contemporary perspective. In M. C. Whittrock (Ed.), *Handbook of research on teaching* (pp. 3–36). New York: Macmillan.

Related Readings

Anthony, R. J., Johnson, T. D., Mickelson, N. I., & Preece, A. (1991). *Evaluating literacy: A perspective for change*. Portsmouth, NH: Heinemann.

Brandt, R. (Ed.) (1992). Theme issue on Performance Assessment. *Educational Leadership 49*(8).

Briggs, C. L. (1986). *Learning how to ask: A socio-*

linguistic appraisal of the role of the interview in social science research. Cambridge, England: Cambridge University Press.

Clandinin, D. J. (1985). Personal practical knowledge: A study of teachers' classroom images. *Curriculum Inquiry, 15,* 361–385.

Gearing, F. O., & Hughes, W. (1975). *On observing well: Self-instruction in ethnographic obersvation for teachers, principals, and supervisors.* Amherst, NY: Center for Studies in Cultural Transmission.

Glazer, S. M., & Brown, C. S. (1993). *Portfolios and beyond: Collaborative assessment in reading and writing.* Norwood, MA: Christopher-Gordon.

Graves, D. H., & Sunstein, B. S. (Eds.) (1992). *Portfolio portraits.* Portsmouth, NH: Heinemann.

Herman, J. L., Aschbacher, P. R., & Winters, L. (1992). *A practical guide to alternative assessment.* Alexandria, VA: Association for Supervision and Curriculum Development.

Paulson, F. L., Paulson, P. R., & Meyer, C. A. (1991). What makes a portfolio a portfolio? *Educational Leadership 48*(5), 60–63.

Rhodes, L. K. (Ed.) (1993). *Literacy assessment: A handbook of instruments.* Portsmouth, NH: Heinemann.

Schnitzer, S. (1993). Designing an authentic assessment. *Educational Leadership 50*(7), 32–35.

Simon, A., & Boyer, E. C. (1967). *Mirrors of behavior: An anthology of classroom observation instruments* (6 vols.). Philadelphia: Research for Better Schools.

Tierney, R. J., Carter, M. A., & Desai, L. E. (1991). *Portfolio assessment in the reading-writing classroom.* Norwood, MA: Christopher-Gordon.

Valencia, S. W., Hiebert, E. H., & Afflerbach, P. P. (1994). *Authentic reading assessment: Practices and possibilities.* Newark, DE: International Reading Association.

Yancey, K. B. (Ed.) (1992). *Portfolios in the writing classroom.* Urbana, IL: National Council of Teachers of English.

Chapter 13

The Process of Guidance and Support (Dimension Four)

A critical and most rewarding component of the Transformational Helping Professional model is the guidance and support provided to the teacher participant. It is here that the helping skills, communication skills, and assessment and diagnosis are orchestrated to formulate a strategy and system for enhancing the personal and professional growth of the individual teacher who is provided the assistance. The process of guidance and support requires a delicate balance between providing leadership for personal growth and change that affects performance, and a focus on technical assistance. The necessity of creating a supportive environment conducive to addressing a broad range of teacher personal and professional needs serves as context for fundamental and long-lasting transformation.

Guidance and support primarily deal with the process of change and eventually transformation. Change in a positive direction, or growth, is a complex process. Promoting growth requires that the Helping Professional not only has the specific skills needed to work with teachers undergoing change, but also the ability to weave these skills together in an artistic fashion for their maximum utilization at appropriate times for the particular individual.

In this chapter the guidance and support process for both the personal-psychological and instructional-professional domains will be examined. We will refer extensively to the knowledge and skills identified in previous chapters that the Helping Professional must call upon in order to function effectively in the guidance and support dimension.

Guidance and Support within the Personal-Psychological Domain

In Chapter 4 we identified several categories of need within the personal-psychological domain. These include physical, emotional, intellectual, social, and spiritual needs. In the previous chapter we described how to assess and diagnose these needs. Now we will analyze how to use this information in the process of guidance and support.

Physical Needs

One of the physical needs is for a sufficient level of energy or stamina to maintain the desired lifestyle. One form of guidance is to suggest that the teacher develop a plan to look at ways in which more energy may be derived from daily habits. The teacher and the support provider can review this plan together, look at options, and set realistic goals and expectations. This might include consultation with a professional, such as dietitian or family physician, who can advise on exercise or other factors related to lifestyle and energy. On the other hand, it may simply be a matter of ensuring that sufficient sleep time is scheduled to meet the individual's needs.

Developing a plan and sticking with it are obviously two different things. Research at the Baylor Nutrition Research Center as reported by John Foreyt indicates people stay motivated for about 42 days (6 weeks) and then discontinue their program. It is important to establish a means of monitoring the individual's progress. The Helping Professional can offer support to help the individual maintain the commitment.

The area of calmness can be of particular importance to teachers, who often have very busy lifestyles and hectic work schedules. The Helping Professional's function is to work with the teachers in looking at what was learned during assessment and diagnosis, particularly noting what needs to be focused on. Part of this process involves identifying what can or cannot be changed. These realistic expectations through analysis are important in order to develop a meaningful response.

Polls have revealed that in today's classrooms the number one issue of concern is school safety. Reports from the National Center for Education Statistics and the Carnegie Foundation indicate verbal abuse, physical threats, and physical attacks on teachers to be of primary concern (*USA Today*, October 25, 1993). This has received attention from professional organizations such as ASCD (Johnson & Johnson, 1995) and others. The increase of violence among students and of assaults on teachers clearly has an impact on the instructional process. Although there are a number of programs emerging for dealing with school violence, it is seldom considered as a factor in professional development programs or in assisting teachers in meeting their particular needs. No matter how well prepared teachers may be in terms of the instructional-professional areas, when they have concerns about their safety in the classroom, their effectiveness will probably be seriously diminished.

If a teacher's assessment results indicate that there are safety concerns, it would be valuable to explore in some depth with the teacher what those factors might be. This would include both home and school conditions, as both influence the teacher's psyche and potentially classroom performance.

Teachers are notorious for having poor eating habits due to their hectic schedules, both at school and at home. Most teachers take considerable work home and spend many hours working with their instructional plans, grading papers, planning curriculum, and so forth. The result is that many suffer from health problems due to insufficient attention to healthy eating and overall health habits.

Assessment of this area focuses on the eating program in particular. The Helping Professional could review this with teachers and assist them in developing a health plan. The health plan should identify what aspects of eating or other general health issues might be of concern and thus be a focus for consideration. How to address these also would be important in terms of modification of habits.

Physical fitness is an area that relates to issues such as stamina, energy levels, and general health. As noted in the discussion of the assessment of general stamina, exercise may be an area that needs attention. Again, a support person is essential and either an individual or a group may serve this function. The Helping Professional can help teachers identify a support person who can work with them in some type of exercise plan. In this type of arrangement with another person or group, individuals become accountable to the others in fulfilling their requirements.

The last area of physical fitness concerns the degree of rest individuals may have. By linking the feeling of being rested with the amount of rest they actually get, a determination can be made as to the amount of rest that is needed in order to function optimally. The Helping Professional can assist by encouraging teachers to construct a log and monitor their progress.

Emotional Needs

The emotional questionnaire in Chapter 4 may lead to significant insights on the part of the individual responding to the instrument. Each of the emotional needs can have a profound effect on the way one functions. It is essential to understand the degree to which each is being met for the individual seeking assistance.

The area of security has different facets. Certainly financial security has always been a concern of teachers. Obviously the Helping Professional cannot provide a financial supplement; however, she or he can guide teachers in terms of systematically approaching their financial situation.

A related aspect of security is that of relationships. The status of relationships can have a very significant influence on the way one functions. This affects both personal and professional levels of performance. An important strategy in the guidance process is to assist the individual in recognizing that relationships that are not fulfilling may contribute to a need not being met. The assessment process should provide some insight; however, it is necessary for the teacher to become more cognizant of that need and its extent. Awareness then can be translated into strategies for trying to meet the relationship need in a variety of ways.

The teaching profession has one of the highest rates of burnout among all professions. It has been identified as one of the most stressful professions (*Men's*

Health, 1991). Much of teachers' difficulties in performing their professional roles comes from their inability to cope with the pressures and stresses of the job (Farber, 1991; Gold & Roth, 1993). The need for serenity and harmony is particularly relevant to teachers, the work they perform, and the schools in which they work.

Time management is often a critical factor in reducing stress. The Helping Professional could assist teachers by identifying key resources, such as *How To Get Control of Your Time and Your Life* by Lakein (1974). Later, discuss how the individuals are applying the concepts to their own lives.

Issues such as self-acceptance, self-confidence, and self-esteem are somewhat complex and require deeper levels of understanding to change. The assessment and diagnosis instruments provided in Chapter 4 can help teachers begin to recognize the extent of their needs in these areas. A first step is recognizing them and accepting that there are some unmet needs in their lives, and then planning specific ways to meet them. This is followed by a willingness to work on these areas. If one is not willing to make a commitment to work on them, then clearly these needs will not be addressed. The Helping Professional can guide teachers through the process of recognition and toward a willingness to move forward. Reviewing the first phases of the change model can be helpful here for the Helping Professional.

Emotional stability can be a very critical factor in the area of emotional needs. Stability relates to the degree to which individuals feel they have pressures or in some instances a crisis that contributes to the feeling of instability throughout the crisis period. If assessment reveals that individuals feel they are in a time of instability in their lives, the need for support becomes even greater until the crisis is resolved. As noted before, the more one can identify specific concerns related to the identified need, such as a crisis, the better one is able to develop a plan for addressing it and learning how to handle it.

If someone does not feel a sense of stability over a period of time, it is helpful to determine as many of the reasons as possible why the individual feels this way. Examples could be elicited to help the individual clarify feelings of instability. Guidance and support can be provided by exploring with the teacher what might be needed in order to develop a sense of stability.

An important part of this element related to emotional need is for the individual to learn how to identify and cope better with pressures over which they have little or no control. Stressful and threatening types of situations and people can be very difficult for some personalities. Chapter 14 on managing stress and preventing burnout will be of significant help in handling events over which we have no control. We will deal with this issue in more detail in that chapter.

Having a sense of worth is an essential human need. The Helping Professional can assist teachers in developing a sense of being worthy by referring to situations in which they have been successful and by encouraging them to engage in activities in which they have particular strengths.

Intellectual Needs

One of the areas most frequently overlooked or forgotten for a professional educator is that of intellectual stimulation. Student teachers and beginning teachers have just spent an intensive period of time totally immersed in academic study. Being thrust into new situations that are very intense and time-consuming and that usually are quite stressful precludes the teachers from engaging in intellectual activities. This is also true of experienced teachers who were accustomed to academic studies as part of the preparation for their profession. The net effect of this withdrawal from intellectual stimulation is felt as an unmet need.

In reviewing the responses to the questions in the Intellectual Needs Inventory in Chapter 4, and the areas suggested here, it would be of value for teachers to think about what aspects or activities would make their life more stimulating intellectually.

The link to instructional-professional needs need not be limited to improvement of specific instructional practices, such as new methodologies or activities. Probing into the nature of the profession more deeply can go beyond instructional and technical issues into the intellectual bases of the profession, such as the nature of the learner or philosophical perspectives. The type of intellectual stimulation needed may well vary with the stage that the student teacher or experienced teacher is in at the time.

Social Needs and Support Groups

As noted in Chapter 4, teachers clearly must be more aware of social needs and the various ways they can be met. Time and again we find in our seminars, workshops, and classes that teachers at all stages struggle with unmet social needs because of the drain on their personal lives from excessive workloads and the nature of commitment needed to function at the levels of excellence they expect of themselves.

An important part of the strategy is to identify which social needs are significant to individuals, particularly those that are not being met. Subsequently, the Helping Professional can discuss with them the opportunities for meeting these needs. A most effective option for many individuals, of course, is finding a supportive other. This is a role that the Helping Professional can fulfill to some extent, but the helping relationship should not become too personal and lose the objectivity that is necessary. Instead, the relationship may be a model for developing relationships with others.

In general, it is found that the need for affiliation and the related need for communication are significantly heightened when an individual works in an isolated environment, as teachers do. When these feelings become chronic over a period of time, increased levels of loneliness and ultimately discouragement begin to appear. Options must be identified and opportunities provided to assist the teacher in meeting these needs. The role of the Helping Professional is to assist the teacher in understanding the options and being aware of opportunities.

Some further helping relationships might be found in support groups that the Helping Professional may suggest. Suggestions might include the types of groups to begin affiliating with, who might participate in these kinds of groups, and how often they desire and have time to get together.

Different types of groups are structured so that individuals can come together to meet a variety of interests and personal and social needs. We use such groups to exchange information, help us work through dilemmas, and learn more about ourselves.

In our experiences with guided groups we have found that they develop their own sense of bonding and fulfill a particular social need to some extent. They begin by committing to confidentiality and building a sense of trust. Individuals are guided to find ways in which they are able to express themselves candidly, and they become more willing to risk in their openness and in discussions of their needs. (The reader may wish to review the discussion of group support in Chapter 8.)

One of the purposes of the group is to allow each participant free expression without evaluating, condemning, or judging. All individuals must feel that they are validated by the group. This means that they must feel that they are heard and understood, and that the others in the group recognize their feelings and understand as best they can the particular situations in which they are involved.

The Helping Professional's role is of great significance in providing interpersonal support as individuals go through the change process. Interpersonal support can help them stay on course, stay encouraged, and continue to find ways to address their social needs.

Spiritual Needs

As has been noted earlier, spiritual needs often are neglected. It is felt that they are too personal, too controversial, or too far removed from the realm of the educational setting. We have used a broader definition of spirituality here that enlarges the area of discussion.

One of the things we recommend is that teachers have a clear conception of what spirituality means to them. This also is true for the Helping Professional. When these two engage in conversations, it is important that they understand their own beliefs and be respectful of the other person's. If this is an area the helpee desires to discuss, they can feel more comfortable about not only what they mean by spiritual needs, but that the helper understands the teacher's perspective.

It is important that the teacher and Helping Professional establish the boundaries within which they would feel comfortable when discussing the spiritual needs area. When this common understanding has not been established between the Helping Professional and the teacher, the issue can actually get in the way of developing a working relationship.

We have found in our work that a firm belief system is an essential foundation for virtually all that we do. The educational belief system undergirds instructional practice. The belief system of the Transformational model underlies the process of mentoring and supervising as a Helping Professional. Beneath all of these, however, are individuals' basic belief systems about themselves, human nature, and fundamental purposes of life. The way people view the world through their belief systems influences the beliefs they develop in all aspects of their personal-professional life. Taking time to understand this factor, to get more in touch with what one's belief system is, and to understand any unmet needs in these areas can make a most significant contribution to an individual's professional health.

Instructional-Professional Needs

The domain that receives virtually all of the attention in professional literature is that of the instructional-professional. This is related clearly and directly to one's professional responsibilities.

Exploring Teacher Thought Processes

In Chapter 5 we indicated that the primary focus of instructional competence is on teachers' thought processes as they relate to and influence teacher behavior. One purpose of the guidance and support component is to help the teacher think through the relevance and appropriateness of the thought strategies engaged in during instructional practice. Once a teacher has engaged in diagnosing and assessing his or her instructional thought processes, the Helping Professional can provide guidance and support toward growth in this area to produce improved practice, as detailed also in Chapter 12.

One way to capture thoughts is the thinking aloud method, in which the teacher verbalizes his or her thoughts and these are recorded and coded. As the teacher looks at the verbalized or coded thoughts, a key question to ask is "What do they mean?" The Helping Professional and teacher mutually inquire into the teacher's thoughts and questions with inquiries such as the following: "Were the appropriate questions raised during decision making?" "Did the questions reflect a clear understanding of where the teacher is going, or did they show a degree of doubt?" "Are the right kinds of questions or issues being raised during the instructional process?" (For example, is the focus on the needs of the students, the subject matter, the need to complete the content for the day, etc.).

The stimulated recall and journal keeping approaches use similar questions in providing for guidance and support. One of the advantages of both the stimulated recall and journal keeping is that they also provide some reference to the context in which the decision making and instructional practices were occurring. Teacher decision making is context-specific, and a variety of variables need to be accounted for in the analysis.

Analyzing thinking is precisely one of the objectives that guidance and support processes intend to achieve. The purpose is to stimulate teachers to think about the thought processes they engage in during instructional activity. It is intended to encourage them to think about what decisions they are making, why they are making these decisions, and what variables they are accounting for when such decisions are made. Of related importance is determining the issues or factors for which they are *not* accounting. Focusing on teacher planning can also reap significant benefits in the guidance and support process.

Professional Knowledge and Understanding

As we noted earlier, the translation of knowledge into planning requires understanding of learners and learning, of curriculum and context, of goals and objectives, of pedagogy, and of subject-specific knowledge of pedagogy. It is here in the guidance and support phase that the Helping Professional assists teachers in drawing from these various knowledge sources in order to reconstruct lessons or devise new ones that more appropriately translate or transform knowledge into forms that are accessible by students in their particular classes.

In looking at lesson plans, it is useful to inquire into how the particular knowledge was selected for the students at that time. Teachers can be assisted in analyzing, contrasting, and developing greater self-direction in their teaching through structured questions and reflecting on their processes.

An area of particular importance in the Transformational Helping Professional model as it relates to instructional and professional needs is that of the constructivist view. A key role of the Helping Professional is to assist and guide the teacher in understanding the context of learning and what the students bring to the classroom.

In the area of planning for instruction and developing the curriculum, the Helping Professional can be of assistance by seeing that the subject matter is not only put into usable forms, but also considered in terms of how it might be perceived by the learner. Seeing the subject matter from a learning perspective may put it into a very different light. Moving from logical pieces of subject matter to learners' perspectives of subject matter is not an easy transition.

Two ways of helping the teacher get at these issues are questioning strategies and student feedback. The teacher may ask, for example, for students' explanations or interpretations of concepts, principles, and relationships. This might reveal differences between linear-sequential perspectives of thinking and more global and multidimensional types of thinking.

Teachers need to understand when students will need to accommodate and thus adjust their existing structure with new perspectives or perceptions of content or concepts. This requires a great deal of inquiry into students' thinking and how they are manipulating the content in the learning process.

Professional Development

The role of the Helping Professional clearly extends beyond the immediate assistance given in improving instructional practice. There are professional needs that must be addressed through long-term strategies. Developing a constructive and realistic professional development plan is part of the Helping Professional role.

One area we discussed earlier in the realm of professional needs was that of teacher stages. One of the ways to help teachers in their professional development is through understanding the nature of stages. By discussing the issue of teacher stages, teachers are able to identify better where they are in the stage sequence and then clarify their developmental process. Thus, the role of the Helping Professional in the area of teacher stages has to do with raising teachers' consciousness levels, helping them assess what stages they may be in, and helping them find ways to move to subsequent stages.

In Chapter 5 we referred to six principles related to professional development proposed by Little (1993). In designing the individual's professional development plan, these six principles can be used to test the meaningfulness of the program.

We often see professional development as focused on the improvement of the individual through a personal program that may be somewhat isolated. Another perspective is to use a group approach in which a number of teachers come together on a common ground and pursue similar objectives for their professional development. A common plan is then established that provides not only for common experiences, but also for group dialogue on issues as they go through the processes. Using focused study groups, teacher collaboratives, and long-term partnerships with the assistance of the Helping Professional can be most productive. What this also tends to do is remove the teacher from isolation and into group inquiry. In a sense, this is the process of creating a professional support group that not only addresses social needs, but the broad spectrum of professional needs as well.

Conferencing with Teachers

The process of conferencing with teachers is an ongoing interaction during the helping relationship. In these conferencing sessions the Helping Professional integrates communication and helping skills articulately to respond to teachers' needs and promote their professional growth. This section, therefore, will focus on the skills and strategies one uses in conferences before and after classroom observations.

It is important to be clear about why we engage in conferencing. The reasons involve certain basic beliefs about the process that guides the selection of specific skills that constitute the conferencing procedure. These basic beliefs that form the foundation of conferencing are listed here.

1. The focus of the observational process is on insight and change. As part of the change process, therefore, it must take into account the factors and variables which influence individual change.
2. Professional development results when the individual makes a commitment to growth and the respective changes needed. The role of the Helping Professional in the observation process is to provide conducive conditions and enhance the commitment to change on the part of the teacher.
3. A primary purpose of the observation process is to promote the capacity of the teacher to make appropriate decisions regarding his or her professional growth.
4. Helping Professionals should model the skills and strategies for instructional effectiveness, as well as teacher helping skills required in a classroom as teachers interact with their own students.
5. Helping Professionals must have a broad repertoire of skills and strategies to use in the conferencing process. This includes working knowledge of various observation and data collection techniques, as well as the skills and strategies for interacting with the teacher regarding lesson design and implementation.
6. Helping Professionals and teachers should view the conferencing process as one that is mutually beneficial.

7. Personal and professional growth require some type of feedback. This feedback is best when it is specific, nonevaluative, and descriptive, in contrast to general and judgmental.
8. Self-analysis is a critical part of the conferencing process. The more insight there is, the more the teacher will internalize the ideas leading to more significant change.
9. Diagnosing and understanding needs of teachers and Helping Professionals is a fundamental factor in the observation process.
10. The teacher has the responsibility and choice to identify issues and concerns and through self-analysis to provide for improved instructional practice.
11. Feedback is best received when based on documented evidence rather than on inferences or value statements.
12. One outcome of the conferencing process is to provide teachers with the capacity to experiment, adapt, and hypothesize, based on documented evidence.
13. Goals for the improvement of the teacher will be developed by the teacher and the Helping Professional as they confer during the helping relationship.

The Process of Observation

As noted in Chapter 12 on assessing and diagnosing, both formal and informal observations can be used in the assessment process. A more focused, structured, or formal observation requires a certain degree of planning. The extent of this planning will depend upon the purpose of the observation, how well formed the relationship is between the Helping Professional and the teacher, and the kind of agreement made between the two for the observation cycle.

Although a variety of specific steps can be identified, there are four basic phases that must be considered in the observation process. The first of these is the *Preparation Phase*. This involves the necessary planning prior to conversing with the teacher about the observation and conferencing process.

The second phase is the *Planning and Collaboration Phase*. This is the actual engagement with the teacher in a pre-teaching discussion of what will occur in the classroom, what the observation might focus on, and how the Helping Professional and teacher will collaborate and work together in mutual inquiry.

The third phase is the actual observation of the teacher in the classroom (*Observation Phase*). This is the major component of the assessment and diagnosis process that concentrates on instructional practice.

Phase four is *Post-Teaching Reflection and Consultation*. The primary emphasis here is on analysis of the information collected and active involvement in the guidance and support process. Guidance and support also are provided for in the Planning Phase prior to observation, but it is at this time that the most significant part of the guidance and support through consultation usually takes place.

One of the important points we wish to make is that these phases do not need to be implemented to the same extent in every situation. A premise of our Helping Professional model is that procedures should be adapted to the needs of the individual. There is no set protocol or standard procedure to use in dealing with the observation cycle for all individuals.

In addition, within each of the phases one need not use all of the specific strategies identified. The Helping Professional will need to know when to use the various skills, and weave them together as she or he practices the art of helping. The point being emphasized here is that the various skills, strategies, and phases are to be considered as alternatives, not prescriptions.

The Preparation Phase

The time available to work with the individual teacher is usually very limited. As a scarce resource, time must be carefully planned to maximize its use and accomplish the greatest amount possible. It is thus of great importance that the Helping Professional be aware of what he or she intends to accomplish and how it will be approached.

Helping Professionals need to put themselves into a mode of thinking that is diagnostic, individually focused, and personalized. With this as the context, the Helping Professional might engage in some of the following thought processes and/or steps that constitute the Preparation Phase:

1. Review needs assessments. The key element in this preparation process is for the Helping Professional to be sure to know the teacher as well as possible, as the helping relationship is more than a technical one. Becoming as familiar as possible with the teacher is of vital importance.
2. The purpose should be clear.
3. Focus on identification of issues. This identification will be a mutually explored process during the initial engagement in the Planning Phase. The Helping Professional needs to decide whether an identified issue indeed will be a major focus, and how it will be approached.
4. Reflect on the approach that the Helping Professional will take in the conference with the individual teacher. This refers to the particular style the Helping Professional will use.

Context Information

Another important consideration in preparing is to think about the context in which the teacher is working. The Helping Professional should have information about the various characteristics of the setting. There should be an understanding of the context within which the teacher is functioning, both in the classroom and the school itself.

Context factors could include the number of students in a class, gender and ethnic distribution of students, the number of students with handicapping conditions and the nature of these conditions, the number of students with limited English proficiency, the nature of the home backgrounds of students, and information about the community in which the students reside. All of this information can be very helpful in working with teachers and understanding significant factors in their daily classroom environments.

Information and Materials
There are many kinds of information and materials the Helping Professional can bring to the planning and collaboration session. For example, prior observations with the teacher could be considered during the planning stage. In general, this material might relate to instructional strategies, classroom management, ideas for lessons, examples of script taping, or other information that might be of use to the teacher in gaining professional insights.

Outcomes
Finally, the Helping Professional might think about the outcome expected from the Planning and Collaboration Phase. Kindsvatter and Wilen (1991, p. 528) proposed four questions to ask before conducting the conference.

1. What do I expect to be the optimal outcome of the conference?
2. What verbal and nonverbal behaviors will I use to build a supportive climate?
3. What questions will I ask in order to have the teacher identify problem areas?
4. Which of the other conference skill areas will I particularly attend to during the conference?

Planning and Collaboration Phase

The Planning and Collaboration Phase is critical in that it sets the stage for the subsequent observation and the Post-Teaching Reflection and Consultation Phase as well.

One of the first issues to deal with is that of respective roles in the process. Clarifying each person's role helps avoid confusion and makes expectations more clear. Another area of clarification is the purpose of the Planning and Collaboration Phase. For example, the Helping Professional may wish to have a statement of objectives or expectations for the lessons to be observed. Clarification of roles and expectations is a basic condition that must be established to provide a productive working relationship.

Effective implementation of the Planning and Collaboration Phase requires appropriate skills as well as an understanding of the conditions necessary for creating a conducive environment for these interactions. The context and conditions that should be considered during the Planning Phase are reviewed in the pages that follow.

Instructional Context
Instructional context provides for identification of the teacher's instructional goals and objectives and the rationale for these goals in relationship to the overall

curriculum and to precedent and subsequent lessons. This also provides for identification of the methods that will be used, as well as rationale for the selection of these methods or activities in the learning process. It includes selection of particular behaviors the teacher intends students to demonstrate during class participation.

The Relationship Investment and Two Aspects of Engagement

A condition of particular importance is the nature of "relationship investment" between the Helping Professional and the teacher. The relationship and the processes they engege in are viewed as part of an interpersonal commitment. It also means that there is a personal contract between the two about being committed to the process and to each other in terms of mutual growth. Many authors advocate a series of steps to use in the interaction with the teacher. Our perception of the process is somewhat different in that it focuses on two fundamental aspects of the engagement process in the observation cycle. One fundamental component is the development of appropriate conditions to create an effective working relationship. The second component relates to the specific skills that may be used as the interaction progresses through the various stages of the collaboration process.

Psychological Contract and Confidentiality. Perhaps the most frequently mentioned and essential aspect of establishing appropriate conditions is the development of a psychological contract between the Helping Professional and the teacher. This is adapted from Levinson's early work (1968) on the relationship between an individual and an organization. For our purposes it means development of an understanding between the two individuals in terms of processes, expectations, and respective roles. More importantly, the psychological contract involves creating rapport so that there is enough trust to interact in a meaningful, open, and productive manner. This psychological contract establishes the climate in which both will function in the helping relationship. It consists of many specific components, and the overall thrust is to provide for a mutually supportive and growth-producing environment.

Another essential element in the psychological contract is to establish, confirm, and agree upon confidentiality in the process and in the relationship. This means that none of the information will be divulged to other individuals, either formally or informally. The teacher also agrees to confidentiality in that he or she will not relate concerns or other issues related to the helping relationship to persons not involved in this situation. It is necessary for the Helping Professional to put this issue on the table and have it openly discussed and clarified. Ignoring the issue would not be productive, and it could lead to some degree of doubt in the mind of the teacher.

Trust and Rapport. Demonstrating positive regard and establishing confidentiality contributes to another important condition: trust. We more thoroughly discussed trust in the helping relationship in Chapter 8. Trust is developed through reflecting an openness and genuine caring for the helpee's needs. It is a critical aspect of the helping function.

Another aspect in the development of trust is rapport. It means that the individuals involved are communicating and relating in a positive and close working relationship. There is mutual confidence in each other. Once one has an ongoing expression of positive regard and has established trust, rapport can be developed and nurtured. Rapport is built through genuine praise, reflection of listening, and a feeling of being understood. The helping and communication skills described in prior chapters are some of the important ways to establish rapport.

Dealing with Resistance

A component sometimes avoided in the issue of building a working relationship is resistance. Resistance may be overt or subtle, a very strong objection or a small, yet irritating disagreement. Whatever the source or nature of resistance, it is important that it be dealt with openly. Chapter 3 on the change process will be most helpful in regard to resistance and the helper's role.

The Helping Professional should handle teacher resistance through positive actions and should avoid responding defensively. For example, trying to break resistance down by threats or reasoning is counterproductive. Negative strategies such as avoiding resistance by ignoring it, trying to make the other person feel guilty, or belittling it or indicating that it is of little importance only increase the resistance.

Resistance opens opportunities for understanding each other better. As noted by Waite (1995), a "teacher's resistance is ripe with implications for supervisors and supervision. Resistance, rather than being categorically and transcendentally defined, ought to be examined for its meaning and potential, that is, assuming supervisors are interested in emancipation rather than oppression for themselves and for teachers" (p. 91).

Growth Aspects

One of the more obvious yet pervasive conditions that must clearly be recognized is that the purpose is to promote the growth of the teacher. It is also recognized that in virtually every situation the helper grows as well, and this is understood as part of the process.

A primary element in teacher development is the enhancement of the teacher's ability to function in a diagnostic-prescriptive manner. This is a fundamental theme of the Transformational Helping Professional model. This analytical model applies to the way teachers guide their own professional growth. Part of the guidance and support process is to enable teachers to monitor their instructional and professional practice; to analyze their behaviors, processes, and outcomes; and to evaluate where they are at a given point in time in order to develop new professional growth plans. This is an application of the diagnostic-prescriptive process.

Planning and Collaboration Phase

The various clinical models contain a variety of specific steps one might pursue in the collaboration phase. Most of these have developed a rather detailed approach to the conferencing process (Acheson & Gall, 1992; Florida Performance Measurement System, 1985; Goldhammer, Anderson, & Krajewski, 1993; Kindsvatter & Wilen, 1991).

One common set of steps for a conference in the planning process is as follows:

1. Provide some time for establishing a comfort level such as use of an "icebreaker."
2. Establish and clarify the purpose of the session.
3. Specify outcomes of the procedure that might be expected.
4. Clarify respective roles.
5. Discuss procedures that will be followed, both in the conferencing and observation process.
6. Identify concerns the teacher has.
7. Provide for translating concerns into specific goals.
8. Identify the context variables in the school and particularly the classroom.
9. Discuss the nature of the information that may be needed to respond to the area of concern and how it might be recorded and analyzed.
10. Provide for closure to the planning.
11. Analyze the conferencing process itself.

As we have suggested, the specific steps do not constitute a protocol or prescription, but rather a series of alternative actions and skills one might employ throughout the helping relationship. These emanate from the conditions we described in the preceding sections.

Purpose and Outcomes
One of the first steps that may be taken is clarification of purpose. This provides for identification of purposes of the relationship that may not yet be understood.

Process
A subsequent step is to reach an understanding on the nature of the process that will be engaged in during this planning session. What will the collaborative process be like, how will one go about it, and what will be the ground rules? Some of the issues here relate to how often the Helping Professional and teacher will meet, what the scope of discussion will be, what issues will be delved into, and what issues one prefers not to explore. The process should be consistent with the respective roles.

Identifying Issues and Concerns
One of the early steps is working with the teacher to assist in her or his diagnosis of needs, interests, and concerns. Part of this may be focused on determining the teacher's general philosophical orientation to learning and the teaching process. Given this background on the teacher's philosophical orientation, the Helping Professional and teacher can begin to explore how they may wish to plan the lesson. This is where the Helping Professional serves as a collaborator in the planning process.

Throughout the entire Collaboration Phase the Helping Professional must use her or his helping and communication skills. The basic strategy is to help teachers think through where they are at this particular point in time and to encourage them to be as specific as possible.

Context
An issue of importance we emphasized is having a clear understanding of the classroom context in which the teacher will be working. This is a review of the specific variables that might have an influence on the situation and will be useful in planning the teacher's lesson. Of particular importance is not just the static details, but the classroom dynamics.

Reviewing the Lesson
The Helping Professional collaborates with the teacher in planning the lesson, using a diagnostic approach. Together they look not just at the content to be acquired by the students, but also to the most appropriate content and instructional strategies or processes for these particular students. This review is based on a diagnosis of the individuals in the classroom and their particular needs at this time.

In monitoring, the Helping Professional checks for understanding and involvement in the activities. Evaluation will determine the extent to which objectives are being met and goals have been achieved by the end of the lesson.

Closure
The purpose of closure is to bring the discussion to a point where there is an understanding of what will be done and what the contribution of the Helping Professional in particular will be. The closure also needs to provide a conclusion to the agreement on the logistics, such as the time of observation, length of observation, type of data to be collected, instruments that might be used, scheduling the post-teaching, consultation meeting, whether or not there will be immediate feedback after the observation, and how the information might be summarized for analysis in the subsequent meeting.

Analysis of the Process
It is often valuable before leaving the planning and collaboration session to openly discuss the nature of the process engaged in and the degree to which this has been helpful. Questions for opening the discussion might be: "How helpful has this process been for you?" "What things would you change in the ways in which we approached this?" "What are some of the kinds of issues that this made you think about?"

Post-Teaching Reflection and Consultation Phase

As noted in Chapter 5 on instructional and professional needs (Domain Two), a major emphasis in this model is to engage teachers in reflecting on their practice. Helping teachers think through the rationale for their instructional plans and activities is the cognitive emphasis. The model also stresses reflection on teachers' own thinking processes, or metacognition. A major purpose is to enable teachers to assess and diagnose their own instructional needs, collaborate on analysis and planning, and utilize the consultation of the Helping Professional. Reflection is a key term that pervades this particular process.

The follow-up of the observation in this Consultation Phase may take place at different points in time. It is most useful to provide some immediate feedback to teachers about performance. Teachers are anxious to know how they have done in respect to the goals that were mutually established. They are interested in another perspective on their classroom dynamics as well as their particular performance. Being somewhat apprehensive about being observed, teachers will need to get some feedback as soon as possible in order to alleviate some of this concern.

The use of an immediate feedback conference alone is usually a pragmatic decision. Time may not be available for in-depth conferencing and review of data. We believe under these circumstances, however, the quality of the supervision and growth of the teacher will suffer. It is usually not possible to delve in depth into issues such as rationales and teachers' thought processes. Deeper reflection on issues is not feasible in a short post-observation review. This does not allow teachers the opportunity to review, self-diagnose, and gain the skills of diagnosis. It becomes more of a one-way conference rather than a true consultation and reflection in which there is mutual exploration of the data.

The purposes of the Consultation and Reflection session are to provide information for the teacher and Helping Professional to review, to enhance the professional growth of the teacher, and to increase the teacher's diagnostic and analytical skills regarding his or her own instruction and thought processes.

Engaging in the Conference
Presenting the data collected during the observation assists teachers in acquiring a clear picture of what happened in the classroom. It also provides a means for them to hone their skills in observing and diagnosing their own instructional practice. This review of the record of the classroom can be the most sensitive part of the consultation process. When specific information is given through documented examples that teachers can see for themselves, there not only is less of a threat, but teachers may draw their own inferences, which is a major purpose of the process.

Analysis of Data
Analysis of data will vary depending upon the nature of the instruments used to collect the information. Some instruments are focused on specific areas of content, such as classroom management, verbal interaction, student engagement in productive activities, et cetera. The analysis of data may be done in terms of specific objectives established by the teacher and Helping Professional, or it may be done in terms of providing an overall picture of the classroom environment and dynamics. One area that needs to be a focus, of course, is teacher behaviors. What are the behaviors the teacher is demonstrating in the classroom, how are they consistent with what was intended, and to what extent do they reflect the goals of the lesson?

Student behavior also is an area of focus. In particular, one needs to look at whether or not the students are engaged in activities that the teacher has intended.

Finally, one needs to infer from the lesson what changes might be made in future lessons. Reasons for these changes need to be derived from review of the data and variables of the classroom that should be taken into account. It is important that these changes be specific so the teacher knows clearly what to do in subsequent lessons.

Consultation Approaches and Questions
There are several general approaches to this interaction phase that have been proposed by various writers. Hunter and Russell (1990) suggest that script taping be analyzed through labeling. The purpose of this is to select potential discussion topics for the conference. Labeled items might be parts of a lesson such as anticipatory set or guided practice. Hunter and Russell suggest that the observer label two types of evidence: (1) behaviors that were enabling learning, and (2) behaviors for which there may be questions. The most critical part of the observation cycle is assisting the teacher in understanding what occurred in the lesson so that he or she can gain diagnostic skills and project ways to improve practice in the future.

Conference Outcomes
There are a number of outcomes that may result from the conference. Some of these can be identified as goals or expectations of the conferencing. One of the essential keys to effective conferencing is developing new directions or new targets. Where will the teacher go with the information that has been acquired? What are new, specific targets or goals that have been identified? There also must be some type of commitment from both parties regarding the process and future actions.

Rarely identified, but often the most critical factor, is whether or not the relationship and conference have been personally satisfying. The teacher and Helping Professional must feel they have derived something that is of value or specific use to them as an individual and professional.

Kindsvatter and Wilen (1991) propose questions for reflection on the conferencing process itself: (1) To what extent did I achieve my conference goals? (2) How did the teacher respond to the climate I created? (3) How can I improve in formulating and asking questions? (4) Which conference skill area should I focus on in my next conference?

Closing Remarks

The process of reflecting and consulting with the Helping Professional has the potential for creating significant teacher growth. It is here that the Helping Professional exercises and pulls together all of his or her competencies such as helping skills, communication skills, instructional skills, and guidance and support skills. The importance of this consulting process also is magnified by the fact that it is revisited several times during the helping relationship experience. An investment

Issues and Questions for Review and Reflection

1. What is the role of the Helping Professional in guiding and supporting the teacher in the personal-psychological domain?
2. Interview several teachers and ask them about their concerns with how their district is meeting teachers' physical needs.
3. Discuss the area of emotional needs. To what extent are they of concern to teachers in your school or district?
4. In what ways are teachers in your school or district meeting their intellectual needs? Are they sufficient? If not, what can be done to improve them?
5. How does the school or district provide for meeting some of the teachers' social needs?
6. How do you interpret spiritual needs? How can the Helping Professional assist with these?
7. Review the various strategies for assisting teachers in analyzing their thought processes. In groups of three, role play using one or more of these strategies. Person A role plays the teacher, B is the Helping Professional, and C serves as observer of the process. Discuss the interaction and the strategy itself. Repeat the process until each person has a turn at each role.
8. Discuss the post-teaching and consultation phase. How do the conditions for positive interactions relate to this phase?
9. How do the communication skills such as paraphrase and questioning fit into the Consultation Phase?

References

Acheson, K. A., & Gall, M. D. (1992). *Techniques in the clinical supervision of teachers: Preservice and inservice applications* (3d ed.). New York: Longman.

Day, C., Calderhead, J., & Denicolo, P. (Eds.) (1993). *Research on teacher thinking: Understanding professional development*. New York: Falmer Press.

Farber, B. A. (1991). *Crisis in education: Stress and burnout in the American teacher*. San Francisco Jossey-Bass.

Florida Performance Measurement System (1985). *Specialized domain: Counseling*. Tallahassee: Florida Department of Education.

Foreyt, J. P. (1987). Issues in the assessment and treatment of obesity. *Journal of Consulting and Clinical Psychology, 55*(5), 677–684.

Gold, Y. (1996). Beginning teacher support: Attrition, mentoring, and induction. In J. Sikula (Ed.), *Handbook of research on teacher education*. New York: Macmillan.

Gold, Y., & Roth, R. A. (1993). *Teachers managing stress and preventing burnout: The professional health (PH) solution*. New York: Falmer Press.

Goldhammer, R., Anderson, R. H., & Krajewski, R. J. (1993). *Clinical supervision: Special methods for the supervision of teachers* (3d ed.). New York: Harcourt Brace.

Hunter, M., & Russell, D. (1990). *Mastering coaching and supervision: Principles of Learning series*. Thousand Oaks, CA: Corwin Press.

Johnson, D. W., & Johnson, R. T. (1995). *Reducing school violence through conflict resolution.*

Alexandria, VA: Association for Supervision and Curriculum Development.

Kindsvatter, R., & Wilen, W. W. (1991). A systematic approach to improving conference skills. *Educational Leadership, 38*, 525–529.

Lakein, A. (1974). *How to get control of your time and your life*. New York: Penguin Books.

Levinson, H. (1968). *The exceptional executive: A psychological conception*. Cambridge, MA: Harvard University Press.

Little, J. W. (1993). Teachers' professional development in a climate of educational reform.

Educational Evaluation and Policy Analysis, 15(2), 129–151.

Men's Health. (1991). July/August.

Schön, D. A. (1987). *Educating the reflective practitioners*. San Francisco: Jossey-Bass.

Waite, D. (1995). *Rethinking instructional supervision: Notes on its language and culture*. London: Falmer Press.

Weinstein, C. E., & Mayer, R. E. (1986). The teaching of learning strategies. In M. C. Wittrock (Ed.), *Handbook of research on teaching*. New York: Macmillan.

Related Readings

Anderson, R. H., & Snyder, K. J. (Eds.) (1993). *Clinical supervision: Coaching for higher performance*. Lancaster, PA: Technomic.

Dannefer, D., & Perlmutter, M. (1990). Development as a multidimensional process: Individual and social constituents. *Human Development, 33*, 108–137.

Dorr-Bremme, D. W. (1990). Contextualization cues in the classroom: Discourse regulation and social control functions. *Language in society, 19*(3), 379–402.

Educational Leadership (1987). Theme issue: Staff development through coaching. 44(5).

Grimmet, P. P., & Housego, I. E. (1983). Interpersonal relationships in the clinical supervision conference. *The Canadian Administrator, 22*, 1–6.

Hargreaves, A., & Dawe, R. (1990). Paths of professional development: Contrived collegiality, collaborative culture, and the case of peer coaching. *Teaching and Teacher Education, 6*(3), 227–241.

Joyce, B., & Showers, B. (1982). The coaching of teaching. *Educational Leadership, 40*(1), 4–10.

Ovando, M. (1993). The post-observation conference from the teacher's perspective: A collaborative process. *Wingspan, 9*(1), 8–14.

Pajak, E., & Glickman, C. (1989). Informational and controlling language in simulated supervisory conferences. *American Educational Research Journal, 26*(1), 93–106.

Sergiovanni, T. J. (1985). Landscapes, mindscapes, and reflective practice in supervision. *Journal of Curriculum and Supervision, 1*(1), 5–17.

Smyth, W. J. (1991). Problematising teaching through a "critical" approach to clinical supervision. *Curriculum Inquiry, 21*, 321–352.

Waite, D. (1990/91). Behind the other set of eyes: An ethnographic study of instructional supervision. (Doctoral dissertation, University of Oregon). *Dissertation Abstracts International, 51*, 3708A.

Waite, D. (1992a). Instructional supervision from a situational perspective. *Teaching and Teacher Education, 8*, 319–332.

Waite, D. (1992b). "Supervisors" talk: Making sense of conferences from an anthropological linguistic perspective. *Journal of Curriculum and Supervision, 7*, 349–371.

Waite, D. (1993). Teachings in conference: A qualitative study of teacher-supervisor face-to-face interactions. *American Educational Research Journal, 30*(4), 675–702.

Zeichner, K. M., & Liston, D. (1985). Varieties of discourse in supervisory conferences. *Teaching and Teacher Education, 1*(2), 15.

Chapter 14

Managing Stress and Preventing Burnout: Keeping the Flame Burning Brightly

*Men are not worried by things, but by their
ideas about things. When we meet with
difficulties, become anxious or
troubled, let us not blame others,
but rather ourselves, that is,
our ideas about things.* —EPICTETUS

The joy of helping others grow and mature has long been the desire of many people who choose teaching for their life's work. Unfortunately, the passion that once existed is too often consumed by the insidious flames of burnout. Tensions, unrealistic demands, and degrading conditions increase over time and feed the fire of discontent in teachers who once believed that they could make a difference in the lives of their students and in the profession itself.

The degenerating morale of teachers mirrors the stressful conditions that they are experiencing today. This low morale is reflected in various reports that describe the profession as being in a crisis. Wendt (1980) called it "a sense of crisis," Wangberg (1984) wrote an article called "Educators in Crisis: The Need to Improve the

Teaching Workplace and Teaching as a Profession," and Farber's (1991) book is aptly titled *Crisis in Education: Stress and Burnout in the American Teacher*. These discouraging conditions led to the 1990 Carnegie Report that announced: "Nearly 40 percent of the teachers stated that if they had it to do over, they would not become a public school teacher" (Carnegie Foundation, 1990, p. 5).

Many teachers are demoralized and discouraged, believing that they are not leading productive or meaningful professional lives. Stress is a major contributor to their feeling overwhelmed and exhausted, while burnout is the insidious disease that over time robs teachers of the joy of teaching and leaves them disillusioned and unable to carry on.

Because stress and burnout are not synonymous, it is important to understand their similarities and differences, as well as their differential influences on one's personal and professional life. This chapter will review the basic characteristics of each and also will discuss their importance for the Helping Professional. Various diagnostic instruments and coping strategies for personal management of stress and burnout will be provided, as well as suggestions for assisting those who need help.

A Conceptualization of Teacher Stress

Due to the increasingly higher rates of teacher turnover (Cunningham, 1982), attention has been focused on the problem of stress among public school teachers. Having high levels of stress was not entirely new for teachers because it was identified as a problem as early as the 1930s (Hicks, 1933), and has continued to be a concern in the profession ever since. However, it was only when teachers began leaving the profession in greater numbers that interest within the research and literature increased. In the 1980s, Kottkamp, Provenzo, and Cohn (1986) reported that 13.1 percent of teachers in their Florida study recorded feeling dissatisfied with their work. It also was reported by Long, Avant, and Harrison that "there is little question that teachers are facing serious difficulties in their jobs and that this is taking a toll on the quality of education in this country" (1986, p. 19). Looking at the 1990s, Farber (1991) maintained that "30–35 percent of teachers are strongly dissatisfied with the teaching profession" (p. 42).

It is easy to see that stress is a major problem that affects the lives of hundreds of teachers, creating consequences for them as well as the students they teach. Stress is linked to mental health problems and physical problems. Because of the grave consequences associated with teachers' stress, researchers began to take a more careful look at it and examined the various definitions within the literature.

The Evolving Definition of Stress

One of the early researchers of stress, Hans Selye, indicated as early as 1956 that stress was difficult to define. He drew from his medical background and described it as:

the wear and tear caused by life, a state manifested by a specific syndrome of biological events and can be both pleasant or unpleasant, the mobilization of the body's defenses that allow human beings to adapt to hostile or threatening events, and is dangerous when it is unduly prolonged, comes too often, or concentrates on one particular organ of the body. (Selye, 1956)

After considerably more experience and a great deal of research, Selye (1974) gained new insights that led to a significantly revised definition. At this time he modified his earlier definition and stated that "stress is the nonspecific response of the body to any demand made upon it" (1974, p. 27). Unfortunately, Selye's definition conceptualizes stress as something that affects people in an almost mindless, reflex-like way, and doesn't take into account intellectual or cognitive evaluations of the situation. However, it is important to remember that Selye was one of the pioneers in the field and he contributed much to our understanding of stress.

With the interest in stress increasing, psychologists also began researching it. R. S. Lazarus (1966, 1971) pointed out the limitations of the definitions that described stress in terms of the physiological responses of the body to the demands made upon it. He believed that events do not in themselves produce stress reactions. Drs. Woolfolk and Richardson (1978), consistent with Lazarus's beliefs, defined stress as being "in here," within the human brain, and stated that "stress is always linked to some act of understanding resulting from the interaction between the environment and the organism" (p. 7).

With the increased attention on teachers, a number of investigators began to define teacher stress. Galloway, Boswell, and Pankhurst (1981) believed that the most useful perspective on stress is one that investigates the interaction or "fit" between teachers and their work. According to these investigators, stress arises when there is a "lack of fit" between the needs and the capacity of individuals and the conditions existing in their environment. A few years later, Kyriacou (1989) stated that, "Teacher stress refers to the experience by teachers of unpleasant emotions such as anger, tension, frustration, anxiety, depression, and nervousness, resulting from aspects of their work as teachers" (p. 27).

More currently, as a result of their research, Gold and Roth (1993) defined teacher stress as "a condition of disequilibrium within the intellectual, emotional and physical state of the individual; it is generated by one's perceptions of a situation, which result in physical and emotional reactions. It can be either positive or negative, depending upon one's interpretations" (p. 17).

In examining these definitions, many believe that stress is an individual response. What one individual finds stressful another may not. Individuals perceive what they believe to be potentially threatening situations according to their own needs, perceptions, and coping resources. Individual differences exist in the sources and degree of stress experienced.

Sources of Teacher Stress

A multitude of factors that precipitate stress for teachers have been identified by a number of researchers. We have found it helpful to organize the sources of stress into two categories: personal stressors and professional stressors (Gold & Roth, 1993).

Personal Stressors

Factors that are associated with personal stressors can be grouped into four major areas: (1) health concerns; (2) relationships, which include family, friends, and associates; (3) financial pressures and living conditions; and (4) recreational concerns.

Health Concerns

Health concerns have long been high on teachers' lists of complaints. Research on teacher stress and investigation into the consequences to their health are greatly needed at the present time. However, what we do know is that stress is costly. Figures from a variety of sources give us some idea of the devastating impact of stress. One source, Pelletier and Lutz (1988), estimated that anywhere from 60 to 90 percent of all visits to health care professionals are for stress-related disorders. In 1993, it was reported by Williams (1993) that coronary heart disease is America's number-one killer. "In its major manifestation, heart attack accounts for nearly half of all deaths in the United States every year" (p. 66).

Because many teachers are in high stress positions, education about stress and training on how they can manage it are essential. Quick-fix stress reduction programs are short-lasting. What is needed is a program that has long-term results (Gold & Roth, 1993).

Relationships

Relationships are often an important reason for selecting teaching as a profession. Most teachers are very people-oriented, and they enjoy interacting with colleagues. However, relationship problems are too often the causes for stress among educators. This is mainly due to the fact that teachers give so much to others and therefore have little left for family and friends (Schwab, Jackson, & Schuler, 1986). Many teachers have told us that they feel depleted after a long and exhausting day at school. They have many responsibilities at school and at home that add to the many stressors they are trying to handle. When personal relationships are strained, the stress level accelerates (Jenkins & Calhoun, 1991). Teachers need assistance in learning techniques for handling relationship issues.

Financial Pressures and Living Conditions

A large number of teachers express concerns about financial problems (Kyriacou & Sutcliffe, 1978). Inadequate salary scales in comparison with many other professions affect their living conditions and their quality of life. When their families are affected by inadequate living conditions, teachers experience even greater stress.

Many young teachers are not in a financial position to purchase their own home, and their children are raised in economic areas that are lower than they desire. For individuals who have spent 4 or 5 years in college, the financial returns do not equal the investment.

Recreational Concerns

Recreational pursuits also are limited for many teachers whose families are living on budgets that must include only the daily necessities. Many young teachers share with us that they are not able to continue the type of recreational activities they once enjoyed when they were living with their parents.

Professional Stressors

A number of factors in the professional realm that contribute to teacher stress are: disruptive students (Gold, 1985; Okebukola & Jegede, 1989), heavy workload (Dewe, 1986), time demands (Payne & Furnham, 1987), work conditions (Laughlin, 1984), teaching older students in grades 5–12 (Borg, Riding, & Falzon, 1991; Gold, 1985), incompetent administration (Dewe, 1986), role conflict and role ambiguity (Schwab & Iwanicki, 1982a), and lack of educational resources (Coats & Thoresen, 1976). These factors are among the most researched areas.

Additional sources of teacher stress relate to the increasing changes in society. Teachers must modify their thinking, teaching, and ways of relating to others as they try to cope with population increases, diversity in school populations, crime on their campuses, and the language barrier for many of their students.

How teachers perceive the new professional demands they face will to a large degree determine how great a level of stress they will experience and how they will make necessary changes. Some individuals will adjust more quickly than others to stressful circumstances, because stress is caused by an individual's perceptions of threatening events and situations. Thus, individual differences exist in the sources and in the degrees of stress experienced.

Effects of Stress on Teachers

The effects of stress from a teacher's work and home situation can be categorized into physical, psychological/emotional, social, intellectual, and behavioral areas. Physical effects of stress are manifest in frequent headaches, hypertension, fatigue, sleep disturbance, tightening of the muscles, and high blood pressure, to name a few (Poteliakhoff & Carruthers, 1981). Psychological/emotional effects of stress include depression, anxiety, nervousness, general uneasiness, and loss of confidence (Gold & Roth, 1993; Woolfolk & Richardson, 1978). Social effects of stress involve depersonalization, arguments, impatience, and divorce or separation from friends and family. Behavioral effects include low productivity, absenteeism, procrastination, and withdrawal from teaching (Dewe, 1986).

Studies over the past several years have strongly supported the belief that the physical, psychological/emotional, intellectual, and spiritual aspects of an individual's life are inseparable and that they are vital for a healthy lifestyle (Leonard,

1980). Teachers must be given the necessary knowledge and skills to handle the stress associated with each of these areas of their lives. They need to be prepared for the challenges and demands of their personal and professional lives.

Assessing Stress Level

It is important to take time for diagnosing the sources of stress in our lives. When specific areas that are high sources of stress are identified, definite plans can be made for dealing directly with the stressors, which will reduce harmful effects.

The following instrument will help teachers diagnose many of their professional sources of stress. Taking time to respond to each item will be of assistance in learning to identify specific areas. Helping Professionals will need to take the instrument to assess their own stressors and to become familar with the instrument.

Work-Related Stress Evaluation Instrument

Directions: Listed here are actual events at work that have been identified by mentors as stimulating stress reactions. Rate each statement on a scale from 0 to 5, with 5 being the highest extent to which the event produced a stress reaction in you. If you have not experienced the specific stressor, respond with NA (not applicable).

Event   My Stress Reaction

1. I recently experienced a significant change in my environmental conditions (lighting, noise, temperature, space, etc.) that was highly stressful for me.   _____
2. I recently experienced a transfer to a different school even though I had not requested it. It was difficult to leave.   _____
3. Recently I was not selected for a position that I wanted in our school.   _____
4. My closest friend at school left.   _____
5. I was transferred to another grade level and had not requested it.   _____
6. A new program was proposed for our school to help the ESL students.   _____
7. I was not granted my request for a transfer to a new grade level.   _____
8. I will be giving a workshop for my district in the next 2 months.   _____
9. I did not receive my promotion to a new position that I had requested.   _____
10. A new principal was transferred to our school.   _____
11. A new housing development is opening and we received a significant number of new students to our school.   _____
12. We hired a number of new teachers for our school this year.   _____
13. My schedule has been changed considerably over the past few months.   _____
14. I am encountering a major change (increase or decrease) in my teaching assignment due to technology (computer, techniques, etc.).   _____
15. I am not being supported by my principal as I had been.   _____

List, in order, the item numbers of the three events you personally felt to be the most stressful, or identify others if they rank in the top three.

1. _____   2. _____   3. _____

After you have completed the instrument, make a list of those items that you ranked with a 3 or higher. Having listed each of these, identify any similarities. Write out your observations and conclusions. It would be helpful to discuss what you learned with others who took the instrument.

Stress on the job causes disruptions in a person's life and usually triggers a chain reaction that requires certain personal adjustments. The items on the inventory represent a few of the types of changes that can cause stress. When we experience a stress response triggered by any type of work event, it is likely that we will become ill (Holmes & Rahe, 1967). An example of this was shared with us by Sylvia, a teacher in an elementary school in a rapidly growing population area.

I had no idea how stressed I was at school. There have been many changes recently due to the new housing around the school. When I made my list after I had completed the "Work-Related Stress Evaluation Instrument," I couldn't believe what I learned. I had marked 3 or above on the following items: (1) I had not been selected to be a mentor in my school because the principal wanted to give other teachers a turn. (I was devastated at first. I really enjoyed my work helping others. Now I feel an emptiness.) (2) My closest friend was transferred last year without even being notified. (I feel so isolated without her. We always talked about so many things. My support is gone!) (3) I was transferred to another grade level because our enrollment increased so rapidly. (I didn't even have an opportunity to select the grade I wanted). (4) We were asked to begin a new reading program to meet the needs of the ESL students. (I must have special training that will take one evening per week. I really don't feel like taking time away from my family.) (5) We were notified that we will be getting a new principal in 3 months. (We all feel concerned about who is coming.) And (6) We need four new teachers to help us handle all of these new students. (No wonder I have been ill so much the past few months. I have more stress than I realized. I'm not sure what I can do to change anything. What can a teacher do when all of these changes are taking place? I feel so helpless.)

We certainly can understand why Sylvia feels so much stress. She has a number of stressors at the present time and she isn't sure what she can do to handle all of them.

In evaluating your responses, if you discover that you have stressors that are not listed on the instrument, add these to your list. After you review your list, identify any stressors you could change. Plan specific ways you could handle the situation to minimize your stress. Remember, stress is caused when you perceive something to be a threat to you. Identify what the threat is. Ask yourself whether you could perceive the situation in another way so that the threat is minimized. Sylvia was able to do this with some of her stressors after further reflection on the issues and circumstances.

After you have identified some of your personal and professional stressors, you will find it helpful to categorize each of them more specifically such as relationships/family problems, financial concerns, health problems, and so on. When you have clearly identified your major stressors, the next step is to develop coping strategies that will help you manage your stress. This type of growth experience also will assist you when you are helping others identify their stressors.

Guidelines for Stress Management and Lifestyle Changes

Daily living requires personal and social changes that inevitably produce pressures, strains, and difficulties. Life also presents economic uncertainties and international problems and tensions that will continue. The world in which we live is an imperfect one that has many challenges. How we handle pressures associated with challenges in life is of utmost importance. Virginia Satir, a well-known family therapist and writer, died of cancer in 1989 after a long and distinguished career. In her obituary in the *Los Angeles Times* (1989, p. 24) she was quoted as saying,

> *Life is not the way it's supposed to be. It's the way it is. The way you cope with it is what makes the difference. I think if I have one message, one thing before I die that most of the world would know, it would be that the event does not determine how to respond to the event. That is a purely personal matter. The way in which we respond will direct and influence the event more than the event itself.*

What a challenging and inspiring message! Most of us want to handle life's problems and respond with this kind of courage and dignity. The next section of the chapter concentrates on the process of coping and discusses what coping is, the stages of coping, and a variety of coping resources. Each of these areas will assist you in responding to the challenges that you encounter in life and as a Helping Professional.

The coping process involves three major areas of concern: (1) what coping is, (2) the stages of coping, and (3) coping resources.

Coping: What It Is

Any coping response is defined as what people think they do as they deal with the demands in their life. When people mature and gain new insights about themselves, they modify existing coping strategies or learn new ones. Therefore, coping is a process that changes over time. Individuals' coping responses are modified as they react to and adapt to specific situations and people throughout their life. Everyone repeats learned patterns of coping which have become their coping style. Joseph's coping style is described in the following paragraph.

> *Joseph came to his first teaching job excited and eager to practice the many things he had learned in his teacher training. He had been raised in a working-class family with a great deal of support from his father, who held the family together. His mother, a drug addict, had left the family when Joseph was in high school. He had two brothers, and the father had developed a strong family bond between them. Joseph worked through*

high school and college to help support himself. He learned to manage his time carefully, and he was encouraged by his father to develop strong friendships for support. Joseph refused drugs in high school and college. During student teaching he was confident and worked hard to be successful. He also worked 20 hours a week waiting on tables in a local restaurant. He was rated outstanding in student teaching and the principal encouraged him to apply for a teaching position in the same district. Clearly, he coped actively and constructively.

Bruno's coping style contrasted sharply to Joseph's.

Bruno entered his first year of teaching at the same time as Joseph. He had attended the same university. He came from a middle-income family where mother stayed at home and life was relatively easy and predictable. His parents were respected members of the community. Bruno enjoyed the privileges of parents who provided money and support for their two children. Throughout high school and college, Bruno received an allotment from his father, so he didn't have to work. He joined a college fraternity and was soon accepted into the popular crowd. He went to most of the parties, used alcohol excessively on a number of occasions, and had a very active social life. Because of his lack of disciplining himself, he did only the minimum amount of work to complete his teacher training and to graduate. During student teaching he felt overwhelmed with the amount of work. He had developed a habit of procrastinating, and the supervising teachers spent a great deal of time working with him. Because of his pleasant personality and winsome ways, the teachers in the school liked him and were eager to give him the help he needed, believing he had the potential to be an effective teacher. Unfortunately for Bruno, he wasn't developing the necessary coping skills to deal with the demands of teaching. When he got his first teaching job in an inner city high school, he was unable to handle the discipline problems. His lessons weren't prepared on time, he was consistently late to faculty meetings, and he rarely attended the beginning teacher support seminars because he had other things he wanted to do after school. Because he stayed out late with his friends, he didn't get enough sleep and as a result caught the flu twice during the first 3 months of teaching and missed a total of 10 working days. By the end of the first semester he was still unable to face the fact that he needed to make some drastic changes in his life. Undeniably, Bruno's coping style is maladaptive.

Both of these new teachers faced multiple stressors during their first year of teaching. They responded to the stressors in patterned ways that they had learned in their life. Each had developed coping styles that by now had been practiced for many years. Bruno's style will remain the same until he becomes aware that he must change maladaptive patterns for more constructive ones in order to be successful in teaching.

Lazarus and Folkman (1984) believed coping to be "... constantly changing cognitive and behavioral efforts to manage specific external and/or internal demands that are appraised as taxing or exceeding the resources of the person" (p. 141). Unless individuals become aware that their coping style is maladaptive, they will continue cognitive and behavioral patterns that are dysfunctional.

Helping Professionals need to know their own coping styles. They need to become aware of any maladaptive patterns, learn new and healthy coping styles, and practice them until changes are made. It is essential that Helping Professionals remain open to their own growth and that they be active participants in the growth process.

Stages of Coping

Lazarus and Folkman (1984) believe that people go through three stages as they cope with difficult situations. The first stage is labeled the *primary appraisal* stage, in which the individual actually appraises the stressor. It is at this point that the person perceives the situation to be threatening or not. If the situation is perceived to be safe, the coping process ends. If, however, the situation is perceived to be potentially threatening, the stress-coping process continues.

The second stage is called *secondary appraisal*. This is when the individual assesses her or his resources for dealing with the stressor. In their studies of these stages, Holroyd and Lazarus (1982) stated that this assessment is influenced by "previous experiences in similar situations, generalized beliefs about the self and the environment, and the availability of personal (e.g., physical strength or problem-solving skills) and environmental (e.g., social support or money) resources" (p. 23). One of the important aspects of this secondary appraisal is an assessment of how much control a person has over the situation. The less the perceived control, the more threatening the situation will be and the greater the probability of mental and physical distress.

Coping is the term given to the third phase. In this phase, people take whatever actions seem appropriate to them. The response selected may involve action or merely involve a cognitive adjustment—redefining the situation through self-talk. A number of authorities believe that a coping response is helpful and constructive for a person depending on the person's perceptions of the outcome (Frese, 1986; Krohne, 1986; Laux, 1986).

Personal and Professional Coping Resources

There are numerous coping resources available to people. Some of these are:

- A positive belief system
- Problem-solving strategies
- Self-talk strategies
- Communication skills
- Exercise routines
- Social support
- Material resources
- School and community resources

We all have these resources to choose from to help us cope in healthy ways. Some hindrances in choosing to use them are: lack of confidence, unexpressed anger, fear, guilt, perceived social restraints, resistance to asking for help, poverty, and dysfunctional backgrounds where maladaptive coping skills were learned. Becoming aware of one's coping style and learning new, effective skills will help a person change old patterns that have been hindering them.

Maladaptive Coping Strategies
Maladaptive coping strategies include the following:

- Smoking
- Chemical abuse (alcohol, drugs, and excessive use of prescriptions or over-the-counter drugs)
- Overeating
- Excessive use of cola, coffee, or tea
- Physical and verbal abuse
- Projection (blaming others)
- Overworking
- Playing the victim (helpless)
- Denial (pretend it isn't there)
- Escapism (flight into TV, drugs, fantasy, etc.)

People use these maladaptive coping strategies largely because they are trying to relieve temporary distress. Even though we all use some of these coping strategies during stressful times in our life, alcohol, drugs, overeating, and overworking become personally destructive when used over an extended period of time.

If we are to help ourselves and others, maladaptive reactions to stress must be identified and changed. To assist in identifying personal reactions to stress, we have constructed "My Stress Reaction Profile." In completing the profile, you may gain valuable new insights.

My Stress Reaction Profile

Directions: For each item, ask yourself, "How often have I used each of the following methods during the past 4 months for the purpose of trying to reduce physical and emotional tension?" Check one of the four choices ("Never," "Infrequently," "Sometimes," "Often") for each.

		Never	Infrequently	Sometimes	Often
1.	Exercise				
2.	Drink alcoholic beverage				
3.	Pray				
4.	Take aspirin or some type of pain reliever				
5.	Do deep relaxation				
6..	Eat				
7.	Smoke				
8.	Use humor				
9.	Pretend it isn't there and keep going				

My Stress Reaction Profile *Continued*

		Never	Infrequently	Sometimes	Often
10.	Feel helpless and unable to complete the task	_____	_____	_____	_____
11.	Grin and bear it and work longer hours	_____	_____	_____	_____
12.	Listen to soft music	_____	_____	_____	_____
13.	Take a day off or a mini vacation	_____	_____	_____	_____
14.	Change my way of dealing with the problem	_____	_____	_____	_____
15.	Take a tranquilizer, sleeping pill, or other prescribed medication	_____	_____	_____	_____
16.	Drink (caffeinated) coffee, cola, or tea	_____	_____	_____	_____
17.	Take a leisurely walk	_____	_____	_____	_____
18.	Do deep breathing to relax me	_____	_____	_____	_____
19.	Refocus the problem to a more positive mind set	_____	_____	_____	_____
20.	Escape into TV, books, or something else	_____	_____	_____	_____
21.	Blame someone else	_____	_____	_____	_____
22.	Take an over-the-counter relaxant	_____	_____	_____	_____
23.	Talk to a friend	_____	_____	_____	_____
24.	Meditate	_____	_____	_____	_____
25.	Use drugs	_____	_____	_____	_____
26.	Take it out on others through verbal attacks	_____	_____	_____	_____
27.	Other _____				
28.	Other _____				

After you have completed responding to the items, look over the list of maladaptive coping strategies that were previously given (e.g., items 2, 10, 25) and see how many you marked as using sometimes or often. Also, review all the items you marked "often" and see if these areas are becoming maladaptive coping strategies. Become more aware of your behavior for a week. It would be helpful to keep a journal (Table 14-1) and record personal stressors and your reactions. One Helping Professional shared his profile with us and asked for our support. He wanted to stop using maladaptive coping strategies and replace them with healthy ones. His profile can be seen in Table 14-2.

TABLE 14-1 Coping Strategies Journal

Stressor	Time	Situation	Coping Strategies	Effects

TABLE 14-2 Sample Coping Profile

Stressor	Time	Situation	Coping Strategies	Effects
Long hours at school	7:30 a.m. to 6:00 p.m.	Grading papers and writing reports	Eat Smoke Escape into work	Short-term relief Relaxing Gets my mind off problems

Peter is willing to look at himself and take responsibility for his actions. He also has the courage to ask for support during the time that he is learning new coping strategies. When he makes the necessary changes, he will be healthier and better prepared to assist others who need help.

Adaptive Coping Strategies

We often have Helping Professionals and people at workshops and conferences ask us to discuss healthy coping strategies. The following list has proven to be extremely helpful.

- Social support: giving and receiving
- Positive self-talk
- Relaxation techniques
- Music
- Solitude (serene, peaceful, quiet activities—alone)
- Play (dancing, running, cards, games, etc.)
- Intimacy
- Prayer and/or meditation
- Hobbies
- Constructive problem solving
- Humor
- Massage
- Thought stopping
- Exercise
- Enjoyable activities (bubble bath, pets, watching a sunset, etc.)
- Perception adjustment
- Professional assistance

The Deleterious Consequences of Burnout

Many people confuse high levels of stress with burnout. It is true that stress can contribute to burnout; however, the two phenomena are not identical. To better understand burnout, a review of selected definitions of burnout from researchers in the field will be provided.

Definitions of Burnout: A Need for Clarification

Herbert Freudenberger

A number of researchers since the 1970s have attempted to define burnout. The first of these was Herbert Freudenberger, a clinical psychologist practicing in New York, who used the term in 1973 in a professional psychology journal. During the 1960s, the term "burned out" had been used in reference to the effects of drug abuse by chronic users. Freudenberger felt that many professionals were burning out because they were exhausted from working too hard and giving too much of themselves.

In evaluating Freudenberger's description of burnout, it is evident that individuals who are experiencing disillusionment, frustration, and exhaustion fit into this category. They are people who are hard on themselves, set high standards, and pursue them fiercely. They have a difficult time accepting themselves for who they are. They strive beyond the limits of their own health as they are constantly driving themselves (Freudenberger with Richelson, 1980).

Maslach and Pines

Two research-oriented professionals, Maslach and Pines, investigated burnout from the perspective of the social-psychological. In 1973, at a major psychological conference, Maslach presented a paper discussing how role-related stress in professionals could lead to the dehumanized treatment of their clients. Her emphasis was on emotional exhaustion, depersonalization, and personal accomplishment. The data she collected were from workers who were involved in human service jobs.

Pines was conducting research on stress for the Israeli army and collaborated with Maslach. They identified specific environmental conditions that contribute to burnout and listed specific symptoms that characterize it. Their research led to the *Maslach Burnout Inventory* (Maslach & Jackson, 1981, 1986) that assesses three factors in measuring burnout in individuals: emotional exhaustion (feeling used up or drained); depersonalization (feeling emotionally hardened and treating recipients as if they were impersonal objects); and, third, lack of personal accomplishment (feelings of inadequacy and ineffectiveness). Maslach and Pines view the burned-out professional as being less idealistic, with nothing left to give.

Cherniss

During the 1970s, Cherniss and his colleagues were also conducting research on burnout, but they concentrated on specific job stresses of the "public professional" (individuals who provide some type of service that requires a high degree of skill and/or formal training and who work in public institutions).

Cherniss (1980a, 1980b) believed that burnout was essentially caused by a mismatch between what workers feel they are getting in return from their work and what they feel they are giving to others. If we accept Cherniss's definition of burnout, an individual who is committing herself or himself to a cause or to a formal ideology may receive a positive effect that prevents burnout. One can see that

Cherniss's views of burnout differ from Freudenberger's. However his symptoms of burnout are similar to those that were suggested by Freudenberger, Maslach, and Pines.

Farber
A recent definition of burnout by Farber (1991) stated that burnout is a work-related syndrome that stems from individuals' perceptions of a significant discrepancy between their effort (input) and the reward (output) they receive. He believed that individuals' perceptions of effort and reward are influenced by individual, organizational, and social factors. Also, Farber argued that burnout occurs most often in those individuals who work face to face with needy clients. It is typically marked by withdrawal from and cynicism toward their clients; by emotional and physical exhaustion; and by various psychological symptoms such as anxiety, irritability, sadness, and lowered self-esteem.

Gold and Roth
Gold and Roth investigated burnout from a psychotherapeutic perspective. In their book on stress and burnout, they presented their Professional Health definition of burnout as "a syndrome which emanates from an individual's perceptions of unmet needs and unfulfilled expectations. It is characterized by progressive disillusionment, with related psychological and physical symptoms which diminish one's self-esteem. It develops gradually over a period of time" (1993, p. 41). Their major emphasis is on the needs of individuals and the expectations they have of meeting their needs. When people's needs are not met, the authors believe that these unmet needs will be manifested in numerous psychological and physical symptoms that will lead to disillusionment and eventually burnout.

Common Threads
There are a variety of definitions of burnout to be considered. Common threads that run through the definitions are as follows: (1) People who are in a state of burnout manifest symptoms of disillusionment, frustration, depression, and exhaustion; (2) burnout victims are individuals who at one time began their profession idealistic and eager to help others; (3) burnout stems from individuals' perceptions of a significant discrepancy between their effort and the rewards they receive; (4) the needs (emotional, physical, social, and intellectual) of these people are not being met; therefore they struggle with a loss of purpose and commitment in their work; (5) a slow disconnectedness from other people takes place, and these individuals alienate themselves from others due to emotional and physical exhaustion; and (6) a sense of sadness and loss develops that diminishes self-esteem.

It is essential to note that the burnout syndrome develops over a period of time and that the victim often is not aware of the deleterious consequences. The slow process of disillusionment is itself not burnout, but rather stages of its development. The end result, when the individual walks away from the job saying, "I have nothing left to give," is the extinguishing of a flame that once burned brightly—this is burnout.

Teachers Burning Out

Even though burnout was a problem for teachers before the 1980s, little was done to investigate it. In 1979, Willard McGuire, president of the National Education Association (NEA), referred to the emergence of burnout in teachers, stating that "a major malady has afflicted the teaching profession and threatens to reach epidemic proportions if it isn't checked soon "(1979, p. 5). The NEA selected teacher burnout as the central theme of its convention that same year.

Little was known about teacher burnout until empirical studies began reporting the progressive course of burnout. The majority of the studies used the *Maslach Burnout Inventory* (MBI) (Maslach & Jackson, 1981, 1986) to measure perceived levels of burnout. There was some criticism regarding the use of the MBI with teachers because the original population for the instrument was taken from a wide variety of professional groups within the helping professions. To test the validity of the MBI, Iwanicki and Schwab (1981) sampled 469 Massachusetts teachers using the instrument. They reported that the MBI did measure the same basic constructs of factors as those identified in investigations that used individuals in the helping professions as their samples. These constructs were emotional exhaustion, depersonalization, and personal accomplishment.

In 1984, Gold sampled 462 elementary and junior high school California teachers using the MBI to provide further evidence of the construct validity of the instrument for a sample of teachers from a different population. She concluded that the two scoring systems of frequency and intensity could be expected to yield comparable factor structures and equivalent constructs. It appeared that either scoring would suffice in identifying teachers who are becoming burned out in terms of self-perceptions (Gold, 1984). These two studies made significant contributions toward identifying teachers who are becoming burned out and led to a compilation of the following information about teacher burnout.

Factors Associated with Teacher Burnout

There are a number of factors identified in the research studies that are linked to teacher burnout. These major factors—demographic, social, self-concept, student behavior, administrative, and role-related—will be reviewed here.

Demographic Factors and Background Variables

From the research studies reported in the literature, a number of demographic variables have been associated with burnout in teachers. A review of these demographic variables in the most relevant studies will be presented.

Using the MBI, a number of demographic variables have been linked with burnout in teachers. These research studies have consistently reported that burnout is more likely to occur in men than in women (Anderson & Iwanicki, 1984; Beer & Beer, 1992; Farber, 1984; Gold,1985; Russell, Altmaier, & Val Velzen, 1987); in those who teach in higher grade levels such as fifth, sixth, junior high, middle, or senior high school (Anderson & Iwanicki, 1984; Farber, 1984; Gold, 1985; Schwab

& Iwanicki, 1982b); in those who are single (Farber, 1984; Gold, 1985); in those teaching in suburban or rural environments (Farber, 1984; NYSUT, 1979); and in different ages, which varied with each study (Friedman, 1991; Friedman & Lotan, 1985; Gold, 1985; Russell, Altmaier, & Van Velzen, 1987).

There were differing reports regarding age level and burnout in teachers. Friedman and Lotan (1985) found that burnout rises with age and years of experience in teaching until it reaches a peak at the age of 41–45 and then declines, while Gold (1985) reported younger teachers who are single scored higher on the emotional exhaustion and depersonalization scales. The need for social interaction is extremely important for teachers and especially in the population of young single teachers, which we have consistently found in our support seminars.

The Need for Social Support

Teachers' need for support from colleagues has been discussed throughout the literature, and a lack of social support has been found to lead to burnout in several of the studies. Pines, Aronson, and Kafry (1981) reported that social support included six functions that need to be taken into consideration. These functions are: (1) listening, (2) professional support, (3) professional challenge, (4) emotional support, (5) emotional challenge, and (6) the sharing of social reality. In their study, they found that listening (listening without giving advice or making judgments) and emotional support (having someone who is on your side and who appreciates what you are doing) were the most important factors in alleviating burnout.

Holt, Fine, and Tollefson (1987) reported in their research that teachers who scored low on the burnout scale were less alienated than teachers who scored high on the burnout scale, suggesting the importance of social support from colleagues. Burke and Greenglass (1989) and Connolly and Sanders (1988) also confirmed the importance of social support for teachers as a means of preventing burnout.

The essential nature of social support and assistance should not be minimized when discussing the importance of handling and preventing burnout in teachers. Support groups and their function have been addressed in a number of chapters in this book, thus emphasizing the vital nature of support.

Burnout and Teachers' Self-Concept

An infrequently investigated but critical factor in the study of teacher burnout is self-concept. Self-concept was defined by Rogers (1951) as one's perception of self (traits, abilities, and aims) in relation to others and the environment. Another definition by Combs and Snygg stated that self-concept includes "perceptions about self which seem most vital or important to the individual himself" (1959, p. 127).

A small number of studies have examined the relationship between self-concept and burnout. Anderson and Iwanicki (1984) reported that the lack of self-concept in teachers was correlated significantly with the emotional exhaustion and depersonalization subscales of the MBI. Malanowski and Wood (1984) found that teachers whose self-actualization needs were unmet were more likely to experience burnout. Similar findings were reported for student teachers as measured by dimensions of self-concept and correlated with the MBI. Substantial evidence was reported that student teachers who scored high on the positive self-concept scale tended to register low scores on the burnout behaviors (Gold & Michael, 1985).

More currently, Friedman and Farber (1992) examined professional self-concept as a predictor of burnout in 641 Israeli elementary school teachers. They used a modified form of the MBI and a composite measure of professional self-concept. The results indicated that the teachers in this sample who feel satisfied by their work are least likely to feel burned out. One of the most interesting findings of part of the study regarding teachers' perceptions of how others viewed them was their sense that both parents and principals overestimate their teachers' professional satisfaction.

Results of these studies on burnout and its effects on teachers' self-concept indicate it is essential that teachers are made aware of how they view themselves. Helping teachers become aware of their personal and their professional needs must be a priority for any Helping Professional. Teachers must develop feelings of satisfaction in their work if they are to avoid burnout, and they need to feel that parents, students, and others understand something of the complexity, responsibility, and stress involved in teaching if they are to survive the pressures of their profession.

Student Violence, Abuse, and Disrespect
One of the major causes for the degenerating morale of teachers, which leads to burnout if it is prolonged, is lack of respect from students. In the "Second Gallup Poll" (Elam, 1989) about half of all teachers who responded to the survey viewed discipline as either very serious or a fairly serious problem. Also, a qualitative study of the teacher labor market (Berry, Noblit, & Hare, 1985) reported that if teachers left teaching due to their dissatisfactions, it was usually because they "can't handle disadvantaged kids" or they were "frustrated with the lack of disciplinary action taken by administrators" (p. 106).

Even in the late 1970s, disruptive and disrespectful students were a problem for teachers. A National Education Association poll (1979) stated that nearly three-fourths of all teachers felt that discipline problems affected their teaching effectiveness. In fact, the problem didn't improve in the 1980s. A study by Gold (1985) using the MBI and correlating it with discipline problems reported that teachers who perceive student control as having become more difficult for them were likely to report greater depersonalization and a lower sense of personal accomplishment.

The studies reviewed provide two common themes to be considered when assisting teachers: First, many teachers are dissatisfied with their teaching because they feel frustrated with the lack of support from parents and administrators regarding students who are discipline problems; and, second, a large number of teachers perceive student discipline and disrespect to be a serious problem for them.

Administrative Pressures and Burnout
In the face of declining enrollments, an investigation into the influence of administrators as a determinant of teacher burnout is necessary. In fact, it is essential, because it has been reported that burnout is related to a lack of support for teach-

ers by administrators, to a lack of sensitivity by many administrators to teacher-related problems and to school-related problems, and to principals' lack of participatory management (Blase, Dedrick, & Strathe, 1986; Jackson, Schwab, & Schuler, 1986). With this bleak view, additional information on a study of new teachers was collected in 1992 and published in the Metropolitan Life Survey (Harris & Associates, 1992). This study supported the earlier research by stating that one of the reasons for new teachers leaving the profession was the lack of support from school administrators. Another study surveying former public school teachers (Bobbitt, Faupel, & Burns, 1991) reported "dissatisfaction with teaching as a career" (p. iii) to be one of the main reasons for their leaving the profession, and "26.4% cited inadequate support from the administration" as their main area of disatisfaction" (p. iii). Teachers in inner city or urban locations also reported that "the lack of support from school administrators was a major factor in their decision to leave teaching" (Harris & Associates, 1992, p. 12).

It is undeniable that the role of the administrator is essential in the life of a teacher. Criticism about the lack of administrative support is not new; it has been cited for a number of years. Increased attention to this problem could improve the life of the teacher, and hence the school culture and student learning.

Role Conflict and Role Ambiguity
It is evident to anyone who works with teachers that they desire to have clear job descriptions. They also want to be involved with the development of school goals, objectives, and curriculum development in order to feel worthwhile and that they are making a significant contribution to the profession. Unfortunately, a number of teachers have reported a sense of confusion when they are faced with inappropriate, inconsistent, and incompatible demands. When two or more sets of these types of demands are experienced by a teacher, role conflict results.

Early research by Kahn et al. (1964) isolated constructs of role conflict and role ambiguity as being important aspects of organizational stress. Years later, Kahn (1978) argued that burnout may be related to situational factors of role conflict and role ambiguity. Studies that built on Kahn's research reported that role conflict and role ambiguity in various professions significantly affect a person's stress and satisfaction (Van Sell, Brief, & Schuler, 1980).

These early studies implied that role conflict and role ambiguity may be related to burnout. The relationship had not been researched directly until Schwab and Iwanicki (1982a) investigated it using the MBI with a sample of 469 classroom teachers. They reported that role conflict and role ambiguity were related to burnout in their sample, especially in the feelings of emotional exhaustion and depersonalization.

A more recent study by Lunenburg and Cadavid (1992) examined the relationship between teacher burnout (MBI) and teacher locus of control and pupil control ideology. Their results indicated a relationship: The teachers who rated themselves as being more burned out were more likely to have an external locus of control (looked outside themselves) and a custodial orientation toward the control of pupils. Individuals with an external locus of control may be considered to have fewer coping strategies, or "even [be] depleted of coping strategies" (p. 19). The authors felt that "these individuals are evidently experiencing burnout and not properly making appropriate adjustments to their situational problems. They may be perceiving these events as being outside their control" (p. 19).

An analysis of the research specifically reveals that teachers need to have clear job descriptions, be involved in the development of school goals and objectives, be reinforced for their belief in their own control (internal locus of control), and feel that they are making significant contributions to their students and to their profession.

Who Escapes the Destructive Flames of Burnout?

People who are most vulnerable for burnout are those who are the most dedicated, competent, and productive in their work and those who work in one of the helping professions. One may be certain then, that teachers who fit these criteria will need to be even more alert to the dangers of burnout. Therefore, understanding coping styles and characteristics of teachers who do not burn out can be insightful for individuals who are more prone to this phenomenon.

Effective Coping to Prevent Burnout

A review of the studies on teacher burnout described those teachers who are more prone to it. They are the ones who have not learned coping strategies to keep them from the negative effects that lead to disillusionment and a need to leave teaching. We have listed effective coping strategies such as physical exercise, social support, a positive belief system, and others earlier in the chapter. Another characteristic of those who survive burnout is of hardiness.

Hardiness

A number of studies on hardiness in the 1980s reported positive findings regarding hardiness as a personal resiliency factor (Hull, Van Treuren, & Virnelli, 1987; Kobasa, Maddi, & Kahn, 1982). In fact, hardiness has received considerable attention as a psychological resiliency factor against stress and illness. Kobasa (1979) proposed the idea of psychological hardiness as a way to explaining why some executives experience debilitating illness when faced with stressful life events while others do not. That is, the executives who demonstrated psychological hardiness were the ones who could handle the stress and pressure better than those who did not demonstrate it. Interestingly, Kobasa, Maddi, and Kahn (1982) view hardiness as a personal characteristic that functions as a source of resistance to stress. They believe it to be made up of three interrelated dispositions: (1) control, which refers to the belief that life experiences are predictable and controllable (the individual is influential rather than helpless); (2) commitment, or the tendency to involve oneself in and believe in the importance, value, and meaningfulness of life's activities; and (3) hardiness, which consists of a sense of challenge, a "belief that change rather than stability is normal in life and that the anticipation of changes are interesting incentives to growth rather than threats to security" (p. 170).

Helping Professionals may use the findings from these studies with teachers as prevention type strategies against burnout.

Strategies to Prevent Burnout

One of the most important outcomes when studying burnout is that it can be prevented if it is identified early and treatment programs are established. The psychological symptoms of discouragement, frustration, anger, and disillusionment are signs that an individual's needs are not being met and they must be attended to. The needs instruments in Chapter 4 are relevant here. Physical symptoms such as headaches, exhaustion, hypertension, and anxiety signal that changes must be made within the individual's life or the consequences will be severe. Social symptoms like isolation, lack of support, few friends, and a lack of security in one's life are also strong symptoms of needs not being met.

Too often, teachers are not even aware that they are in a state of disillusionment. It is important to remember that burnout is an insidious disease. Victims rarely are aware of the symptoms because they develop gradually over time. Not being aware of the danger signals, people are unable to develop effective coping strategies. Many talented and creative people are lost to the profession that was once an exciting and rewarding career for them.

Helping Professionals are key agents of change where burnout is concerned. First, they must be aware of the symptoms. Second, they must have the knowledge to know what to do, and, third, they must have learned effective coping strategies to assist teachers who are at risk.

A Burnout Inventory

If you wonder whether or not you are a candidate for burnout, here is a way to test yourself for symptoms that lead to burnout. Put an "X" in front of each statement with which you find yourself in agreement.

Personal Burnout Inventory

_____ 1. I feel a great deal of pressure and responsibility at work as of late.

_____ 2. I feel very unfulfilled and discouraged about my job.

_____ 3. I feel like a failure at work most of the time. All of the work I've accomplished just doesn't seem worth it.

_____ 4. I often think, why bother? My work really doesn't make any difference.

_____ 5. I feel as though my work just isn't good.

_____ 6. I often have feelings of hopelessness. No one really cares.

_____ 7. My concentration isn't as good as it used to be.

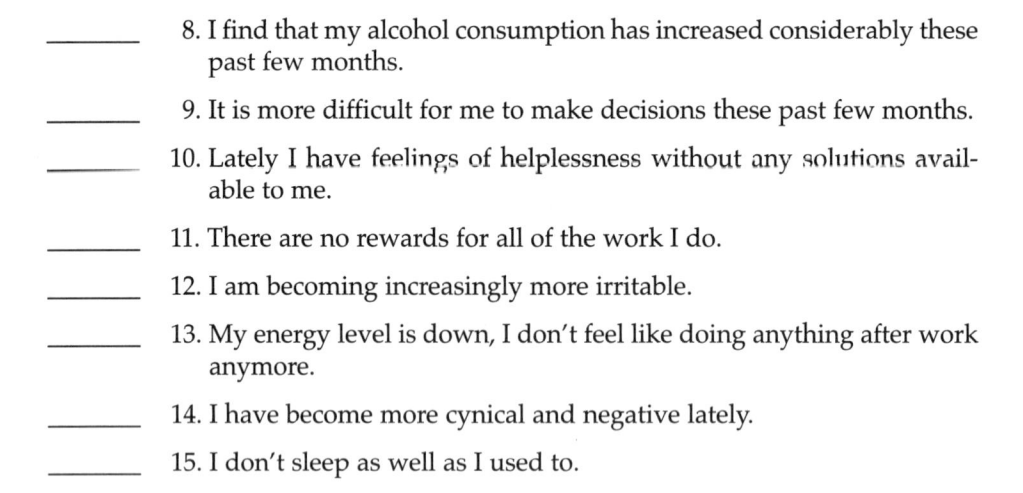

_____ 8. I find that my alcohol consumption has increased considerably these past few months.

_____ 9. It is more difficult for me to make decisions these past few months.

_____ 10. Lately I have feelings of helplessness without any solutions available to me.

_____ 11. There are no rewards for all of the work I do.

_____ 12. I am becoming increasingly more irritable.

_____ 13. My energy level is down, I don't feel like doing anything after work anymore.

_____ 14. I have become more cynical and negative lately.

_____ 15. I don't sleep as well as I used to.

After you have taken the inventory, look over the items you marked with an "X." If possible, share your responses with a support person or a support group who will listen and not give advice. Discuss ways you might improve some of the situations you have marked. If some of the ideas you discussed appeal to you, write them down and begin to apply them in your life. Continue to monitor the items you marked. Work on one at a time, and take control of the areas that you can change. Wherever you can, restructure your negative thinking by writing out positive statements that are acceptable to you. When you become aware of negative thoughts, use thought stopping and get out your positive statements and read them over a number of times. Use your positive self-talk statements throughout the day. Also, refer to the following list of Strategies to Conquer Burnout and apply the ones that will help you. Use your support people to get positive feedback for your successes and your progress.

If you marked an "X" by three or more of the items, you are probably a candidate for burnout. You can plan an intervention program and reverse the direction you are now heading. The process of burnout can be reversed if you will begin prior to leaving teaching. Rarely can the process be reversed once a person experiences burnout and leaves the job.

Helping Professionals can be agents of change by first identifying where they are on the burnout inventory and then applying coping strategies to prevent burnout. When Helping Professionals have learned to recognize burnout and to reverse it before they get to the stage of leaving the profession, they can be extremely helpful in assisting others who demonstrate the signs of burnout. The strategies listed next have proven to be highly successful for us as we work with teachers who manifest symptoms of burnout.

Effective Coping Strategies to Prevent Burnout
Assist teachers to:

1. Perceive themselves as problem solvers who identify problems, plan strategies for solving them, and who feel that they have the power within themselves to make necessary changes.
2. Keep their work expectations in line with reality.
3. Learn to resolve conflict situations with skills that are effective.
4. Restructure negative thinking and use cognitive restructuring.
5. Identify their unmet needs and plan specific ways of meeting them.
6. Take action and take control of their life.
7. Take care of their physical needs through exercise and healthy eating .
8. Develop relaxation techniques.
9. Use self-talk to change destructive thinking.
10. Develop support people and support groups.
11. Learn effective communication skills for interacting with others and for improving personal relations.
12. Identify signs of emotional exhaustion, depersonalization, and low personal accomplishment.
13. Monitor negative coping strategies to become aware of maladaptive ones.
14. Clearly identify their role expectations.
15. Develop a wellness program, monitor their progress, and include support agents.

Concluding Remarks

We have looked at the destructive forces of both stress and burnout, have concentrated on the essential elements of each, and have focused on what an individual can do to handle stress and prevent burnout. Helping Professionals are in a strategic position to assist teachers who are suffering the ill effects of these powerful and dangerous diseases. We label them diseases because this is exactly what they are. The negative statistics on the number of stress and burnout victims are astonishing.

We have presented the problem and have provided you with prescriptions that will turn the tide of these ever-growing illnesses. Like any prescription, it can only be written; it cannot act as the cure. The responsibility for bringing about healing rests in the hands of every individual who reads the information, chooses to act upon it, and then shares it with others. Our confidence rests with Helping Professionals who will make the necessary changes in their own lives, and who will also apply the knowledge they have gained in ways that will protect themselves and others from the dreaded diseases of stress and burnout that destroy great numbers of productive and meaningful careers.

We have seen many lives changed when individuals commit themselves to identifying their levels of risk in both burnout and stress, in meeting their unmet needs, in planning programs to change destructive coping strategies, and in forming support groups that will encourage one another as the members experience the difficult phases of the change process.

It is possible to change oneself, and hundreds are now finding success through making commitments to their own programs of healthy growth. We believe that as individuals we are responsible for ourselves and for how we live our life. This is an element of the Transformational philosophy. We have no power to change another person, only ourselves. Also, we believe that we have responsibilities to the profession and to the thousands of teachers who are being lost to the destructive flames of burnout.

Lastly, there are generations of youth who have the potential to help build a better life for themselves and for others. They may never know the excitement of learning from a teacher who once was enthusiastic and inspiring, but then lost the zeal for helping others in the ashes of a once shining career. Helping Professionals can help prevent the burnout before it is too late.

References

Anderson, M. B., & Iwanicki, E. F. (1984). Teacher motivation and its relationship to burnout. *Educational Administration Quarterly, 20*(2), 109–132.

Beer, J., & Beer, J. (1992). Burnout and stress, depression and self-esteem of teachers. *Psychological Reports, 71*(3, pt. 2), 1331–1336.

Berry, B., Noblit, G. W., & Hare, R. D. (1985). A qualitative critique of teacher labor market studies. *Urban Review, 17*(2), 98–110.

Blase, J., Dedrick, C., & Strathe, M. (1986). Leadership behavior of school principals in relation to teacher stress, satisfaction, and performance. *Journal of Humanistic Education and Development, 24*(4), 159–171.

Bobbitt, S. A., Faupel, E., & Burns, S. (1991). *Characteristics of stayers, movers, and leavers: Results from the Teacher Followup Survey, 1988–89.* Washington, DC: Office of Educational Research and Improvement.

Borg, M. G., Riding, R. J., & Falzon, J. M. (1991). Stress in teaching: A study of occupational stress and its determinants, job satisfaction and career commitment among primary schoolteachers. *Educational Psychology, 11*(1), 59–75.

Burke, R. J., & Greenglass, E. R. (1989). Psychological burnout among men and women in teaching: An examination of the Cherniss model. *Human Relations, 42*(3), 261–273.

Carnegie Foundation for the Advancement of Teaching (1990). *The condition of teaching: A state-by state analysis.* Princeton, NJ: Author.

Cherniss, C. (1980a). *Professional burnout in human service organizations.* New York: Praeger.

Cherniss, C. (1980b). *Staff burnout: Job stress in the human services.* Beverly Hills, CA: Sage.

Coats, T. J., & Thoresen, C. E. (1976). Teacher anxiety: A review with recommendations. *Review of Educational Research, 46*(2), 159–184.

Combs, A. W., & Snygg, D. (1959). *Individual behavior: A perceptual approach to behavior* (rev. ed.). New York: Harper Collins.

Connoly, C., & Sanders, W. (1988, Feb.) The successful coping strategies—the answer to teacher stress? Paper presented at the annual meeting of the Association of Teacher Educators, San Diego, CA.

Cunningham, W. G. (1982). Teacher burnout: Stylish fad or profound problem? *Planning and Changing, 12*(4), 219–244.

Dewe, P. (1986). *Stress: Causes, consequences and coping strategies for teachers.* Wellington, N.Z.: New Zealand Education Institute. (ERIC Document Reproduction Service No. ED 280-807.)

Elam, S. M. (1989). The second Gallup/Phi Delta Kappan poll of teachers' attitudes toward the public schools. *Phi Delta Kappan, 70*(10), 785–798.

Farber, B. A. (1984). Stress and burnout in suburban teachers. *Journal of Educational Research, 77*(6), 325–331.

Farber, B. A. (1991). *Crisis in education: Stress and burnout in the American teacher.* San Francisco: Jossey-Bass.

Frese, M. (1986). Coping as a moderator and mediator between stress at work and psychosomatic complaints. In M. H. Appley & R. Trumbull (Eds.), *Dynamics of stress: Physiological, psychological, and social perspectives* (pp. 183–206). New York: Plenum Press.

Freudenberger, H. J., with Richelson, G. (1980). *Burnout: The high cost of high achievement.* New York: Bantam Books.

Friedman, I. A. (1991). High- and low-burnout schools: School culture aspects of teacher burnout. *Journal of Educational Research, 84*(6), 325–333.

Friedman, I. A., & Farber, B. A. (1992). Professional self-concept as a predictor of burnout. *Journal of Educational Research, 86*(1), 28–35.

Friedman, I., & Lotan, J. (1985). *Teacher stress and burnout in Israel (In elementary education).* Jerusalem, Henrietta Szold Institute. (Hebrew with English summary).

Galloway, D., Boswell, K., & Pankhurst, F. (1981, Dec.). Stress in teaching. *National Education,* 204–206.

Gold, Y. (1984). The factorial validity of the Maslach Burnout Inventory in a sample of California elementary and junior high school classroom teachers. *Educational and Psychological Measurement, 44*(4), 1009–1016.

Gold, Y. (1985). The relationship of six personal and life history variables to standing on three dimensions of the Maslach Burnout Inventory in a sample of elementary and junior high school teachers. *Educational and Psychological Measurement, 45*(2), 377–387.

Gold, Y., & Michael, W. (1985). Academic self-concept correlates of potential burnout in a sample of first semester elementary school practice teachers: A concurrent validity study. *Educational and Psychological Measurement, 45*(4), 909–914.

Gold, Y., & Roth, R. A. (1993). *Teachers managing stress and preventing burnout: The professional health solution.* Washington, DC: The Falmer Press.

Harris, L., & Associates (1992). *The Metropolitan Life Survey of the American teacher. The second year: New teachers' expectations and ideals.* New York: Metropolitan Life Insurance.

Hicks, F. P. (1933). *The mental health of teachers.* Nashville, TN: George Peabody College for Teachers.

Holmes, T. H., & Rahe, R. H. (1967). The social readjustment rating scale. *Journal of Psychosomatic Research, 11,* 213–218.

Holroyd, K. A., & Lazarus, R. S. (1982). Stress, coping, and somatic adaptation. In L. Goldberger & S. Breznitz (Eds.), *Handbook of stress: Theoretical and clinical aspects* (pp. 21–35). New York: Free Press.

Holt, P., Fine, M., & Tollefson, N. (1987). Mediating stress: Survival of the hardy. *Psychology in the Schools, 24* (1), 51–58.

Hull, J. G., Van Treuren, R. R., & Virnelli, S. (1987). Hardiness and health: A critique and alternative approach. *Journal of Personality and Social Psychology, 53*(3), 518–530.

Iwanicki, E. F., & Schwab, R. L. (1981). A cross validation study of the Maslach Burnout Inventory. *Educational and Psychological Measurement, 41*(4), 1167–1174.

Jackson, S. E., Schwab, R. L., & Schuler, R. S. (1986). Toward an understanding of the burnout phenomenon. *Journal of Applied Psychology, 71*(4), 630–640.

Jenkins, S., & Calhoun, J. F. (1991). Teacher stress: Issues and intervention. *Psychology in the Schools, 28*(1), 60–70.

Kahn, R. (1978). Job burnout: Prevention and remedies. *Public Welfare, 36*(2), 61–63.

Kahn, R., Wolfe, D., Quinn, R., Snoek, J., & Rosenthal, R. (1964). *Organizational stress: Studies in role conflict and ambiguity.* New York: Wiley.

Kobasa, S. C. (1979). Stressful life events, personality and health: An inquiry into hardiness. *Journal of Personality and Social Psychology, 37*(1), 1–11.

Kobasa, S. C., Maddi, S. R., & Kahn, S. (1982). Hardiness and health: A perspective study. *Journal of Personality and Social Psychology, 42*(1), 168–177.

Kottkamp, R. B., Provenzo, E. F., Jr., & Cohn, M. M. (1986). Stability and change in a profession: Two decades of teacher attitudes, 1964–1984. *Phi Delta Kappan, 67*(8), 559–567.

Krohne, H. W. (1986). Coping with stress: Dispositions, strategies, and the problem of measurement. In M. H. Appley & R. Trumbull (Eds.), *Dynamics of stress: Physiological, psychological, and social perspectives* (pp. 207–228). New York: Plenum Press.

Kyriacou, C. (1989). The nature and prevalence of teacher stress. In M. Cole & S. Walker (Eds.), *Teaching and stress* (pp. 24–34). Milton Keynes, U.K.: Open University Press.

Kyriacou, C., & Sutcliffe, J. (1978). A model of teacher stress. *Educational Studies, 4*(1), 1–6.

Laughlin, A. (1984). Teacher stress in an Australian setting: The role of biographical mediators. *Educational Studies, 10*(1), 7–22.

Laux, L. (1986). A self-presentational view of coping with stress. In M. H. Appley & R. Trumbull (Eds.), *Dynamics of stress: Physiological, psychological, and social perspectives* (pp. 233–254). New York: Plenum Press.

Lazarus, R. S. (1966). *Psychological stress and the coping process*. New York: McGraw-Hill.

Lazarus, R. S. (1971). *Behavior therapy and beyond*. New York: McGraw-Hill.

Lazarus, R. S., & Folkman, S. (1984). *Stress, appraisal and coping*. New York: Springer.

Leonard, G. (1980). The holistic health revolution. In J. D. Adams (Ed.), *Understanding and managing stress: A book of readings* (pp. 21–36). San Diego, CA: University Associates.

Long, S. W., Avant, A. H., & Harrison, T. R. (1986, November). An investigation of the prevalence, symptoms, and sources of anxiety, stress, and burnout among classroom teachers, and implications for interventions. Paper presented at Mid-South Educational Research Association, Memphis, TN. (ED 279-629.)

Los Angeles Times. (September 12, 1989). Obituaries, Satir, V.P., p. 24.

Lunenburg, F. C., & Cadavid, V. (1992). Locus of control, pupil control ideology, and dimensions of teacher burnout. *Journal of Instructional Psychology, 19*(1), 13–22.

Malanowski, J. R., & Wood, P. H. (1984). Burnout and self-actualization in public school teachers. *Journal of Psychology, 117*(1), 23–26.

Maslach, C., & Jackson, S. (1981). The measurement of experienced burnout. *Journal of Occupational Behaviour, 2*, 99–113.

Maslach, C., & Jackson, S. (1986). *The Maslach burnout inventory*. Palo Alto, CA: Consulting Psychologists Press.

McGuire, W. H. (1979). Teacher burnout. *Today's Education, 68*(4), 5.

National Education Association (NEA) (1979). *Nationwide teacher opinion poll*. Washington, DC: Author. (ED 178-533.)

New York State United Teachers Research and Educational Services (NYSUT) (1979). *NYSUT teacher stress survey*. Albany, NY: Author.

Okebukola, P. A., & Jegede, O. J. (1989). Determinants of occupational stress among teachers in Nigeria. *Educational Studies, 15*(1), 23–36.

Payne, M. A., & Furnham, A. (1987). Dimensions of occupational stress in West Indian secondary school teachers. *British Journal of Educational Psychology, 57*(2), 141–150.

Pelletier, K., & Lutz, R. (1988). Healthy people—healthy business: A critical review of stress management in the workplace. *American Journal of Health Promotion, 2*(3) 5–12.

Pines, A., Aronson, E., & Kafry, D. (1981). *Burnout: From tedium to personal growth*. New York: Free Press.

Poteliakhoff, A., & Carruthers, M. (1981). *Real health: The ill effects of stress and their prevention*. London: Davis-Poynter.

Rogers, C. R. (1951). *Client-centered therapy*. Boston: Houghton Mifflin.

Russell, D. W., Altmaier, E., & Van Velzen, D. (1987). Job-related stress, social support, and burnout among classroom teachers. *Journal of Applied Psychology,72*(2), 269–274.

Schwab, R. L., & Iwanicki, E. F. (1982a). Perceived role conflict, role ambiguity, and teacher burnout. *Educational Administration Quarterly, 18*(1), 60–74.

Schwab, R. L., & Iwanicki, E. F. (1982b). Who are our burned out teachers? *Educational Research Quarterly, 7* (2), 5–16.

Schwab, R. L., Jackson, S. E., & Schuler, R. S. (1986). Educator burnout: Sources and consequences. *Educational Research Quarterly, 10*(3), 14–30.

Selye, H. (1956). *The stress of life*. New York: McGraw-Hill

Selye, H. (1974). *Stress without distress*. Philadelphia: Lippiincott.

Van Sell, M., Brief, A., & Schuler, R. (1980). *Role conflict and role ambiguity in work organizations:*

A review of the literature. Iowa City, IA: College of Business Administration.

Wangberg, E. G. (1984, March). Educators in crisis: The need to improve the teaching workplace and teaching as a profession. Paper presented at the annual conference of the Association for Supervision and Curriculum Development, New York.

Wendt, J. C. (1980). *Coping skills: A goal of professional preparation*, Project description No. 141. (ERIC Document Reproduction Service No. ED 212 604.)

Williams, R. B. (1993). Hostility and the heart. In D. Goleman & J. Gurin (Eds.), *Mind body medicine* (pp. 65–83). New York: Consumer Reports Books.

Woolfolk, R., & Richardson, F. (1978). *Stress, sanity, and survival.* New York: Sovereign Books.

Zager, J. (1982). The relationship of personality, situational stress, and anxiety factors to teacher burnout. Doctoral dissertation, Indiana University.

Chapter 15

Revitalizing the Helping Professional (Dimension Five)

Where in my life did I stop dancing?
Where in my life did I stop singing?
Where in my life did I stop being enchanted with stories?
Where in my life did I become uncomfortable
with the sweet territory of silence? —ANGELES ARRIEN

One of the greatest liabilities for any Helping Professional is to be unaware of having given too much. It is true that assisting others can and does bring many rewards. However, sharing ideas and giving of their emotional and physical energy over long periods of time to a variety of individuals often leave helpers feeling as though they are drained and have little left for themselves. It is essential, then, that helpers be able to identify when they have given too much emotionally, intellectually, and/or physically.

When helpers recognize what they need, they are more likely to focus on taking care of themselves. Helpers must be able to identify their own needs. Reviewing Chapters 4 and 5 will assist in this process.

The purpose of reviewing the needs instruments is to become aware of any areas you are neglecting at the present time. Also, planning specific ways to take care of yourself is essential for your well-being. Beyond needs identification is the entire area of self-revitalization. When we are able to meet many of our needs, we can develop our potential for creative living and experience life in new and fulfilling ways.

To revitalize is to give "new" vitality and vigor to life. This process can be an exciting adventure for anyone who chooses to embark upon it. The remainder of the chapter will focus on ways a Helping Professional can find new vitality in life—the process of revitalizing.

Recognizing the Risks of Helping

Because one of the greatest risks for Helping Professionals is ignoring when they are at risk, it is essential that they take time throughout their career to identify these areas. However, knowing how to assess one's needs is not always an easy task.

Assessing Helpers' Needs

The following inventory was developed to assist helpers in becoming aware of their risk areas. It has helped many to gain insights into their unmet needs for the purpose of planning a program to take better care of themselves. Taking time to read the inventory and answer the questions will provide insight into potential problem areas that can rob helpers of vitality.

At Risk Inventory

Directions: Answer "Yes" or "No" to the following questions. Your first response is most often the accurate one.

_____ 1. I find that I am less patient with my co-workers.

_____ 2. I am needing to spend more time alone to do some of the things I enjoy.

_____ 3. There are more times lately that I avoid social gatherings because I don't have enough energy.

_____ 4. My comments to others are less positive than they previously were.

_____ 5. Assisting someone else is less rewarding than it was 6 months ago.

_____ 6. I feel less energetic than I did 3 months ago.

_____ 7. I am spending less time on my own interests and hobbies.

_____ 8. I find that I am making less time for my close relationships.

_____ 9. As of late, I have less enthusiasm about my professional work and want to work on more challenging and creative projects.

_____ 10. I need some type of change in my life to add novelty and vitality.

_____ 11. I become easily frustrated with the daily demands placed on me.

Having completed the questions, take a few minutes to evaluate the items to which you responded "Yes." It is helpful to write down any insights you gained from your responses. These insights often will help you identify your unmet needs. An example one Helping Professional gave was:

I responded with a positive answer to numbers 3, 5, and 8, and learned that I am not enjoying my time with others like I used to. I seem to need to get away from people. I have little left to give after a day of helping others. I am exhausted when I get home. My physical need for calmness isn't being met. I'm too pressured every day with all of the demands placed upon me. I am now aware that I am at risk for burnout and I must make some changes.

Another Helping Professional remarked:

I did not realize I had so many negative feelings about helping others. I need to stop and listen to my own messages. Maybe I need to take a break from helping others and concentrate on my own teaching. I think I'm neglecting my own work and the kinds of creative things I want to do that take more time. My intellectual need for creativity isn't being met and I am at risk according to numbers 5, 9, and 10.

When Helping Professionals share their insights with other helpers in their group, it encourages understanding and growth in everyone. The first step toward change, then, is recognizing areas in your life that need attention. Before you can begin to concentrate on revitalizing yourself, you need to know the areas of your life that are at risk and begin changing what you can.

Consequences of Helping Too Much

Recognizing the consequences associated with helping others is an important part of taking care of oneself that can help motivate individuals to look at their own personal and professional needs. Also, the importance of pacing one's activities to achieve maximum challenge and fulfillment in life is without question.

If Helping Professionals are to continue in the role of helper, they must be able to gain a sense of gratification when they help people confront their problems. They also must experience feelings of satisfaction when they assist others in developing appropriate solutions to their problems. Helpers must learn to become stronger as they handle the concerns of others, rather than allowing others' problems and pressures to drain their own strength and vitality.

Helping Professionals need to recognize signs of overscheduling that bring on fatigue. They must reverse the process by developing coping skills to help them stop and reflect on their schedule. They must be aware of danger signals such as: (1) physical and emotional exhaustion, (2) having a desire to get away from others for longer periods of time, (3) feeling restless to try something new, (4) needing more time for creative projects, and (5) experiencing impatience with one's self and others.

If Helping Professionals recognize the hazard signs of working with people, they can set limits and boundaries for themselves and learn ways to revitalize. Also, being aware that taking time to develop one's interests and talents is a necessary part of living a fulfilling life.

Personal Fulfillment

There are a number of ways that people find fulfillment in life, such as through families and close friends, work and accomplishments, use of free time, and creative endeavors. In order to have the energy to accomplish all of the things people want to, they need to have good health, emotional stability, intellectual challenge, and a spiritual belief that offers them hope and gives them purpose. For some people this balance is easier to achieve than it is for others. Because of the tendency to focus on others, helpers need to take time to evaluate their own life and to concentrate on what is fulfilling. To accomplish this they must know themselves and what is enjoyable and revitalizing.

Taking Time for Yourself

As we become more aware of ourselves, we find that we are made up of different attitudes, experiences, interests, and habits. These different parts are what make us human. What is detrimental is when we ignore a part of ourselves in an attempt to avoid internal conflict. An example would be when we have been working extra hard for a period of time and we need to take time off to relax and do something revitalizing for a while. To deny this need and allow the demands of work to be in control most of the time will tend to produce a rigid personality. Creativity and freedom are lost when this takes place. The more we deny our options and limit our freedom to explore a variety of experiences, the more we replace the flexibility in our life with rigid controls that can prevent healthy growth. Choices can only be available to us when we encourage different points of view within our own thinking. It is important to maintain an attitude of having unlimited options and being willing to explore those that are healthy.

One of the Helping Professionals we worked with, Flo, is an example of someone committed to the helping process at the expense of herself.

Flo is a successful Helping Professional in her school. She came in for counseling because she was feeling depressed. She said she was having a difficult time keeping up with everything. When she went home at night, she didn't feel like doing anything with her family. All she wanted to do was be alone and go to sleep early. After a period of time her husband asked her to go see a counselor and get some help. He was worried about her. When she came for her first visit, we talked about what she thought was missing in her life. Flo said that she wanted to enjoy herself again. She wanted to have the energy to play golf with her friends and go dancing with her husband. I asked her to share enjoyable experiences she had over the past few months. Each experience that she shared was work-related. We talked about how people can get locked into one part of their personality, and in her case it was the work part. She had been neglecting the fun, playful parts of herself as she had become more involved in her work. In the beginning her work was enjoyable for her—in fact, so enjoyable that she became so focused on it that she neglected other parts of herself that were also rewarding. We discussed some ways that she could set limits for herself regarding her work schedule, and how she could plan activities that allowed her to experience other enjoyable parts of her life such as sports, hobbies, and friendships.

Flo is similar to many Helping Professionals who became so involved in their work that they neglect other parts of their life. We have found this to be a common problem for many helpers.

We all have a remarkable capacity within our minds and bodies to stretch ourselves in new areas. The more we use our mind and body, the more flexible and versatile we become. We really do not know what we can do until we try.

The following activities are especially helpful for assessing the use of your mind and body. Begin with the first activity and see how much you can learn about yourself as you respond to each one. When you have completed them, sharing what you learned with a special friend can be most insightful and rewarding.

1. Keep a diary for 1 week. Write in it any time you want to throughout the day. At least one entry per day is necessary. Discuss what made you feel good about yourself, what made you feel sad, lonely, angry, etc.
2. Write a brief description of how you see yourself. Then write how you think others see you. Next ask someone who will be honest with you to write a brief description of you. Then compare the descriptions. What did you learn about yourself?
3. Write a brief statement about what intellectually challenges you. Then see if you are taking time for this type of experience.
4. Pay attention to your emotional reactions throughout the day. Write some of these down. Use them as information about yourself. What do you notice about yourself? Do you like what you see? If not, why not? What do you want to do?

Many people are concerned that they will become selfish and self-centered if they concentrate on meeting their own needs. Focusing on one's own needs and interests does not need to produce selfishness and self-centeredness. It can encourage healthy understanding of one's ethical standards and beliefs, which will contribute to one's self-respect and self-esteem. Learning to revitalize oneself adds energy and vitality to life and life becomes more rewarding.

Selfishness or Selfness

Throughout the book we have taken a close look at the needs of the Helping Professional. We have also discussed the importance of recognizing unmet needs and planning specifically to change areas that need to be changed. We have suggested two major strategies to assist the helper in achieving the growth she or he desires. These are individual growth and social consiousness.

One of these strategies focuses on individual growth, with the emphasis on developing one's own potential. This strategy is essential if people are to understand themselves and work toward developing a balanced life. Some critics have called this strategy "narcissistic" and selfishness. They see it as self-absorption and as lacking in social awareness or commitment. We, along with others who propose developing one's own potential, find that personal enhancement does not need to be built around selfishness. If we are to help others grow and mature, then we must begin within. If we cannot love ourselves and respect ourselves, how are we to genuinely love and respect others? Thus, developing one's potential does not need to be selfish and narcissistic.

Robert Samples (1977) calls the individual strategy "selfness" and explains that it is "the state in which self is celebrated in a nonexploitative mode" (p. 2). It is distinct from selfish, which he defines as the exploitation of others for the benefit of oneself. Selfness is the growth and development of oneself for the benefit of self and others. We find his explanation to be compatible with ours.

The second strategy we propose is one of social consciousness and change. This strategy includes discovering ways to bring about change in organizations, such as the school, family, and home, to enhance the lives of everyone involved. Taking responsibility for encouraging and bringing about the growth and betterment of the community of people is a major aspect of this strategy.

We find that the two strategies complement one another. Deep inner exploration of oneself contributes the development of a healthier, more knowledgeable individual. As a result, this person is now better prepared to assist others as they enhance the quality of their life and the quality of the organization.

Because growth is a choice and cannot be forced on anyone at any time, helpers must become knowledgeable about themselves and their own growth to be in a better position to encourage growth in others. The benefits affect both individuals and organizations.

The Challenges of Personal Fulfillment

One of the most important considerations when discussing personal fulfillment is to look at how an individual defines the term. When asked how they define fulfillment, many people say for them it is amassing all the money, power, and possessions they can. This interpretation of the term is characteristic of a culture that is engaged in what is called the anhedonic struggle for the part of success that is related to money, power, possessions, and sex. (*Anhedonic* is derived from the Greek *an* [not] and *hedone* [pleasure] and refers to the inability to experience pleasure.) Therefore, people are unable to enjoy the success they do have.

We subscribe to a definition of personal fulfillment that encourages people to acquire knowledge and skills that will empower them to enjoy their life and to experience inner joy that comes from healthy interactions with family members and close relationships, good health, spiritual beliefs, personal integrity, and the enjoyment of giving to others. As human beings, we are created with a nearly unlimited capacity for growth. We can achieve depth of understanding, quality of experience, and lasting satisfactions in life if we accept the challenge to do so and acquire the knowledge and skills to develop each of these in our life. The more we pursue this challenge, the more we will be revitalized.

A Quest for Fulfillment
We all are unique individuals who are responsible for knowing what we truly want out of life. A measure of our success in accomplishing a fulfilling life is how well we create inner joy and satisfaction that is the result of well thought-through values and a life that is lived consistently with them, which will then enhance our personal integrity and revitalize us.

In our quest for fulfillment we can discover opportunities almost every day that will help us express our talents and our abilities. We can also learn to create a grateful attitude even when circumstances are difficult. Finding meaning in our work can be highly rewarding, and we can know that what we contribute helps make the world a better place for many individuals. All of these aspects add to our own fulfillment. Thus, life is more rewarding and we look for even more opportunities to grow and mature.

But what about failures or setbacks? No matter what our vision for our life, there always will be personal costs that we had not considered. Achieving our vision will rarely be consistent with all of our expectations.

What produces growth and strength of character is learning to create in our life an attitude of appreciation even when plans we have made do not work out as we had expected. Defining our own fulfillment eliminates the need for status symbols to prove to ourselves and to others that we made it, that we are a success. We don't need to judge ourselves by what others think of us. We live our life consistent with our beliefs and true to our integrity. When we live this way, the major issues in life for us are those that center around our personal values, beliefs, and satisfactions. Helping Professionals who are able to achieve this type of lifestyle are able to model these types of values for others. They demonstrate a strength of character to others that helps to revitalize a faculty. They do not need to prove who they are, and others are comfortable with them. Teachers learn to trust them because they see trustworthiness in their behavior. They are the kind of persons that others look to for guidance and support. They also know when to take a break and revitalize their own lives to maintain a vital balance.

Assessing Your Fulfillment Profile
Once you have defined fulfillment for yourself, the key issues for you to consider are related to your personal values. Questions such as "Am I enjoying my life fully?," "Am I enthusiastic about new programs and practices?," and "Am I living my life at home and school consistent with my values?" will become major considerations for you.

In our work with Helping Professionals, teachers, and hundreds of others in workshops and the therapy room, we have identified indications of a fulfilled life. These may be helpful in assessing your own lifestyle, providing you answer each question as honestly as you can. There are no right or wrong answers. It is important for you to describe your behavior as accurately as possible. Answers range between 1 (not true of me) and 5 (very true of me).

After you answer the questions, carefully review your responses. List each question that you responded to with 1, 2, or 3, and write down the main concept of the question. For example, see Table 15-1.

Fulfilled Life Profile

At the present time:

1. My life has a great deal of meaning.
    Not true - 1 - 2 - 3 - 4 - 5 - Very true
2. I live consistent with my values and beliefs.
    Not true - 1 - 2 - 3 - 4 - 5 - Very true
3. I am able to truly enjoy my leisure time.
    Not true - 1 - 2 - 3 - 4 - 5 - Very true
4. I spend the right amount of time with my family and friends.
    Not true - 1 - 2 - 3 - 4 - 5 - Very true
5. I finish my work at school.
    Not true - 1 - 2 - 3 - 4 - 5 - Very true
6. I know my success is due to my insights and creativity.
    Not true - 1 - 2 - 3 - 4 - 5 - Very true
7. I value my commitments to marriage, children, and friends.
    Not true - 1 - 2 - 3 - 4 - 5 - Very true
8. I have a clear vision of the future.
    Not true - 1 - 2 - 3 - 4 - 5 - Very true
9. I have a strong desire to make contributions that make the world a better place.
    Not true - 1 - 2 - 3 - 4 - 5 - Very true
10. I am successful in my intimate relationships.
    Not true - 1 - 2 - 3 - 4 - 5 - Very true
11. I am excited about my work.
    Not true - 1 - 2 - 3 - 4 - 5 - Very true
12. I enjoy taking time to go on vacations.
    Not true - 1 - 2 - 3 - 4 - 5 - Very true
13. I am becoming increasingly patient through the years.
    Not true - 1 - 2 - 3 - 4 - 5 - Very true
14. I feel confident in my job.
    Not true - 1 - 2 - 3 - 4 - 5 - Very true
15. I try to discover opportunities every day to express my talents.
    Not true - 1 - 2 - 3 - 4 - 5 - Very true
16. When things don't work out, I try to find meaning and enjoyment in alternatives.
    Not true - 1 - 2 - 3 - 4 - 5 - Very true
17. I find a great deal of pleasure in most of my relationships.
    Not true - 1 - 2 - 3 - 4 - 5 - Very true
18. My personal integrity is important to me.
    Not true - 1 - 2 - 3 - 4 - 5 - Very true
19. I am able to relax without feeling guilty.
    Not true - 1 - 2 - 3 - 4 - 5 - Very true
20. I have achieved a healthy balance in my life between overstriving for success and not striving at all.
    Not true - 1 - 2 - 3 - 4 - 5 - Very true

TABLE 15-1 Analyzing Your Fulfillment Profile

Item Number	Concept
1	*Lack of meaning in life.*
2	*I compromise my values.*
3	*I need to enjoy my leisure time.*
8	*I need a clear vision of the future.*
12	*I need to enjoy my vacations.*
17	*I need to find more pleasure in my relationships.*
19	*I need to feel positive about relaxing.*
20	*I need to assess the balance in my life regarding how I strive.*

After you have looked over each of the concepts you have written, take time to write a statement about how you could fulfill that part of your life. Examples of responses we have received from Helping Professionals are:

Question 1. I need to take more time to develop the relationships in my life. Intimate relationships that are rewarding bring more meaning in life for me. I have been neglecting mine.

Question 2. I now realize one of the reasons why I feel so much stress. I have been compromising my values because I have been afraid that I will not be successful. I've gone along with others on the faculty even when I have not agreed with the outcome. I will begin changing this in my life.

One of the best ways to develop appreciation of your life and to find fulfillment each day is to assess your own fulfillment levels. You now have a profile that gives you important information about yourself and what you need to change. When people are aware of the importance of adding vitality to their lives and of developing a more enjoyable lifestyle, they can plan to achieve it. The outcomes are well worth the effort.

Caution: Roadblocks Ahead

We hope that you have decided you want to begin to revitalize your life. One impediment you will find is the psychological reward you are now getting for remaining exactly the way you are. Chapter 3 described why it is difficult for people to make necessary changes. This is true even when the reward is an improved lifestyle. People need to become aware of the resistances they experience when they begin to change. This is important if they are going to overcome barriers to growth. We have identified several roadblocks that we have found to be common for Helping Professionals:

1. **Your current ways of performing may be masking your fears and doubts about your personal values and beliefs.** Many people resist asking themselves questions about their values and beliefs because they feel they will

need to change familiar ways of handling their lives. Changing is not the important consideration at this point—evaluation is. The consequences of refusing to look at their beliefs are great because peoples' vitality and joy of living are affected when they refuse to make personal changes that are necessary for growth. Asking questions such as "What do I really want out of life?", "Is there something I would rather be doing?", and "Am I satisfied with my life as I am now living?" is important in evaluating our present condition. All of these questions help us to evaluate whether or not we are living consistent with our values and beliefs, even though our answers to the questions may not be simple, or even clear in some instances. Holding on to a lifestyle that is inconsistent with our values and beliefs creates internal conflict and robs us of enjoying our life. Ultimately this type of living will be defeating.

To revitalize ourselves, we must find alternatives that help us change old, maladaptive patterns. What we need is a commitment to be honest with ourselves and to accept what we must change. We also need to be willing to use the Change Model as a guide

2. **Success can become addictive for many people who are not aware that it may be a defense mechanism to cover up their insecurities.** When we strive for success and achieve it, over time we can begin to feel worthwhile because we are successful. If this false sense of importance develops, it will rob us of knowing the satisfactions that come regardless of how successful we are. Too often people put the major part of their energies into their work as a defense against facing personal issues such as insecurity. The result is short-term rewards. Major problems occur in all lives, and people who run from their problems are not prepared to handle them. They lack the inner strength.

    An example of this is when people strive hard to recieve recognition from others as a means of feeling good about themselves. Almost everything they do is directed at having others comment on their achievements. They win awards and recognition from many sources in their professional life. Without being aware of it, they are developing a sense of security from what they do rather than from who they are. When they no longer are able to receive recognition for their efforts, they do not know how to handle the feelings of rejection and discouragement they experience. Their self-esteem is built on their feeling successful. Awards and recognition in and of themselves are great for the moment, but they are short-lived. Being able to enjoy what one does and basing self-worth on one's value are healthier and far more rewarding.

3. **Many people throw themselves into long hours of work to avoid loneliness and interpersonal problems.** When people have difficulty in their personal relationships and do not have the skills to work problems through, their work can become a hiding place to escape painful feelings. Work can become the classic excuse for avoiding confrontations. Many people of this

type say they are working long hours to help their family, which sounds very self-sacrificing. When this is true, both the individual and the family lose. Relationship tensions often increase, and interpersonal problems become more pronounced.

When people run from facing their personal problems, they rob themselves of the opportunity to resolve their problems and to develop inner strength in their lives. When difficult situations are prolonged, these types of people often are unable to correct them. When a crisis occurs, and it eventually will, the desire to work issues through and the skills to do so are not available to this type of person. Rarely is conflict worked through when it progresses to a crisis. Unfortunately, these people choose avoidance over growth, and they suffer the consequences.

Assessing Your Roadblocks to Revitalization

Read the discussion of the three roadblocks carefully. Take time to write out your own responses to each. For example, look at number 1 and identify your values and beliefs. Write them down. Then evaluate your behavior. Check to see if you are consistent in how you act and what you believe in. In areas where you find inconsistency, list your fears and your doubts and see how they influence the decisions you are making. The next step would be to talk with a trusted friend and get some feedback. Lastly, decide what you need to do to live consistent with your values and beliefs. Map out a plan to help you clarify what you need to do. After you begin to change your behavior, check and see how you feel. Are you feeling differently about yourself?

What you will find is that when you are consistent with what you believe and how you live your life, you will develop an integrated personality. You will feel more secure, and you will be more successful in your interactions at work and with your family and/or friends. You will make better choices between your personal growth and your personal ambition and between your enjoyment in life and your achievements. You can find excitement in helping others, and you can plan time to enjoy your personal relationships. You can work hard and get a great deal of satisfaction from it, and you can enjoy taking time to relax to revitalize yourself without feeling guilty.

One of the most important outcomes of being open to what you need to work on is the development of an inner sense of peace and well-being even when you have demanding days. You can learn to more fully enjoy your personal and professional life. The results will include being able to feel more successful and more competent. The journey toward a healthy, balanced lifestyle is well worth the time and effort.

How Can I Revitalize Myself?

Let's assume that you sincerely want to revitalize yourself, and you wish to begin enjoying your life in ways that you have not in the past. The first thing you will

TABLE 15-2 Sally's Revitalization Record

Activity I Enjoy	Feelings	Thoughts	Resistances	Desires
Oil Painting	Guilty Anxiety Pressure Selfish	"I am taking time from my family"	"Stop playing and get to work." Avoidance	"I really want to paint."

need to do is to write down all of the things you enjoy doing. Once you have recorded all of your ideas on paper, examine them carefully. Select one of the things that you enjoy and develop a plan of how you will integrate it into your life. The following steps are useful:

1. List one of the activities that you enjoy the most.
2. Record your feelings.
3. Record your thoughts, resistances, and desires.

The example of Sally shown in Table 15-2 will assist you. It is easy to see that Sally is having difficulty doing what she really wants to do. She feels guilty for taking time for herself. She feels that she must first concentrate on her work and that her painting is a lesser priority. Her confusion centers on the fact that she desires to paint, yet she feels guilty when she does take time for her painting. Sally looked carefully at her feelings and realized that she felt a great deal of anxiety and pressure when she took time for her painting. She felt selfish for wanting to do something that was enjoyable for her. Sally shared her experiences with the support group:

As she became more aware of her negative thoughts, Sally began to realize that she was allowing what other people thought about her to control her life. She was rewarded at school for the heavy workload she was carrying. Other teachers often commented about the great job she did planning all the staff development days and coordinating the new teacher program in the district. She decided to separate her work schedule from her personal fulfillment schedule. Sally told the support group that she needed to free herself from living her life according to the expectations of others. She wanted a balanced life of work and personal activities. She said that she was going to plan specific times just for her painting. Allowing this time for her creative expressions helped to revitalize her. After a few weeks, Sally said she felt more energized to carry out her responsibilities at school and at home. Sally began to plan time for herself and her painting. She told us months later at the support group meeting that she will be having a showing of her paintings at a local gallery at the end of the year. She feels so proud of herself. She said, "I feel energized and more alive then I have in years."

Each of us must discover our own enjoyable areas that revitalize us. For some people this is an easy task, but for many others it is not. We know that within each of us there appears to be a strong impulse to grow. In fact, we desire to be more than we are. According to Arkoff, "Each of us will have our own ideas of what we wish to become. Perhaps more informed and knowledgeable, or more understanding and loving, or more capable and creative, or more joyful and serene" (1993, p. 278). We need to know ourselves and what it is that we value and want for our life, and then we must begin the necessary changes to bring it about.

One of the barriers to growth is the anxiety we experience when we begin something new. We all feel comfortable with areas of our lives that are safe and familiar. When we cling to old, familiar ways of living, we block our possibilities for growth. We must be willing to take risks and to experiment with our talents and interests as we try new things. Our chapter on change provides insights and strategies to encourage risk taking.

There are those who believe that humans have a powerful impulse to make the most of their potential. Carl Rogers (1975) believed that every living organism is born with an inherent tendency toward developing all of their capacities in various ways that serve to enhance or maintain the organism. Albert Szent-Gyoergyi, a research biologist and two time winner of the Nobel Prize, stated that there is an "innate drive in living matter to perfect itself" (1974, p. 14).

Even when we are meeting many of our needs and finding success in our professional life, there is a deep longing or restlessness to develop our potential. We have a drive toward enhancement of self. Failure to acknowledge our potential is a red flag that signals future discontent. We must be in a state of striving toward meeting our potential to feel fulfilled. Giving too large a portion of ourselves to others and leaving little time and energy for revitalizing ourselves leads to discontent and dissatisfaction.

The Rewards of Revitalizing Yourself

Many people want to change, yet they don't know how. Throughout the book you have been learning to understand yourself, and if you have been an active participant, you have already begun the growth process. Understanding yourself and learning to use the knowledge you have acquired is a lifelong process. Part of the process includes becoming a mature Helping Professional who has a clearly defined system of beliefs that provide trustworthy guidelines for developing personal and professional thought as well as practice. In order to continue your growth, you must have a strong commitment to process. We find that helpers who are willing to look carefully and honestly at themselves are more successful in helping themselves and the people with whom they work.

Becoming a Helping Professional is a very personal matter, and no two individuals will follow the exact same path. However, support groups of Helping Professionals can be of considerable assistance in refining and extending one's belief system. Sharing ideas and beliefs with others stimulates thinking and contributes to clarifying one's own perceptions. Feedback from others whom we trust and admire can be a powerful stimulus for growth. This process is also true as helpers seek to revitalize themselves.

Throughout the process of revitalizing there are significant rewards that prove to be powerful motivators for growth:

- *Relationships:* Taking time to nourish relationships that are important to you will not only be revitalizing; it will also enhance the quality of your relationships.
- *Creative endeavors:* Because we are individuals who have strong drives and desires to use our creative capabilities, when we do begin to develop these potentials the rewards are extremely gratifying.
- *Intellectual challenges:* Human beings seem to have powerful impulses to make the most of their potential. Planning specific types of intellectual activities for yourself will greatly enhance this part of your life.
- *Emotional stability:* If you have followed the principles and strategies in the book throughout the past weeks and/or months, the growth you are experiencing will significantly enrich your life. By now you are beginning to see the results of your commitment and work. When your emotional needs are being met and you are growing in your feelings of self-acceptance, self-confidence, security, and self-esteem, to name a few, you truly feel revitalized.
- *Good health:* Being able to enjoy life because you feel healthy, experience high levels of energy, feel physically fit, and are able to enjoy periods of calmness and serenity is not only revitalizing; it is one of life's greatest rewards.
- *Spiritual enrichment:* The spiritual dimension of one's life acts as a unifying force that integrates the other dimensions: physical, mental, emotional, and social. It creates for the person or brings into focus the meaning in life. It serves as a powerful drive for personal meaning and accomplishment. Without some meaning in life, the will to live is lost. Chapman (1987), a researcher who developed a definition of spiritual health, stated that it is the ability to develop our spiritual nature to its fullest potential. He believed it is the ability to discover and to articulate our own basic purpose in life. It is the ability to learn how to experience love, joy, peace, and fulfillment. It is also the experience of helping ourselves and others achieve full potential.

Concluding Thoughts

Learning to revitalize yourself is an exciting and challenging journey. You will learn a great deal about yourself as you participate in the process. We all are hesitant in the beginning, and we experience powerful feelings that let us know there is risk involved. Without developing the courage within ourselves, we will refuse to venture forward. However, each time we face our fears and resistances and move forward, we grow and mature and become stronger. Each bit of strength encourages us to continue the journey because we see the results in our life.

Knowing that we are not alone in this process and joining with other professionals who offer encouragement and support will make the journey more exciting and rewarding. The end result is well worth the struggle, for we can then know we have developed the resilience and strength to face adversities. We also learn that we can take time to enjoy ourselves and reach new heights through new discoveries about ourselves. We can give vitality to ourselves. To experience revitalization is to keep the excitement for living and growing alive, which in turn benefits everyone we encounter.

Activities for Revitalizing

1. You and your friends have been invited to attend a popular talk show. When you arrive, they ask you and your friends to make a list of ways people could achieve personal fulfillment. You have 2 hours to prepare, and then you will present it on national TV. What do you come up with?

2. Take a 30-day calendar and make suggestions for each day that include ways to revitalize your life. When you are finished, share your suggestions with others.

3. You have just received a million-dollar grant to design a "professional health clinic" for the future. Outline what you suggest for the recipients. What will you include in your clinic that will promote both physical and emotional health? Include a description of the services that will be offered.

4. You are assigned the responsibility of planning a "Revitalizing Day" for your faculty. Plan a range of creative energizers that will meet the needs of a wide variety of people.

5. Design a "revitalizing birthday party" for someone in the group. Be sure to celebrate emotionally, physically, intellectually, spiritually, and socially with the birthday person.

6. List all the things you can think of that make you laugh. When you are finished, discuss these with your group. See how many join you in the laughter.

7. With a partner, take a long walk where you can clear your mind as you exercise. Pay attention to the thoughts that enter your mind. Verbalize the thoughts to your partner. Say out loud anything that enters your mind. Your partner will listen and refrain from giving any advice. Switch roles at the midpoint of the walk. When you get back, discuss how you both feel now.

References

Arkoff, A. (1993). The meaning of personal growth. In A. Arkoff (Ed.), *Psychology and personal growth* (pp. 278–292). Boston: Allyn and Bacon.

Chapman, L. S. (1987). Developing a useful perspective on spiritual health: Love, joy, peace, and fulfillment. *American Journal of Health Promotion, 13*.

Rogers, C. R. (1975). Client-centered psychotherapy. In A. M. Freedman, H. I. Kaplan, & B. J. Sadock (Eds.), *Comprehensive textbook of psychiatry* (vol. 2) (pp. 1831–1843). Baltimore, MD: Williams & Wilkins.

Samples, R. (1977). Selfness: Seeds of transformation. *AHP Newsletter*, May, pp. 1–2.

Szent-Gyoergyi, A. (1974). Drive in living matter to perfect itself. *Synthesis, 1*, 14–26.

Related Readings

Arrien, A. (1993). *The four-fold way: Walking the paths of the warrior, teacher, healer, and visionary.* San Francisco: Harper.

Brammer, L. M., & Macdonald, G. (1996). *The helping Relationship.* Boston: Allyn and Bacon.

Buscaglia, L. (1982). *Living, loving, and learning.* New York: Holt, Rinehart, and Winston.

Gazda, G. M., Asbury, F. R., Balzer, F. J., Childers, W. C., Phelps, R. E., & Walters, R. P. (1995). *Human relations development.* Boston: Allyn and Bacon.

Luks, A., & Payne, P. (1991). *The healing powers of doing good: The health benefits of helping others.* New York: Ballentine Books.

Peck, M. S. (1978). *Road less traveled: A new psychology of love, traditional values, and spirtual growth.* New York: Touchstone.

Richards, A. C. & Combs, A. W. (1992). Education and the humanistic challenge. *The Humanistic Psychologist, 20*(2 & 3), 372–388.

Chapter 16

Now the Vision Shall Be Real

The Transformational Helping Professional model may best be characterized as a vision. It is a vision of how Helping Professionals enhance their own lives, how they assist teachers, what the culture of schools should be, and how the profession can be enhanced to achieve higher levels of effectiveness and significance.

In the preceding chapters we have provided the descriptions, models, and tools to transform the vision into reality. A vision that cannot be implemented or is not operationalized is an unfulfilled promise. Implementation models often are imperfect representations of the vision they reflect, due to the complexities of practical application in the real world. It thus takes significant effort to make it work and function effectively, even in its best operational form.

Our task in this book is to pursue the vision and seek to fulfill the promise. The vision holds promise for the children and youth who we hope ultimately will benefit, for the teachers whose growth and fulfillment we cherish, for the Helping Professionals to whom we dedicate our work, and for the education profession to which we have committed our professional lives and which we hold in the highest regard.

The composite of beliefs, values, concepts, dispositions, and methodologies of the Transformational Helping Professional model provides the structure and substance of the vision. This, however, is not sufficient. It is essential for practitioners to capture the spirit of the vision and model. This is the essence of the process of transformation and the nature of the Helping Professional.

Transforming the vision to reality thus requires capturing the spirit. It necessitates that Helping Professionals believe in the vision and embrace its philosophy. In this regard, we are reminded of a children's story that serves as a metaphor for the means by which the vision becomes real. The story is *The Velveteen Rabbit* (Williams, n. d.), and the message is how a spirit and vision become real.

The story begins by relating that there once was a velveteen rabbit who was really splendid. On Christmas morning he sat atop a boy's stocking, the best of all the gifts. For a couple of hours the boy loved him, but the rabbit was soon forgotten in the bustle of the day. The rabbit was snubbed by all the other toys and made to feel very insignificant and commonplace. The only one kind to him was the old, worn Skin Horse, who was the wisest of all the toys. "'What is REAL?' asked the rabbit one day.... 'Real isn't how you are made,' said the Skin Horse. 'It's a thing that happens to you. When a child loves you for a long, long time, not to just play with, but REALLY loves you, then you become Real'" (pp. 13–17). The Skin Horse goes on to explain that sometimes loving hurts, and that becoming real doesn't happen all at once. He advises the velveteen rabbit that being real wears away some parts of you, "'But these things don't matter at all, because once you are Real you can't be ugly, except to people who don't understand'" (pp. 13–17).

As the story continues, Nana puts the velveteen rabbit in the boy's arms at bedtime. The boy hugged the rabbit and held him very tight as he talked to him. The boy took the rabbit with him during the day wherever he went. One night the boy said, "Give me my bunny, he isn't a toy, he's Real." Then one day the boy contracts scarlet fever, and his toys are to be burned. The velveteen rabbit is saved by a magic fairy who turns him into a real rabbit. "'Wasn't I Real before?' asked the little Rabbit. 'You were Real to the boy,' the Fairy said, 'because he loved you. Now you shall be Real to every one'" (pp. 38–40).

The velveteen rabbit metaphor carries insights into our message of the Transformational Helping Professional model. For the model to be real, those who use it must believe in it and live its philosophy. It is not the mere use of the skills, instruments, and strategies that make it work. Just as the velveteen rabbit was not "Real," or meaningful, until it was truly assimilated into the little boy's life, the philosophy of the model must be integral to the Helping Professional's belief system or it is not real.

The velveteen rabbit story has other parallels to the model as well. The worth of the individual is a common theme, be it rabbit or person. Once valued, the rabbit became real. Also, the rabbit was transformed, just as Helping Professionals are transformed through their own growth and in return assist others in transformations.

There is one apparent discrepancy, however, between the velveteen rabbit story and the Transformational model. In the Transformational model, worth is not dependent upon the value placed on the individual by others, but is derived from one's own meaningful set of values and beliefs, acting consistent with these, and helping others in their personal and professional development. In our view, this is the deeper message of the Fairy to the velveteen rabbit. Being "Real" means to know our own worth and value and to offer the nurturing and support to others who will discover it for themselves.

The concepts, practices, and culture of the Transformational model are critical to the health of our schools and the profession. They create an environment of mutual support and freedom to learn. As the Helping Professional models these dispositions, they permeate the system, affecting teachers and their students. Teachers are professional helpers as well, and as they are engaged in the processes and ethics of the model, they become transformed as individuals, as teachers, and as Helping Professionals themselves.

The future of education depends upon how well our teachers function in the classroom. This, in turn, is related to the support and guidance they receive and the learning environments they work in. The Helping Professional provides for and creates this support and a conducive environment. This is both a heavy responsibility and a great opportunity.

We envision schools of the future that are characterized by a culture of significance. The Transformational Helping Professional model is a vehicle for achieving this. As we have suggested, the climate created by Helping Professionals will bring about transformations that have great influence on achievement and meaningfulness in the lives of all who attend.

The reins are now put in the hands of the reader. It is your charge to create the schools of the future that fulfill the vision. We all must take responsibility for our legacy and for the transformation of teachers, schools, and the profession.

Reference

Williams, M. (n. d.). *The velveteen rabbit, or how toys become real*. Garden City, NY: Doubleday.

Index

Achievement, and motivation, 30
Adjustment phase, change process, 60, 63-64
Administrative behaviors, and burnout, 270–271
Assessment
    assistance to teacher, 188–192
    content-assessment approach matrix, 229
    content in, 185–186
    guidance/support, 125–126
    as helping dimension, 123–124
    of instructional-professional needs, 217–229
    and multiple intelligences, 201, 202
    observation, 187–190
    of personal-psychological needs, 211–217
    process component of, 186–187
    purposes of, 124, 209
    structure of assessment model, 186
    teacher performance measures, 206–207
Awareness phase, change process, 58, 63

Burnout, 265–275
    and administrative behaviors, 270–271
    coping strategies, 272–275
    definitions of, 266–267
    demographic factors, 268–269
    and locus of control, 271–272
    measurement of, 266, 268
    prevention of, 273–274
    versus revitalization, 127–128
    and role conflict/role ambiguity, 271–272
    and self-concept, 269–270
    social support needs, 269
    and student behaviors, 270
    teaching profession, 268

California Beginning Teacher Support and Assessment Program (BTSA), 7
California Mentor Teacher Program, 6
California Standards of Program Quality and Effectiveness, 206
Catharsis, in groups, 158
Change
    conflict theory, 44
    educational change, 47–55
    and helping process, 26
    holistic model of, 45–46
    organismic model of, 44
    social learning approach, 44
    in Transformational Helping model, 36, 56
Change process, 55–66
    adjustment phase, 60
    awareness phase, 58
    continuation phase, 62
    new commitment phase, 60–61
    new insights phase, 58
    readiness for change phase, 59–60
    resistance phase, 58–59
Chapters on School Supervision (Payne), 2
Clinical supervision, 5
    models of, 5
Clusters
    exercise for, 175
    and nonverbal communication, 174
Cognitive development
    cognitive complexity, 198–200

of teacher, 21
Commitment, of helping professional, 125–126
Communication
    conditions for quality communication, 167
    listening, 170–173
    nonverbal communication, 173–175
    objectives of, 166
    paraphrasing, 177–178
    process behaviors, 167–168
    questioning, 175–177
    styles, classification of, 167
    validating, 179
Communication skills, 20
    and interpersonal effectiveness, 122–123
    practicing of, 169
Concerns-based adoption model (CBA), educational change, 54
Conferencing, 241–242
    goals of, 241–242
    guidance/support for teachers, 241–242
Confidentiality, and psychological contract, 245
Conflict theory, of change, 44
Congruence, and nonverbal communication, 174
Constructivism, 102–104
    example of use, 103–104
    principles of, 102–103
Content
    in assessment, 185–186, 229–230
    cognitive complexity, 198–200
    as meaning, 197–198
    standards for teachers, 203–207
    and student intelligence, 200–203
Content knowledge, 100–102
    curricular knowledge, 101
    pedagogical, 101
    subject matter, 101
Continuation phase, change process, 62, 64
Coping, 260–265
    adaptive strategies, 265
    with burnout, 272–275
    definition of, 262
    and hardiness, 272–273
    maladaptive coping strategies, 263
    meaning of, 260–261
    positive coping strategies, 262
    stages of, 262
    stress reaction profile, 263–265
Curricular knowledge, 101

Data analysis, scope of, 249–250
Data collection, and observation, 225–226
Demographic factors, in burnout, 268–269
Developmental theory, teachers/student teachers, 95–96

Diagnosis. *See* Assessment
Diversity, in groups, 159–161
Don't Smile until Christmas: Accounts of the First Year of Teaching (Ryan), 2

Educational change, 47–55
    assistance for teachers during, 50–51
    concerns-based adoption model (CBA), 54
    and financial limitations, 48
    issues related to, 55
    organizational development model, 53
    problem solving model, 52
    Rand Change Agent Study, 53–54
    reform levels, 47–48
    research, development, and diffusion model, 52
    restructuring for, 48–49
    scope of, 49–50
    social interaction model, 51–52
Educational Testing Service, Praxis/Pathwise, 185, 206
Efficacy, development of, 32
Elementary and Secondary Education Act
    Title III, 53
    Title IV, 53
Emotional needs, 75–80
    assessment of, 214–215
    and burn out, 235–236
    coping, relationship to helping, 140–142
    evaluation of, 78
    personal log for tracking of, 80
    types of, 78, 215
Emotions, and illness, 77–78
Empathy, 138–140
    characteristics of, 139–140
    meaning of, 138
    positive aspects of, 139, 140
Evaluation, versus helping, 10–11, 13
Evidence, types of, 250

Federal programs, change agent programs, 53
Financial problems, of teachers, 256–257
Flanders Interaction Analysis Category System, observation, 226, 227
Florida Beginning Teacher Assessment Program, 185
Florida Performance Measurement System, 206
Focusing, and listening, 171

Groups, 155–162
    caring in, 157
    catharsis in, 158
    commonality in, 156
    diversity, 159–161
    group cohesiveness, 156–157
    information sharing in, 157–158
    insight, acquisition of, 159

modeling in, 158
structured exercises, value of, 161–162
trust in, 156
Growth
dynamic in Transformational Helping model, 33
growth assessment tools, 143–144
and guidance process, 246
motivators for, 293
Guidance-support, 124
conferencing, 241–242
and emotional needs, 235–236
as helping dimension, 123–124
instructional-professional needs, 239–240
and intellectual needs, 236–237
and observation, 242–250
and physical needs, 234–235
professional development, 240–241
and social needs, 237–238
and spiritual needs, 238

Handbook of Research on School Supervision (Glanz), 4
Hardiness, and coping, 272–273
Health
and stress, 256
See also Physical needs
Helping
beliefs/values of, 22–27
philosophy of, 21–22, 38–39
qualities of helper, 162–163
Helping dimensions
assessment/diagnosis, 123–124
guidance/support, 125–127
interpersonal effectiveness, 122–123
revitalization of helping professional, 127–128
self-enhancement, 121–122
Helping model
cognitive development of teacher, 21
communication skills, 20
individual competency/technical proficiency, 20
interpersonal relationships, 19
motivation and growth, 20
personal growth in, 21
role model/leader, 20
self-responsibility, 20
support provider/helper relationship, 19
Transformational Helping model, 22–40
Holistic model, of change, 45–46
Human relations model, philosophy of helping, 38, 39
Human resources supervision theory, 4–5

Identity map, 160
Illness
and negative emotions, 77–78
optimism versus pessimism, 76

Identification, with others, 133–134
Individual change theory, 44
Individualization, and helping, 31–32
Informal observation, 225
Information sharing, in groups, 157–158
Insight, and group processes, 159
Instructional-professional needs, 104–110
development of, 108–109
instructional needs inventory, 106–107
inventory of needs, 109–110
Instructional-professional needs assessment, 217–230
content assessment, 229
interviews, 220–221
observation, 223–228
portfolios, 222
questionnaires, 221
teacher thinking assessment, 217–219, 239
Intellectual needs, 80–83
assessment of, 215–216
evaluation of, 81–83
types of, 80–81
Intelligence, multiple intelligences model, 200–203
Interpersonal effectiveness
with groups, 155–162
as helping dimension, 122–123
and interpersonal support, 150–151
and rapport, 151–153
and trust, 153–155
Interstate New Teacher Assessment and Support Consortium, 205
Interviews, instructional-professional assessment, 220–221
Intrinsic motivation, 31

Journal keeping technique, 219

Leadership Resource book, 6
Learning, constructivist view, 102–104
Listening, 170–173
exercise for, 173
focusing, 171
listening skills, types of, 172–173
verbal strategies, goals of, 172
Locus of control
and burnout, 271–272
meaning of, 76
positive development of, 76–77

Maslach Burnout Inventory (MBI), 268
Mature helping professional, characteristics of, 144–146
Mentor, definitions of, 9
Mentoring
evaluation versus helping, 10–11, 13
historical view, 6–7

mentor preparation, 7–8
programs, 6–7
roles/responsibilities, 8–9
compared to supervision, 3–4
Metacognitive questions, 177
types of, 177
Modeling, in groups, 158
Morale problems, teachers, 71–72, 123
Motivation, 29–31
and achievement, 30
intrinsic motivation, 31
Multiple intelligences model, 200–203
and assessment, 201, 202
assessment of, 201
curriculum development related to, 201, 202–203
and teaching strategies, 202
types of intelligences, 200–201

National Association of State Directors of Teacher Education and Certification, 205
National Board for Professional Teaching Standards, 204
National Council for Accreditation of Teacher Education, 204, 204–205
Nation at Risk, A, 47
Neo-scientific model, philosophy of helping, 39
New commitment phase, change process, 60–61, 64
New insights phase, change process, 58, 63
Nonverbal communication, 173–175
and clusters, 174
and congruence, 174
range of behaviors in, 173–174
types of messages, 173
North Carolina Mentor/Support Team Training Program, 7, 19, 20

Observation, 187–190, 223–228, 242–250
and assistance, 187–189
and confidentiality, 245
and context, 243–244, 248
data collection in, 225–226
Flanders System, 226, 227
goals of, 189
informal observation, 225
instructional-professional assessment, 223–228
Pathwise System, 228
planning/collaboration phase, 244–246
post-teaching reflection/consultation phase, 248–250
preparation phase, 226–227, 243–244
psychological contract in, 245
and relationship investment, 245
script taping, 227
specific focus approach, 224

structured approach, 223, 224
unstructured approach, 224–225
Ohio Department of Education Training Program, 20
Optimistic explanatory style, 76
positive aspects of, 76
Organismic model, of change, 44
Organizational development model, educational change, 53

Paraphrasing, 177–178
exercise for, 178
purposes of, 178
types of paraphrase, 178
Pathwise System, observation, 228
Pedagogical content knowledge, 101
Personal fulfillment, 283–288
fulfilled life profile, 287–288
Personal-psychological needs, 73–90, 211–217
emotional needs, 75–80
emotional needs assessment, 214–215
intellectual needs, 80–83
intellectual needs assessment, 215–216
physical needs assessment, 212–214
professional health assessment, 216
social needs, 83–88
social needs assessment, 216
spiritual needs, 88–90
spiritual needs assessment, 216
Philosophy of helping
helping resources model, 39
human relations model, 38, 39
human resources model, 39
neo-scientific model, 39
scientific model, 38, 39
usefulness of, 21–22, 38–39
Physical needs, 73–75
assessment of, 212–215
needs analysis, 74–75
physical fitness concerns, 235
physical needs plan, 75
school safety, 234–235
types of, 73, 213
Planning by teachers, and teacher thought, 99–100
Policy capturing technique, 219
Portfolios
content/organization of, 222
functions of, 222
instructional-professional assessment, 222
usefulness for assessment, 222
Praxis/Pathwise, 185, 206
Problem solving model, educational change, 52
Process behaviors, 167–168
and assessment, 186–187
Professional development

developmental stages in, 95, 240
helping professional, role in, 105
and instructional needs, 104–107
and professional needs, 107–110
programs for, 113–114
socialization of teachers, 110–113
teacher needs, meeting of, 115–116
thought process, development of, 96–100
Professional health, assessment of, 216–217
Psychological factors
    in Transformational Helping model, 28–29
    See also Personal-psychological needs

Questioning, 175–177
    to elicit thinking, 175
    exercise for, 177
    metacognitive questions, 177
    questions, types of, 175
    reflective analysis questions, 175–177
Questionnaires, instructional-professional
    assessment, 221

Rand Change Agent Study, educational change, 53–54, 54
Rapport, and interpersonal effectiveness, 151–153
Readiness for change phase, change process, 59–60, 63–64
Reflective analysis questions, 175–177
    types of, 176
Repertory grid technique, 219
Research, development, and diffusion model
    educational change, 52
Resistance phase
    change process, 58–59, 63
    dealing with, 246
Restructuring, for educational change, 48–49
Revitalization
    barriers to, 288–290
    guidelines for self-revitalization, 290–292
    for helping professionals, 127–128
    importance of, 292–293
    personal fulfillment, 283–288
Right-to-Read program, 53
Role conflict, and burnout, 271–272

Safety, school safety, 234–235
Script taping, observation, 227
Self, view of, 132–133
Self-concept, and burnout, 269–270
Self-enhancement
    and empathy, 138–140
    and growth, 131
    growth assessment tools, 143–144
    as helping dimension, 121–122

mature helper, characteristics of, 144–146
and needs identification, 140–141
and relationship to others, 133–134
Self-Enhancement Profile, 146–147
    and self-esteem, 134–137
    and self-realization, 142–143
    and self-valuing, 132–133
    tips for, 131
Self-esteem, 134–137
    evaluation, quiz for, 135–137
    and helping others, 134–137
    meaning of, 134
Selflessness, versus selfishness, 128, 284–285
Self-realization, 142–143
    growth strategies, 142–143
Self-valuing, 132–133
Social interaction model, educational change, 51–52
Socialization of teachers, 110–113
    process, example of, 110–111
    psychoanalytic view, 112–113
Social needs, 83–88
    assessment of, 216
    evaluation of, 85–86
    and support groups, 86–88, 237–238
    types of, 84–85, 86
Social resources, components of, 83–84
Social support
    functions of, 269
    lack of and burnout, 269
Specific focus approach, observation, 224
Spiritual needs, 88–90
    assessment of, 216
    belief system, 238
    fulfillment of, 88–89
    types of, 89
Standards for teachers, 203–207
    Interstate New Teacher Assessment and Support Consortium, 205
    National Association of State Directors of Teacher Education and Certification, 205
    National Board for Instructional-Professional Teaching Standards, 204
    National Council for Accreditation of Teacher Education, 204–205
    of professional organizations, 203–204
    state standards, examples of, 205–206
States, standards, examples of, 205–206
Stimulated recall technique, 219
Stress, 254–265
    assessment of, 258–259
    definitions/concepts of, 254–255
    effects on teachers, 257–258
    personal stressors, types of, 256–257
    professional stressors, types of, 257–259

304   Index

risks of helping, 281–282
work-related assessment, 258–259
See also Burnout; Coping
Structured approach, observation, 223, 224
Student behaviors, and burnout, 270
Student teaching
   phases in, 95–96
   supervision, 5
Subject matter, content knowledge, 101
Success, addictive nature of, 289
Supervision
   clinical supervision, 5
   definitions of, 9
   evaluation versus helping, 10–11, 13
   general supervision, 4–5
   helping model, components of, 19–21
   historical development, 2–3, 4–5
   human resources approach, 4–5
   compared to mentoring, 3–4
   student teacher supervision, 5
   supportive supervision, 11, 21
Support groups, and social needs, 86–88, 237–238
Supportive supervision, 11, 21

Teacher Advisor Project, 6
Teacher Expectations and Student Achievement (TESA), 206–207
Teachers
   developmental stages of, 95, 240
   morale problems, 71–72
   physical needs, 73–75
   professional development, 95–116
   psychological needs, 73–90
Teacher thinking, 96–100
   categories of, 98
   model of thought/action, 98–99
   relationship to helping professional, 99
   research on, 97
   teacher planning, 99–100

Teacher thinking assessment, 217–219
   journal keeping technique, 219
   policy capturing technique, 219
   repertory grid technique, 219
   stimulated recall technique, 219
   subject matter knowledge, 220
   think aloud technique, 218–219, 239
Teaching, competence, areas of, 191–192
Think aloud technique, 218–219, 239
Thought processes of teachers. See Teacher thinking
Transformational Helping model, 22–40
   beliefs/values of, 22–27
   change in, 31
   characteristics of Helping Professional, 34–37
   competence as goal, 32
   conducive conditions, creation of, 33–34
   definition of Helping Professional, 40
   dispositions, in, 33
   efficacy as goal, 32
   growth capacity, 31
   growth dynamic, 33
   individualized focus, 31–32
   personal-psychological foundation of, 28–29
   role of Helping Professional, 63–64
   transformation of helping profession, 33
   view of motivation in, 29–31
Trust
   elements of, 153, 245–246
   in groups, 156
   integrity evaluation, 154–155
   and interpersonal effectiveness, 153–155

Unstructured approach, observation, 224–225

Validating
   in communication, 179
   exercise for, 179
   introduction of validating statements, 179
   support statements for, 179